D0787191

FIRST
FLOWERING

FIRST FLOWERING

THE BEST OF
THE
HARVARD ADVOCATE

Preface,
"Our Man at Harvard,"
by
NORMAN
MAILER

Introduction
by
ROBERT
FITZGERALD

RICHARD M. SMOLEY
Editor

ADDISON-WESLEY PUBLISHING COMPANY

Reading, Massachusetts • Menlo Park, California
London • Amsterdam • Don Mills, Ontario • Sydney

"Circe's Palace," "Spleen," "Humouresque," and "Nocturne" by T. S. Eliot are reprinted by permission of Faber and Faber Ltd. from *Poems Written in Early Youth*. United States rights controlled by Farrar, Straus & Giroux, Inc.

"Gentlemen and Seamen" by T. S. Eliot is reprinted by permission of Mrs. Valerie Eliot and Faber and Faber Ltd. © in this edition Valerie Eliot.

"The New Art," "Summer Silence," "Sunset," and "Of Nicolette" by E. E. Cummings are reprinted by permission of Harcourt Brace Jovanovich, Inc.

"Sweet Jane," "Pain," © 1971 by Louis Reed.

Photos of John Berryman by Daniel Alexander.

ISBN 0-201-02736-4
ABCDEFGHIJ-HA-7987

Library of Congress Cataloging in Publication Data

Main entry under title:

First flowering.

    Includes index.
    1. College prose--Harvard. 2. College verse-- Harvard. I. Smoley, Richard M. II. The Harvard advocate.
PS508.C6F5   810'.8'0923797444   76-55634
ISBN 0-201-02736-4

CONTENTS

PREFACE
Norman Mailer

INTRODUCTION
Robert Fitzgerald

1898–1915

❦❦❦

1915–1928

1929–1943

1947–1960

1961–1976

OUR MAN AT HARVARD

Norman Mailer

Let me tell you about the Somerset Maugham party that we gave at the *Advocate* in the Spring of 1942. The magazine was housed then in a dark gray flat-roofed three-story building across the street from the stern of the *Lampoon* (and indeed we were much aware of being in their wake—*Lampoon* editors usually went to *Time*; ours to oblivion). In those days the *Advocate* building was as ugly from the exterior as it is now. A few small and dingy stores occupied the ground floor, some mysterious never-seen tenants were on the second, and the *Advocate* offices took up the third. They were beautiful to me. One climbed a dull carpeted staircase as dusty as a back road in Guerrero, used one's *Advocate* key to go through the door at the top, and the suite opened, an entire floor-through of five rooms, five mystical chambers full of broken-down furniture, and the incomparable odor that rises from old beer stains in the carpet, and syrup-crusted empty coke bottles in the corners. It is a better odor than you would think, sweet and alcoholic and faintly debauched—it spoke of little magazines and future lands of literature, and the offices were almost always empty in late afternoon when the sunlight turned the dust into a cosmos of angels dancing on a pin. Magicians would have felt a rush of aphrodisia amid all this pendant funk and mote. Maybe I loved the *Advocate* offices more than anyone who was taken in my competition—I spent the Spring of Sophomore year at Harvard drinking cokes by a table at the window that faced on the *Lampoon,* and I read old issues of the magazine. Once I was an authority on the early published work in the *Advocate* of T. S. Eliot, Edwin Arlington Robinson, Van Wyck Brooks, John Reed, Conrad Aiken, E. E. Cummings, and Malcolm Cowley—it must have been the nearest I ever came to extracting genealogical marrow from old print. Occasionally Marvin Barrett, the President, or Bowden Broadwater, Pegasus, would come through the office, give a start at seeing me at the same chair and table where they had glimpsed me on the last visit and go off to do their work.

The following academic year, '41–42, Bruce Barton, Jr. was elected President and John Crockett became Pegasus. We had troubles instantly. Barton,

called Pete, was the son of Bruce Barton, Sr., an advertising magnate as well-known in his period as Nicholas Murray Butler, and for that matter one could find similarities. (Barton must have been the last of the advertising tycoons who believed passionately in a strenuous Jesus with muscles.)

His son, in compensation, was a gentleman. Pete Barton was the nicest guy a lot of us met at Harvard, and with his blond hair, good if somewhat pinched features and fundamental decency, he could have passed for Billy Budd if he had not (1) gone to Deerfield, which left him a little more patrician than yeoman in manner, and (2) if he had had more beef. But he was gentle, he was quietly literary, and his father had millions. Since the *Advocate* was in its usual cauldron of debt, no other man would have been so appropriate to serve as President. Barton might even have had a benign, well-financed, and agreeable administration if not for the new Pegasus, John Crockett, a man as talented as Claggart, and equally riven in his soul by detestation of our Billy Budd.

Being innocent of Crockett's propensities for literary evil, we were a happy group coming into office. The magazine would be ours. We would print what we wished. Our first issue, therefore, consisted of each of us putting in his own story. Crockett then took our pearls to a printer in Vermont. This was, I think, in November. By February we still did not have a magazine. Crockett kept assuring us the printer would soon deliver. None of us ever called him. Crockett had assured us that the inexpensive rate he had managed to extract from the linotype mills of the Vermont woods would be ruined forever if we broke any of our voices on the printer's ear. Therefore, we waited. Nervously, impatiently, suspiciously, we waited for the issue with our stories.

Instead Crockett came back with the (75th) anniversary edition of the *Advocate,* a little work of love Crockett had gotten together by himself over the last year, in truth, a prodigious push of Pegasusmanship collecting poems, pieces and comment from the fine ranks of Wallace Stevens, Horace Gregory, Djuna Barnes, Marianne Moore, Robert Hillyer, Frederic Prokosch, Mark Schorer, John Malcolm

Brennan, Richard Eberhart, Bowden Broadwater, and William Carlos Williams, plus a poem by John Crockett, "The Sulky Races at Cherry Park." It was a mammoth virtuoso critico-literary crypto-CIA affair back in March '42, and none of us on the *Advocate* had had the first clue to what Crockett was cooking. As for our issue with the stories—Crockett promised to get to that next. The expression on his young but sour face told us what he thought of our stories. Crockett, incidentally, while not as well-featured as John Dean, had a great resemblance to him—I remember his tortoise-shell glasses, high forehead and thin pale hair.

Pete Barton had been agitated for weeks at the long wait of our first issue. Painfully aware of his father's weight in the world, he was invariably over-scrupulous never to push his own. He had suspended himself into a state of forbearance worthy of a Zen warrior considering the immense agitation the late appearance of the magazine had caused. When the anniversary issue appeared (to rich critical reception in the Boston papers, worse luck!), Barton finally demonstrated his father's blood. He called an emergency meeting where he calumniated himself for his derelictions of attention, took the full blame for the financial disaster of the issue (it had cost something like three times as much as more modest issues; our debt on the consequence had doubled overnight) and —Billy Budd to the last—absent even to intimations of a further notion to evil, stated that he would not ask for Crockett's resignation if he could expect his cooperation on future projects.

Crockett replied with a nod of his head and a profound turning of our collective head. Having heard, he said, that Somerset Maugham would be in the Boston area during April, he had sent an invitation to Maugham to come to a party that the *Advocate* would be happy to throw in his honor; Maugham had accepted. Maugham had accepted.

That piece of news ran around the ring of Cambridge like a particle in a cyclotron. Nothing in four years at Harvard, not Dunkirk, Pearl Harbor, or the blitz, not even beating Yale and Princeton in the same season for the first time in ten years could have lit Harvard up more. Not to be invited to that party was equal to signifying that one had mismanaged one's life.

The literary grandees of the faculty sent their early acceptance, F. O. Matthiesen, Theodore Spen-

cer, and Robert Hillyer in the van; the officers of the *Lampoon* sucked around; house-master's wives asked how things were *going* at the *Advocate*. On the night of the party, four hundred souls in four hundred bodies as large as Patrick Moynihan's and as delicate as Joan Didion's came to the small rooms on the third floor and packed themselves in so completely that you ended by bringing your drink to your lips around the wrist of the forearm in front of your face. The noise of cocktail gabble anticipated the oncoming shapings of time—one would not hear the sound again until the first jet planes fired up their engines at an airport. Drinks were passed overhead. If you did not reach at the right time, another hand plucked the drink. It did not matter. More was on its way. Glasses bounced like corks over white choppy Harvard hands. From time to time, word would pass like wind through grass that Maugham had just entered the building, Maugham was having trouble getting up the stairs, Maugham was through the door, Maugham was in the other room. We formed phalanxes to move into the other room; we did not budge. A phalanx cannot budge a volume that is impacted. The lovely smile of resignation was on the lips of faculty wives: It is the establishment smile which says, "Life is like that—the nearest pleasures are not to be tasted." After a half hour of such smiling into the face of a stranger as one brought one's arm around her neck to get at one's drink, the wind came through the grass again. Maugham, we heard, was at the door. Maugham was slowly going down the stair, Somerset Maugham was gone.

Hands passed drinks above the impacted mass. Eyes flashed in that hard gem-like smile of pride retained when opportunity is lost. In another half-hour, there was a lessening of pressure on one's chest, and bodies began to separate. After awhile, one could walk from room to room. What was the point? Maugham was gone.

It was only on the next day, after the claims of liars had been checked against the quiet evidence of reliable witnesses who had found themselves analogously empretzeled in every room and on the stairs, that the news came back. By every sound measure of verification, Somerset Maugham had never been in the *Advocate* building that night. Crockett, now confronted, confessed. Out of his unflappable funds of phlegm, he allowed that he had known for weeks Somerset Maugham was not coming—the great author had been kind enough to send a telegram in answer to the invitation. "Certainly not" the telegram said.

It was too late to ask Crockett to resign. Due to the war and an accelerated graduation, our term as *Advocate* officers was up; the new President and Pegasus were in. Because of the party, we left with a debt that had just doubled again. The *Advocate* has never been solvent since.

A postscript: Pete Barton became a navy officer and commanded a ship, came home, worked as quietly for *Time* as if he had been a *Lampoon* man, and died before he was forty. The only time I saw John Crockett again was about ten years ago in New York on a reunion at the Harvard Club. He was now in the State Department and had been stationed for years in Yugoslavia. He told delicious stories about idiotic conversations with Madame Tito at banquets in Zagreb. He looked to be as wicked as ever. Our cause was being well-served in Yugoslavia. It occurs to me that the mag across the street never knew what a talent it missed when the *Advocate* got Crockett. Rest in peace, Pete Barton.

INTRODUCTION

Robert Fitzgerald

❡ "... I sat up the better part of a night writing [an editorial] to suit myself, to the great disgust of my chum, who could not sleep while the gas was burning." That was a spring night in 1866, and the young man toiling under the gas light was F. P. Stearns. He had thought up a new student publication at Harvard, given it the name *Advocate,* and arranged to get it printed—all in mild defiance of college authority. What he and his friends advocated were undergraduate points of view and a magazine in which to express them, and from that day to this the *Advocate* has been fully independent, representing its editors and contributors and no one else. But defiance has in fact rarely been necessary at a university more and more patient of idiosyncrasies and receptive to new ventures in art and thought.

The intent of the present volume is literary, of course, as one would expect from what has developed into the primary literary magazine of Harvard's undergraduates. But the anthology also offers an historical record, as the format indicates and as the present editors of *The Harvard Advocate* intended in putting it together. In this it differs from the *Harvard Advocate Centennial Anthology,* published in 1966, in which the literary interest predominated. The two collections necessarily overlap, but the new one is more comprehensive. The reader will find here not only the changing moods and styles of student verse and fiction at Harvard during the past 110 years but, often and overtly enough, the intellectual life of Harvard students.

How far has the work of the young men, and later the young women, of Harvard reflected the life of their country, not to mention that of the great world? I am not a cultural historian and cannot answer this question precisely, but I find myself making one or two cautionary notes. Even while becoming a great university in ambition and aspect, Harvard remained at heart, for most undergraduates, what George Santayana called "a local Puritan college" well into the twentieth century. After the Civil War, for example, few Southerners went to Harvard, and the Southern experience, the mind of the South, is scantily represented in these pages. Homesteaders pushing West, cattlemen on the Great Plains, rail-roading and industry, immigration and labor, slum life, and the life of the *nouveaux riches*—these nineteenth-century scenes and struggles are not often, glimpsed in *Advocate* writing of those days.

On the other hand, what got into the *Advocate,* early and late, makes a rich and curious record in its own right. If in the early years the bending Charles enclosed what in retrospect seems a literary backwater for Harvard undergraduates, it would be sad to undervalue the élan with which they splashed in it. Samuel Eliot Morrison, Harvard's historian, has written of the "old-fashioned shabbiness and jollity" that lingered in the college a hundred years ago, when water still came in buckets from the Yard pumps and studies were heated by coal grates. In the '80s, as Owen Wister gently recalled twenty years later in his story *Philosophy 4,* an undergraduate with "sand" could quit cramming in favor of a day's outing in a buggy through the green meadows of Brighton and get "fogmatic" over port at a country inn. And Santayana himself remembered how students in another season, "standing packed in the tinkling horse-car, their coat-collars above their ears, and their feet deep in the winter straw, jigged in a long half hour into Boston, there to enjoy the delights of female society, the theater, or a good dinner."

Such was the life out of which nineteenth-century *Advocates* came. It would be late in the century before more than a very few students became acquainted outside the classroom with any of the great presences by whom letters and philosophy were being cultivated in Cambridge, let us say in the days when Samuel L. Clemens would come out from Boston by horse-car to call on William Dean Howells. Almost until the First World War, undergraduates browsed at random in the inviting pastures of President Eliot's elective system, often apparently wasting four years. But as Santayana observed, "manhood and sagacity ripen of themselves; it suffices not to repress or distort them," and *The Harvard Advocate* bears witness to that sufficing freedom.

"Don't yelp with the pack," William James told his students on the occasion of the Spanish American War, putting Harvard independence in terms that anyone could understand. If students were free to waste their time, they were also free to cultivate critical detachment and respect for dissent—qualities that would be even more valuable in coming generations. In the new century Harvard students and Harvard writers would not fail to register the conditions of mankind at large; the local Puritan college became one of the world's great centers for that registration.

Henry James, revisiting Cambridge at the end of summer in 1904 after many years abroad, found the newly fenced-in Yard reminiscent (as he fancied with all due irony) of a cloister amid American commercialism; but the vastly extended university gave him an impression of potency that he could not quite pin down: "the figure of the rich old Harvard organism . . . brooding through the summer night, on discriminations, on insistences, on sublime and exquisite heresies to come. . . ." Not that he conceived these heresies as artistic. He missed Lowell and Howells and felt no premonition of anything to make up the loss. "We see," he wrote, "the great university sit and look very hard, at the horizons of possibility, across the high table land of her future; but the light of literary desire is not perceptible in her eye (nothing is more striking than the recent drop in her of any outward sign of literary curiosity). . . ."

When these words were published in *The American Scene* (1907), the literary curiosity of young Mr. Eliot of St. Louis had already begun, at Harvard, a work that reanimated and in some sense transformed literary tradition. This and other twentieth century "insistences" (to use James's word) were first heard in Cambridge, or would echo there. The present anthology evokes the changing atmosphere between the Great Wars: the gradual conquests of Modernism in the arts, the not-so-gradual turn toward Social Consciousness in the '30s when so many Harvard men took part in the New Deal of F. D. Roosevelt, '04, or contributed to the thinking that went into it. Memorable pieces from this era are Lincoln Kirstein's 1934 memoir of *The Hound & Horn* and Arthur M. Schlesinger, Jr.'s article on the Republican Party in 1936. After the interruption of the Second War, the *Advocate* has persistently tended toward that coming of age that in its best years it has closely approached, as a more than local and better than amateur publication. Its special numbers, especially, have a place in literary history. The deadlier consequences of professionalism seem happily unlikely.

In 1930, when my own first contribution appeared, some friends and I celebrated with dinner in Boston at the Athens Olympia, where wine, then illegal, could be had in coffee cups. A number of cups made it seem possible to climb the smokestack of the abandoned power house where Eliot House now stands. We climbed it in complete darkness by rungs set in the mortar of the interior. As the mortar had crumbled with age, every now and then a rung would give way sickeningly under hand or foot. On finally scrambling out at the top, we could not see one another's pallor as we stood sweating and shivering in the midnight breeze off the Charles. But, having made it up, we felt the odds were in favor of our getting down again. As it turned out, I had not in fact made my last contribution to the *Advocate*.

The premises then consisted of a small frame house up an alley off Mount Auburn Street—a secluded sanctum, never violated by mop or dustcloth, for the life of the imagination. When he wanted to work on a story for a few days, James Agee once or twice holed up there, sleeping on the ancient couch. On one of my first visits I found in the office an editor whom I had never seen before, reading manuscript with his hat shoved to the back of his head—a skinny boy who looked up with burning black eyes. "I suppose you like T. S. Eliot," he said to me, who had given him no reason to suppose anything. "Well, I like John Masefield." I still relish the comedy of that moment, typical somehow of the *Advocate* life of the time.

If I were to choose a moment to epitomize *Advocate* life in a later time, I might pick the occasion in 1966 when I was asked, as a new member of the Harvard staff, to introduce an *Advocate* reading by the Soviet poet André Vosnesensky. There were no *Advocate* readings in 1930; for that matter, so far as any of us knew, there were no Soviet poets. Now in a changed and larger world I went over to Lowell Lecture Hall to welcome the guest, who appeared as a pale stripling in a pullover sweater with the kind of diamond pattern favored by American high-school kids in the '20s. A translator at his side would provide the English renderings. I made my introduction brief because, as I said, the audience had not come to hear me but to hear Mr. Vosnesensky. I spoke better than I knew. The stripling made himself heard, all right, as from that apparently frail thorax emerged a voice like a section of brass, making the whole auditorium tremble. Of Russian reading style it must have been a revelation to many auditors besides myself, a revelation that may exemplify the *Advocate's* latter-day scope and initiative.

ACKNOWLEDGMENTS

The creation of a book of this kind involves debts that cannot be fully repaid in any acknowledgments page. And it involves many people whom an editor never meets or knows. I must unwillingly limit my thanks to those whose help has touched me directly. To them I am greatly indebted indeed.

Special thanks must go to Professor Robert Fitzgerald: both this anthology and its editor owe much to his interest and expertise.

Grateful acknowledgment is made to Dr. Harley Holden and the employees of the Harvard University Archives, who have been most cooperative in assisting us in research and production.

At the *Advocate* itself, I give my hearty gratitude to Messrs. Douglas A. McIntyre and Steven A. Ballmer for their indispensable aid in organizing and finding the publisher for this project. Mr. William Maroni selected the photographs and art, with the assistance of Miss Emily Kane and in cooperation with the design and layout department of Addison-Wesley.

I would also like to thank my good friends Sam K. Seymour IV and Antoinette LaFarge, who gave me much encouragement and advice in the selection of pieces and in the writing of the chapter introductions.

Finally, I thank the many members of the Addison-Wesley staff whose intelligent concern and careful attention to detail have guided the book over many difficulties to its present form.

Cambridge, Massachusetts   Richard M. Smoley
December, 1976

Founders of the Advocate (W.G.I.)

Leatham   Gage   Sanborn   Fox   Stearns   William

1886–1882

The *Advocate* began its life stormily, and as a different publication. *The Collegian,* its immediate predecessor, published essays critical of such college ordinances as compulsory chapel attendance ("Memorabilia"), and so proved obnoxious to the Harvard faculty. As a result it lasted for half the spring semester of 1866, the only Harvard publication to die from suppression rather than indifference. In May the *Advocate* appeared and, though it bore the brave motto *Veritas nihil veretur,* won the right to exist by a conciliatory tone and by subtle disassociation from its parent ("Our Paper").

The new magazine, renamed *The Harvard Advocate* three years later, was the only Harvard periodical until 1873, and as a result it had to serve many functions: it reported baseball scores, club activities, undergraduate opinion, and major events of the college like President Eliot's inauguration in 1869.

Editorials were sometimes abrasive, but often they predicted and influenced great changes at Harvard. "The Propriety of Admitting Women into Our College" preceded the founding of the Harvard Annex (later Radcliffe) by thirteen years; and "Harvard for Women" showed the magazine's support for the venture when its time came.

Yet it was literature rather than news or opinion that provided the *Advocate* with its main reason for existence. Writing at that time tended to take the form of droll college anecdotes and sentimental verse; occasionally Harvard lore ("Legend of Harvard") and journalism appeared as well. Nor were critical essays lacking, and "Zukunftmusik" and "Walt Whitman" indicate the standards of student taste when Wagner was still avant-garde and Whitman unacceptably coarse.

THE FOUNDING OF THE ADVOCATE

From the Harvard Advocate of May 18, 1892.

During the autumn of 1865 Gage and Peckham of the Class of '67 were seen much together. Gage was the most popular man in his class, and until Fred Loring came the following year, the best poet and wit in college. He was a genial, light-hearted, dreamy fellow, and very little of a student. Peckham was a boy of fourteen when he entered, a precocious scholar, too critical to be popular, but full of driving Yankee energy. Both were of a decidedly radical turn of mind,—this and their keen intelligence was the bond of sympathy between them,—and having by mistake been taken into a religious society, the Christian Union, they and others of '67 proceeded to turn it topsy-turvy with the best intentions possible. This probably was what first led the college faculty to look upon them with suspicion. Their next move was to hatch together the plan of a college periodical. The old *Harvard Magazine* had died a slow paralysis some time in the previous year, and there was no longer any chance for public opinion among the students to find expression. In No. 4 of the second volume of the ADVOCATE will be found an article called "The ADVOCATE's Natal Day," referring to the first conception of their plan. They went with their project to Sanborn of '67, who was always either first or second scholar in the class, an older man than themselves and a vigorous writer. He readily joined them, and then these three consulted with members of the Senior class, from whom Perry, Curtis, and A. K. Fiske were finally selected by mutual agreement. No class meetings, as I remember, were held on the subject, no special authority conferred on the editors. It was decided that the new paper should be a fortnightly publication called the *Collegian.*

The tone of the *Collegian* was from the start a trifle saucy; more independent certainly than was pleasing to the college government. In the first number Sanborn led off with an able argument against the strictness of the college law in regard to Sunday service, and followed it up in the second number, also, where Gage came to his assistance with a witty and facetious article upon morning prayers written in the manner of the Platonic dialogue. It ended in the following manner:

SOCRATES—Do you not, then, say that in the temple, as in the Agora and in the Peireus, that the matter about which most were busy was the business of the meeting, and not that about which the few?

GLAUCON—I do, indeed, by Jupiter! and tomorrow morning I will go to roll-call and not to prayers. Come and breakfast with me, Socrates.

Now that twenty years later morning prayers have been abolished, Gage and Sanborn appear as the pioneers in a salutary movement of reform, but in those days they were considered dangerous innovaters. In the third number, however, I can find nothing which the college faculty could take offence at, except a Latin parody by Peckham called *Carmen Horatii,* which few were able to translate, but which was clearly intended as a satire on the methods of our Latin professor. There was general surprise among the undergraduates when shortly after this the editors were summoned to the president's office and informed there that if they continued to publish the *Collegian* they would do so at their peril.

The students had already taken a fancy to the paper, and a good deal of indignation was expressed at what was termed the "despotic" action of the college faculty. Gage, who was a New Hampshire democrat of the old style, said he could even feel sympathy now with the early abolitionists. At Mrs. Wells' club table, where he was the leading spirit, public feeling ran high, and Landon Longworth even talked of open rebellion and raising the black flag. During that afternoon it occurred to me that the publication of the paper might be continued with safety by changing the name, and choosing new editors for it, whose names were not to appear, as those of the *Collegian* had, upon the first page. Suppose the new paper was called the ADVOCATE, an advocate of the students' interests,—the name came to me at that moment,— what would the college faculty have to complain of? They had suppressed a paper called the *Collegian,* not the ADVOCATE. The editors of the *Collegian* need take no active part in the matter, and, if summoned, could plead not guilty with a clear conscience. If the first number of the ADVOCATE met with no opposition, the former editors could unite with the new set, and continue quietly on in the old way. Of one thing I saw the necessity most clearly, that the new paper should in all matters be most respectful.

I soon encountered Peckham and communicated my design to him as the one amongst the *Collegian's* editors who had the least fear of being offended. He approved of it most cordially. I next went to E. W. Fox. He was a man of nobly independent character (whose early death must always be regretted), and had proved himself as equally good a prose writer as Gage was in verse. He had a strong sense of humor, and practical jokes on a large scale were his special delight. I think this side of the question interested him quite as much as the moral side, the rights of the undergraduates. He entered heartily into my plan, but as it happened did little to help me beyond writing an excellent article on Pedestrianism, in style nearly equal to that of Irving, and devoting one Saturday afternoon to the correction of proof. Since it was necessary to keep the affair as secret as possible, and as the editors of the *Collegian* could write nothing for us, we soon found a difficulty in obtaining sufficient copy to fill the paper. John E. Leonard, who afterward went to Congress from a Louisiana district, wrote an editorial for us, but the tone of it did not seem sufficiently earnest, so I sat up the greater part of a night writing one to suit myself, to the great disgust of my chum, who could not sleep while the gas was burning. This was called "Our Paper," and Leonard's somewhat modified, appeared under the title of "The *Collegian*." Finally I was obliged to write a full half of the paper myself.

At this time my father was supporting for political purposes a weekly paper called the *Right Way*. He was absent in Washington himself, so, thinking it would be more prudent to publish the first number of the ADVOCATE in Boston than in Cambridge, I went to Mr. Thayer, the editor of the *Right Way,* and laid our case before him. He took the matter up with alacrity, and arranged with Rand & Avery to do the printing. Rand & Avery, however, were slow and negligent. They wasted so much time that a large portion of the paper became stale matter and more copy had to be written. The spring term was hurrying on to its close, and I was almost in despair of getting the ADVOCATE published in season to do its work, and have the effect I was hoping for. At the Wells table, too, as soon as the secret became known, Lowell and some others did not hesitate to tell me that I was an unfit man for such an enterprise; but Gage tipped me an encouraging wink, and Longworth magnanimously offered to pay whatever deficit there might be in my account with the printer; though my father afterwards preferred to do this himself.

At length, on the evening of May 10th, the package of four hundred copies of the new paper arrived at Richardson's book-store. I went at once to John Wilson's and had him print me a dozen square posters as follows:

A NEW COLLEGE PAPER

FOR SALE AT RICHARDSON'S BOOKSTORE

TO-MORROW

With these I went to Fox's room, and told him our mine was ready for the explosion. "Good!" said he; "now, Frank, go and get a good night's rest. My chum and I will look after this business." His chum, J. W. Reed was remarkably fond of nocturnal adventures, and about midnight Fox and he together pasted up the notices in conspicuous places. It gives a double relish to mischief when it is done in a good cause. That night I slept soundly and cared little whether I was suspended or not. The following morning (Friday) there was a general rush for Richardson's, and the greater part of our edition was sold off at once. Then we sent copies of the paper by mail to every member of the Corporation and Board of Overseers of the college, as well as to the Boston daily papers, from which we obtained highly favorable reviews of it. The statement in our editorial that the college faculty might at least have allowed the editors of the *Collegian* an opportunity to correct their mistakes and mend the error of their ways, was an argument too strong to be refuted.

What would happen next Monday night was the problem now. A little after 10 P.M. I heard rushing feet on the stairs and Peckham's vigorous knock at my door. With cool audacity he had interviewed the president himself on the way home from faculty meeting. Dr. Hill said there had been some discussion that evening concerning the ADVOCATE, but the faculty had finally decided to drop the question for the present and let the paper live or die on its own merits. "I have read it myself," said he, "and liked it very well. There is one poem in it which is really excellent,—'You kissed me in my Dreams,' by a young lady of Cambridge,—only it is perhaps a trifle too amorous." Good for the president so far! The next forenoon there was a joyful meeting of old and new editors in Gage's room. Those of the class of '66 had long since disappeared from our horizon, and Moses Williams of '68 was elected to make up the complement of six. Gage and Peckham agreed to take the next number in charge, and we never had any further trouble with the college authorities. Many years afterwards one of the professors informed me that they had no suspicion as to who the first editors of the ADVOCATE were.

A much less pleasant business still remained to be accomplished. We were publishing a newspaper without any subscribers. It was expected that the subscribers to the *Collegian* would stand by us, and so most of them did; but every man had to be interviewed and the money collected from him. The senior class was on the eve of graduation, and took little interest in the matter. Some of them were glad of a chance to escape their obligations. There were only about three hundred and sixty students in Harvard at this time.

I saw if we were to make both ends meet, there were no dollars to be lost. Unwilling to trust to others a work which needed to be thoroughly done, I went myself, to every room in the college building, and to a good many outside, and argued, coaxed and entreated for subscriptions. Perhaps there are those who still remember how disagreeable I made myself. The Harvard nine went to New York in the May recess to play a series of matches, and I went with them as a substitute and reporter. The account of these games occupied a large space in the ADVOCATE, and gave our paper the strong support of the baseball interest.

F. P. Stearns

THE
COLLEGIAN.

MARCH 23, 1866.]   "DULCE EST PERICULUM."   [VOL. I. — No. 2.

MEMORABILIA.

[Translation.]

Socrates. Good-morning, Glaucon.

Glaucon. Good-morning, O Socrates!

Socrates. Tell me now, Glaucon, are you just from the temple?

Glaucon (who has seen Socrates before). I should say so.

Socrates. Whether is the business there worship, or to see if any of the young men be absent?

Glaucon. Give it up.

Socrates. Is it not right that all men should be eager to learn?

Glaucon. Most certainly, O Socrates!

Socrates. Are you not, then, a man?

Glaucon (who has seen the Sphynx). You bet.

Socrates. It is plain, then, that you wish to listen to me.

Glaucon (somewhat mixed). It must be so.

Socrates. Tell me, then, if you were to go into the Agora, and there see many citizens noting and discussing the affairs of the city, and only two or three who were selling figs, would you not say that the object of the meeting was politics, and not fig-peddling?

Glaucon. Most assuredly. If I should deny it, I should be very foolish.

Socrates. And if there should be a crowd around me, some time in the Peireus, listening to my wise words, if perchance they might learn something, and two only should be matching obuli, of what would you say the crowd was composed? Ahem!

Glaucon. Of your disciples, certainly, O most wise Socrates!

Socrates. Tell me, then, Glaucon, in the temple this morning how many were engaged in worship.

Glaucon. One, indeed.

Socrates. Whether was one conducting the worship and many listening, or do you say that no one was listening?

Glaucon. Not one, in truth, save by accident.

Socrates. And were there any who were busy marking the young men if they were absent?

Glaucon. You will find no one to deny it.

Socrates. How many, then, were there?

Glaucon. Four, O reverend sage!

Socrates. Then it seems that four were busy about the affairs of men, and one only about those things which concern the gods.

Glaucon. Thus it certainly was.

Socrates. Do you not, then, say that in the temple, as in the Agora and in the Peireus, that the matter about which most were busy was the business of the meeting, and not that about which the few?

Glaucon. I do, indeed, by Jupiter! and, to-morrow morning, I will go to roll-call, and not to prayers. Come and breakfast with me, Socrates.

Δ.

THE
ADVOCATE.

MAY 11, 1866.]   "VERITAS NIHIL VERETUR."   [VOL. I. — No. I.

OUR PAPER.

THE "Collegian" was started two months ago as a Cambridge newspaper, intended to represent the views and opinions of Harvard students. Its prosperity was great; it had a long list of honorable subscribers, among both graduates and undergraduates, and was favorably spoken of by the leading periodicals of Boston. Soon after the issue of its third number, the editors of the "Collegian" were summoned, and informed that their publication must be discontinued. No direct reason was assigned for this unexpected step; and all attempts at conciliation and compromise on the part of the editors, who offered to bind themselves to any restrictions whatever, were unavailing. Deterred from further pursuance of their undertaking by threat of a most severe college censure in case they continued it, the editors stopped their paper, and squared accounts with their subscribers. Impressed with a feeling that some such newspaper as was the "Collegian" is sorely needed here to express the wishes and opinions of the students, we propose to issue this, our present publication, as long as it is supported.

We do not make our attempt in any spirit of blind malignity to those who govern and instruct us, nor do we consider it mere schoolboy sentiment which animates this appeal to our right of free journalism. As boys, we were prejudiced against our masters; and there may be some of that instinct lingering about us still: but we believe ourselves, on this occasion, to be actuated by other and more liberal motives.

It seems to us as if "leave to plead our own cause" had been asked for, and refused. It is from no idle whim, nor in any spirit of unmeaning opposition, that we try to assert that we consider ourselves slighted by this relentless course of our rulers in overlooking our dearest wishes. The good order and correct discipline of the College is far more likely to be demoralized by one instance where all explanation of the disputed point has been refused, than it could be by many midnight revels in front of University. It is true that two or three articles in the "Collegian" contained indistinct allusions to those to whom we are rightfully expected to pay the highest deference; but such were hardly discernible to any save ourselves, and were not intended to be understood beyond the limits of a department or of a certain class. We admit that it may have been a mistake to have published such articles in the "Collegian;" but we are positive that such a practice would have been entirely stopped as soon as it became known that they were a source of annoyance to their subjects. Harmless by-play the editors thought it, which no one need be offended at.

Here are four hundred young men, the greater number of whom have now passed that age at which law prescribes that they shall become their own masters. All these have individual opinions, feelings, ideas, more or less, of their own. It would be absurd to attempt to gratify all their whims and tastes; yet, when a majority concur in claiming a right to this privilege or that privilege, we know there is some reason for it, which ought to be investigated. And we think, that, if we are to be responsible at all, we ought to be allowed a voice, or at least some expression of appeal, on the subject of those rules and customs here which determine so nearly our habits of thought and action throughout life. We confess that undergraduates are inexperienced, and, as compared with older heads, are ignorant enough of the realities of the world. "Yet he that wears the shoe alone knows where the shoe pinches." The scholarly senior, who knows well where the discipline of each day serves him as an assistance and a guide, also knows best of all where the chafing of his harness impedes free motion. "Times change, and men change with them." Is it expected that we should find suited to our best purposes those regulations which were framed for the government of our grandfathers? If a change is to be allowed at any time, it is possible that one time may demand it as well as another.

We disclaim having received any assistance or co-operation in our project from the former editors of the "Collegian." Not even are they responsible for the original idea of our attempt. They were not alone in their belief that a newspaper of some sort was needed among the undergraduates, both for the purpose of expressing their sentiments to each other, and also their impressions of college matters to the world. We are not a small and insignificant minority, nor are the principles on which we act cherished within the breasts of a few proselytes. They have been for a long time echoed and re-echoed in college talk and society debates. We assure the public that our columns are open to all who desire to make fair, unbiased statement of their judgment on these subjects on or any others. Nothing abusive, nothing personally libellous, nothing which in the judgment of the editors would be likely to excite disobedience or disorder, will be received.

With this exposition of "our purposes," we intrust to the mercy of our readers the first number of the "Advocate."

THE PROPRIETY OF ADMITTING WOMEN INTO OUR COLLEGE.

MESSRS EDITORS, — I cannot praise too heartily the various articles upon University Reform which have appeared in your magazine; and Dr. Hedge's most excellent address upon the same subject (which I had the pleasure of hearing) receives entire approval from me: but there is one branch of reform which, I believe, has not as yet been touched upon in your magazine, — a reform of paramount importance, and in regard to which, I will ask your attention to a few words from me.

I mean that advance upon our present state of civilization which will no longer exclude one-half of the human race from the walls of our college; which will no longer tolerate the barbarous idea that our sisters have not as good a right to a liberal education as ourselves.

Said a young lady to me on a certain occasion, "I would have given all that I could earn in five years, if I could have been allowed to be graduated from Harvard College. I went through a high school with five young men as classmates: these entered Harvard; but I, who had stood at the head of the class, was compelled to leave New England, and seek the doubtful advantages of Antioch College." I felt ashamed for my College, and blushed for the inconsistency of New-England civilization which tolerates such a manifest injustice in its pet colleges.

When our College was founded, the state of things was far different from what it is now. School-teaching then was confined almost entirely to men; now a great majority of our teachers are women; a large number of our students are prepared for college chiefly by women; and are we to set the same standard now for women's education as then?

I confess that I am unable to see what possible harm can result from throwing our College open to every person, male or female, who is desirous of entering it; on the contrary, I think that great good would be the result. It has been suggested by one of your contributors, that, if the expenses at Harvard were reduced, she would no longer be compelled to depend upon the immediate neighborhood for a supply of students: but I can inform him of a way by which a much more satisfactory result could be attained without half the difficulty attending his suggestion.

At the next examination for admission, let a notice be circulated throughout the country, that young ladies as well as young gentlemen will be received as candidates; and, if I am not mistaken, the result will be that in five years' time our number of students will be doubled. Then our expenses can be reduced to one-half the present amount, and we can properly say that we belong to a University; for I do not believe that we can justly call an institution *a University* which is confined to one-half of mankind.

It is often urged as an objection against receiving women into our larger colleges, that several colleges have been established exclusively for females, and several others are open both to males and females; and that women ought to be contented with these colleges, and not aspire to the dignity of becoming students of Harvard or Yale. This trifling argument is as applicable to men as women.

Why do so many young men leave their Western homes, and come all the way to New England for an education, ignoring the hundreds of little colleges, so called, which are struggling into existence on their boundless prairies? The simple reason is, that they are attracted by the superior advantages which our Eastern institutions afford; and, for the same reason, our sisters, who desire a collegiate education, cannot but feel disappointed to see us entering a first-class college, while they must put up with an Antioch or Oberlin. What a disgraceful sight! — an Eastern girl forced to leave her home in New England, so famous for its educational advantages, and seek the State of Ohio, as a place where she can enjoy even tolerable advantages!

If sectionalism is dangerous in government, it certainly must be so in education. Nature has placed boys and girls together in families, that they may mutually benefit each other; but, at the very age in which they are in the greatest need of each other's assistance, they are ruthlessly separated. What a glorious era it will be in American civilization, when a brother and sister, after attending school together during their younger days, can finally be received under the classic shades of Harvard, hand in hand, and continue here together for four happy years! A blessed day, too, will it be for the morals of our College, when the young men have the restraining influence of woman's society before them during their college course.

Alumni, the task is yours! See that this criminal exclusiveness be eradicated. Open the doors of your Alma Mater to all who desire and deserve her maternal care. Do away with this false distinction between the two sexes; and let the blessed light of civilization permeate the barriers of bigotry and injustice.   Lux.

LEGEND OF HARVARD.

NO. I.

I WILL tell the story as it was told me by a member of '66, as we were trudging home one dark night, from one of the neighboring towns. The loneliness of the situation caused the story to make a deep impression on my mind. I walked boldly on, whistling a merry tune, though I must say my eyes roamed furtively round when passing dark places. All stone-walls were objects of interest, and I engaged in pleasant speculations as to the size of his Satanic Majesty, and whether he could conceal himself behind the bush ahead. I short, I think I could have detected the smell of brimstone a long way off. Of course, I wasn't frightened; oh, no! I was only a little nervous, that's all. Being a meek and unassuming Freshman, I did not dare to question the truth of my companion's story. Any doubts, however, that I might have had at the time have since been removed; and I have the satisfaction of assuring my readers, that my story is, in the main, true. Not that I would guarantee the truth of the common version, hobgoblin and all, but I *do* say, that the story rests on a real foundation. But to my tale.

Once upon a time — or many years ago — there was a certain society in college which went under the name of the " League of Reason." It was composed of some four persons, and their avowed object was to combat the spread of religion. The society's acknowledged head and founder was a man of great force of mind, though a thorough sceptic, while his associates were men of no mean parts; but all four had the reputation of being rather reckless, devil-may-care fellows. And well was their reputation for foolhardiness borne out by the character of their meetings, in which nothing was too holy to escape their jeers and scoffs. But to hasten to the *denouement*. One winter's eve, they were holding high carnival together, and over their wine they became more than usually blasphemous. As they were about to separate, their president proposed, " Here's to the Devil, wishing he were here." No sooner had this been uttered than a crash was heard; the side of the room fell in, the apartment was filled with sulphurous fumes, and amid blue flames, standing in the midst of the room, was seen — the Devil, in traditional costume. ——— In the morning, the bodies of the two principal members of the society were found amid the ruins, — dead. The bodies of the other two were taken up insensible. One died in a short time, while the other never seemed the same person as before, and lived, a mystery to all who knew him. Being questioned on the events of the evening, he maintained the truth of the foregoing, and did so throughout his life, though most loath to allude to the subject in any way whatever.

So much for the Senior's story; and this is the form in which you sometimes find the story flitting about the college yard. At the time of hearing it, I gave it no more than a passing thought; but I have since learned that it rests on fact. In the college records of the year 1765, there is this entry made under the date of Nov. 3: " Last night a sad affair happened, which has cast a gloom over all the college. During a sudden and severe thunder storm, the new hall (Hollis was built in 1763) was struck with lightning, and two of our promising young men were suddenly and awfully deprived of their lives, while two others were seriously injured. The names of the dead are William Church Ga—n, of Boston, in this Commonwealth of Massachusetts, and John F——b, of the same place." The record goes on to state, that a society, styled " Reason's League," was holding its session at the time in the room No. 25 Hollis. At the side of the page, and in a different hand, were some pencillings to this effect: " From this learn to believe on the Lord, and tempt not by thy unbelief the wrath of the Holy One." I am indebted for these facts to the kindness of one of the Faculty.

And, to give plausibility to my story, until within a few years, the room designated bore the marks of extensive repairs; but the industry of our carpenter removed not long since all traces of the first, but I fear not the only, visit of Mr. Devil to the shades of Old Harvard.

PRICE ONE DOLLAR

A.D. 1636 — 1878.

HARVARD AND ITS SURROUNDINGS

BY MOSES KING AND T. P. IVY.

L. S. IPSEN DEL.

HARVARD COLLEGE CAMBRIDGE ❖ MASS.

PUBLISHED BY MOSES KING

CHEMICAL ENG. BY R. H. MANCEL, BOSTON

AN ELEGANT GUIDE-BOOK TO HARVARD.

100 pages, 5 × 6 inches. Paper covers.

This work will contain eighteen plates of *heliotypes* (which include about forty views), and numerous wood engravings, illustrating every building connected with the College, and others in its vicinity; with sixty pages of letterpress descriptions. Subscriptions received by T. P. Ivy, 29 Matthews; Moses King, 12 Story Street.

INAUGURATION OF PRESIDENT ELIOT.

TUESDAY, October 19, 1869, brought with it the most imposing college ceremonies in which it has been the fortune of any of the present undergraduates to participate. The undergraduates assembled at two under the following marshals: Seniors, Thayer, G. Adams, and Rich; Juniors, Clifford, M. Rotch, and Boyd; Sophomores, Hickox and Gambrill; Freshmen, Pritchard, Gambrill, and Ware. The marshals were in full dress.

The standing about incident to the formation of every procession was then endured for about half an hour. The waiting of the Seniors was enlivened by the attempts of one of Sarony's men to take some views of the class; but as some youthful Ethiopian or member of the Germania Band would persist in walking between the camera and the class, doubts have been expressed as to the success of the pictures.

THE PROCESSION

started at about half-past two, and secured places in the church by three. It was arranged as follows: —

CHIEF MARSHAL. — Leverett Saltonstall.
ASSISTANT MARSHALS. —Joseph P. Gardner; Arthur T. Lyman; Robert T. Paine, Jr.; J. Lewis Stackpole; Benj. W. Crowninshield; Henry S. Russell; Stephen M. Weld; Charles S. Sargent; James R. Chadwick; William E. Silsbee; Charles T. Lovering; Francis H. Appleton.

Band.
Undergraduates of the College.
Members of the Scientific and Professional Schools.
Members of the Corporation.
Ex-Presidents Walker and Hill.
Former Members of the Corporation.
The Overseers.
Professors and other Officers of Instruction.
Librarian, Steward, and Secretary.
President of the Overseers and President elect of the University.
His Excellency the Governor, and Aids.
Ex-Governors of the Commonwealth.
His Honor the Lieut.-Governor.
Committees to visit the University.
Officers of the Army and Navy.
Gentlemen specially invited.
Presidents and Professors of other Colleges.
Government of the Massachusetts Institute of Technology.
Judges of the State Courts.
Mayors of Boston and Cambridge.
Alumni.

The Alumni formed the most interesting feature of the procession, containing representatives of classes as far back as 1804.

AT THE CHURCH.

The exercises were begun with music by the Germania Band, followed by the choral, "Let us with a gladsome mind," sung by Harvard men, under the direction of Mr. Paine.

PRAYER

was then offered by Dr. Peabody, who, after alluding to the great and good who had held high places of trust in this University, invoked the Father's blessing and support for "Thy servant, who this day assumes the sacred and holy charge.

THE CONGRATULATORY ADDRESS

was then delivered, in Latin, by Mr. John S. White, of the Senior Class. Mr. White was frequently interrupted by applause, which was particularly significant in support of his encomium on Dr. Peabody.

THE INDUCTION INTO OFFICE

by Hon. J. H. Clifford, President of the Board of Overseers, followed. This ceremony consisted of an interesting address, by Mr. Clifford, to which President Eliot replied, briefly and earnestly.

The chorus, " Domine, salvum fac Præsidem nostrum," by Mr. Paine, was then sung, and most favorably received by the audience.

ADDRESS OF PRESIDENT ELIOT.

Our limited space prevents our publishing the President's address in full. We have, therefore, selected those portions bearing upon Elective Studies, the Rank List, the Opportunities for Poor Men at Harvard, the Woman Question, and the Relations of the University and the Public. We advise every one to read the other portions of the address at their earliest opportunity.

THE SYSTEM OF ELECTIVE STUDIES.

" Only a few years ago, all students who graduated at this College passed through one uniform curriculum. Every man studied the same subjects in the same proportions, without regard to his natural bent or preference. The individual student had no choice either of subjects or teachers. This system is still the prevailing system among American colleges, and finds vigorous defenders. It has the merit of simplicity. So had the school methods of our grandfathers, — one primer, one catechism, one rod for all children. On the whole, a single common course of studies, tolerably well selected to meet the average needs, seems to most Americans a very proper and natural thing, even for grown men.

As a people, we do not apply to mental activities the principle of division of labor; and we have but a halting faith in special training for high professional employments. The vulgar conceit that a Yankee can turn his hand to any thing we insensibly carry into high places, where it is preposterous and criminal. We are accustomed to seeing men leap from farm or shop to court-room or pulpit, and we half believe that common men can safely use the seven-league boots of genius. What amount of knowledge and experience do we habitually demand of our lawgivers? What special training do we ordinarily think necessary for our diplomatists? In great emergencies, indeed, the nation has known where to turn. Only after years of the bitterest experience did we come to believe the profes-

sional training of a soldier to be of value in war. This lack of faith in the prophecy of a natural bent, and in the value of a discipline concentrated upon a single object, amounts to a national danger.

In education, the individual traits of different men have not been sufficiently attended to. Through all the period of boyhood, the school-studies should be representative; all the main fields of knowledge should be entered upon. But the young man of nineteen or twenty ought to know what he likes best and is most fit for. If his previous training has been sufficiently wide, he will know by that time whether he is most apt at language or philosophy or natural science or mathematics. If he feels no loves, he will at least have his hates. At that age, the teacher may wisely abandon the school-dame's practice of giving a copy of nothing but zeros to the child who alleges that he cannot make that figure. When the revelation of his own peculiar taste and capacity comes to a young man, let him reverently give it welcome, thank God, and take courage. Thereafter, he knows his way to happy, enthusiastic work, and, God willing, to usefulness and success. The civilization of a people may be inferred from the variety of its tools. There are thousands of years between the stone hatchet and the machine-shop. As tools multiply, each is more ingeniously adapted to its own exclusive purpose. So with the men that make the state. For the individual, concentration, and the highest development of his own peculiar faculty, is the only prudence. But for the State, it is variety, not uniformity, of intellectual product, which is needful.

These principles are the justification of the system of elective studies which has been gradually developed in this College during the past twenty years. At present, the Freshman year is the only one in which there is a fixed course prescribed for all. In the other three years, more than half the time allotted to study is filled with subjects chosen by each student from lists which comprise six studies in the Sophomore year, nine in the Junior year, and eleven in the Senior year. The range of elective studies is large, though there are some striking deficiencies. The liberty of choice of subject is wide, but yet has very rigid limits. There is a certain framework which must be filled; and about half the material of the filling is prescribed. The choice offered to the student does not lie between liberal studies and professional or utilitarian studies. All the studies which are open to him are liberal and disciplinary, not narrow or special. Under this system the College does not demand, it is true, one invariable set of studies of every candidate for the first degree in Arts; but its requisitions for this degree are nevertheless high and inflexible, being nothing less than four years devoted to liberal culture.

It has been alleged that the elective system must weaken the bond which unites members of the same class. This is true; but in view of another much more efficient cause of the diminution of class intimacy, the point is not very significant. The increased size of the college classes inevitably works a great change in this respect. One hundred and fifty young men cannot be so intimate with each other as fifty used to be. This increase is progressive. Taken in connection with the rising average age of the students, it would compel the adoption of methods of instruction different from the old, if there were no better motive for such change. The elective system fosters scholarship, because it gives free play to natural preferences and inborn aptitudes, makes possible enthusiasm for a chosen work, relieves the professor and the ardent disciple of the presence of a body of students who are compelled to an unwelcome task, and enlarges instruction by substituting many and various lessons given to small, lively classes, for a few lessons many times repeated to different sections of a numerous class. The College therefore proposes to persevere in its efforts to establish, improve, and extend the elective system. Its administrative difficulties, which seem formidable at first, vanish before a brief experience."

THE RANK LIST.

" Many excellent persons see great offence in any system of college rank; but why should we expect more of young men than we do of their elders? How many men and women perform their daily tasks from the highest motives, — for the glory of God and the relief of man's estate? Most people work for bare bread, a few for cake. The college rank-list re-enforces higher motives. In the campaign for character, no auxiliaries are to be refused. Next to despising the enemy, it is dangerous to reject allies. To devise a suitable method of estimating the fidelity and attainments of college students is, however, a problem which has long been under discussion, and has not yet received a satisfactory solution. The worst of rank as a stimulus is the self-reference it implies in the aspirants. The less a young man thinks about the cultivation of his mind, about his own mental progress, — about himself, in short, — the better."

HARVARD COLLEGE NOT EXCLUSIVE.

" Harvard college has always attracted and still attracts students in all conditions of life. From the city trader or professional man, who may be careless how much his son spends at Cambridge, to the farmer or mechanic, who finds it a hard sacrifice to give his boy his time early enough to enable him to prepare for college, — all sorts and conditions of men have wished and still wish to send their sons hither. There are always scores of young men in this University who earn or borrow every dollar they spend here. Every year many young men enter this College without any resources whatever. If they prove themselves men of capacity and character, they never go away for lack of money. More than twenty thousand dollars a year are now devoted to aiding students of narrow means to compass their education, besides all the remitted fees and the numerous private benefactions. These latter are unfailing. Taken in connection with the proceeds of the funds applicable to the aid of poor students, they enable the Corporation to say that no good student need ever stay away from Cambridge, or leave college simply because he is poor. There is one uniform condition, however, on which help is given, — the recipient must be of promising ability and the best character. The community does not owe superior education to all children, but only to the *élite*, — to those who, having the capacity, prove by hard work that they have also the necessary perseverance and endurance. The process of preparing to enter college under the difficulties which poverty entails is just such a test of worthiness as is needed. At this moment there is no college in the country more eligible for a poor student than Harvard on the mere ground of economy. The scholarship funds are mainly the fruit of the last fifteen years. The future will take care of itself; for it is to be expected that the men who, in this generation, have had the benefit of these funds, and who succeed in after life, will pay many fold to their successors in need the debt which they owe, not to the college, but to benefactors whom they cannot even thank, save in heaven. No wonder that scholarships are founded. What greater privilege than this of giving young men of promise the coveted means of intellectual growth and freedom? The angels of heaven might envy mortals so fine a luxury. The happiness which the winning of a scholarship gives is not the recipient's alone: it flashes back to the home whence he came, and gladdens anxious hearts there. The good which it does is not his alone, but descends, multiplying at every step, through generations. Thanks to the beneficent mysteries of hereditary transmission, no capital earns such interest as personal culture. The poorest and the richest students are equally welcome here, provided that, with their poverty or their wealth, they bring capacity, ambition, and purity. The poverty of scholars is of inestimable worth in this money-getting nation. It maintains the true standards of virtue and honor. The poor friars, not the bishops, saved the Church. The poor scholars and preachers of duty defend the modern community against its own material prosperity. Luxury and learning are ill bed-fellows. Nevertheless, this College is deeply indebted to those who, bringing hither from refined homes good breeding, gentle tastes, and a manly delicacy, add to them openness and activity of mind, intellectual interests, and a sense of public duty.

To lose altogether the presence of those who in early life have enjoyed the domestic and social advantages of wealth would be as great a blow to the College as to lose the sons of the poor. It is as high a privilege for a rich man's son as for a poor man's to resort to the academic halls, and so to take his proper place among cultivated and intellectual men. The interests of the College and the country are identical in this regard. The country suffers when the rich are ignorant and unrefined. Wealth is an unmitigated curse when divorced from culture. Harvard College is sometimes reproached with being aristocratic. If by aristocracy be meant a stupid and pretentious caste, founded on wealth and birth, and an affectation of Europern manners, no charge could be more preposterous: the College is intensely American in affection, and intensely democratic in temper. But there is an aristocracy to which the sons of Havard have belonged, and let us hope will ever aspire to belong, — the aristocracy which excels in manly sports, carries off the honors and prizes of the learned professions, and bears itself with distinction in all fields of intellectual labor and combat; the aristocracy which in peace stands firmest for the public honor and renown, and in war rides first into the murderous thickets."

WOMEN AT HARVARD.

" The attitude of the University in the prevailing discussions touching the education and fit employment of women demands brief explanation. America is the natural arena for these debates; for here the female sex has a better past and a better present than elsewhere. Americans, as a rule, hate disabilities of all sorts, whether religious, political, or social. Equality between the sexes, without privilege or oppression on either side, is the happy custom of American homes. While this great discussion is going on, it is the duty of the University to maintain a cautious and expectant policy. The Corporation will not receive women as students into the College proper, nor into any school whose discipline requires residence near the school. The difficulties involved in a common residence of hundreds of young men and women of immature character and marriageable age are very grave. The necessary police regulations are exceedingly burdensome. The Corporation are not influenced to this decision, however, by any crude notions about the innate capacities of women. The world knows next to nothing about the natural mental capacities of the female sex. Only after generations of civil freedom and social equality will it be possible to obtain the data necessary for an adequate discussion of woman's natural tendencies, tastes, and capabilities. Again, the Corporation do not find it necessary to entertain a confident opinion upon the fitness or unfitness of women for professional pursuits. It is not the business of the University to decide this mooted point. In this country the University does not undertake to protect the community against incompetent lawyers, ministers, or doctors. The community must protect itself by refusing to employ such. Practical, not theoretical, considerations determine the policy of the University. Upon a matter concerning which prejudices are deep, and opinion inflammable, and experience scanty, only one course is prudent or justifiable, when such great interests are at stake, — that of cautious and well-considered experiment. The practical problem is to devise a safe, promising, and instructive experiment. Such an experiment the Corporation have meant to try in opening the newly established University courses of instruction to competent women. In these courses, the University offers to young women who have been to good schools, as many years as they wish of liberal culture in studies which have no direct professional value, to be sure, but which enrich and enlarge both intellect and character. The University hopes thus to contribute to the intellectual emancipation of women. It hopes to prepare some women better than they would otherwise have been prepared for the profession of teaching, the one learned profession to which women have already acquired a clear title. It hopes that the proffer of this higher instruction will have some reflex influence upon schools for girls, — to discourage superficiality, and to promote substantial education."

THE UNIVERSITY AND THE COMMUNITY.

"What can the community do for the University? First, it can love, honor, and cherish it. Love it and honor it. The University is upheld by this public affection and respect. In the loyalty of her children she finds strength and courage. The Corporation, the Overseers, and the several Faculties need to feel that the leaders of public opinion, and especially the sons of the College, are at their back, always ready to give them a generous and intelligent support. Therefore we welcome the Chief Magistrate of the Commonwealth, the Senators, Judges, and other dignitaries of the State, who, by their presence at this ancient ceremonial, bear witness to the pride which Massachusetts feels in her eldest University. Therefore we rejoice in the presence of this throng of the Alumni, testifying their devotion to the College which, through all changes, is still their home. Cherish it. This University, though rich among American colleges, is very poor in comparison with the great universities of Europe. The wants of the American community have far outgrown the capacity of the University to supply them. We must try to satisfy the cravings of the select few, as well as the needs of the average many. We cannot afford to neglect the Fine Arts. We need groves and meadows as well as barracks, and soon there will be no chance to get them in this expanding city. But, above all, we need professorships, books, and apparatus, that teaching and scholarship may abound.

And what will the University do for the community? First, it will make a rich return of learning, poetry, and piety. Secondly, it will foster the sense of public duty, — that great virtue which makes republics possible. The founding of Harvard College was an heroic act of public spirit. For more than a century the breath of life was kept in it by public spirit of the Province and of its private benefactors. In the last fifty years the public spirit of the friends of the College has quadrupled its endowments. And how have the young men nurtured here in successive generations, repaid the founders for their pious care? Have they honored freedom and loved their country? For answer we appeal to the records of the national service, to the lists of the Senate, the Cabinet, and the diplomatic service, and to the rolls of the army and navy. Honored men, here present, illustrate before the world the public quality of the graduates of this College. Theirs is no mercenary service. Other fields of labor attract them more and would reward them better; but they are filled with the noble ambition to deserve well of the republic. There have been doubts, in times yet recent, whether culture were not selfish; whether men of refined tastes and manners could really love Liberty, and be ready to endure hardness for her sake; whether, in short, gentlemen would in this century prove as loyal to noble ideas, as in other times they had been to kings. In yonder old playground, fit spot whereon to commemorate the manliness which there was nurtured, shall soon rise a noble monument which for generations will give convincing answer to such shallow doubts; for over its gates will be written, "In memory of the sons of Harvard who died for their country." The future of the University will not be unworthy of its past."

The Address was followed by the Chorus from the Antigone of Sophocles: "Πολλὰ τὰ δεινὰ κοὐδὲν ἀνθρώπου δεινότερον πέλει," "Wonders in Nature we see" (Mendelssohn), which was warmly applauded.

Dr. Walker then pronounced a benediction, and the audience left the church at about half past five.

A reception was held through the evening at the President's house.

ZUKUNFTSMUSIK.

THE recent performance of *Lohengrin* at the Globe Theatre was an event of considerable importance, as it was the first opportunity given to Bostonians to judge of the new school of music, — the Music of the Future. The selections occasionally heard at concerts could at best give but an imperfect idea of the value of Wagner's operatic music. A concert must fail completely in illustrating one of his great principles, — the thorough union of the drama and the music. These considerations, and the fierce war which has so long been raging in the world of art between this and the old "classic" school, had raised expectations to the highest pitch; and, as far as we are able to judge, there are very few who are not now more anxious than ever before to hear the productions of the composer of *Lohengrin*.

Critics have not been wanting. One small class of musical people, whose feelings have been injured by Wagner's literary polemic against the tendencies of modern society, religion, and art, make it a point to condemn *in toto* his musical compositions, including even those in which he deviates least from the established and familiar forms of previous composers.

It is instructive to observe the grounds of their condemnation. They say that the forms of his music do not correspond to their idea of what these forms should be. By pointing out this incongruity, they assume that they have proved the worthlessness of his music. But the first principle from which Wagner starts is that these ideals of theirs, these previously established forms, are too narrow and not suitable for the highest musical expression. The case is parallel to that of a distinguished professor whom we recently heard refuting doctrines of Spinoza by applying to them *Cartesian* definitions.

We will endeavor to show how Wagner's operas differ from earlier dramatic music, and in what his real superiority consists; but, we regret to say, want of space will allow us to touch upon only a few of the chief points.

In the first place, Wagner believes that the opera should be a work of art in which there ought always to be an intimate, necessary union of all the arts. Between the libretto and the music this intimate union is so essential that they ought both to proceed from the same mind. In pursuance of this principle, Wagner has always written his own librettos.

In almost all Italian and German operas the librettos are of the most worthless character, and altogether incapable, from their want of emotional elements, of inspiring a composer to make the music an exact copy of the sentiments of the libretto. Where the language is unmusical, — that is devoid of emotion, — the composer has no means of expressing it. Accordingly, an Italian opera is nothing but a string of arias, occurring every ten or fifteen minutes, between which the intervals are filled up with dry, uninteresting recitative, without orchestral accompaniment. It is scarcely too much to say that the librettos of any two Italian operas might be interchanged without much injury to the operas themselves. Let any one who has heard Wagner's operas try to conceive of the same being done with two of them, and he cannot fail to observe that the story and its sentiments are expressed not only by the acting and singing, but also in a wonderful manner by the orchestra, thus rendering separation impossible.

In the Italian opera the orchestra is merely a "monstrous guitar" for accompanying arias. There the voice alone has the task of interpreting emotions; but, in the hands of Wagner, the orchestra exerts the full power of its rich resources, and with its aid he touches our inmost feelings in a manner equalled by no other dramatic composer. Even those of our musicians who pretend not to admire Wagner are the foremost in imitating him in his instrumentation.

It is not only over Italian composers that Wagner thus triumphs, but also over his German brother-artists, who stand high above the Italians. Coming after Weber and Mozart, he could notice the strong and the weak points in their operas. At an early age he became director of the Dresden Opera House, and it was by noticing the most remarkable effects in the operas which he constantly heard and studied that he formed his ideal of the opera. His operas are free from those stupid, unaccompanied recitatives which disfigure even "Don Giovanni." Beethoven made a great advance over Mozart in the discovery of wonderful harmonic combinations, and one of the great merits of Wagner is his application of these discoveries to the dramatic field. He has advanced even still farther into the yet unexplored wonderland of sound. Compare the Ninth Symphony, or Leonore, overture No. 3, with the introduction to "Tristan und Isolde," and you will see what I mean.

Probably the objection most frequently urged against Wagner is that in his operas we find no melodies. It is said that after we have left the theatre we can recall no particular air, and have only a vague impression of the whole. Far from being a defect, this is the ideal perfection of his work. We hear his operas, and the impression left upon us is like that we have after enjoying some beautiful scene of nature, We walk, some summer day, in a beautiful park. Trees, flowers, birds, a thousand other objects, meet our eyes, and inspire us with a peculiar feeling of elation and happiness. And yet, when we leave the park, we do not remember, nor care to remember, any particular flower or butterfly. If we want the pleasure renewed, we must take our walk over again. So it is with Wagner's operas. Every time we recur to them, we discover new beauties, none of which we feel able to carry away, without impairing the unity of the whole or detracting from the perfection of the individual. In every perfect work of art, the parts are of one mould and inseparable. Any detached portion is imperfect and uninteresting. In the opera this perfect unity is attained only by Wagner. His "infinite melody" takes the place of arias, and monotonous cadences make way for new and striking modulations. We may admire the arias of a Mozart, but their proper place is the parlor or concert-hall, rather than the dramatic stage.

Music is the only key to the world of sound, which is as wide and wonderful as the world of sight, — to some minds even more so. What can be more silly than to suppose that all its wonders have been discovered by past generations, and that no unexplored fields remain for future artists? When people get rid of this ridiculous notion, and make themselves familiar with the history of musical development, there will be less ignorance and less opposition to the Music of the Future.

F.

WALT WHITMAN.

THE works of Walt Whitman have lately been very much reviewed in England, while in this, his native country, he has rarely been noticed. In America, through ignorance of all the characteristics of his works, the little value he possesses as a poet has been denied him; while in England, chiefly through ignorance of the American people, Mr. Whitman has been greatly overestimated. Between his admirers and his enemies, Mr. Whitman has fared ill, — the former praising him too highly, out of all proportion to his deserts, the latter praising him not at all, seeing nothing but faults in him. The one is extravagantly delighted with the hidden music of his verse, the other calls him a noisy impostor; the one says he is Shaksperean in "balance and sanity" of mind, the other is utterly disgusted with the "confused jumbling together of the component parts of the dictionary;" — the loudest applause and the severest censure.

Whitman is spoken of in England as preeminently the poet of Democracy and of America, the first of Democracies; but we are not definitely told why. One English critic has gone so far as to style Whitman the "*sacer vates* to the growth of the American youth*,*" implying, I think, that he is benefiting us and is well known to us. But, mortified though we must be to admit it, we believe the youth of America know very little of their "*sacer vates;*" and, upon those of us who do know something of his works, it were just to deny that the effect produced is at all commensurate with the effect claimed.

We indignantly abjure Walt Whitman as a "*sacer vates,*" or as a true representative of our national thoughts and feelings. Because he spreads American names over his pages, foreigners consider him as the long-looked for herald of Democracy! An excellent chance, forsooth, for any madman to be flatteringly belauded and crowned America's poet, by merely mumbling and writing down in broken-legged verse the names of his country's physical features, its fowls, brute kind, its institutions, and numerous occupations! Either we refuse to Mr. Whitman his claim to be the exponent of our national thoughts, ambitions, hopes, and progress, or we submit ourselves to be looked upon as a people whose marked characteristics are illiteracy, sensuality, clownishness, and an utter absence of delicacy in manners, thought, and feelings; in other words, as a people of Pariahs. This is a distasteful alternative, but I see no other. Englishmen and other foreigners have been eagerly looking for something decidedly original in American literature; they have believed with Buckle that America must place a peculiar stamp on the foreheads of all her distinguished men; some of them have thought Lowell, Longfellow, and Bryant clever imitators, because their genius is but slightly tinted by the circumstances which in this country surround them. Something abnormal was wanted, and at last is at hand: they have found a man of a nature less poetical than his pretensions would have us believe, but yet poetical; and, as his works show, possessed of a character the most eccentric and marvellous. Their joy at this discovery is boundless, and Americans cannot comprehend it. To us, such violent admiration of Whitman seems to be the sputtering of diseased minds; for their admiration of him extends to matter, the construction of which is opposed to every well-established rule of poetical form, and the vulgarity of which is revolting to the sense and distasteful to the intellect. There are times when Whitman is the poet; but at such happy times there is in him no more evidence of the influence of Democracy than in any other American poet.

But let us quote a few lines, which, chosen with a view to give true impressions, will show at once the worthlessness of his claims as a poet, and at the same time expose some of those literary monstrosities which his English and American friends admire. Our bard's - admirers say that one of his most excellent poetical qualities is the faithful reflection of his character in his poems. If this is true, the following quotations tell a sorry story of his life, and will also help to explain his mysterious individuality, his governing motives, &c. He says he is —

"Turbulent, fleshy, and sensual, eating, drinking, and breeding," and not a " dainty, dolce affetuoso."

He takes a curious delight in repeating to his readers that he is sensual and lusty, without a greater fondness for the clean and respectable than for their opposites.

"No more modest than immodest."

" I am not the poet of goodness only — I do not decline to be the poet of wickedness also."

" I am myself just as much evil as good, and my nation is. And I say there is in fact no evil."

Whitman declares this repeatedly, as if he were afraid that some one would deny to him those qualities which he asserts that he has. But his glory, in so far as it depends on his sensuality, may rest safely; for in his earlier works his declarations are supported by passages sufficiently gross and indecent.

He tells us he is untranslatable; that when we think we have caught his meaning, — presto! it vanishes. He thinks his accumulations of words are : —

"Man's, woman's, child's, youth's, wife's, husband's, mother's, father's, young man's, young woman's poems;
Head, neck, hair, ears, drop and tympan of the ears,
Eyes, eye-fringes," etc., etc., from " toe-joints " to " jaw-hinges,"
" O, I say now these are the soul."

To discuss such unmeaning trifles would be to insult the good sense of the reader.

In his effusion headed " Salut au Monde," he applies to himself the question, " What do you see, Walt Whitman?" and his reply is embracingly poetical, consisting of a bare list, not in rhyme, rhythm, or reason, of every range of mountains, of every body of water, of every city, noted in a comprehensive geography. And this, we are told, indicates in him a vocabulary more fruitful than that possessed by Shakspere.

Whitman is a materialist, and chants his belief thus : —

"Divine am I inside and out, and I make holy whatever I touch or am touched from;
The scent of these arm-pits, sweeter than the aroma of prayer,
This head more than churches, bibles, and all the creeds."

It is not the subject of his poems, but its treatment, that we may justly complain of; and there is no one of his thousand and one poems, which exemplifies better than the preceding his disgusting taste.

He says if he worshipped any thing it would be his own body. Discussing one's duty to God makes our poet sick; so he would like to leave the society of those who do so discuss, and live with animals, — if they permitted it. He howls of the heavens, stars, moon, time, and space, leaping without difficulty from the infinite to the finite. Nothing too low or high but must bear the burden of his song. Whitman has no idea of delicacy, and supposes none in the reader. He penetrates our closets, accompanies us to the bath, pursues us through the day, passes the evening with us, sees us into bed, and then, unasked, jumps in with us. If we rebuff him, he reproaches us with " gossamer delicacy," taunts us with purism. Indeed, his sense of propriety is utterly dead.

Whitman harps long on the soul. It is at once spiritual and material, the body and not the body. Wonderful and obscure as the soul has hitherto appeared, under Whitman's hand it has become doubly wonderful, doubly obscure. Scattered among such dignified topics are verses forming repositories for the most repulsive nastinesses, while others are loaded with the most sickening of absurdities.

In some few verses there is a sad, sweet air gently moving, hand in hand, however, with only a pleasant rhythm; for he has thought it best to scorn metre, making rhythm in its stead sometimes furnish the music to which his verses dance. Rhythmical movement, unfortunately, does not sharply enough distinguish his verse from prose. Time after time we fancy ourselves reading disjointed prose, and our fancy does not deceive us.

In fine, then, we see nothing in Whitman, either in form of expression or in poetical nature, which does not grossly violate those standards by which the claims of the best of poets have been measured. Should we allow Whitman to embrace us, as he again and again says he wants to do, we should be erecting for ourselves a new standard of poetic thought and expression. His English admirers would carry Whitman in triumph over the muddy road which they have strewn with flowers-torn from the tombs of the greatest poets. But we will not join them in their frenzied march. When, however, Whitman shall have given us noble thoughts or elevating ideals, he may be sure the youth of America will appreciate him; but nobody can force us to drink from the polluted bucket which a maniac has filled, and which English sensualism raises to our lips.

HARVARD FOR WOMEN.

LAST fall, our most prominent professor in Greek received a letter from a young lady who wanted to study under him. He wrote, in reply, that it was impossible for him to take private scholars. She was not daunted by his refusal, but explained to him that she had resolved to give up Greek unless she could go on with it under his direction. He was naturally complimented by her persistence, and consented to try her. Thereupon she came to Cambridge, and, showing herself a brilliant scholar, has continued till now her lessons in Greek, besides studying Latin and Anglo-Saxon under equally distinguished professors. This is the beginning of the Woman's College at Harvard.

A few Cambridge ladies, thinking that there is room for more than one lady-student in Cambridge, have formed a plan by which our professors shall teach regular classes of girls. They are making arrangements for giving these girls boarding-places, and for hiring recitation-rooms. The common-sense college thus formed is to be run with as little red tape as possible. It will fit girls for the Harvard Examinations for Women, if they choose, or if the students prefer a less circumscribed course, they can have that. Of course, there is no intention, as yet, of forming four classes, or setting up the stupid machinery of required studies which we still retain: all the members of the college will have the same liberty as our special students, or as students at a German university.

Until the college is regularly endowed, it will be, to a certain extent, dependent on the caprice of our instructors, though they have very generally given their cordial support to the scheme. It is easily seen that the trouble of repeating a lecture or recitation already prepared is small, compared to the addition to a salary which a large outside class could give. If the University is rigorous in its exclusion of women from the laboratories, there will be, at first, some difficulties in obtaining about the apparatus necessary to the study of chemistry and physics; but these can be remedied in two or three years.

Of course, the college will give no degree at first; but it is hard to see that that will make any difference. "She has studied two years at Harvard" will always mean more than "she is a Neophogen A. B.;" and to those who study for study itself, a degree is of minor importance. It is, however, easy to anticipate that this college will early be included in the University, taking the place which Girton College holds at Oxford, if it is not absolutely made a part of our College. What will be more easy than for an instructor with two small sections to obtain leave to have them recite together? What more just than that a few of the vacant U. E. R. desks be filled, for this occasion only, by ladies who have the same course? And, with the entering wedge thus introduced, to what shall we not come?

"Where there's a will there's a way." The powers that be have thundered against co-education; but seven ladies of Cambridge are strong enough to snap their fingers in the powers' faces, and bring the girls here to study. Unless the professors who consent to take private pupils are cashiered unmercifully, it is probable that the powers will have to lump it.   M. B.

The Harvard Advocate

HELIOTYPE PRINTING CO. BOSTON.

1882–1898

"Our Predecessors and Our Contemporaries," written in 1885, describes the flourishing of Harvard magazines after the *Advocate* had cleared the path. They made new claims on student attention and allowed the older publication to shed some of its journalistic duties and concentrate on literature, which had always been its first love. Harvard writers were beginning to keep a closer eye on the continent, and realism, as exemplified by Zola and Tolstoy, attracted attention and inspired imitators. The essays by M. D. Mitchell ("Realism in French Literature") and Lloyd McKim Garrison ("Count Tolstoy and Modern Realism"), which analyze this trend, represent the best college criticism of the period, and, true to the spirit of the early *Advocate,* are edged with a certain taste of acid.

Another current flowed at this time. The aesthetic movement at Harvard could trace its origins to Oscar Wilde's 1882 lecture ("The English Renaissance"). It was Wilde, as publicized by his own appearances and by Gilbert and Sullivan's *Patience,* who brought the aesthetic fashion to popularity in the United States as well as in Britain. But even in the nineties this style did not dominate the *Advocate,* though the magazine did sometimes publish "decadent" verse ("Les Fleurs du Mal") and macabre stories almost until the First World War. The high standards of decency then prevalent kept really scurrilous writing from public print; morals were strict enough so that even an innocent story like "Yumé" could arouse private indignation.

But on the whole the styles of realism and aestheticism were subordinated to more conventional tastes. Arthur Cheney Train's "The Wrong Scent" shows the better side of standard *Advocate* stories; these still favored the well-told anecdote, usually in a light or sentimental tone and sometimes with an amusing twist at the end. George Lyman Kittredge's "Caunterbridge Tales" exemplifies a type of writing that was to become more and more outdated toward the century's end, although it was still popular in 1882. The technique lay in parody of an author commonly read at college (Latin parodies had been published in earlier days) as a means of attacking some old and vulnerable institution. In this case Kittredge uses Chaucer to mock the dining hall system, which seems to have been no worse then than it is today.

The *Advocate* boards of the early eighties included the first men to make names for themselves in the larger world of letters: Kittredge, the later Shakespearean critic, is perhaps the best known of them, but Charles Grandgent and Charles Townsend Copeland would also prove to be great scholars at Harvard. It was not until the early nineties that Edward Arlington Robinson appeared, the first major American poet to serve his apprenticeship on the *Advocate.* "Ballade of the White Ship" and "Villanelle of Change" represent the best of late nineteenth-century student verse, both in lofty subject and in careful control of metrical and stanzaic forms.

THE CAUNTERBRIDGE TALES.

"PARFAY," than quod our hoste, and lokde aboute,
"Who next shal telle his tale in all the route?
For goddes love give us no ribaudye
But som hey historie or tragedye.
Methinkth, Sir Borsair, thou schalt be the man
Which that a tragik tale telle can,
For that thou spekest wordes fewe and sharpe,
Ne wilnot never pleye with us and carpe."

Then fiersly him answerde this Borsair, "No:"
And semde he wordes speken wolde na mo.
But on a sodeyn chaunged was his mynde
And forth he tolde his storye, as i finde.

THE BORSAIRES TALE.

Forsoth ther livde in ages long ygo
A Borsair kind, god yeve his sawle wo,
Which that so gentil was and curteys eek,
And bar his heye offices so meke,
That lovd he was of students fer and nerre.
— This Borsair was an olde man, i here, —
And hadde o daughter for his mikele pride,
Angelika, no child hadde he biside,
And mycel bi hire fader lovd was sche,
Whose wif ful mani yeres deed had be.
He kepte hir as the apel of his yë,
Ne tak he any kepe — i will not lye —
Of printing-press nor eek of non biccyle,
This fader lovde Angelika so mycel.

It chauncede ones, that this fayre may,
Bitok hirself to walke upon a day,
Right in the parke, which cleped is commoun,
The pride and the delite of thilke toun
Of Cauntabrige, which that god saufe and se
For it is bred and boter unto me!

As sche about the moniment gan go
Walking amonges the cannon to and fro,
She was war of a litel freshman bolde
— A yonge thing, nat sixteen yeres olde —
Yet soth a stikke hadde he in his honde, —
For after Christes masse, ich onderstonde,
Even the freshmen blossomen out in stikkes,
And to the theatre goon, with other trickes.

Now whan this freshman sey Angelika,
He blente, like Arcite, and cride "A!"
As if he hadde be smiten thurgh the herte.
And with that worde out of the bussches sterte,
Fulfild with pride and rage, a sophomore.
But when he sey the maid i saide before,
He al so blente, he al so cride "A!"
Whan that he sey the fair Angelika!
Wherat uprist — what nedeth wordes mo? —
A junior and a senior also.
Who, whan they saw the maid Angelika,
They torned pale bothe and cride "A!"
Som man will ax, "How cometh it, Sir Borsair,
That al these wightes foure at ones were ther?

We may nat take the tale as it is tolde."
But i to hem make answere and bidde hem holde;
Ful mani thing hath happd, and happneth yit,
Of which the cause ne wot no human wit.
Who runnth the hal that highte Memorial,
Ne wight ne wot ne telle never schal.
How that the bill hath risn from four til five,
Is known, god wot, to not a manne alive;
Who is the mastir — who that wot mays aye —
Of Haverford in Massachusetts-Baye,
Whethir he dwelleth in the great white halle
(Which that containth the regioun infernale)
Clept Université, or on the hille,
Or els the Wadsworth wher man payth his bille,
Or Corporacioun highte or Faculté,
If ani knowth, i wot what man is he.
For thei ben mysteries, everichon
And fer beyond our feble senses gon.

Whan that Angelika to hire hom is gon
This 4 studentes followen everichon,
With lookes askance — hem liste not to pleye —
Thei soughte hir fader and to him gan seye: —

"O Borsair, greet and mihty is thi name,
Thrugh cristen landes is yspred thi fame;
And we, thi servauntes to live or dye,
Bisechen the to caste a pïtous yë
Upon us and to graunte our bone, alas!
For we ben alle, god wot, in sorry cas."

Then seyde he kindeliche, "What woln ye, frendes?
Who hath misboden yow ne doth amendes?
What woln ye han, i charge ye on your lif?"
"Angelika," cride ech, "to ben mi wif!"

"Ay, stant it so?" quod he. "By Seynt Johan,
Is everich of yow a ful proper man.
Yit comth ageyn, and i wil hav a teste
Schal telle me which on of yow be beste."

Thus goeth home ech on with sory chere;
But on the morwe thei ageyn appere,
Ech beting on his breste and crying "A!"
Wold god that thou were min, Angelika!"

Nu in the grete halle of his castel
This Borsair hath hem welcomèd ful wel.
Win brought he out and made hem meri chere, —
But sothely it were to long to here, —
And at the ende he spak, "Lordings," saide he,
"Sith ye woln hav my doghter der fro me,
Her is the test." Then tok he in his hande
A rol of parchment long, ich onderstande,
And yaf it to this freshman wher he stod.
This freshman streytway quok as he were wod,
And rad aloud the wordes were therin: —
"To Harvard College," thus dide it begin,
"Debtor for Bord" (which no man ever thoughte
That it beyond four dollars mighte be broughte,
Though that was served hash seven times ech wek
And coffe colde and therto thin and wek)
"Five dollars wekely," thus ran the bille;
And whan the freshman mervailld hadde his fille,

He yaf the money in the Borsairs hande,
Who put it in his pouche, i onderstande.
  " Ful honestly, mi son, the test thou bore."
Then yaf another to the sophomore.
The soph remembereth his score for beere,
The bils unpayèd of his freshman yere,
Subscripcioun fendes and the *Ekko* man, —
He dropth the bil and fleth as best he can.
" Ha !" quod the Borsair, " what a coward art thou !
But, juniour, it is thi torne now."
" Bi gog," then cride this junior in hy,
" I wil not stand no testes, no, not i !"
With that he smot him sore uppon the hede,
That all his mantel was with blode rede.
But was he not dismayèd, this borsair,
For steyteway he tok him by the hair ;
And thus they strogled as that they were wode,
And ech wolde hav the otheres herte blode.

And as they fohte and wrestleden, they tweye
This senior slily stole the maid aweye,
With sondri bags of ducats that he fond
With which besprinkled was the castel grond,
And by the person married were they
And married livde happily alwey.
  But of the Borsair and the juniore
We liste, lordings, for to seye namore ;
But so much can i seye, without drede,
That they were never seen, ylife ne dede.
And fro that time was there no Borsair
Was kind and curteys til that i cam her ;
And whan i go (which god grante be not scon)
Wher wil ye finden such an othere one ?
Thus ended is mi tale, i saye agen,
Christ kepe us al and saufe our soules, amen !
    Explicit narracio borsarij.

THE ENGLISH RENAISSANCE.

THE impression made upon those who heard Oscar Wilde's lecture last Tuesday, on the English Renaissance, was in many cases far from being an unfavorable one. Many of those who came to scoff remained, if not to pray, at all events to listen, and they were not ill repaid for so doing. The supposition that this man was a pure impostor, — a supposition amounting in the minds of some almost to a conviction, seemed gradually to weaken, till some remarked that Oscar Wilde himself was the only man in the world who really knew whether he was an impostor or not. This idea seems to us wholly unnecessary. What is an impostor? Is he not a man who pretends to be what he is not? Now it is absolutely well known what Mr. Wilde is. He is a young man who has written a volume of poems, and who knows and professes to admire the art of Greece and Italy. Besides this, he has come to America, and here, for private reasons, he takes upon himself to proclaim in public that the Beautiful is a source from which mankind can derive much pleasure, nay, even happiness; and that this generation, though progressing rapidly in many directions, does not gain as much in this particular field as it might.

All this is undoubtedly true. No one who understands the proposition will deny it. Every one is to a certain extent an admirer of the Beautiful; and true æstheticism is something which ought to be felt and believed in by every one who is not a worse than a senseless thing.

It may be said that a man who does not believe in what he says is an impostor as well as one who pretends to be what he is not. This sounds plausible enough, and yet a man may say a thing at one time from his heart, and repeat it at another in a lecture, when he is feeling that he does not care a fig for the matter. Suppose Oscar Wilde leaves the Music Hall, steps into a cab, goes to the best restaurant he can find in Boston, Ober's for example, and has the best supper he can order, with any one he may choose to ask. When the supper is in full sway, " By Jove," cries Oscar (I do not say he ever does or will do this, but simply imagine his doing it), — " By Jove, what unutterable rot it all is. I 've a mind to cut the whole concern. What do you say, old fellow, eh! just pass me the corkscrew, I mean the champ . . . thanks." If Oscar Wilde, I say, were to speak thus it would by no means prove in the slightest degree that he was an impostor. It would simply be his under nature rising for the moment above the structure of his education. If he or any one else really thought that æstheticism was rot, they would be very wrong.

What a man's finer nature has said, his baser nature cannot unsay.

The bar-tender who is said to have composed "I want to be an angel," did probably at one moment feel some such desire, or at all events he was able to appreciate such a desire on the part of another, sufficiently to allow of his writing the familiar words. This fact of itself is enough to warrant a hope on his part of seeing that wish fulfilled. He was not an impostor.

Oscar Wilde has written some verses which are as fine in their way as the hymn mentioned above.

When in the "Humanitad" he speaks of

> "The old Greek serenity
> Which curbs the passion of that level line
> Of marble youths, who with untroubled eyes
> And chastened limbs ride round Athena's shrine,
> And mirror her divine economies,
> And balanced symmetry of what in man
> Would else wage ceaseless warfare — "

he has said something after which he cannot be an impostor in this second sense.

It matters not what else he may have written, or what sort of cravats or trousers he may wear ; this verse is good, and he wrote it.

What then are we to think ? Simply this, that he, being a most enthusiastic follower of the æsthetic movement, — for he is not the leader of it, — has with true unselfishness sat down to consider what the best mode of advancing that movement would be, and he has come to the conclusion that to be ridiculous is to have an audience, and to have an audience is to have power.

He and his friend Gilbert have consulted together how this might best be accomplished.

"I will make myself ridiculous," said Oscar, "and do you write an opera, to which, without mentioning our arrangement, you must get Sullivan to write the music. This will make me all the more ridiculous, and once famous I have power." The scheme was a complete success, financially at least ; and now, after allowing the opera to make a fortune out of him, he has come to make a fortune out of the opera.

REALISM IN FRENCH LITERATURE.

REALISM, or *naturalisme* as it is called in France, is a name which has been applied to the present school of French literature, more than anything else to distinguish it from the preceding school of idealism or romanticism. It was the expressed aim of that school of writers to weave into a pleasing story imaginary characters and incidents which would illustrate the better side of life. The characters could do extraordinary things by extraordinary means, in order to demonstrate the general triumph of virtue over vice. Their best side was shown to us, and if their weaknesses appeared, they were only the ludicrous harmless ones. When a really bad man appeared, he was sure to receive his just reward before the end of the tale, and meet a miserable fate, or else, utterly unmentioned, sink into oblivion. The noblest senti-

ments and actions were displayed that we might be inspired by them to a higher life. One has only to read or recall Georges Sand, Alfred de Musset, Dumas père, Engène Sue and Theophile Gautier to perceive this.

Now, we all know very well that such is not the eternal way of things in real life. A good man does not always succeed, while a bad man is very apt to. There are failures and discouragements in real life, and many a good man has not "come out all right in the end," as similar men in the novel would, because he, physically or mentally, has not the perfection which they have. If there is to be a fictitious world in literature, why have it so one-sided? There must be virtue in mediocrity or there would not be so much of it in the world. Only the fittest survive, and survival means right.

Men saw all this, and thus arose the new school, which deals of life just as it is, with all its strength and weakness. The story is told simply, and it speaks its own moral,—inspiring by its successes, warning by its failures. This is the realism of the modern French school. But to call it new, is to call human nature new. The method only is new. Writers have been realists since the time of the Greek comedians. Among the very idealists, what could be more realistic than "Les Miserables" or "Travailleurs de la Mer"? On the other hand, where is there anything more idyllic than Daudet's "Contes," or Balzac's "Lys dans la Vallée," or even that extreme realist, Zola's "Une Campagne," and parts of "Les Fortunes des Rougon"? Instead of being new, realism is the embodiment of the lasting principles of every school which has ever existed. The code by which realists work is summed up in this single command: paint life. Does such a painting not include all of romance, of ideality and of nobility?

The aim of a novel is to accomplish some ethical good. This will be granted, I think, without discussion. For the very lightest novels, which, you may say, were written to please, do their good in resting the mind from heavier labor or in showing us the happier side of life. But how shall this aim be effected? The romantic writers had two methods of attempting this. By interspersing their novels with moral reflections, and by forcing their characters to climaxes which should easily point to a moral. The first method approached too nearly a philosophical treatise to succeed in a novel. The second was too palpably unnatural to ever affect men in the actions of their lives very much. The general intellectual development of our time rejects as unsound any such forced effects. The method of the realists is, to utter a paradox, in having no method. In painting life simply and truly as possible, they cannot help teaching the highest moral. They are unconscious philosophers of the highest school.

Claude Bernard, the French scientist, has said: "Modern morality aspires to a higher rôle than that of mere arbitrary teaching. It seeks to find the causes, tries to explain them and to act upon them. It wishes, in a word, to be master of good and evil, to develop the one and combat against the other." So the realistic writers aim to know the natural man as thoroughly as the advanced scientists of our time know the physical man. They study him, bound by physical laws, governed by passions and influenced by surroundings. They seek to know what effect a certain passion acting under certain circumstances will produce in man and on society. When this knowledge has been obtained, then in the formation of their novels, they act upon the individual and upon the surroundings in such a way as shall show how to arrive at the highest state, moral and social. Zola has said: "To be master of good and evil, to regulate society, to solve, in the long run, all the social problems, above all to furnish justice with solid foundations by determining experimentally questions of criminal law, what can be nobler?"

One word remains to be said concerning the position of Emile Zola, as the living head of this school. His extreme style is regarded by the great majority of his Anglo-Saxon readers as highly immoral, even obscene. And, taking him as leader, they blindly damn the whole school as harmful, without considering Balzac, Flaubert, Daudet and Tourguéneff. In regard to Zola, nothing could be more grossly unjust, nor farther from the truth. Zola's extreme style is induced from motives altogether outside of realism. He belongs to the realistic school as a writer, but he is using a method of work as a moralist, in his great undertaking, which is entirely his own. That undertaking is the combating against a national immorality. Before we can judge Zola's novels from a moral standpoint we must take into account what they were written for. We must realize the social condition of France.

France is a nation steeped in immorality, and more than that, hardened to it. For, before Zola, within a century, there has hardly been one protester against it whose voice was loud enough to be heard. Think of a country where *liaisons* are smiled upon as mere pranks by parents, and in which *faux ménages* are almost instigated by the action of the government. When this is understood, it will be acknowledged indeed, that extreme measures are needed. Zola saw this, and also saw that the old weak way of telling a pretty tale and pointing a moral was petty and useless. Previous writers had either sentimentalized against vice in a way which nobody took any stock in, or else while they showed the evil effects of it, they made it alluring. Zola has painted vice in all its hideous ugliness, with its shallow joys and its terrible retribution. He has not gone down into all this filth and dirt in order to make obscene stories, but to put a picture of the people before themselves, that they may see their stupidity, their vileness, their bestiality. He is not obscene. You cannot find in all his works a passage which makes vice alluring, or which would excite any feeling other than sorrow and disgust. He is not a writer who plays upon men's baser passions for the gain that is in it. In every one of his works he is a far-seeing, pitying man who is trying by shame and disgust to drive his fellow men away from their lower selves to their higher selves. Compare his work with a novel of Georges Sand or any of the romantic school, where the most noble aims and the most laudable sentiments come from characters who do the most ignoble acts; where passion and sin are excused, and nearly all the characters are represented as weak human beings who sooner or later give way to temptation. This, as Zola says, is but the morality of words, and these characters are more degrading than the veriest Magdalen in his books, because they pretend to nobility and she does not. Such books are vicious. Zola is moral.

COUNT TOLSTOI AND MODERN REALISM.

MR. BERENSON's charming little essay on Tolstoi, in the January *Monthly*, interested me as much as it did everybody else. It is a very clear and just analysis of this remarkable man's most remarkable writings; and if it be truly said of a great author, as has been recently quoted from Hugo, that "the book is the man," Mr. Berenson has given, even to those unacquainted with Tolstoi's writings, a faithful description of Tolstoi himself. And yet his title covered so vast a possible field that certain points were naturally and inevitably left unalluded to. It is with some trepidation that I venture on the dangerous task of amending so clever and interesting a study, especially, since to give a true idea of why modern realism exists, I must seem to dwell comparatively long upon some now almost unknown and very dull writers who are responsible for it.

At the close of the eighteenth century, French literature dominated Europe, and the terrible ghost of that "tyrant of words and syllables," Malherbe, still dominated French literature; but although Malherbe had accomplished a temporarily beneficial reform by "de-gasconnizing" the barbarian court of Henri IV, the furious zeal with which his disciples enforced obedience to his propaganda, made of the supple French literature a stiff, misshapen thing like the wasp-like bodices of the court beauties of the day. Malherbe begat Boileau, and Boileau wrote the "Art Poétique,"—a very Draconian law of poetry,—whose authoritative proscription of all that was natural put an end for two centuries to what the example of Villon and Régnier might have been able to accomplish. "Vulgar fellow"! he sneers at Ronsard; "he makes his peasants talk as they talk in the village"! Malherbe and Boileau crushed the life out of French poetry; Balzac, like them, tried to crush it out of French prose; but, being less able, and vainer than they, he did not succeed as he could have wished; although, such was the ultimate effect of the rule of this unholy trinity, that when the Revolution burst under the toy court of the son of Saint Louis, among the fragments of old forms and traditions, which it scattered to the four winds of heaven, were those of a dead literature.

Nevertheless, during this period of two hundred years, the iron hand of three pedagogues had ruled all the continent. English writers were as little read and appreciated in Europe as Japanese writers are to-day. "Have these English a literature"? said Henri IV to the Sieur de Comminges. "But very little, Sire," was the reply; "there are Bacon, Buchanan, and a certain Miltonius, whose writings are more insidious and infamous than the assassins of his king." Shakespeare was absolutely unknown in France till 1715. And so, when all European writers took their cue from France, and when French writers trembled under the ferules of the three, what wonder is it that both fell into the rut? Everywhere the five-act tragedy with its maddening Alexandrines was insisted on and perpetuated. The worship of Boileau even penetrated to Britain, where the writers of the court of Anne bowed down to the false god; and straightway pastorals and epics began to be once more in fashion, and the great Addison—erstwhile a clever writer—wrote a five-act tragedy,—"Cinna,"—if anything, more stupid than the "Cinna" of Corneille. Happily England was not badly tainted.

The eighteenth century was almost half through, and murmurings of rebellion were heard on all sides. The people chafed under the heels of kings and nobles; men of independence, under the restraints of a rotten church; and young authors, under the heavy yoke of Malherbe and Boileau. The men of mind rebelled the first; Montesquieu, Voltaire, and Jean Jacques Rousseau led the van in France, and Lessing, Schiller, and Goethe, in Germany; but before their work could be peacefully accomplished the bond-slaves uprose in their wrath and overthrew church, state, and literature in one mighty ruin.

The vastness of the revolution had the same effect on literature that a sudden and violent fright has upon the heart: for a moment all movement ceases, and then strong and swift pulsations begin anew. The foreign writers recovered the first, being the least affected, and for a time the heavens, so lately red with conflagration, glowed with the combined brightness of Shelley and Coleridge. Violently attacked at first, and then as ardently appreciated, Byron was their natural successor. Realism in English literature thereafter quietly continued its way without any sudden diverging. In France, just as the restoration of the last of the Louis was made the occasion for the restoration of Boileau, so the sudden revolution of 1830 and the overthrow of the Bourbons was fittingly accompanied by the "romantic" revolution of Victor Hugo and Gautier. They, however, remembering their past wrongs, and being opposed in their struggle for liberty by an army of furious bigots, were correspondingly wanton in victory. Hence Mm. Zola, Guy de Maupassant, and Catulle Mendès; hence Tolstoi and Alphonse Daudet; hence Howells and Henry James and all the other modern "realists."

The Russian people, being "without a spiritual and intellectual past of their own," to use M. Berenson's words, felt at once this nineteenth century renaissance, and hailed it with all the strength of their new-found voice, like a young cock saluting the sun. Poushkin and Gogol, the first, wrote some wonderful poems in their native language, but in form still either Byronic or French-romantic; Turgueneff wrote novels that made a tremendous sensation wherever they were read, and which really introduced Russian literature to the rest of the world; but he violated none of the traditions of the novel as they stood accepted when he began to write; after Turgueneff came Tolstoi and Dostoïevsky,—the first purely Russian, and withal purely realistic writers we know.

Realism means the portrayal of life as it really is, and yet, at the same time, as it appears on the surface. Here lies the difference between the Russian and French realistic novelists. The Russian describes an emperor riding by his troops on a white charger covered with gold trappings. You see the scene as the troops saw and felt it. The Frenchman goes further: he tears away the trappings, and discloses to your view a sore on the brute's back; its presence is as immaterial to the story as it was to the troops; and the description of its disgusting features— merely because they exist—is not only unnecessary, but offensive.

Tolstoi and Dostoïevsky, who are panoramists, are, at the same time, genuine realists. A recent critic said of two characters of Daudet and Howells, two most ambitious modern realists— "Daudet is false to his theory and true to his art. The Nabob is always touched by a soft light from the novelist's heart; poor Silas Lapham shivers in a perpetual east wind." Tolstoi is artless, and being so is far more skilful than either of his would-be rivals. He presents his characters as they are, and as they seem to be to their neighbors, without either warming or chilling them. He makes them live as simply and naturally as he lives himself. The action in his novels is always felt irresistibly tending to an end, but not necessarily to a climax of passion, despair, or death. Everything is natural, quiet; the dramatic arises and is felt—for every human life is quietly dramatic—but it is not allowed to dominate. There is not any more a false note in his whole pretentious works than there is in his descriptions of his childhood; and he would tell you that he were false to art did he strike a note false to nature. He allows the irresistible sweep of a story to seize upon you, till it brings you to the inevitable, but unforeseen conclusion. He lifts a curtain, and lets you peer breathless upon the life and death and birth of countless human creatures; but nowhere does he offend any more than life offends; and doing this, he is a realist; but Miss Austen never lets the victim escape from the suffocating sweetness of the hot house; Zola, from the stenches of the dissecting room.

In Tolstoi's "big" romance, "War and Peace," the reader is swept on by the action as by the current of a river, and yet never once thinking of the author or the style. The scenes are presented so vividly that one feels like a bystander. Let any one read the description of the Russian troops crossing the bridge under fire, or the redoubt at Borodino; he will feel himself, as I felt, an involuntary desire to get a little further out of range; and no realistic author can desire higher praise than this. This is the secret of Tolstoi's strength. He never philosophizes, he never raves, or weeps, or laughs; his characters do so, but in doing so unconsciously expound the Tolstoi creed themselves. Tolstoi, as Mr. Berenson has aptly put it, is the great "tendency-teacher"; given a certain point or crisis in a life he will show just how great and how far-reaching consequences will follow; and by adhering rigidly to the natural and the true he escapes the Scylla of the romanticist and the Charybdis of the analyst.

It is this adherence to theory and abandonment of art which makes Tolstoi so remarkable; and I am surprised that Mr. Berenson did not call attention to what he must surely have perceived, that Tolstoi in regardlessly following his own native instincts has as utterly revolutionized the novel as, fifty years ago, Victor Hugo did the theatre. "Quentin Durward" and "War and Peace"! What a vast gulf lies between them now! The unwritten law which used to govern the novel almost as the code of Boileau did the five-act tragedy, prescribed some ending,—generally a marriage or a death,—to the novel, which closed with a violent outburst of the passion which had been smouldering through its pages. Tolstoi's novel is none the less dramatic in that it is true to life; but he ends the story where fate has decreed it shall end,— not where he sees an opportunity for a startling suicide or duel. Of course the romantic novel cannot endure this kind of a thing for a moment. Fancy Steerforth unpunished and Little Em'ly married! And yet Tolstoi, without exciting either ridicule or hostility, goes beyond the fifth act, and writes, as may suit him, a sixth or a seventh.

In "War and Peace," the heroine, Natacha, is betrothed to Prince Bolkonsky. A handsome libertine named Kouragouine persuades her to reject Bolkonsky and fly with him; the elopement, however, is fortunately prevented in time. Bolkonsky, frustrated in his attempt to kill Kouragouine in duel, enters the army, and is mortally wounded at Borodino; there, in the hospital, he sees his enemy dying on the next cot to his, and, strange enough (to the French realist), he pities his sufferings and forgives him. He survives the capture of Moscow, and while being carried away in an ambulance-train he is discovered by his old love, who has in the meantime bitterly repented of her fault. A reconciliation follows, but Bolkonsky, too weak to rally from his wound, dies a few days later. Here Tolstoi goes beyond the fifth act. The roman-

ticist and the French realist would have made the reconciliation scene in the ambulance-tent the crisis of the story; Miss Austen's Bolkonsky would have fainted dead away, or her Natacha would—one or both,—and after a long and complex series of fevers and a complete recovery, the wounded warrior would have won his bride. Zola's or Daudet's Bolkonsky would have either died cursing the wretched girl at his side; or she, inconsolable at his death, would have taken poison; like the fainting scene in Miss Austen, one or the other would have been inevitable. What solution does Tolstoi find? None; he attempts none. The story glides gently on; Natacha dries her tears after a year or two (for youth and grief are seldom companions long), and marries the real hero of the book, the questioning, philosophizing, Bézoukhof, who has loved her for years; the clearing away of his doubts and fears is shown to be her mission; and this done, the story ends in the midst of peace and quiet, as it was begun in the rattle and hum of war.

In this novel again, the same delicious disregard of the conventional appears in the treatment of the love affair of Natacha's brother Nicolas. He is pledged secretly to his cousin Sonia, and loves her boy-fashion till his return from the war, a decorated and mustachioed officer. Rescuing the sister of the dead Bolkonsky from her revolting serfs, he falls in love with her. He is too manly, however, to break his pledge to Sonia, and tears himself away from the temptation. Natacha and Marie Bolkonsky becoming friends, the mother naturally learns of the reciprocated attachment. Her son's determination to keep his pledge, when by this marriage his heavily mortgaged estates could be redeemed, angers her, and she upbraids the gentle Sonia until she has written a letter to Nicolas absolving him from his pledge. Miss Austen would have had him refuse the sacrifice, elope, and do or die! Daudet would have removed Sonia by suicide, and perhaps made Nicolas, smitten by remorse, follow her *à la Deschelette*. Nothing of the kind happens. Nicolas, tired of Sonia, eagerly accepts her release, marries the princess, redeems his estates, and maintains the family in affluence. And Sonia? She smothers down her grief, and lives the same patient, uncomplaining life as before, sacrificed on the domestic altar, but never forsaking her love, nor once murmuring at her lot.

These are bits of real life. Poison and the knife are uncommon enough among the rich; suicide is far oftener induced by hunger and drink than any other causes; broken hearts are few; the bruised hearts, whose wounds, like Sonia's, heal over on the surface, beat on in silence. This is why Tolstoi is a realist. There is not a false note in his own composition, and he never introduces one into his novels. Unpitying and terrible as he is when he portrays evil, he never excites any other than the truly Christian spirit of indignation at the crime, and pity for the criminal. The villain of "War and Peace," and the villain—if one can call him so—of "Anna Karénina," both escape unjudged from the tribunal of the novelist; the insolent Dologhof is lost sight of in pursuit of the fragments of Napoleon's army over the Bérésina; the wretched Vronsky, enlisting in a Serbian regiment, seeks death in a cause he is indifferent to. Would a violent removal at the hand of the novelist have produced the same effect of awe which one feels over the probable fate of Dologhof, and the pity one feels for that of Vronsky? Was it a mockery when the Lord said, "Vengeance is mine, I will repay"? Must the novelist always judge? And if he judges wrongly does he himself not stand in danger of the judgment?

Tolstoi and Dostoïevsky are at the head of all novelists. The one preaches the resurrection of broken life, virtue, hope, and courage; the other of repentance and charity lifting the souls from misery and crime. Tolstoi is grand and simple. Dostoïevsky is tremendous and overwhelming. Tolstoi is the Beethoven, Dostoïevsky the Wagner of novelists; and no one can turn from these new novels to the Dickens and Scott of yesterday with any more satisfaction than from "Tannhauser" to "Trovatore." For, above the swell of human woe and suffering, rises clear and sweet the continually recurring theme of hope, and love, and peace, like the song of the wren above the clash of streets in the early morning.

L. MCK. G.

OUR PREDECESSORS AND OUR CONTEMPORARIES.

IN the early years of this century, when newspapers had but just begun to be, and magazines of the highest literary character had, for the first time, assumed the direction of the thought of the period, a desire to imitate the example of their elders entered the heads of undergraduates at Harvard.

The year 1810 was that which ushered into the world Harvard's first literary offspring, *The Harvard Lyceum*. Founded by Edward Everett, the "first scholar" of his class (1810), this magazine made its appearance on July 14, 1810; a pamphlet of 24 pages, uncut, with blue cover, and published every two weeks. The articles were composed somewhat in the style of those in English magazines of the day, the *Edinburgh Review*, for instance, and *Blackwood's*. High literary ability was demanded for the contributions published in the new bi-monthly, and for nine months Everett and his six co-editors worked hard and well to keep up to the standard they ever had in mind. But they had miscalculated the temper of their readers. The numbers were too purely literary to suit the tastes of the times, and the magazine was stopped in March, 1811, for lack of financial support. Everett, then only in his 17th year, wrote the valedictory for the last number, warning all would-be editors to refrain from giving their productions to an ungrateful world.

Profiting by this sad example, no one dared to undertake the publication of a second magazine until 1827, when Cornelius Conway Felton, he who was afterward the distinguished president of the college, then in his senior year, undertook, with two classmates, the task of editing a monthly pamphlet of 32 octavo pages, called the *Harvard Register*. When these three were graduated, nine men of the class of '28 succeeded to their duties. Of the later board of editors, George S. Hilliard was the most prominent. The concluding address in the last number, February, 1828, was by his pen: "We lament, in common with all scholars, that spirit of literary indifference which has given a death blow to far more ambitious projects than the *Harvard Register*." Complaint of indifference is, we see, no new thing at Harvard.

There soon appeared in the college firmament a brilliant literary comet, *The Collegian*, of which the first number was published in February, 1830. John Osborne Sargent, with four others, conducted the paper. Oliver Wendell Holmes was its most talented contributor. In *The Collegian* were first published his "Spectre Pig," "The Dorchester Giant" and those ever laughable verses, "The Height of the Ridiculous." Six issues brought this magazine to a close, to be followed four years later by the initial number of *Harvardiana*. Among the names of the editors of the last volume of this periodical are those of Nathan Hale, Jr., Rufus King and James Russell Lowell. The preface to this volume says, with surprised self-admiration: "A college periodical has survived its fourth year, and, wondering at itself, goes tumbling to its grave." Among its more prominent contributors were Samuel T. Hildreth, Charles T. Russell, Jones Very and Charles Hayward.

Not until twelve years later, in December, 1854, was another college magazine started. At that time *The Harvard Magazine* appeared, conducted by such men as Frank B. Sanborn, Phillips Brooks and J. B. Greenough. For ten years this magazine lived on with varying fortunes, but at length succumbed to its fate in 1864.

We have now reached a division line, broad and well defined, parting the older forms of college literature from the new. All the periodicals published up to this date had been in magazine form, edited with high desire to imitate their neighbors in the outside world; to devote their space to articles of high literary worth alone, rather than to attempt to print any less ponderous articles on college notes. Henceforth the tone of the college press is lighter and more pleasing; better adapted also to the changing character and tastes of the college world.

On March 9, 1866, appeared the first number of a new monthly, *The Collegian*. It took as a motto the words "Dulce est periculum." With foolish design and silly bravado it endeavored to show its contempt for existing authority, and, as a natural consequence, was stifled by orders of the faculty. But three numbers were issued; like its forerunner of the same name, its life was short. A feeling, however, existed in the college at the time that a college periodical was needed. Within five weeks after the suppression of *The Collegian* the first number of *The Advocate* was issued, with the words on the title page, "Veritas nihil veretur;" a reference to the sad fate of its immediate predecessor and to its own honest purpose. This motto remained undisturbed on the title page for some years, but in May, 1868, it was deemed best to strike out the words. Nothing was substituted for them. The phrase is, however, still the motto of the paper. On March 16, 1869, the name was altered to *The Harvard Advocate*.

On January 24, 1873, *The Magenta*, modelled much after the plan of its existing contemporary, opened its first number. *The Advocate* said editorially at this time, "We have long felt that there was room, nay, even a demand for another paper here, and we have occasionally expressed a hope that some one would try the experiment. The *Magenta* now appears to fill this void and to satisfy this demand—we heartily welcome it."

In May, 1875, when the college color was changed from *magenta* to *crimson*, the name of the paper also was altered.

A new departure in college journalism was made when *The Harvard Lampoon* was first published in February, 1876. The only humorous and illustrated paper published by college students, its success has been remarkable. F. G. Attwood and Robert Grant are names always to be connected with the paper. The first series of nine volumes was brought to a close in June, 1880. The second series was begun in March, 1881. The successful founding of the *Lampoon* stimulated others to other work in the journalistic field. December 9, 1879, was the birthday of the first daily paper published at Harvard. The reason given for its existence was that Harvard ought not to be outdone by Yale "in any literary enterprise," by which was meant the *Yale News*. The names of the editors of the *Harvard Echo* were kept secret for two years. It was but natural that a journal conducted in this way should not be a complete success. But in spite of its many faults all were surprised when the first number of another daily, the *Harvard Herald*, appeared January 3, 1882. Of course there was not room for two daily papers to succeed in college, and the *Echo* proved the weaker of the two. Its publication was suspended in June, 1882. To the *Echo* was due the suggestion, which has borne much good fruit, that of founding a Co-operative Society. In the autumn of 1883 it was deemed best, by the respective boards of the *Herald* and the *Crimson*, to consolidate under the name of *The Herald-Crimson*. This was done, but in September, 1884, the name was changed to *The Daily Crimson*.

We have still to record the recent appearance of our new and admirable contemporary *The Harvard Monthly*. Founded by energetic and capable men, it has before it every prospect of success.

We have purposely delayed till the last all mention of one magazine. The *Harvard Register*, the younger of the name, decried and severely criticized by its college contemporaries, was published monthly by Moses King, an undergraduate at the time, from January, 1880 to June, 1881. In it are stored up a mass of most valuable facts relating to Harvard, which will be of inestimable value to the future historian of the college.

In summing up this cursory review, we see that from the ambitious attempts of past generations of students, a system of college journalism has been devised which admirably meets the wants of our students. A *Daily Crimson* is needed to supply the news of the day, a "*Lampy*" to lighten our heavy scholastic burdens with his jokes, a *Harvard Monthly* to lift our souls to a higher and nobler plane of thought, and the *Advocate* to fill its own particular sphere, let us hope quite as acceptably now as at any time during the past twenty years.

TWENTY YEARS AGO.

"In olde days of the king Artour
All was this lond fulfilled of faerie.
The Elf quene with hire joly compagnie
Danced full oft in many a grene mede.
The grete charite and prayeres
Of limitoures and other holy freres
This maketh that ther ben no faerie."

SOME owe it to Carlyle and Emerson and the bloodless transcendentalists, and some thank Professor Bowen and the easily contented Scotch metaphysicians for the fact that such a Paradise as the Mussulman looks forward to is no longer for us. The fancy and the affections find nothing better to linger around with us in the ruggedness of American business life, than college memories. Our visions are still firelight pictures in Holworthy rooms. We think less, virtuous and logical as we were taught to be, of fair-ankled Hebe and of damsels with a dulcimer. For us it is better to let the mind run back to the well-bred beauties who came to our Class Days and wandered on the green. The pulse thrills still with the memories of triumphs over Yale, on the Field and on the Lake, when the college "Hurrah" told of proud victories. It is hard therefore to realize that there was something which needed righting in the kingdom of Harvard twenty years ago.

To Harvard men of the years from 1860-1870 college memories are especially rich and varied. Youths of noble spirit were going to the war and coming back with tales of glory, or dying to leave immortal names to be recorded in Memorial Hall. When Dr. Peabody gave his last warning and blessing "to those about to go forth into the battle of life" his words had a very present meaning. Rustication was no more a terror but a ready release from the objection of parents to joining the army. When Hazard Stevens was suspended for screwing in his tutor in Greek, did he not thereby shortly become the youngest general in the Grand Army? Did it profit that fellows should spend the fleeting years in delving out the stories of ancient worthies, fellows who knew Robert Shaw and the Lowells and Barlow and the two Hallowels and hundreds like them? Cambridge girls did not

recommend the ancients as sole exemplars of the fashion of men who could win them. But they told of the reply which his true-love gave to General Bartlett when he wrote her : My dear, it breaks my heart : but there is so little left of me that I think I ought to offer to release you from your engagement. Her answer was : So long as there is enough left to bear the name of Frank Bartlett, he is the only man I want to marry.

The war spirit was in the college both before and after the war. One famous colonel of cavalry had three claims on fame in the freshman myths. He had been stroke of the crew, he had cut a very huge rebel from shoulder to hip, and previously he had fearlessly sent our chapel Bible to Yale and likewise endowed our chapel with Yale's Bible. And after the war E. W. F. complained in the *Advocate* that the faculty had not the sense to realize that "the same blood was spent" in some midnight college exploit "which watered the plains of Gettysburg and in front of Battery Wagner." Seriously, there was where the first trouble began. The faculty had little knowledge of, or sympathy with the students. They were far more ancient men than the active professors of to-day. Harvard especially invited to Commencement "the venerable ministers who have a parish." Of that class of guests many abided. They were good men, something more or less than human. Some Yale men are saying now that they have too many such, and too few others. By the way, one of your old editorials about some Yalensian discussions is righteously entitled "Small fowles maken melodie." The contemporaries of the early editors of the *Collegian* and the *Advocate* were ripened for the war-time, and when they were partially ripe there was no war. They had to attack some wrongs. Nobody of account did otherwise then. They pitched into the ancient errors nearest at hand. Out of this came the *Advocate*, the story of whose beginning the present editors ask for. There were errors. It was wrong to force men daily before light in winter and thrice on Sundays to religious services. It seemed a bitter error that irreligion and profanity should thus be fostered. The President himself was a grievous error. The change first to Dr. Peabody and later to President Eliot of itself was enough to mark the dawning of a new and better day. The educational and religious system was hostile to its subjects as a thing of another day always is.

Those were the days to burst the bonds. The college was ready to become a great university. Some of the men and all of the rules were cramping the destiny of Harvard. They were not of the size of the times. How could the flock look upon the shepherds as intellectual leaders when the office of the professors most closely brought home to the students was to take marks from the scholarship of such as kept a dog, or wore other than a black coat on certain days, or rejected oatmeal metaphysics, or walked on the grass, or pared the nails, or went to sleep in the cold chapel? The professors thus did their duty as ordained of old in the college laws.

Students were treated, or operated on, upon ancient general principles without any recent reflection as to methods. *Experimentum in corpore vili* had always been a scholastic precept. The student in America had never been asked how he thought it worked on him and never took occasion to tell until the *Collegian* and *Advocate* were founded. This was the object of their beginners. Perhaps the fight was precipitated on the part of the Lilliputs by the act of the one of the professors who was suspected of being against the war and in favor of slavery. In a moment of irritation he called some of the blood of "Battery Wagner" by a name such as boys apply to one another. Their class, '67, was a class of marked individuality and independence. Soon after the three numbers of the *Collegian* were printed. These contained nothing more revolutionary than a remark ascribed to Socrates. "How many were worshipping in the agora?" Glaucon: "One, indeed." Socrates: "Forsooth to-morrow I will sooner attend a roll call." This was written by the poet-editor. Sanborn the second editor, then first scholar in his class, and one of the most conservative of men, wrote, "It seems a profanity to make the worship of God a mere instrument of police service." The other editor, the present writer, wrote "We want some place and opportunity for the students to meet and become acquainted with the professors. The college has suffered in no small degree for the want of this." Later the other weighty matters above mentioned were likewise discussed. But the beginning sufficed. The three editors were ordered to discontinue the *Collegian*. The college was roused instantly. Everybody wanted to be an editor. The captain of the crew and the captain of the nine tendered physical backing. Possibly the presidents of some of the religious societies offered solace or support. There was no hesitation. E. W. F. the best all around man of our time, and F. P. S. son worthy of the father who equipped John Brown, and M. W. (all ready to become a later leader of the Mugwumps) joined two of the *Collegian's* editors in founding the *Advocate*. The motto of the first was "Dulce est periculum"; of the second "Veritas nihil veretur." When the faculty formally decided on expulsion and announced it, it gave a moment's regret for the old folks at home, but roused a little Spartan feeling likewise, something in replica of the war spirit, something large for the occasion. The ludicrous features are now the plainest. Youth will out. The writer was sixteen. The older and wiser editors were three years older. Some of the new editors' friends pasted the posters announcing the birth of the *Advocate* on the President's house, and on University Hall steps and on the Elms. Lucky it was for the editors that as at Troy the powers above took sides. On the side of the juveniles Dr. Holmes, Dr. Hedge, Col. Higginson, F. B. Sanborn, Professors Gurney, Child, Cutler and all the younger alumni declared themselves. James Russell Lowell, they heard, attended a faculty meeting in the martyrs' behoof. He certainly said to them: "I was something of a revolutionist myself, you know." They doubted if Leonidas had ever received so congenial a tribute. Professor Child gave out Free Speech as the subject for the next forensic, told us to say our say on it, and in a humorous and lovable way added, that for his part he thought boys must have some safety-valve or they might explode. For two years the students printed their thoughts about themselves and their government before the first editors graduated and for eighteen years since. One of the many like articles of those early days is headed: "*Murderer*. We are men my liege? *Macbeth*. Aye, in the catalogue ye go for men." Dr. Hedge and others wrote notable essays on our themes, and the Doctor the same year had the Phi Beta Kappa oration and in stronger words than ours said: "The professors are police-officers. Harvard must be made a university." And Harvard under President Eliot's glorious administration did shortly become a great university. The *Advocate* was the first of college newspapers.

Many others followed. Can they not profitably advocate now the cheapening of education and living at Harvard. Is it not the one blot on President Eliot's administration that in effect the result will be an attempt to gather grapes from bramble bushes only, that is, an attempt to make scholars only out of such as could live in Beck and Weld, and to bar the sons of impecunious literary and professional men whose blood is quite as hopeful of results in scholarship? Neither is it American to say our boys can be sizars or servitors.

College magazine poetry used to be from all too hollow reeds, always excepting Dr. Holmes's.

Some critic with a heart should tell you how the *Advocate* Poets, in the *Advocate* and in the *Century*, *Harper's* and *Life* and elsewhere, rhyming of love, as it is or used to be, and writing of life without pathos, have founded the first purely native and natural school of American poets. This is not too much to say of the verses of Frederic Loring, Soley, Fiske, Pease, Goodwin, Robert Grant, Scollard, Sherman, Lord, Kittredge, Gates, Nutter, and the forty others who since the time of Gage, E. J. Lowell, E. C. Clarke, F. P. Stearns and Leonard of '67, have made your verses.

W. G. PECKHAM, '67.

BALLADE OF THE WHITE SHIP.

DOWN they went to the still, green water —
　　The dim White Ship like a white bird lay;
Laughing at life and the world they sought her,
　　And out they sailed on the silvering bay :
　　The quick ship flew on her roystering way,
And the keen moon fired the light foam flying
　　Up from the flood where the faint stars play,
And the bones of the brave in the wave are lying.

'Twas a king's gay son with a king's gay daughter,
　　And full three hundred beside, they say,
Hurrying on to the lone, cold slaughter
　　So soon to seize them and hide them for aye;
　　But they danced and they drank and their souls grew gay,
Nor ever they knew of a ghoul's eye spying
　　Their splendor a flickering phantom to stray
Where the bones of the brave in the wave are lying.

Through the mist of a drunken dream they brought her
　　(This wild white bird) for the sea-fiend's prey :
The ravenous reef in his hard clutch caught her
　　And whirled her down where the dead men stay —
　　A torturing silence of wan dismay;
The shrieks and curses of mad souls dying.
　　Then down they sank to slumber and sway
Where the bones of the brave in the wave are lying.

L'ENVOI.

Prince, do you sleep 'mid the perishing clay
　　To the mournful dirge of the sea-birds' crying?
Or does blood still quicken and steel still slay —
　　Where the bones of the brave in the wave are lying?

E. A. Robinson.

VILLANELLE OF CHANGE.

SINCE Persia fell at Marathon
  The yellow years have gathered fast —
Long centuries have come and gone.

Any yet (they say) the place will don
  A phantom fury of the past,
Since Persia fell at Marathon;

And as of old, when Helicon
  Trembled and swayed with rapture vast, —
Long centuries have come and gone —

This ancient plain, when night comes on,
  Shakes in a phantom battle blast,
Since Persia fell at Marathon   .   .   .

With mouldering mists of Acheron
  Long have her skies been overcast,
Long centuries have come and gone;

The suns of other days have shone —
  The first has fallen to the last:
Since Persia fell at Marathon,
Long centuries have come and gone.

                              E. A. Robinson.

"LES FLEURS DU MAL."

THE obdurate eyes of awful creatures gleam,
  And in their nakedness uncoiled and bare
In piteous procession there do stream
A thousand horrid shapes : as thin in air
  And abominable through the shifting dream
I hear the mocking laugh of Baudelaire.

John Mack, Jr.

THE HARVARD BELL.

HEAR the recitation bell,
  Brazen bell !
What a dreary, weary hour its rhythmic throbs foretell !
From the tower on Harvard Hall
Comes its irksome lecture-call,
In a melancholy clang,
With a bumping, brassy bang,
From the ugly tower tall
On the top of Harvard Hall.
How it says that for a sour and voluminous long hour
  We shall delve
  On History 12
In the Grind-infested bower !
  How it shrieks !
  How it creaks !
How the perspiration leaks
From the deathly pallid face
Of the Sport, whose hurried pace
  Echoes round
  On the ground !
  How he talks
  As he walks !
  Hear him curse
  In language terse
At the horrid Harvard bell,
Grinding out sweet Leisure's knell !
  At the bell, bell, bell,
  He says, " Hell, Hell, Hell ! "
At the brawling, bumptious banging of the bell.

Daniel Gregory Mason.

YUMÉ.

A FRIEND of mine, a young Japanese philosopher, came back from a journey through the interior of Japan, and told me of a very interesting incident.

About five days after he had started from the city of Tokio, he came to a thickly wooded, mountainous region. At the foot of the mountain he had a little lunch, and then started northward through the narrow path leading to a town on the other side of the mountain. The path ran zigzag to avoid a steep slope. The cedars and firs were so dense that, except when they were moved by the wind, the sunbeams hardly penetrated their needles. Every footstep, every cough, and every murmur of the philosopher, was echoed from all directions, as the sound struck, one after another, a tree or a rock. The path was often hidden by the thickly-growing moss or bush. Sometimes it was broken by the streams running across the path. The philosopher jumped over many streams, but he was often obliged to go into the water, which was clear and extremely cold. He was alone, and during all the afternoon he saw only two houses and half a dozen men.

About five o'clock, he came to the summit. As he climbed on a cliff projecting over the woods, he saw the sun just setting in the western horizon. "What an immense fire-ball! What a magnificent cloud!" he exclaimed. In the west he saw the sunbeams striking the peaks, thence scattering thousands and thousands of golden rays. In the north and the east he saw nothing but several mountain ranges, running like six-folded screens. Those parts of the ranges which were nearest to him were dark blue. As they retreated they grew lighter, and finally the mountains looked gray, blurring themselves in the mist. In the south he saw the plain extending a hundred miles seaward, and disappearing in the horizon just before it touched the ocean. Below was a rich valley. In it he saw several towns, and even steam-cars running busily. But the cars could not take the exhausted philosopher from the solitary summit.

He looked down, and found beautiful moss so growing between the rocks as to give him an unroofed shelter in the cliff. He took a seat on the moss, and said, "Ah! I am tired!" He stretched his hands and legs like a dog. Then he bent his right arm, and rested his head on his hand. His eyes closed.

Suddenly he saw near him a light. "There is my hotel," he exclaimed. He got up, and scrambled hastily over rocks, bushes and water.

At last, he came to a little wooden house. He knocked at the door. There was no answer. He knocked again. Then a woman, with a candle in her hand, came out. She looked surprised, and asked, "Who are you, sir?"

"I am a tourist," said the philosopher. "I am anxious to get to a hotel, for the night has come and I am very tired. But in the darkness I have lost my way, while I was crossing the mountain. I have found your light and came here to beg the shelter of your hotel."

"This is my residence," said the lady, "and I cannot accommodate any tourists. If you want a hotel, you must go about twenty miles northward."

"I am exhausted and cannot walk any more, madam," said the philosopher. "I am not accustomed to sleep in the fields. It is terrible, madam, for I may be attacked by wild beasts. Pray, let me occupy some space in your house over night."

The young lady hesitated a little while and asked, "Whence are you, and what is your name?"

"I am from Tokio," said the philosopher, "and my name is Hara Dokan. My uncle is Count Hara of Mita."

"Well, well," the lady exclaimed; "then you are from my native place; come in, and wash your hands. Alas! their skins are broken." She went into the next room and brought out a bottle of medicine.

They were seated by the fire in the drawing-room, and the young lady bound up the wounds. The fire disclosed her features in detail. Her face was neither round nor long. Her fair, snowy complexion was in harmonious contrast to her rosy cheeks. Her nose was straight and long. Her eyes were large and bright, her eyebrows slightly curved like a new moon. She had occasionally a dimple in each cheek. Her hands were small and smooth, her fingers straight and long. She wore no ring. Her dresses were all silk, and her sash was rich and splendid. Her dark hair shone like a black pearl, and it was fastened in the Shimada fashion which showed that she was not married. She looked noble and refined.

The young philosopher asked her, "Have you a mother?"

The lady having finished the binding of his wounds, lifted her face, and said, "No, sir, I have no mother, father, brother or sister. I am living here alone. I cook for myself and do all kinds of sewing."

The philosopher did not understand why such an angel-like lady could ever live alone in such a solitary place, yet maintaining her beauty and her dignity.

He asked her, "Whence and why did you come here?"

She said, "There is a long story about it, and I think it better not to tell you. Anyhow, you must be hungry, so you must take some supper."

She went to the adjacent room and brought out chestnuts, persimmons, cherries, grapes and all sorts of wild fruits and meats. The philosopher ate but very little and repeated his question. Then the young lady yielded, and began:

"I was born in the city of Tokio. My father was a jeweler. He died when I was little. I lived with my mother. Once, in the spring, we went to Boktai to see the cherry flowers. We were walking among the crowd. A handsome young man in a beautiful carriage came from the opposite direction, led by his footman. He looked at us and passed by. Soon afterward he came back to us and stopped his carriage. He got down from it, and followed us a few steps, and asked us to drive with him. I was indeed frightened. My mother discoursed with him all the time, and declined his invitation. He asked our address, and then went off. About two weeks later, he came to our store and bought many jewels. Then he repeated his call and finally proposed marriage to me. But I declined.

"After two months the Countess of Mita came to my house with some valuable presents, and told my mother that her son was seriously ill because of his disappointment. And if I did not marry him, she said, he would not live. My mother tried to induce me to marry the young Count, but I declined. Two days later, the Countess came to my house with two carriages, one of which was empty, and told my mother that her son was dying in desperation, and unless I would come and see him, his spirit could not ascend to Heaven. I went with my mother, guided by the Countess. I saw the young Count lying on the bed. His face was wrinkled, and his cheek-bones were unusually prominent. Since morning his head had lain motionless on the pillow. His eyes were cast on the floor. He had no power to raise his head. So I knelt down and saw him. He seemed extremely surprised. He looked at my face for a short time and gave a ghastly smile; then tears fell from his eyes. Soon, with great difficulty, he stretched out his hand, and I grasped it in my palm. He was gone. My sympathy and sorrow were so strong that I felt as if my breast was filled with something. I was keenly conscious of my sin in so desperately disappointing the young Count.

"Since then I have determined not to marry anybody. In the ensuing winter my mother died. In the next spring I left Tokio and came here. That was three years ago."

The philosopher asked, "Why did you not marry the young Count?"

The young lady said, with tears in her eyes, "I could not marry him."

"Why?" said the philosopher.

"Because I have a peculiar inheritance from my ancestors," said the lady.

"What is your peculiar inheritance?" said the philosopher.

"I cannot tell you anything about it," said the young lady, and she turned the subject of the conversation.

The clock struck twelve, and the fire was

gradually growing smaller. The young lady showed the philosopher to his bedroom. There he undressed and went to bed. It was pleasant in the silken sheets. Yet, however tired he was, he could not go to sleep, for his mind was occupied with his admiration of the lady. About one o'clock he lifted his head and saw her still sitting by the fireside.

He said to her, "Are you working?"

She answered, "No, sir."

"It is now very late; why don't you retire?" he said.

"Because I do not care to," she said.

The philosopher could not understand why the lady did not retire. He lifted his head again and looked all around the room, and studied the construction of the house. He found that there were only three rooms in the house, namely, kitchen, drawing-room and bed-room. He discovered the reason that she could not go to bed was because he was occupying the bed-chamber. He dressed, came out of the chamber and tried to persuade the young lady to go to bed and let him sleep by the fireside.

But she said, "You must keep the bed, for you are tired."

He answered, "But I have no courage to occupy the hostess' bed-chamber and drive her from it."

She said, "You are a philosopher, and I am a virgin. We have both withstood temptation. We have no inclination whatever to make any mistake. Let us sleep in the same chamber."

The philosopher agreed; she spread out a mattress for him, and they slept in the same chamber.

The next morning he found himself alone, lying on the moss, embracing his satchel.

Suiho K. Nakamura.

18 Grays, May 13th, 1895.

My dear Mr. Kublauch,

I was much surprised to see to-day in the Advocate the story by S. K. Nakamura, printed in its original indecent form. You will remember that when I hunted up the story to give to you, that I pointed out the indecency of its ending, and warned you that it should be changed before publication. I did not think that it was necessary to exact from you an explicit pledge. I supposed that from the fact that you were editor of a paper which must to a certain extent represent the college, you would have the sense of what is fitting and decent; or that at any rate, after I had been at some trouble to find you material, you would naturally respect my wishes. Apart from the indecency of the story, which might be excusable in a foreigner, ignorant of American standards, you seem to me guilty of a breach, if not of faith, at any rate of courtesy; and under the circumstances I shall refuse to help you to any more manuscript from the sources under my charge.

Yours truly,

J. H. Gardiner.

Mr. I. G. Kurthauch.

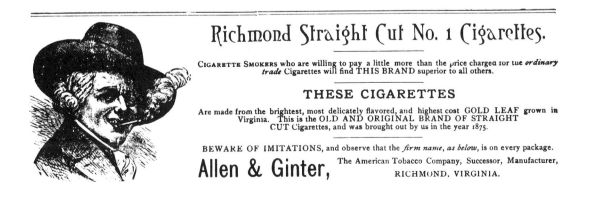

THE WRONG SCENT.

THE TRUE STORY OF A "MAUVAIS QUART D'HEURE."

A COLD shiver passed through the manly frame of Mr. Richard Randolph as he stood before an open box lying upon his centre-table and gazed with perturbed countenance at its contents. The hour was late; that is, it was about a quarter after six, which does not leave much time to spare when one is due at a dinner at seven and must dress and get into Boston from Cambridge within the hour. But it was not lack of leisure that disturbed our friend; in fact, he claimed on ordinary occasions to be able after long practice to perform his toilet and array himself in evening dress in the ridiculously short space of seven minutes; it was not lack of time, I repeat; it was something infinitely worse.

A short retrospection upon our part will be necessary in order fully to understand the situation. Lying upon his writing table was an invitation from a certain society leader of Boston, asking him to dinner upon this very evening, to meet a young and attractive damsel from Baltimore who happened to be visiting her. Richard had of course joyfully accepted, and then as carefully dismissed the whole thing from his mind with his usual nonchalance, only remembering his engagement a few moments before our story opens.

"It's lucky I happened to remember that dinner!" he remarked mentally as he endeavored to find his dress suit. "Mrs. Tyler would have black-listed me!" After a fruitless search in his chiffonier, which failed to reveal any signs of the aforesaid wedding garments, Mr. Randolph realized with a sinking heart that this being his first appearance in society for the season, since it was early in the autumn, his evening clothes were still carefully done up and put away in a box at the top of his closet. "They'll be ruinously creased! I should have sent them to the tailor's ages ago!" he ejaculated as he hastily carried the box out into his study and untied it. Then, as he removed the cover, his courage departed from him. There lay his poor dress suit, creased and crumpled, but that was not all; a strange and noisome odor rose from the box and filled the air,— an odor hated of all men,— a perfume like the mingling of checkerberry, kerosene, and Charles-River-flats-at-low-tide,— the odor of those inventions of Satan that women put in men's clothes to keep out the moths. The smell floated calmly up and tickled the nostrils of our wretched hero; it pervaded the room, hung about his head, and infected his person. He was paralyzed with horror. He remembered how in the spring he had told the "goody" to put away his dress clothes for him, and he now perceived with what thoroughness she had performed her work. Her very words on that occasion returned to his mind: "Dar now, Marse Randolph, Ise done fixed yo' clo's so dey ain't no kind ob insec' can tech 'em. Ise put in some ob my 'moth-balls'!" And he recollected that he had *thanked* her for her thoughtfulness.

He looked at his watch and found that it was just a quarter after six. At first he thought of giving the whole thing up and feigning sudden sickness; then he remembered the Baltimore girl and resolved to go at all hazards. First he subjected the clothes to a vigorous beating; then he hung them out of the window and let the autumn breezes fan them while he got ready to put them on. Nevertheless, after he had dressed, the clothes seemed as odoriferous as ever; the smell was absolutely fiendish. In desperation he seized an atomizer and deluged himself with vaporized cologne; but, strange to say, this seemed to have no effect — in fact, if anything, it appeared to put an edge on the already sufficiently penetrating perfume.

All the way into Boston he stood on the front platform with his coat off and tried to air himself, and as he felt the wind whistling through his coat-tails, while the car buzzed over Harvard Bridge, he began to feel more at ease. He thought of the beautiful girl from Baltimore, and reflected that he had been in worse predicaments than this before and lived through them.

Randolph arrived in good time and was introduced to the damsel for whom the dinner was given, and then followed a tête-à-tête, during which he shuddered and tried to look pleasant by turns. To his excited imagination the room seemed already full of the odor of "moth-balls," and he awaited with feverish anxiety the moment when it should be discovered by the rest of the company. He did not have long to wait. Mrs. Tyler shortly betrayed signs of nervousness.

"I wonder what is the matter with that lamp!" she exclaimed, glancing at a tall piano-lamp in the corner. Dick was on the *qui vive* in an instant.

"Let me fix it!" he suggested, endeavoring to get as near it as possible. The lamp proved to be in a fairly normal condition, however, and Mrs. Tyler apologized for the unpleasant odor, saying that the lamps were always getting out of order. Dick meanwhile mentally hugged himself and tried to turn the conversation.

The host, who was a trifle late, now entered, and after greeting his guests, turned to his wife with, "Er, Mary, what is this peculiar odor? Is there anything the matter with that lamp? Pray have it fixed as soon as possible."

During the confusion of going out to dinner, Richard congratulated himself upon his escape, yet quaked with apprehension at the thought of what later tortures he might have to endure. His uneasiness was not diminished when he found himself placed beside the girl from Baltimore.

There was a good deal of conversation at first, and our hero flattered himself that perhaps his trials were over, but the hope was in vain. A curious and peculiarly searching perfume began to make itself evident most unmistakably. Dick fairly perspired with agitation, being, as he was, absolutely helpless. He wished the house would catch fire, but this was improbable. The girl from Baltimore was seized with a fit of coughing, which did not improve matters. The hostess beckoned to the butler, who carefully examined all the gas jets and then shook his head dolefully at her from the pantry door. The guests moved a trifle uneasily. Conversation languished. The servant who passed Dick the soup turned away and stifled a cough. Someone started to tell an anecdote about General Grant and forgot what he was going to say, when he had reached his description of how "the General sniffed the powder-laden air," and stopped in a plainly embarrassed manner.

Presently there came a dead silence. Dick was racking his brains for a pretext to excuse himself, and had resolved to have an epileptic fit if something did not happen within two minutes. Fortunately or unfortunately, something did happen. He was seized with an uncontrollable desire to sneeze. He felt it coming and whipped out his handkerchief in time to save himself, but to his horror found that three little white balls had flown from his pocket at the same time, and were now rolling and bouncing about the table to the amusement of the startled company. For a moment there was silence, then followed an hilarious burst of laughter. Dick, seeing that all was over, laughed confusedly with the others, and resolving to throw himself upon the mercy of his hostess, got up and told the whole story of his sufferings and begged to be forgiven. His account of the matter was received with much mirth, and he was granted complete and final absolution by all present.

"But Mr. Randolph must write this up into a story," cried someone.

"Yes, yes!" resounded on all sides.

"But what shall I call it?" gasped Dick.

"Call it," murmured the girl from Baltimore, glancing slyly at our hero, "call it 'The Wrong Scent.'" *Arthur Cheney Train.*

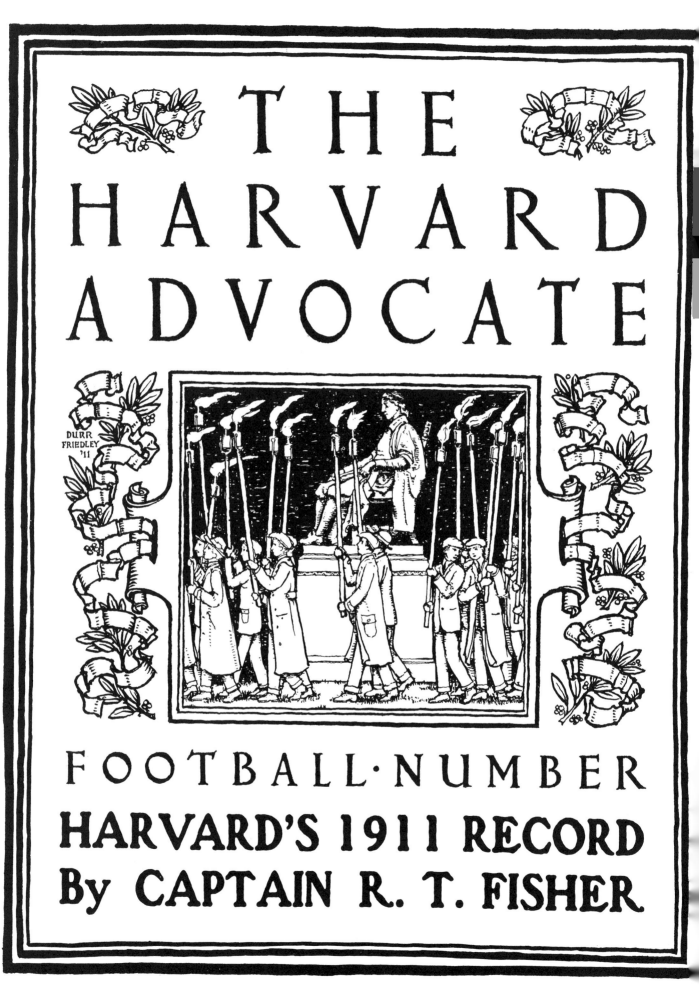

THE HARVARD ADVOCATE

FOOTBALL·NUMBER

**HARVARD'S 1911 RECORD
By CAPTAIN R. T. FISHER**

1898–1915

The time from the turn of the century to the First World War seems to us an heroic age in *Advocate* history, for in retrospect it is dominated by five great men.

Wallace Stevens, '01, comes first. His undergraduate work sometimes disappoints: this is in part because of the twenty-two-year gap between his *Advocate* writing and *Harmonium,* his first volume of mature verse. But the modern reader is familiar with a different poetic idiom than a young writer could have known seventy-five years ago. Stevens helped create the literary revolution of the twentieth century, but we cannot expect to see effects of that revolution in his first poems. We should instead note the tone of refinement and the quiet sophistication that both the young man and the older one share. The aesthetic movement of the nineties did not prevail within the *Advocate,* as we have seen, but it was the most advanced literary school of its time. Such pieces as ''Pursuit'' and ''Street Songs'' bear the influence of aestheticism, and this is especially noticeable if we compare them to the more classical poems, like Robinson's, of the nineteenth century.

Van Wyck Brooks follows Stevens by seven years. In many ways, his college writing is more brilliant: Brooks was fired with wit and argument, as is obvious from even the most casual readings of ''Varied Outlooks'' and ''Last Chapter of 'Smith's Decline and Fall of the World.' '' The latter piece has no counterpart in *Advocate* fiction of the period, for no other young author seems to have been influenced by the science fiction of Jules Verne. Despite its harsh attitudes, ''Varied Outlooks'' shows more of Brooks' concern for literary opinion and prefigures the historian of New England thought.

Thomas Stearns Eliot, '10, is in many ways the *Advocate*'s most distinguished alumnus, and it is fortunate that his college writings can withstand inspection. ''Spleen'' and ''Humouresque'' betray the young man's fondness for the French Symbolists, who figure so importantly in the progress of his later work. ''Nocturne'' not only indicates the development of this influence, but also serves as a stepping-stone toward the elegant disenchantment of ''Prufrock.'' ''Gentlemen and Seamen'' gives another aspect of Eliot, that of the aristocrat honoring the past virtue of his ancestors.

Conrad Aiken, Eliot's junior by a year, ranked among the more prolific contributors to the *Advocate,* less, as one may decide, from abundance of inspiration than from scarcity of editing. Nevertheless, he produced many pieces of value: ''François Villon,'' which is reminiscent of Browning, and ''Rabbit,'' a short story in the macabre mode, are examples from his student years. His contributions did not cease when he left Harvard: 1916 and 1918 yield ''Vaudeville'' and ''Impromptu from 'Senlin' '' respectively.

It is not surprising that e. e. cummings, the last of these great men, proved the most revolutionary of them. One may remark with some amusement that his favorite poetic exclamation seems to have been ''Hark!'' But these poems appeared at a time when the old poetic standards that had guided new writers were in fast decay, and the new ones either unformed or generally despised. cummings' college verse, despite its rawness, shows remarkable innovation and strength: phrases like ''carnal mountains'' and ''the cold ripple sneering on the rocks'' demonstrate a power of expression that did not brook the limits of stock phrases or poetic clichés. ''The New Art,'' delivered in the commencement program for the class of 1915, hints at the direction the young man would take.

These men tower over the age, and justly. Yet they did not obstruct the progress of others and should not obstruct our view of the period. For the most part the *Advocate* during this time maintained a steady balance among literature, opinion, and frivolity. Richard Washburn Child's ''Ultimatum of Nature'' and W. C. Greene's ''Vignette'' serve as examples of less assuming literature of the period, and Robert Benchley's ''Ivy Oration'' for the class of 1912 shows us a piece of youthful work from one of the favorite American humorists of the century.

SONG.

SHE loves me or loves me not,
  What care I ? —
The depth of the fields is just as sweet,
  And sweet the sky.

She loves me or she loves me not,
  Is that to die ? —
The green of the woods is just as fair,
  And fair the sky.

W. Stevens.

VITA MEA.

WITH fear I trembled in the House of Life,
  Hast'ning from door to door, from room to room,
Seeking a way from that impenetrable gloom
Against whose walls my strength lay weak from strife,
All dark ! All dark ! And what sweet wind was rife
With earth, or sea, or star, or new sun's bloom,
Lay sick and dead within that place of doom,
Where I went raving like the winter's wife.

" In vain, in vain," with bitter lips I cried ;
" In vain, in vain," along the hall-ways died
And sank in silences away. Oppressed
I wept. Lo ! through those tears the window-bars
Shone bright, where Faith and Hope like long-sought stars
First gleamed upon that prison of unrest.

W. Stevens.

STREET SONGS.

I.

The Pigeons.

OVER the houses and into the sky
　And into the dazzling light,
Long hosts of fluttering pigeons fly
　Out of the blackened night,
Over the houses and into the sky
　On glistening wings of white.

Over the city and into the blue
　From ledge and tower and dome,
They rise and turn and turn anew,
　And like fresh clouds they roam,
Over the city and into the blue
　And into their airy home.

II.

The Beggar.

Yet in this morn there is a darkest night,
Where no feet dance or sweet birds ever rise,
Where fancy is a thing that soothes — and lies,
And leads on with mirages of light.
I speak of her who sits within plain sight
Upon the steps of yon cathedral. Skies
Are naught to her; and life a lord that buys
And sells life, whether sad, or dark, or bright.

The carvings and beauty of the throne
Where she is sitting, she doth meanly use
To win you and appeal. All rag and bone
She asks with her dry, withered hand a dreg
Of the world's riches. If she doth abuse
The place, pass on. It is a place to beg.

III.

Statuary.

The windy morn has set their feet to dancing —
　Young Dian and Apollo on the curb,
The pavement with their slender forms is glancing,
　No clatter doth their gaiety disturb.

No eyes are ever blind enough to shun them,
　Men wonder what their jubilance can be,
No passer-by but turns to look upon them —
　Then goes his way with all his fancy free.

IV.

The Minstrel.

The streets lead out into a mist
　Of daisies and of daffodils —
A world of green and amethyst,
　Of seas and of uplifted hills.

There bird-songs are not lost in eaves,
　Nor beaten down by cart and car,
But drifting sweetly through the leaves,
　They die upon the fields afar.

Nor is the wind a broken thing
　That faints within hot prison cells,
But rises on a silver wing
　From out among the heather bells.

W. Stevens.

SONNET.

THERE shines the morning star! Through the forlorn
   And silent spaces of cold heaven's height
   Pours the bright radiance of his kingly light,
Swinging in revery before the morn.
The flush and fall of many tides have worn
   Upon the coasts beneath him, in their flight
   From sea to sea; yet ever on the night
His clear and splendid visage is upborne.

Like this he pondered on the world's first day,
   Sweet Eden's flowers heavy with the dew;
And so he led bold Jason on his way
   Sparkling forever in the galley's foam;
And still he shone most perfect in the blue,
   All bright and lovely on the hosts of Rome.

W. Stevens.

PURSUIT.

THE clouds strayed lazily into the sky, like children into an open field, as we began our journey. Our nets tugged in the wind as we made amateur dabs after butterflies; and we had to be very careful to prevent their catching and entangling themselves in the thorns. It was delightful to be in the fields, waist deep in yarrow and the flowers of wild carrot, to creep up behind a pair of fine, black wings, to make a lunge with the net and then to behold those same black wings opening and closing contentedly against the face of some blossom or other a short distance away. We might have had a horde of the little clover and cabbage flies that kept flitting to and fro about our knees; but we were after prey, after booty, and had eyes only for what was bright and rare.

All this was folly to those farmers whom we met. One of them had seen me bound after some invisible thing in the weeds at my feet and, after several mad gestures, rise with a bland smile holding a beetle between my fingers. At the same time my companions had been jumping this way and that like so many furious grasshoppers. The farmer was evidently of a curious turn of mind, for, calling his wife, the two of them came to the edge of the field we were in and, leaning on the fence, watched us inquisitively. I happened to stroll that way, net in hand, and as I approached the pair were talking to one another.

"I guess they think they're fishin'," said the man.

"Um, likely, fishin' in the air," answered the woman with a laugh.

"Sh! Nan, for the love of mercy, don't let the poor fools know you're alaughin' at 'em," he exclaimed in alarm.

"Hi there," cried the woman, ignoring him, "hev you ketched many yet?"

"Oh, yes," I replied, "quite a number,"—at which she burst into a loud laugh which the dismayed husband excitedly tried to check. He put his hand over her mouth and, when he took hold of her and began to beg and demand her to be quiet, her mirth redoubled and peal after peal of laughter rose, until my companions in the middle of the field heard and began to laugh too, unconscious that they were the butt of the uproar.

At this moment, for some reason which I could not see, they began to run about the field in wild confusion. Once they formed a circle and seemed to be pursuing each other like madmen; then they suddenly fell apart and pranced up and down like clowns, at which the husband, finding all efforts at pacification futile, slowly abandoned them. He began to stare at the four men in front, and I felt that his eyes were following me as I joined them. And once on the spot I understood their frenzy; for there upon a wild flower could be seen the slight shimmering of a pair of argent wings. There was infinite delicacy in that frail and glorious thing — such an opening of light, such a closing of radiance, such a big, easy grace of moving wings as almost made us afraid to take a step and struck us with terror when it took flight! After it we went, on tiptoe and in trepidation, five of us abreast, with five gaping nets and wild, anxious eyes. The farmer's wife suddenly stopped her laughing and by degrees was becoming infected with a little of our fear and consternation; as we approached them, the pair stood still and with eyes fastened on us watched as we came stealthily toward them, in pursuit of the splendid creature that seemed so much like an idle leaf continually blown just out of our reach by little opportune gusts of wind. Up it rose in the air and then we leaned forward in horror until it settled again. The eyes of the farmer began to grow wide with wonder while his wife turned paler and paler at our dire approach.

At last the butterfly sailed down in its luxury quite at the farmer's feet and five nets dashed toward the fence. There was a piercing scream and in a wild panic the farmer and his wife were gone. Raising our eyes to look after them we lost a moment's sight of the butterfly and, when we looked for it again, it too had fled. Then we saw its silver wings in apparent pursuit of the big, timid couple. After it we went, heralded in advance by the shrieking woman and the stricken man,— after it over fields and fences, through a hedge, over the ford of a creek, up a hilly road, on and on, — after it to the death, with all manner of shouts among ourselves and harrowing screams from the woman in advance.

We passed her, a breathless heap in the dust — or rather with just enough breath to emit a shrill, fainting cry as we disappeared around a curve in pursuit of her husband. The vanquished clod, upon seeing us, cut across the country through a thicket of tall, pink-blooming milkweeds, and was soon out of our range except for an occasional loud crash as he made his way over some obstruction. The object of our mad chase, indifferently as ever, settled down upon one of the tall, slender weeds, weary of her long flight, and there we caught her. Her helpless beauty struck us with great pity and delight and quite repaid the labor spent in her capture. Her body was very perfect and the long, pure unbroken beauty of her wings together with the rarity of her kind made us forget for a time the events she had brought about. Later, when we remembered, we went back to look for the lady in the dust.

She was gone. *W. Stevens.*

Varied Outlooks

II.

THERE is no cause, I suppose, to prevent one from discussing public tendencies, who has been hitherto a somewhat remote and impersonal onlooker. And, on the other hand, a rather specialized view may express the strong feelings of a minority and provoke other specialized expressions of opinion which may lead to more general sympathy and more general understanding.

It is a natural thing perhaps that the more we tend to mental development, which ought to be a balance for our whole nature, the more we grow away from pure honesty and simplicity. The minute ones' attention is called to human nature, honesty and simplicity become objects of thought to be juggled with like any other idea, and we are soon wondering just what is honest and what *is* simple, and the very conduct of life becomes a distinct problem.

I have been asked to direct my attention particularly to the so-called "aesthetic" side of college. And I desire first of all to make plain that the word "aesthetic" indicates not a flabby, purple and altogether repulsive state of mind, but the outlook on life of certain clear and sensitive persons who are quite honest and straightforward and by no means effeminate. There are indeed persons given to "cults," there are persons who regard athletes as coarse and boorish or enjoy them, if at all, as forms comparable to the Hermes of Praxiteles and expatiate upon the contour of their muscles: there are indeed persons who discuss Ibsen and Yeats in a loud (or perhaps a tender) voice in public places, being totally ignorant of Dickens and Sir Walter Scott. To be aesthetic is not to be discolored: it is to be properly colored. And persons of new culture are a thousand times more distasteful than persons of new fortune. There are a great many fellows in college who have suddenly discovered literature — in whom good taste is wholly factitious. They read their Bernard Shaw or their Chesterton — and of course you are very much impressed. But do they know their

Martin Chuzzlewit? Do they know their *Paradise Lost?* They regard nothing in literature that is not of conversational value, and therefore it is not literature that they regard at all, but conversation,— quite legitimate, no doubt, but not *literary.*

One instinctively respects a man less for having a Mona Lisa in his room when he is the kind of man who ought to have a Gibson girl. And this is quite just, because one realizes that the *state of mind* must first be changed before Mona Lisa becomes appropriate. And the influence of such super-subtle pictures as Mona Lisa upon coarse minds is far more apt to spoil them on the surface than to revolutionize and refine them below. The only safe training for a coarse mind is a study of the sensible, broad, old-fashioned things — the Raphaels in painting and the Dickenses in literature: otherwise the mind stumbles on Oscar Wilde or Bernard Shaw quite out of perspective and is dazzled by them. I do not think that pose is as common in Harvard as it is supposed to be: perfect sincerity has indeed a great many temptations — political ambition, social ambition, preconceived notions of how a literary man must act and think, of what is coarse for an artist and what is unmanly for an athlete. Only it is a great mistake to suppose that all posers are "aesthetic" posers. There are men who pose as democrats and there are men who pose as athletes. I rather think it is less harmful to pass one's self off as a person of exquisite taste than to pass one's self off as a "fine manly fellow" — when one is, after all, merely average in both respects. I fear that there are some who pass themselves off as democrats, who certainly could never be mistaken for anything else. And what a hodge-podge is the mind of a man who laughs at coarse jokes because it shows manliness to laugh at coarse jokes, and then reads Pierre Loti because it shows a refined literary sense to read Pierre Loti! Do we all feel quite sure that we have found our level when we spend an evening over Fielding and

Lamb, or don't we sometimes (when the bed-room door is locked) give ourselves a good treat for once — an honest laugh over George Ade, or a tear silently shed on the pages of Miss Marie Corelli? And do we all look back on our child-hood with more lingering pleasure over the days spent with the Tanglewood Tales than the days before we had to keep up appearances with Ibsen and Shaw, spent with Nick Carter? I wish I might hope so.

What is the earthly use of pretending that we like Leonardo or Walter Pater when we are dis-honest in doing so? Anybody who *really* likes Leonardo or Walter Pater can see through us in a minute, and it is mere vulgar showing-off to pretend such things before people who are igno-rant of either. However in the question of insincerity, I feel strongly that it is more diaboli-cally insincere to pretend to be manly than to pretend to be literary and artistic, when one is really neither literary nor manly. The true sportsman is in many ways the finest man in the world, on the whole the least of a philistine, the most apt to "recognize dynamic force" when he meets it, just as the false sportsman is in many ways the most contemptible man in the world — the athletic poser, the subtle mind which admires itself in running-drawers. How morbid we are on the subject of manliness! I think it is still considered effeminate by many to drink tea in the afternoon — a notion that is contradicted by every impulse other than old prejudice. In college we should test the value of ideas, and we shall soon find that it is a man's business to become tolerant of tea. I once knew a man who would never drink milk because he considered it unmanly; but he was frank enough to say so right out, and therefore only lacked a sense of humor.

The only quality that you admire at first in another man and go on liking forever is honesty. Men who are genial and genuine always take to each other; and nothing stands so much between men as a kind of superficial and facetious literary jargon.

Now there *is* an attitude toward literature of which college men, like any other men, are cap-able, and which is perfectly honest and straight-forward and at the same time passionate. Take two poets, for example, as far apart as Longfellow and Swinburne. The man who wallows in Swinburne's impressionism is quite as false as the man who throws out his chest and dismisses Swinburne as flabby and unhealthy. The one merely falls in with a fad as such, the other merely opposes a fad as such. Both are blind to the vital, human, impulsive, elemental essence of the real Swinburne, the real poet of the sea, of the winds, of humanity, and of hope. Likewise in Longfellow, after all the sneers of the over-civilized and of all in whom the head is developed beyond the heart, there remains after all the sense of a noble, generous, and pure character which is part of the real essence and purpose of poetry. And there is a transcendental way of looking at the most decadent literature. It is perfectly possible for the lover of Tennyson to admit that Wilde and Dowson have written poems of exquisite and lasting beauty; indeed the admission only strengthens his case for Tennyson, for it gives Tennyson the admiration of a broad mind instead of a narrow mind.

Last and falsest and most fatal: in the pro-duction of literature by undergraduates. Why has it become necessary to regard our work as only *college* work after all — as if college were a kind of reproach, as if we were not living in the absolute world at all but in a kind of relative purgatory, from which we may, if we are fortunate, emerge as men, capable of common feelings and ideas? When we turn to college literature, which *is* literature in the truest sense of the word — no matter how immature and faulty — and when we turn to college poetry which is poetry in the truest sense of the word, we at once see how fashionable it is to decry the real impulses of all literature and of all poetry. We are taught that undergraduates *cannot* write poetry; that undergraduates can write only *verse*, as if poetry were anything more than the real and genuine feelings of real and genuine men: as if, indeed, the noblest and strongest and purest and deepest poetry of the world had not been written by men of twenty — Keats and Catullus, Rossetti and Shelley, Tibullus and Heine. Of course under-graduates *usually* do not write poetry, but what a discouraging and deadening assumption that they *never* can! True poetry is quite as likely to come from young men as from old, as a matter of fact, and it is absurd to insist that the most appropriate poetry college men can produce is college poetry; as if "goodies" and "exams" and "lemons" after all were the chief emotions of which sensible men of twenty are capable.

Perhaps "aesthetic" is the wrong word after all. The actual meaning of a word changes when its connotations change, no matter how false the connotations may be.

Van Wyck Brooks.

Last Chapter of "Smith's Decline and Fall of the World."

IT is evident to the reader of my previous chapter that any life on the earth was now only a question of days. Not only had its circular form become egg-shaped, but this violent contortion had erected vast toppling mountains, seven times higher than the Himalayas, and, from their proximity to the sun, white-hot and molten on the summits. Prodigious streams of blazing lava were rushing hither and thither, at a speed of some twenty miles a minute, and hissing like a million cobras. The Pacific Ocean could be spanned and scanned with the naked eye, being scarcely broader than a mill-pond, and all about it for thousands of miles its bed was a vile seething mass of slime. Bodies of vast sea-monsters lay festering among the stagnant weeds, many of them still breathing, ponderously flapping their ulcerous gills, gasping and squirming.

No better test for my aero-car could be conceived. Thanks to the efficient service of the Interplanet Wireless Company, I was able to keep in constant touch with Mars; my own appliances resisted the force of gravitation, and enabled me to remain poised at a distance of half a mile over any spot which demanded my investigation, while my air-tank supplied me with our delicious home-atmosphere, and my radium window-plates kept out the rank vapors and the insufferable heat. Thus I remained for three weeks pursuing my observation in perfect safety.

On the tenth day I passed over the wide valley which I had formerly known as the English Channel, and pushed southward along the coast of Spain. It occurred to me that, with the ocean completely dried up, I might easily find the lost continent of Atlantis. I had always suspected the Azores of being its surviving peaks, and accordingly steered in that directon. Towards evening the land beginning to rise, I found it necessary to steer violently upward in order to avoid precipitating myself into the mud-hills which stood before me. The sun, which had gained so enormously in size that seven fissures were visible upon it, sank in the west. The ground beneath me now rose violently, so that it was necessary for me to pursue my course upward at an angle of seventeen degrees, and as the moon rose, I discovered myself at the foot of a steep ascent which sloped off indefinitely into the sky. At this point I threw out all my extra side-flaps and parachutes and decided to poise for the night. My sleep was disturbed at intervals by a jarring of the basket in which I lay, caused by the perpetual whir of the huge monsters below whose coiling and leaping produced a constant vibration in the air without.

At daybreak I continued my upward progress and towards noon, after rising perpendicularly for two or three miles, the mountain suddenly broke off into a wide plateau, which I recognized instantly from its shape as the island of Teceira. I ascended twenty or thirty miles to gain a bird's-eye view of the Azores, and to ascertain their relation to the rest of the continent. The islands were connected at a distance of not half a mile below the former water-line, and above this they defined themselves as upon a clay map. I approached the village of Angra, to find that the vast cathedral had melted like a candy house, its marvellous mosaics and colored marbles running in streams through the neighboring streets. In two hours I had crossed the entire archipelago. To the west for a thousand miles lay the continent of Atlantis, a flat stretch covered to the horizon in every direction with a layer many rods deep of decayed yellow sea-plants, swarming with life, now wilted and sickly from exposure to the sun. I dropped to within a hundred yards of the surface in order to watch two monstrous clams; when suddenly an unusual jolting of my car caused me to look around. Almost upright to the sky, towering like a water-spout, a vast snake was bearing towards me, his tail swishing along in the slime and weeds, his upper parts propelled by flaps or fins which supported him in the air. His long, sleek, hose-like body glistened, and in his mane or hair streamers of sea-weed were fluttering. I had but a second. Turning on the recoil-valve, my car darted upwards like an arrow, as I felt his hair brush against my hanging basket below. As I continued my flight I saw the huge tower topple, and his whole length fell with a violent splash, cutting the weeds like a sword, and gradually sinking through with a suction on both sides which stirred the mire for many acres.

Towards evening I discerned a distant mountain to the northwest and turning my course in that direction came just at dark upon what appeared to be a vast pyramid. The rise of the moon confirmed this conjecture. It was after the model of the pyramids of Egypt, though many times larger — quite regular in shape, and covered with barnacles of the size of a church spire. I was thus enabled not only to confirm my notions of the lost continent, but to reach rather definite conclusions as to the nature of its civilization.

During the following days, there was a perceptible change in the condition of the earth. The molten state was apparently drying and it was evident that in a few days the entire planet would be one great burnt-out cinder. On the sixteenth day I was in the neighborhood of the South Pole. The snow having entirely melted, another great continent was exposed, which ran for two thousand miles across the pole and up on the other side from Franklin's Land. Almost exactly over the pole were a number of caves or long tunnels which ran into the ground. As I watched one with not unnatural curiosity, I saw a man, a human being, crawl out slowly, followed by a woman. They were scorched quite black and seemed to have lost all power of locomotion. I approached them with the idea of rescue, but seeing them diseased beyond any hope of recovery and moreover in a contagious state, I thought it best in the interests of science to keep myself safe. In this distraction, I had not noticed that a sort of gray pallor was coming over the entire surface of the earth. The man saw it too, for he cried out "Just as I said!" and the woman fell down and worshipped him — and I am convinced that these were the last words spoken on earth. The skeleton of an echo rattled through the cinder hills, just as vast fissures opened everywhere; and suddenly in absolute silence the whole earth gave way. It shot from me with inconceivable speed, revealing more and more of itself, until in an instant I saw the globe spinning off like a cannon ball down the infinite void.

V. W. B.

Humanities.

MANY things are deep and high
   That have no word for such as I:
Thoughts as strong as strong gods are
Spring the way from star to star.

Would you have my love thus, even
Big as earth and big with heaven—
So forgetting the sweet days
We've played at loving, different ways?

What have gods and stars to do
With *You love me* and *I love you?*
Many things are deep and high
That have no word for such as I.

Van Wyck Brooks.

Circe's Palace.

AROUND her fountain which flows
   With the voice of men in pain,
Are flowers that no man knows.
Their petals are fanged and red
With hideous streak and stain;
They sprang from the limbs of the dead.—
We shall not come here again.

Panthers rise from their lairs
In the forest which thickens below,
Along the garden stairs
The sluggish python lies;
The peacocks walk, stately and slow,
And they look at us with the eyes
Of men whom we knew long ago.

T. S. Eliot.

Humouresque.

(After J. Laforgue).

ONE of my marionettes is dead,
   Though not yet tired of the game,—
But weak in body as in head,
(A jumping-jack has such a frame).

But this deceaséd marionette
I rather liked: a common face,
(The kind of face that we forget)
Pinched in a comic, dull grimace;

Half bullying, half imploring air,
Mouth twisted to the latest tune;
His who-the-devil-are-you stare;
Translated, maybe, to the moon.

With Limbo's other useless things
Haranguing spectres, set him there;
"The snappiest fashion since last spring's,
"The newest style, on Earth, I swear.

"Why don't you people get some class?
(Feebly contemptuous of hose),
"Your damned thin moonlight, worse than gas—
"Now in New York"—and so it goes.

Logic a marionette's, all wrong.
Of premises; yet in some star
A hero!—Where would he belong?
But, even at that what mark *bizarre!*

T. S. Eliot.

Spleen.

SUNDAY: this satisfied procession
  Of definite Sunday faces;
Bonnets, silk hats, and conscious graces
In repetition that displaces
Your mental self-possession
By this unwarranted digression.

Evening, lights, and tea!
Children and cats in the alley;
Dejection unable to rally
Against this dull conspiracy.

And Life, a little bald and gray,
Languid, fastidious, and bland,
Waits, hat and gloves in hand,
Punctilious of tie and suit
(Somewhat impatient of delay)
  On the doorstep of the Absolute.

T. S. Eliot.

Nocturne.

ROMEO, *grand serieux*, to importune
  Guitar and hat in hand, beside the gate
With Juliet, in the usual debate
Of love, beneath a bored but courteous moon;
The conversation failing, strikes some tune
Banal, and out of pity for their fate
Behind the wall I have some servant wait,
Stab, and the lady sinks into a swoon.

Blood looks effective on the moonlit ground —
The hero smiles; in my best mode oblique
Rolls toward the moon a frenzied eye profound,
(No need of "Love forever?" — "Love next week?")
While female readers all in tears are drowned: —
"The perfect climax all true lovers seek!"

T. S. Eliot.

Gentlemen and Seamen.

THOSE of us who can claim any New England ancestors may congratulate ourselves that we are their descendants, and at the same time rejoice that we are not their contemporaries. Their sombre faces, with an inflexible contraction of the lips, as they have been stiffened and conventionalized in oils by forgotten artists, suggest natures difficult and unyielding, as the consequence of religious principle and of interminable struggle against the narrow resources of New England. The men of whom I am thinking are the patriarchs of the smaller towns, rather than the merchants of Boston, whom affluence often left more genial than the never prosperous countryfolk. But the representative New Englander is not exclusively a city man by descent, and has quite as much reason for taking pride in his rustic ancestors.

One notable characteristic of those hardy folk is the success with which they supported, in the conflict with misfortune, a gentlemanly dignity. Tradesmen and farmers, most of them, by descent, they were farmers in America; yet here they founded and maintained successfully a plebeian aristocracy, without the training of generations, and under adverse fates. Any task which necessity compelled them to undertake, in their hands became honorable; no privation and hardship lowered their pride or social position. So they were found as merchants and tradesmen, as farmers and printers, according to circumstance, without losing a jot of their dignity. There were many sacrifices. Straightened means confined noble ambitions, and their passion for education was not always gratified. In one of those white clapboard houses which look so tranquil in their decay lived a boy of good family, a hundred years ago, whom lack of means thwarted from his ambition the college education. So, at the age of fifteen, he killed himself.

But most of our New Englanders were stronger, and turned to what vocation they could find; the farm, the printing-press — a hundred years ago there were many local presses — or to the sea. The merchant marine was not the least important career in which New Englanders found distinction. They were the men who carried American commerce to the Levant, to India, to China; who from the Revolution till after 1812 made America an ocean power in war and in peace. They built the fine old ships which we know only from contemporaneous engravings. How stirring are those antique woodcuts. The "*Ajax*," two hundred ton brig, entering Algiers under full sail with a thundering salvo from the city; the ensign very large, triumphantly shaking out its thirteen stars from the end of a yard-arm. Or the "*Poor Richard*," off the coast of Africa repelling pirates; the native feluccas very small in contrast; or the "*Samuel Adams*," passing a sea-serpent in the Bay of Biscay. Built and manned and commanded, every one of the boats, by Yankee seamen; and for them was built the handsome old custom house at Salem, now slumbering in proud uselessness.

Go to Salem and see a town that flourished a hundred years ago in the hightide of New England's naval energy. It seems now to be always in dignified mourning for its former grandeur for the ships which do not leave and the ships which do not return. One feels that noisy mirth is a profanation there, the town is so populous with ghosts. Where is the China fleet now? the clumsy barks that sailed to every part of the world? Every day, a hundred years ago, the crowsnest watched for another homecomer bending past Baker's Island. Of the freights which the boats carried in are left only the shawls,

the ginger-jars, the carved ivory which the captains brought back from the Orient, the gifts which their descendants are proud to display. From New Brunswick to Florida to-day lounge the coasters, manned with Irish and the "bluenose"; the mackerel fleet slants out to the banks under Irish skippers, and the cargoes of the world are borne in steamers owned in Europe. The sea trade of the Yankees is gone.

The captains who handled the old fleet were just the sort of aristocratic plebeians of whom I spoke. Very young, at fourteen or fifteen years, they would enter the service, at the bottom of the nautical *cursus honorum*. They often rose quickly; there were many like the youth who sailed a bark from his father's Portsmouth shipyard to Savannah for lading, thence to London, where he sold ship and cargo at a good profit; and this when he was aged nineteen. His logbook, kept in a neat small hand, shows that he was an able and a conscientious navigator. Such were the men who handled the shipping of New England.

Though we must regret the commerce which has fallen to Germany and to England, we must regret still more the virtues of the old skippers. Thrown from youth among the roughest adventures, with the crudest companions, they emerged at the end as good gentlemen, often, as the more fortunate college-bred. Of these yeomen ancestors we are apt to think as the infantry whom the drums beat to Charlestown, or as the gunners who raked the "*Hornet*," rather than as the founders of commerce or the pioneers of education. But that is half of their importance. We may well mourn for the enterprise which sent American shipping round the world, and started the printing press in many small communities. Nowadays we are thankful that more congenial occupation is open to the industrious gentleman, however needy, than was possible to some of our New England forbears. If along with greater luxury, with more generosity and geniality than was theirs, we have preserved the spirit of our old plebeian aristocracy, we should give them the grace of recognition.

T. S. Eliot.

François Villon.

HOW bitter cold it is! It *looked* like snow ---
 I hear the wolf-wind now; wolf-wind, d' I say?
 Aye, hear the host a-snoring! Fire's gray
With ashes. Hey, you drunkard! Stir your — No; —
He must not wake. I turn my pockets, so —
 And — am I startled? nothing, nothing, falls,
 No laugh of silver mocks me from these walls
So desolate, so bare. Well, here I go
To mill a verse. Ha ha! It's Christmas time!
I want a hollied verse, a berried rhyme—

O sleepy, sleepy eyes! Will verses keep?
 Aye, think of roast-fowl, then,— Lights! Christmas spread!
 Ah, what a vision! (*Smiles — nods low his head*)
O! Verse, d' I say? Aye — (*murmuring, falls asleep*).

C. P. Aiken.

Rabbit.

WE paused on the brow of the hummock, and looked down into the bushy valley below us.

"This is really an excellent place for rabbit," remarked my host softly. "Can't remember coming here without success."

Hardly had he spoken when he jerked his gun to his shoulder and fired at a quiver in the tall bushes. The report echoed harshly across the glade and the smoke began slowly rising in the calm sunlit air; and then suddenly, without the slightest warning, there rose from the bushes a shriek — short, sharp, and ear-piercing. Immediately after it, followed the same warm, Sunday placidity.

"Good Lord!" gasped Jenkins, and stared at me, gaping foolishly. "What was it?"

`"I don't know."

I collapsed to the earth like a consumed fire and stared down at the bushes, which were now quite still.

"A ghost?" I suggested weakly, patting my forehead with a handkerchief.

Jenkins dropped his gun in a cluster of golden dandelions and started walking gingerly down the gentle slope. Then I saw his brown Norfolk jacket and corduroy trousers disappear into the rustling bushes. The green leaves tossed nervously about his invisible figure, and became again motionless. Everything was as silent as if he had fallen into a bottomless pit.

"Jenkins!" I shouted.

A young thrush lighted on the top of a willow sapling and jerked his tail at me defiantly, watching me with his bead eyes, his little head cocked to one side. Hearing something, he flitted off again. The leaves were again tossing and bobbing; and presently Jenkins appeared, holding something in his arms.

"Thank the Lord!" I cried fervently. "Was it only a rabbit?"

I scrambled weakly to my feet and started

to approach him. And then — suddenly — I stopped dead. Jenkins laughed a little, chill laugh,— and stood still too, with his blackly bearded face bent downward. His shadow came just to my feet. I noticed with horror that it appeared quite headless; and then, for the first time, I looked at the object in his arms, with a dim dream-like sense of having done the same thing in a previous life. It was a little boy, about three years old, quite dead. He was dressed in a tiny pair of Scotch kilts, and wore a Scotch cap with a dangling black ribbon. The face was plump and ruddy, and the eyes, now closed, were darkly fringed with long curving eyelashes.

Jenkins raised his head and fastened his narrow yellow eyes on mine.

"It's done," he said slowly. "I wonder where his parents are?"

I could n't answer him, for I was gulping. So I shaded my eyes with a trembling hand and gazed off over the glade. In an instant I had seen the thin blue thread of smoke above the trees.

"There," said I, pointing.

Jenkins looked, and then commenced the descent into the valley. Picking up the gun from the dandelions, I ejected the empty shell, blew out the little ghost-like whiff of smoke still lingering in the barrel, and followed, with hanging head. In Jenkins went, with never a pause, picking an intricate way through the sumach and willow coppice. Birds flew up chirping before us and more than one rabbit flashed away through the long grass; yet Jenkins never once turned his head, till we came to the shallow brook. Here I paused involuntarily. On the further side was a brown tent, ragged and soiled, with its flaps closed. Beside it stood a high-bodied gypsy-cart, white, with green and red trimmings, its shafts resting idly on the ground. A lean-ribbed horse was tethered to one of the wheels, and browsed peacefully in the deep clover. On his back sat a girl, perhaps ten years old, with a golden shock of hair that curled down over a yellow linen dress. She was laboriously playing a bag-pipe.

Jenkins was already half way across the brook, stepping carefully from stone to stone. I followed once more, doubtfully; then sat down in the grass and waited. The yellow-haired girl looked at me with indifference, the pipe still at her lips, the bag under her arm. I noticed a strange dullness in her large brown eyes; yet she was very pretty.

"Hello!" called Jenkins, stopping.

There was a movement in the dingy tent, a bulging against the canvas flaps, and then a man came forth, looking calmly from one to the other of us, and bending slightly forward. He was short and thin, clad in kilts and plaid stockings, and his gaunt face was wholly covered with black hair. Large brown eyes gazed out serenely from beneath great bushy eyebrows. His hands were large and hairy, his arms of unusual length, hanging limply at his sides. He looked entirely primeval.

Jenkins stood before him, still holding the baby in his arms. The perspiration stood on his forehead like dew. And he began talking softly to the man in Gaelic, which I could n't understand. What he said, I have n't the faintest idea, for the Scotchman's face remained perfectly placid throughout; he showed absolutely no signs of feeling. He just stood there, his knees slightly bent, like an ape's, his funny jaw tightly closed, his brown sunlit eyes unblinking.

Jenkins stopped. Slowly winking with his great eyes, the man climbed into the cart and returned with a spade. He and Jenkins then went off silently among the oak-trees and disappeared. I knew well what they were doing. Meanwhile, the golden-haired girl was still kicking with her bare brown legs against the old horse's ribs, and squealing in an ejaculatory manner on the bag-pipes. As for me, I sat still in the shade of the huge oak, near the tent, and sucked a straw.

Presently the two men came solemnly back, Jenkins leading, and the other limping behind with swinging arms and head thrust brutishly forward.

"It's all done," remarked my host unfeelingly. He slipped a golden sovereign in the man's hand, picked up his gun, and started away. When we had reached the other side of the shallow brook, I looked over my shoulder and saw the man smiling inanely at the sovereign, which shone on the palm of his hand.

"They're Gaelic," said Jenkins shortly; "old clan people, so often intermarried that their brains are gone. Almost all of them are tinklers, like him, and harmless enough....Softly now — I must shoot us a dinner. Off to the left, I think ...."

Jenkins went off, the gun cracked, and he came back holding up a rabbit by the hind legs. He started to smile. He was surprised to find me squatting on the ground, and blubbering like a child.

C. P. Aiken.

Vaudeville.

I. THE LEADER.

EACH time the sign flashed 'Hayes and Mayne'
  His frantic heart began to beat.
A fiery music laced his brain.
And through his veins her golden feet
Danced and glistened, danced and turned,
Pirouetted without a sound;
Up and down his blood they burned;
Glided and winked and swished around;
Until he longed to drop his bow,
And break his torturing violin,
And dance with her who witched him so
In a moonlight carnival of sin.
Her partner was a fool, and blind;
He smiled and smiled, and did not guess;
He skipped and hopped with vacant mind
Beside that fiery loveliness, —
Held out his hand for her to take,
And grinned, like a sawdust mannikin....
Sometimes he thought his heart would break;
Sometimes he thought his violin
Would crack to pieces, rather than play
That everlasting idiot tune....
But then he thought of nights in May,
And moonlight seaside nights in June,
And how they'd walk along the sands,
And laugh a little, and hear the sea,
And feel strange magic, touching hands,
And kiss, and shiver....and there would be
Eternities like this....But then
She ran to the wings, and turned, and screamed,
And waved her hand....And once again
The whole thing like a nightmare seemed....
The music changed, the curtains rose,
Two acrobats, in yellow tights,
One with an artificial nose,
Signalled into the wings for lights;
And coldly, above a falling flame
That lately set his pulses wild,
Freezing memory once more came
Of crippled wife and crying child.

II. FRONT ROW.

Day after day she came, day after day
She sat in the front row, fixing her eyes upon him,
And never spoke to him, and never smiled.
Like one in a spell she watched his fingers moving
On the little silver levers, watched his lips,
And how he moistened them before he played;

The blue eyes, slowly gliding across the music,—
The lamplit music; and how, when he was tired,
He sighed, and rested his oboe on his knee.
The people on the stage meant nothing to her:
She'd seen them all before, perhaps, remembered
All that they said and did. They came and went
Silent as thought:
The fair-haired girl who played the violin,
Smiling a fixed and foolish smile; the clowns
Who lifted horrible faces into the spotlight
And sang so out of tune; the screaming monkeys;
The dwarfs, the trapeze artists, the bottle-jugglers;
And the young men who played pianos blindfold....
Pictures upon the white screen flashed and faded,
The music changed, the spotlight cast new shadows
Sharply against the drop; and still, unseeing,
Never lifting her eyes, never applauding,
And only faintly smiling at some old joke,
She sat and stared. So near she was to him,
That sometimes, lifting her dress to cross her knees,
Her slipper brushed his elbow, and he'd turn
And peer at her, one instant, above his glasses,—
Still blowing a tune; and edge his chair away....

What was it like, that unknown world of hers,
Those sinister streets in which no lamps were lighted,
And no doors ever opened, and no voice heard?

Conrad Aiken, '11.

IMPROMTU FROM "SENLIN"

Death himself in the rain . . . death himself . . .
Death in the savage sunlight . . . skeletal death . . .
I hear the clack of his feet,
Clearly on stones, softly in dust,
Speeding among the trees with whistling breath,
Whirling the leaves, tossing his hands from waves . . .
Listen! the immortal footseps beat and beat! . . .

Death himself in the grass, death himself,
Gyrating invisibly in the sun
Scattering grass-blades, whipping the wind,
Tearing at boughs with malignant laughter . . .
On the long echoing air I hear him run!

Death himself in the dusk, gathering lilacs,
Breaking a white-fleshed bough,
Strewing the purple spikes on a cobwebbed lawn,
Dancing, dancing,
Drunk with excess, the long red sun-rays glancing
On flourishing arms, skipping with hideous knees,
Cavorting his grotesque ecstasies . . .
I do not see him, but I see the lilacs fall,
I hear the scrape of his hands against the wall,
The leaves are tossed and tremble where he plunges among them,
And silence falls, and I hear the sound of his breath,
Sharp and whistling, the rhythm of death.

It is evening: the lights on a long street balance and sway
In the purple ether they swing and silently sing,
The street is a gossamer swung in space
And death himself in the wind comes dancing along it
And the lights, like raindrops, fall and tremble and swing. . . .

Hurry, spider, and spread your glistening web,
For death approaches!
Hurry, rose, and open your heart to the bee
For death approaches!
Maiden, let down your hair for the hands of your lover,
Comb it with moonlight and wreathe it with leaves,
For death approaches! . . .

Death, colossal in stars, minute in the sand-grain,
Death himself in the rain, death himself,
Drawing the rain about him like a garment of jewels . . .
I hear the sound of his feet
On the stairs of the wind, in the sun,
In the forests of the sea . . .
Listen! the immortal footsteps beat and beat$_2$

Conrad Aiken, '11

Summer Silence.

(Spenserian Stanza.)

ERUPTIVE lightnings flutter to and fro
　　Above the heights of immemorial hills;
Thirst-stricken air, dumb-throated, in its woe
Limply down-sagging, its limp body spills
Upon the earth.　A panting silence fills
The empty vault of Night with shimmering bars
Of sullen silver, where the lake distils
Its misered bounty.— Hark!　No whisper mars
The utter silence of the untranslated stars.

E. E. Cummings, '15.

Sunset.

GREAT carnal mountains crouching in the cloud
　　That marrieth the young earth with a ring,
Yet still its thoughts builds heavenward, whence spring
Wee villages of vapor, sunset-proud.—
And to the meanest door hastes one pure-browed
White-fingered star, a little, childish thing,
The busy needle of her light to bring,
And stitch, and stitch, upon the dead day's shroud.
Poises the sun upon his west, a spark
Superlative,— and dives beneath the world;
From the day's fillets Night shakes out her locks;
List! One pure trembling drop of cadence purled —
"Summer!"— a meek thrush whispers to the dark.
Hark! the cold ripple sneering on the rocks!

E. E. Cummings, '15.

Of Nicolette.

DREAMING in marble all the palace lay,
　　Like some colossal ghost-flower, born by night,
Blossoming in white towers to the moon;
Soft sighed the passionate darkness to the tune
Of tiny troubadours, and, phantom-white,
Dumb-blooming boughs let fall their glorious snows,
And the unearthly sweetness of a rose
Swam upward from the moonlit dews of May.

A Winged Passion woke, and one by one
There fell upon the night like angels' tears
The syllables of that ethereal prayer.
And as an opening lily, milky-fair,
When from her couch of poppy petals peers
The sleepy morning, gently draws apart
Its curtains to reveal the golden heart,
With beads of dew made jewels by the sun,

So one fair, shining tower, which, like a glass,
Turned light to flame, and blazed with silver fire,
Unclosing, gave the moon a nymph-like face,
A form whose snowy symmetry of grace
Haunted the limbs as music haunts the lyre,
A creature of white hands, who, letting fall
A thread of lustre from the opened wall,
Glided, a drop of radiance, to the grass.

Shunning the sudden moonbeams' treacherous snare,
She sought the harboring dark, and, catching up
Her delicate silk,— all white, with shining feet,
Went forth into the dew.　Right wildly beat
Her heart at every kiss of daisy-cup,
And from her cheek the beauteous courage went
At every bough that reverently bent
To touch the yellow wonder of her hair.

E. E. Cummings, '15.

The New Art.

(Commencement Part.)

E. E. CUMMINGS.

THE New Art has many branches,— painting, sculpture, architecture, the stage, literature, and music. In each of these there is a clearly discernible evolution from models; in none is there any trace of that abnormality, or incoherence, which the casual critic is fond of making the subject of tirades against the new order.

It is my purpose to sketch briefly the parallel developments of the New Art in painting, sculpture, music, and literature.

I.

Anyone who takes Art seriously, who understands the development of technique in the last half century, accepts Cezanne and Matisse as he accepts Manet and Monet. But this brings us to the turning point where contemporary criticism becomes, for the most part, rampant abuse, and where prejudice utters its storm of condemnation. I refer to that peculiar phase of modern art called indiscriminately, "Cubism," and "Futurism."

The name Cubism, properly applied, relates to the work of a small group of ultra-modern painters and sculptors who use design to express their personal reaction to the subject, i. e.— what this subject "means" to them,— and who further take this design from geometry. By using an edge in place of a curve a unique tactual value is obtained.

Futurism is a glorification of personality. Every so-called "Futurist" has his own hobby; and there are almost as many kinds of painting as artists. For instance, one painter takes as his subject sounds, another, colors. A third goes back to old techniques; a fourth sees life through a magnifying glass; a fifth imposes an environment upon his subject proper, obtaining very startling effects; a sixth concerns himself purely with motion,— in connection with which it is interesting to note the Japanese painters' wholly unrealistic rendering of the force of a river.

The painter Matisse has been called the greatest exponent of Cubist sculpture. At the 1912 exhibition the puzzled crowd in front of Brancusi's "Mlle. Pogany" was only rivalled by that which swarmed about the painting called "Nude Descending a Staircase." "Mlle. Pogany" consists of a more or less egg-shaped head with an unmistakable nose, and a sinuous suggestion of arms curving upward to the face. There is no differentiation in modelling affording even a hint of hands; in other words, the flow of line and volume is continuous. But what strikes the spectator at first glance, and focusses the attention throughout, is the enormous inscribed ovals, which everyone recognizes as the artist's conception of the subject's eyes. In the triumph of line for line's sake over realism we note in Brancusi's art the development of the basic principles of impression.

II.

Just as in the case of painting, it is a French school which brought new life to music; but at the same time, Germany has the honor of producing one of the greatest originators and masters of realism, Richard Strauss.

The modern French school of music finds its inspiration in the personal influence of César Franck. Debussey, Ravel and Satie all owe much to this great Belgian, who (like Maeterlink and Verhaeren), was essentially a man of their own artistic nationality.

It is safe to say that there will always be somebody who still refuses to accept modernism in music, quoting in his defense the sovereign innovator, Beethoven! On a par with the sensation produced by the painting and sculpture of the Futurist variety was the excitement which the music of Strauss and Debussey first produced upon audiences. At present, Debussey threatens to become at any moment vulgarly common; while Strauss is fatuous in his clarity beside Schönberg, who, with Stravinsky, is the only god left by the public for the worship of the esthetes.

Erik Satie is, in many respects, the most interesting of all modern composers. Nearly a quarter of a century ago he was writing what is now considered modern music. The most striking aspect of Satie's art is the truly extraordinary sense of humor which prompts one of his subjects, the "sea cucumber," to console himself philosophically for his lack of tobacco.

The "Five Orchestral Pieces" of Arnolo Schönberg continue to be the leading sensation of the present day musical world. Their composer occupies a position in many respects similar to that of the author of the "Nude Descending a Staircase." I do not in the least mean to ridicule Schönberg; — no lawlessness could ever have produced such compositions as his, which resemble bristling forests contorted by irresistible winds. His work is always the expression of something mysteriously terrible,— which is probably why Boston laughed.

I have purposely left until the last the greatest theorist of modern music,— Scriabin. Logically, he belongs beside Stravinski, as leader of the Russian school. But it is by means of Scriabin that we may most readily pass from music to literature, through the medium of what has been called "sense-transference," as exemplified by the color music of the "Prometheus."

This "Poem of Fire" is the consummation of Scriabin's genius. To quote the Transcript: "At the first performance, by the Russian Symphony Society, on March 20, for the first time in history a composer used a chromatic color score in combination with orchestration....At the beginning of the orchestration, a gauze rectangle in about the position of a picture suspended on the back wall became animated by flowing and blending colors. These colors were played by a "color-organ" or "chromola," having a keyboard with fifteen keys, and following a written score."

III.

The suggestion of an analogy between color and music leads us naturally to the last branch of the New Art,— to wit, literature. Only the most extreme cases will be discussed, such as have important bearing upon the very latest conceptions of artistic expression.

I will quote three contemporary authors to illustrate different phases and different degrees of the literary parallel to sound painting — in a rather faint hope that the first two may prepare the way for an appreciation of the third. First Amy Lowell's "Grotesque" affords a clear illustration of development from the ordinary to the abnormal.

"Why do the lilies goggle their tongues at me
When I pluck them;
And writhe and twist,
And strangle themselves against my fingers,
So that I can hardly weave the garland
For your hair?
Why do they shriek your name
And spit at me
When I would cluster them?
Must I kill them
To make them lie still,
And send you a wreath of lolling corpses
To turn putrid and soft
On your forehead
While you dance?"

In this interesting poem we seem to discern something beyond the conventional. The lilies are made to express hatred by the employment of grotesque images. But there is nothing original in the pathetic fallacy. No one quarrels with Tennyson's lines

"There has fallen a splendid tear
From the passion-flower at the gate" —

Let us proceed further,— only noting in the last three lines that brutality which is typical of the New Art,— and consider the following poem by the same author:

"The Letter."

"Little cramped words scrawling all over the paper
Like draggled fly's legs,
What can you tell of the flaring moon
Through the oak leaves?
Or of an uncurtained window, and the bare floor
Spattered with moonlight?
Your silly quirks and twists have nothing in them
Of blossoming hawthorns,
And this paper is chill, crisp, smooth, virgin of loveli-
  ness

Beneath my hand.
I am tired, Beloved, of chafing my heart against
The want of you;
Of squeezing it into little ink drops,
And posting it.
And I scald alone, here under the fire
Of the great moon."

This poem is superb of its kind. I know of no image in all realistic writing which can approach the absolute vividness of the first two lines. The metaphor of the chafed heart is worthy of any poet; but its fanciful development would have been impossible in any literature except this ultra-modern.

I shall now quote from a sonnet by my second author, Donald Evans:

"Her voice was fleet-limbed and immaculate,
And like peach blossoms blown across the wind
Her white words made the hour seem cool and kind,
Hung with soft dawns that danced a shadow fête.
A silken silence crept up from the South,
The flutes were hushed that mimed the orange moon,
And down the willow stream my sighs were strewn,
While I knelt to the corners of her mouth."

In the figure "Her voice was fleet-limbed," and the phrase "white words," we have a sought-for literary parallel to the work of the "sound painters." It is interesting to compare Dante's expressions of a precisely similar nature, occurring in the first and fifth cantos, respectively, of the Inferno — "dove il Sol tace," and "in loco d'ogni luce muto."

From Donald Evans to Gertrude Stein is a natural step,— up or down, and one which I had hoped the first two might enable us to take in security. Gertrude Stein subordinates the meaning of words to the beauty of the words themselves. Her art is the logic of literary sound painting carried to its extreme. While we must admit that it is logic, must we admit that it is art?

Having prepared the way, so far as it is possible, for a just appreciation, I now do my best to quote from the book "Tender Buttons," as follows:

(1)   A sound.
      Elephant beaten with candy and little pops

and chews all bolts and reckless, reckless rats, this is this.

(2)   Salad Dressing and an Artichoke.
      Please pale hot, please cover rose, please acre in the red stranger, please butter all the beefsteak with regular feel faces.

(3)   Suppose an Eyes.
      . . . .
      Go red, go red, laugh white.
      Suppose a collapse is rubbed purr, is rubbed purget.
      Little sales ladies little sales ladies little saddles of mutton.
      Little sales of leather and such beautiful beautiful, beautiful beautiful.

The book from which these selections are drawn is unquestionably a proof of great imagination on the part of the authoress, as anyone who tries to imitate her work will discover for herself. Here we see traces of realism, similar to those which made the "Nude Descending a Staircase" so baffling. As far as these "Tender Buttons" are concerned, the sum and substance of criticism is impossible. The unparalleled familiarity of the medium precludes its use for the purpose of esthetic effect. And here, in their logical conclusion, impressionistic tendencies are reduced to absurdity.

The question now arises, how much of all this is really Art?

The answer is: we do not know. The great men of the future will most certainly profit by the experimentation of the present period. An insight into the unbroken chain of artistic development during the last half century disproves the theory that modernism is without foundation; rather we are concerned with a natural unfolding of sound tendencies. That the conclusion is, in a particular case, absurdity, does not in any way impair the value of the experiment, so long as we are dealing with sincere effort. The New Art, maligned though it be by fakirs and fanatics, will appear in its essential spirit to the unprejudiced critic as a courageous and genuine exploration of untrodden ways.

✖ ✖ ✖

Harvard Advocate

1866 Class Day 1915

Vignette.

A TEA: the hostess suavely circumspect,
    Three score of ladies, and a score of men;
A well-bred hum of smiling platitudes;
The day "just lovely,— but so hot, my dear."
Soft click of cups, and whir of fevered fans;
Eau de Cologne and orchids; faint, the mild
Remonstrance of a weary orchestra;
The drowsy nod of boredom,— four to six.

W. C. G.

An Ultimatum of Nature.

BRAMTON threw aside a page of notes and a cigarette and scuffed hastily up the stairs into the big hall with its rows of benches, its "kitchen" chairs, and its white plaster walls. Once seated in a far corner of the room before a "blue book" his nervousness caught the unrest in the atmosphere of the room: his hand trembled as he took out his watch, it shook as he wrote his name. Then he listened for the bell until his ears throbbed with the rhythm of imagined sound. Quite unconsciously he cursed the man in front of him for his confounded ease and precision of manner, cursed him because the back of his neck looked white and cool. Bramton knew the back of his own neck was red and hot — he could feel the blood pounding there. A shaft of sunlight which lay across the floor wriggled like a snake in agony. Bramton wondered if, after all, it payed to stay up all night to "cram" an examination.

It had been most necessary to study until the last minute. The instructor was young and in his callowness, he would doubtless try to impress the faculty that his course was "scholarly"; he had even announced to the class that he would demand definite answers rather than generalities, a remark which had been jeered by a hundred foot-beats.

Two days before Bramton could not even remember, in a definite way, what the course was about; since that time he had lived and fought with disgustingly fat books in the library and with eye-trying notes in his own room, until the whole mass of facts whirled about in his brain like the details of a bad dream.

When the night before the examination came, it found Bramton hot headed and nervous — still striving. When a light hearted, care-free acquaintance dropped in at midnight, whistling the finale of the harem scene, he found Bramton imbibing great beakers of cold tea and beating on his forehead with a pencil to keep awake.

"Go to bed, you ass!" he said in laconic playfulness.

"Very sorry. Getting a critical and analytical bead on the course. Step out, will you?" He went on turning pages with an uncertain hand.

Morning, gray cold dawn and a flurry of snow — day had come and Bramton had arisen stiffly from his chair, blown out the lamp, stared blankly out at a telephone wire which the eye could never focus and turned again to the desk with its chaos of books, diagrams and papers.

And now as he sat waiting for the bell, with the chill of an empty stomach and the dizziness of a sleepless night upon him, he wondered if all night sessions in preparation for mid-years was not — just then the bell rang.

Bramton saw the proctors divide and redivide between themselves piles of clean looking examination papers, and in his obscure corner, he waited, plucking at his collar. He wondered at his own frantic nervousness; he wondered at the rudeness with which he finally snatched at the paper. Then he felt the cool printed sheet between his unsteady fingers.

"This sort of thing is absurd, sleep or no sleep," said he straightening up in his chair with somewhat the same determination to be clear headed which comes to men befuddled with liquor, but still mindful of their dignity. He turned to scan the questions on the paper and as he read one after another a wonderful peace came over his mind, a restfulness, a luxurious relaxation. The examination was a farce.

Bramton wondered that the man across the aisle with the thin hands and the gold cuff buttons should look troubled. It was all so easy, so elementary, so childish. He had studied far beyond the requirements of any such test as this.

It would bore him to write these answers — it was like answering engraved invitations.

Engraved invitations? Why, no! because the sun streamed in through the window and lay down on the floor very quietly. There were little sprouts growing wherever there was sunlight. And waves — soft waves — lapping this way and that — very softly. They were gone. But right away they were back again — lapping on the edges of sunlight and a quiet sound,— louder, harsher, nearer. Then came the crash of reality.

"The examination will close in five minutes."

Bramton once more, could see the neck of the man in front of him cool and white and he cursed him for his confounded ease of manner.

Richard Washburn Child, '03.

Ivy Oration.

ROBERT C. BENCHLEY.

IMAGINE my surprise — my confusion — at just now being called upon to address you at this meeting. Nothing could have been farther from my thoughts as I sat listening to the other speakers here this afternoon, than that my modest voice should be desired to lend a touch of dignity to this occasion. Why, a quarter of an hour ago I was sitting in my room, looking for a position for next year, when the Bursar, that Prince of Good Fellows, that Shylock of Melancholy Dane, came bounding up the stairs, and laying a sympathetic hand on my shoulder said "Bob, old man, aren't you coming down to say a few words to the Big Red team? The boys are all calling for you down there." Then it all came over me like a flask — this was Class Day! I did remember having seen a program of the week, in which somewhere between ball-games with Yale and Phi Beta Kappa Exhibits there was made casual mention of a Class Day Exercise, but I understood that it was to be held only in case the ball-game at New Haven was called off on account of rain, and besides, I really did not dare to leave the Yard, for fear lest I had not the right colored ticket and that, once out, I could

never get back in again to get my clean clothes for the summer vacation. So here it was Class Day, and there I was in my room, hemming napkins. Quickly I drew on a pair of shoes and my cap and gown, and breaking into a run — and a perspiration, soon found myself, unless I am mistaken, here.

On this day, when all minds are turned to the National Prize Ring in Chicago, where Harvard and Yale are again demonstrating that the rules of the game need changing before next season, and at a time when the air is so charged with personal politics that it threatens to destroy the crops, what could be more out of place or thoroughly disagreeable, than for me to give my speech a political flavor? With true Harvard indifference then, I shall proceed to deliver a political speech which our paternal and conservative Administrative Board refused me permission to deliver in the Thayer Common-room, stigmatizing it as unnecessarily impolite and improper propaganda.

I shall divide my speech into three quarters, or halfs; 1st the Peroration, containing what I consider to be one of the most virulent attacks

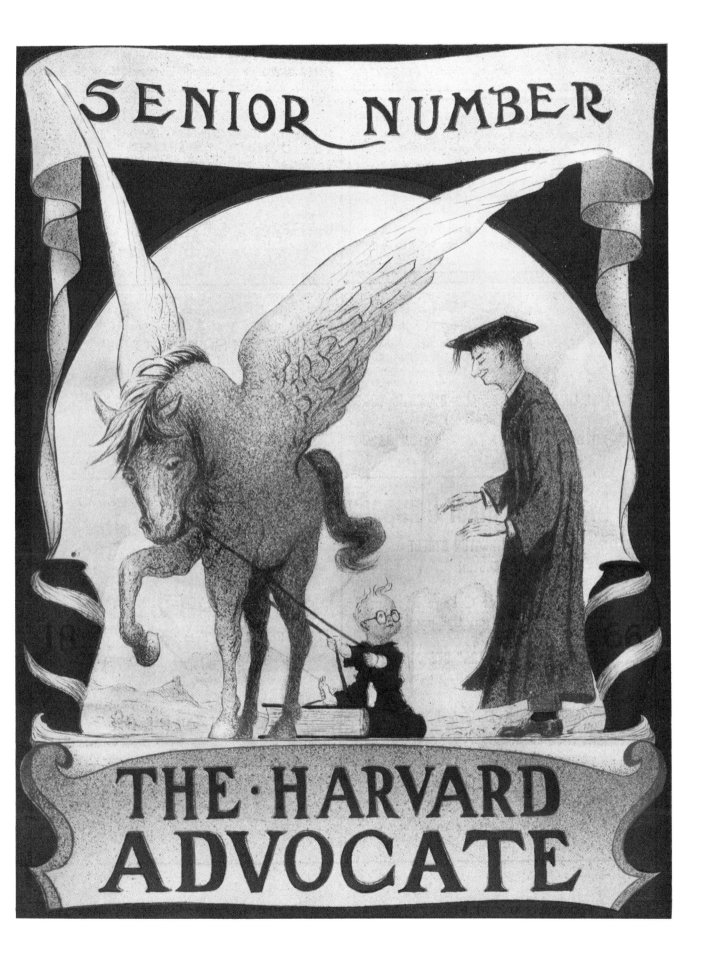

against the Malefactors of Great Health yet voiced in the present campaign. 2nd the Oration Proper, or Improper, dealing in the large with the great issues of the day, such as the Class Day Issue of the Lampoon and the Recall of Faculty Decisions. In this I shall embody a sweeping denunciation of the goodies. Thirdly, and inevitably, will come the Anti-Climax or Oporation, in which, with a burst of mature rhetoric seldom found in one so young I shall revile in bitterest terms the Social Usurpation of our Colleges, dealing with the underground method in which the Social Set at Harvard derives its stimulus from Boston, the annual, exclusive, five-day cruise of the Yale crew along the Themes, to be celebrated again Friday, and the recent election and inauguration of Sam White as President and Fellows of Princeton, on the magnanimous endorsement of our intrepid cheer-leader, our heritage from the class of 1911. These are vital questions, Classmates, and must be met at Harvard Squarely.

You have my ultimatum. If you are resigned and ready, I shall proceed, without further parsley, to dissect my Peroration. If there are any timid or super-sensitively nervous ladies or members of the Harvard Equal Suffrage league present in the arena, they may retire now inconspicuously by the trap-door opposite, where the elephants enter. I will answer any questions that may be put to me after the lecture.

1st Peroration: Roman numeral I — small letter (a).

Voters and Votaries — and Conservative Republicans.

We are gathered here to-day in this June sunshine (if it had been raining I should have been **quick-witted** enough to substitute for that, "We are gathered here in this June rain." By a lucky coincidence the "June" part would be equally fitting in both cases, you see.) We are gathered here in this June sunshine, under the leafy boughs of these grand old elms, to celebrate the fourth anniversary of the passing of our entrance English examinations. As our witty Latin orator so aptly puts it "Non sequebantur, sed in felicitate demonstrandum nunc nobis ad libitandum esse." What more can be said? Father Garcelon, in his prime, from his taxi-

chariot, could say no more. Were it not for the fact that all you nice people had melted all the way down here just to hear my words and to say that they were n't nearly so funny as you had expected them to be, I should let it go at that, and call the whole thing right off now. But I will not. Rather will I turn from this, our Peroration, to the second section of the speech— the Oration Proper. If the Malefactors of Great Health do not like what I have just said about them, they may petition the Administrative Board at its next secret practice.

Oration Proper — Section A, under the General Heading of Cotton Goods and Steel Rails. Roman numeral V. (Personally I think the speech drags a little at this point.)

As I look into your bright young faces here in the shade of these grand old rock-maples, I am oppressed with the conviction that never before in her history has our country been face to face with such a grave financial crisis. It is with the customary Class Day mingled emotions of pleasure and regret that we bask here to-day, and with eyes dimmed by Bolyston St. dust look back over the seventeen pre-digested courses that have constituted our educational banquet. Let us ponder ponderously on these things. What have we accomplished? What new visions have we seen? When and why does all this mean? O, Brothers, we are all unthinking in this extremity. We have waited and the innumerable caravan has gone without us. We have sung, and the echo has not come back. And now I ask you, what has the Republican party ever done for you — the working man? Temporary platforms, unfilled pledges and dinner-pails, and these mute, defenseless colonnades confront us, and with tier upon tier cry out "Give us the man."

You are brave men. You have given your lives without a murmur to the Class-Album Committee, lives padded, it is true, by Vice-Presidencies of the Soap and Brush Club, but lives, nevertheless, young, virile lives. Even now, with that intrepid fearlessness born of youth you recline here in the new-mown grass before this altar raised to machine-made wit, defying at once hay-fever, and Owen Johnson's accusation that Harvard's social set is based on the dry grass of the fields, which, like Memorial toast, is cast into the oven and withereth away.

You have heard with calmness the dictatorial warnings of the Class Day Committee that pajamas are not to be worn under the caps and gowns until the caps and gowns have been removed, and that anyone attempting to leave the Yard by more than one gate at a time without a yard mileage ticket properly endorsed by the Secretary of the Navy, will have to stay in the yard all night, and cry himself to sleep under the red-oak saplings, or else leave the yard immediately. And yet we are Romans, and this is Rome, that from her throne of beauty ruled the world! O, ingrates! Sluggards! Undesirable citizens!

And now I think that you will agree that I have come logically to the crux of my argument on which I base my claim for the nomination. You have gone through much, besides your June allowances. You have survived the embroidered salmon of last night's spread, where your class-mates and their class-mates tread on your light fantastic toe. You have gone through that most democratic of institutions, the Senior Picnic, where one sees more of the other men in one's class than at any other gathering. And right in connection with the Senior Picnic I wish to make the announcement that I have learned the name of the man who slapped me on my sun-burned back the morning after the Picnic, and I give him warning that I shall hound him to-day, from spread to spread, forcing him to eat one dollar's worth of food at each place, till at last I see him sink bubbling beneath the banana-strewn Red Sea at Beck.

And now, as Tupper's lightning artist says, as the one-thirty bell rings on a lunchless noon, "Now for the last and best!" My speech so far has dealt mainly with the economic aspects of the matter at hand. I shall now close by a few concrete references to the proposed Freshmen Sanitarium, and the Conservation of our National Resources in general.

As a result of a clubbing offer with the HARVARD ADVOCATE I shall omit this section of my speech in delivering it here this afternoon, but a complete copy of it, with footnotes and errata, may be found in the current issue of the ADVOCATE on page 409. It is for sale almost anywhere, and offers two prizes — a second and a third prize, the amounts to be announced at its awarding for the best essay on "How the Ivy Oration (printed in this number) might be improved."

I do not claim that the principles enunciated in this speech will take effect immediately. You are young men yet. But think them over, Brothers. Take them home and confront yourselves with them when you are alone to-night shaking the confetti from your clothes, standing on a packing box full of old neck-ties which Max won't buy and which you hate to throw away. Then, in the silence, ask yourself if your life has been such that you could face with calmness a disclosure to the world of all that Terry knows about you.

When the time comes to fee the goody with an I. O. U. and when, with some one else's diploma in one hand, and a Bursar's card, to show that you are a real Harvard man, in the other, you sit on the old college fence, and gaze over your Lyendecker Arrow collar across the old college campus to where the sun is setting in a crimson glow behind the old college pharmacy, then allow a tear to trickle unnoticed down your cheek, and thinking of what I have said to-day about the Ideal College man and the community, give a regular Harvard cheer for yourself, gird up your loins and be brave.

Go forth now, and, like the gypsy-moth, spread to your hearts content. The only distressing feature of Class Day is now over. Go and live to-day out to its fullest measure, rejoice and be glad, for you are existing to-day in that Golden Age, to which, when again we assemble here as a class, we shall longingly refer as the good old Halcyon Days when we were in College.

THE DIAL

APRIL 1925

NEO-PLATONIC LOVE. BY R. E. PEETS.

1915–1928

The outbreak of the First World War aroused little immediate concern at Harvard; *Advocate* editors were disposed to treat the whole matter as a trifle and made lame jokes in editorial pages about "General Penandink" summoning men to fight at "Advograd." But interest in the war grew as it became likely that the United States would become involved. Teddy Roosevelt, who had been a rather perfunctory editor for the 1880 board, published an article warning Harvard men that they should prepare themselves for the struggle. In 1915 the *Advocate* offered a prize for the best war poem submitted: the winning poem (entitled "Gottmituns") outraged a German professor, who insisted that President Lowell take disciplinary action against the magazine and resigned when his demand was refused. And David W. King, who had left Harvard to serve with the French at Verdun, caused a minor sensation by sending a firsthand account of the battle through Professor Grandgent ("Letter from Verdun").

The war itself, once we were in it, did not help the *Advocate*'s fortunes, though the magazine was lucky, and unique in the university, in that it could continue publication uninterrupted. But issues were printed in a smaller size to save paper, and talented writing did not abound. Only Malcolm Cowley stands out from that time. He served on ambulance duty in France and sent back his impressions of the war in such poems as "To a Dilettante Killed at Vimy."

Cowley's "A Theme with Variations" appeared in the magazine while the war was still in progress, but points to a direction the *Advocate* would take when it was over. After a brief infatuation with political awareness (which produced a competent if uninteresting *Supplement*—"a non-partisan journal for the free discussion of political and economic problems"—that lasted three issues), the *Advocate* returned to normalcy with a series of parodies. A few, like Stedman Buttrick's "Book Reviewing in the United States," appeared in regular numbers, but the magazine had already begun full-length parodies with the *Atlantic Monthly* in 1921. Its success encouraged similar endeavors; a year later, in April 1922, "Mirrors of Grub Street" was published, containing pieces by "Jsph Cnrd" and "Grg Brnrd Shw" as well as "Dgr L. Mstrs' " "Charles River Anthology." *Advocate* parodies reached the height of notoriety in 1925 with a *Dial* issue containing verse by O. O. Goings, Marianne Most, and T. S. Tellalot, all of it quite harmless, but a line drawing called "Neo-Platonic Love" proved too lurid for Bostonian tastes, and the issue was removed from the stands by local authorities.

In poetry little of value appeared in the twenties, no great voices. The prestigious Garrison prize, named for the *Advocate* president of 1888, was given in 1923 to "Sonnets to Mussolini." Even if we ignore political considerations, we can hardly suppose that these verses were much admired. Only Dudley Fitts, '25, constitutes an exception: "Two Translations in Sonnet Form" foreshadows the witty versions of Aristophanes that would later distinguish Fitts as one of the finest Greek translators of his generation.

Fiction fared much better. Oliver LaFarge, '24, began by writing sea stories and legends ("Captain Tom and Mother Carey's Chickens"), and late in his college career turned his attention to the Indians of the Southwest. This interest produced several *Advocate* stories and the novel *Laughing Boy,* which would win the Pulitzer Prize in 1929. James Gould Cozzens, the future novelist, and John Finley, who later became a Harvard professor of Greek, also arose in the twenties. As an undergraduate, Finley had a strong and ultimately futile concern for the election of John W. Davis to the United States Presidency in 1924: that campaign not only colored "The Hobgoblin Defeated" but also inspired a vitriolic article entitled "The Republican Menace," in which he attacked the complacency of the Coolidge era.

The later twenties betray a certain flaccidity in the *Advocate*'s attitude. Occasionally came reports on athletics or Harvard clubs (always favorite topics for analysis), or articles exposing the power and corruption of the American Legion, but on the whole these years do not offer much. It would require the intellectual crisis of the Depression to stir the *Advocate* from its complacency.

Harvard and Preparedness.

By Theodore Roosevelt, '80.

HARVARD ought to take the lead in every real movement for making our country stand as it should stand. Unfortunately prominent Harvard men sometimes take the lead the wrong way. This applies pre-eminently to all Harvard men who have had anything to do with the absurd and mischievous professional-pacificist or peace-at-any-price movements which have so thoroughly discredited this country during the past five years. These men are seeking to chinafy the country; and, so far as they have any influence, they are tending to chinafy Harvard too. The pacificist of this type stands on an exact level with the poltroon. His appropriate place is with the college sissy who disapproves of football or boxing because it is rough.

In all our history there have been few movements more detrimental to our people and no movement more essentially ignoble than the professional pacificist or peace-at-any-price movement which has reached its zenith during the past five years. This movement became part of our official governmental policy when five years ago the effort was made to adopt the all-inclusive arbitration treaties under which we covenanted to arbitrate questions of national honor and vital interest (specifically, this means questions such as the murder of American men, women and children on the high seas and the rape of American women, for instance.) A couple of years ago we actually adopted certain ludicrous arbitration or commission-for-a-year's-investigation treaties which, when the proposal was made to reduce them to practice, were instantly repudiated by the very administration that had made them. Much harm has been done to America by crooked politicians and by crooked business men; but they have never done as much harm as these professional pacificists have sought to do and have partially succeeded in doing. They have weakened the moral fibre of our people. They have preached base and ignoble doctrines to this nation. For five years they have succeeded in tainting our foreign policy with mean hypocrisy.

I abhor wanton or unjust war. I believe with all my heart in peace, if peace can be obtained on terms compatible with self-respect. Even a necessary war I regard as a lamentable necessity. But it may be a necessity. It may be a necessity in order to save our bodies. It may be a necessity in order to save our souls. A high-minded man or woman does not regard death as the most dreadful of all things, because there are some things worse than death. A high-minded nation does not regard war as the most dreadful of all things, because there are some things worse than war.

Recently there have actually been political buttons circulated in this country with "safety first" as the motto upon them in the fancied interest of one of the party candidates for the Presidency next year. This is the motto which in practise is acted upon by the men on a sinking ship who jump into the lifeboats ahead of the women and children. Even these men, however, do not, when they get ashore, wear buttons to commemorate their feat.

This country needs to prepare itself materially against war. Even more it needs to prepare itself spiritually and morally, so that, if war must be accepted as the alternative to dishonor or unrighteousness, it shall be accepted with stern readiness to do any duty and incur any hazard that the times demand. It would be well if Harvard would establish as part of its curriculum an efficient system of thorough military training — not merely military drill, which is only a part of military training, and indeed a small part. I believe heartily in athletics; but from the physical and moral standpoint such a system of military training would be better for all the men in Harvard and would reach far more men than are now reached by athletics.

In addition, however, to such military training, and even if at present it proves impossible to get such military training, let Harvard men, graduates and undergraduates alike, start at once to practice and to preach that efficient morality which stands at the opposite pole from the milk-and-water doctrines of the professional pacificists. Remember that sentimentality is as directly the reverse of sentiment as bathos is of pathos. It is right and eminently necessary to be practical; it is right and eminently necessary to take care of our own fortunes, of our own bodies. Each man must do it individually; and the nation must do it in its corporate capacity, acting for all of us. But in addition, both men and nation must have the power of fealty to a lofty ideal.

No man is worth his salt who is not ready at all times to risk his body, to risk his wellbeing, to risk his life, in a great cause. No nation has a right to a place in the world unless it has so trained its sons and daughters that they follow righteousness as the great goal. They must scorn to do injustice, and scorn to submit to injustice They must endeavor steadily to make peace the handmaiden of righteousness, to secure both peace and righteousness. But they must stand ready, if the alternative is between peace and righteousness, unhesitatingly to face suffering and death in war rather than to submit to iniquity or dishonor.

Letter from Verdun

Bureau de Paris, Brooklyn-New York Daily Eagle, 53, Rue Cambon.

March 31, 1916.

Dear Professor Grandgent,

It may interest you to know that a Harvard undergraduate has helped stem the German tide at Verdun, so I take the liberty of sending to you a copy of a letter I have just received from him.

His name is David W. King, and his home is in New York. When he enlisted, he was a Sophomore, so I suppose he would be a Junior by now had he stayed. He enlisted early in the war with the other American volunteers, went through the trench warfare of last winter on the Craonne plateau west of Rheims, and later in the chalk of Champagne east of the same city. Last fall he went through the whole of the Champagne battle, but unlike most of the other Americans, he was not hurt. He has now come through the Verdun battle without so much as a scratch, though pretty well tired out. "Poor King deserves a little wound, so he can get some rest in a hospital" say his comrades.

At the end of his letter he adds: "You won't have a very fine opinion of English A when you see my spelling mistakes, but after a year in the trenches I am so mixed up with French and English spelling, that I do not know where I stand, and I haven't the courage to go over it and correct."

Personally I think "English A" may be very proud of David W. King; and I should like to suggest that his letter be either read aloud to every section, or else be printed in one of the Harvard undergraduate papers, such as the Illustrated or the Advocate. I leave that to your judgment. I do not know who has charge of English A this year.

From a study of the French and German official reports of the events that he describes at close range, I feel certain that Mr. King was present at the very highest tide of the

German advance, the attacks on the villages of Vaux and Douaumont the first week in March. By the time he was relieved, they had begun to attack on the west bank of the Meuse.

Outwardly the life in Paris has not changed much since you were here. Very few wounded have been brought here from Verdun, and I hear all the Paris hospitals are practically empty, waiting for action nearer the capital. The Verdun fighting drags on, but there is no anxiety that they will break through at this date.

With my best regards and greetings to the College, I am,

Yours sincerely,

NABOTH HEDIN, '08.

March 25, 1916.

Dear Mr. Hedin,

You asked for the story of Verdun, so I am going to give it to you just as I saw it.

In the first place let me state that our division are troops of attack and when the trouble started, were "en repos" getting ready for the spring. But doings began to get warmer and they moved us up by forced marches and autos, regiment by regiment, from town to town like cabs at a cab rank. When we started we were told that we had seven army corps (300,000 men) before us. On February 18 we left the repose town in autos. We went about 80 kilometers and spent six days there. The morning of the sixth day we started marching. We had made 25 kilometers but when we got to the town where we were to halt, orders came to push on 15 more that night. From there on it was forced marching. We left a town at six o'clock the morning of the 25th day of February and marched till 3 A. M. the morning of the 26th. We had soup before starting but nothing else till the next day.

The rest of the 26th, until ten o'clock, was put in a fort on the outskirts of Verdun. At ten we marched through Verdun on our way

forward. This was in broad daylight and three Boche planes spotted us, flew over the column and let four or five bombs go. Luckily no one was hurt but this was my first experience with aero bombs. I don't like them. Things began to get more and more lively. We took up our positions in a wood and waited for orders. I will call this wood the Bois de H. . . . Pretty soon orders came to move up as the Boches had taken a fort and our line had been bent. Then the famous French formation for marching under feu de barrage (curtain fire) began. It reminded me of Champagne. We halted on the slope of a wooded hill and waited there till dark. They were hunting for us with their big ones but they burst just back of us. That night we pulled up a notch and went forward as supports. We got into our new quarters, another wood, about three in the morning of the 27th. It was at this point that we began to realize what the Boches had in the way of artillery. All that day they sprinkled the woods with "105" shrapnell and an occasional 210 marmite, for the batteries or for good luck. They kept this up day and night. That night our third batallion with the other regiment of our brigade attacked to try for the famous fort of D. . . . To this day I don't know if they got it or not, but I know that only 60 men of that batallion came back. The next day we lay there still and the night of the 28th came orders to go up and relieve a regiment in a little redoubt at Vaux. The Boches were pounding this night and day. There was no boyau (communication-trench) leading to it, no trenches in front of it and we were told if we were attacked in force to hold out till the end, but no supports could be sent to us. We arrived here after seven hours hard walking in mud and "sac au dos" and without one halt. When we got there we had to wait half an hour while the occupants got their wounded out. Things began to look as cheerful as they were painted.

The 29th passed remarkably quietly in the little fort. We only had three men wounded. They shelled us now and then but nothing to speak of. The night of the 29th we worked at trenches before the village of Vaux. One special unit was mounting guard over a 240 naval gun stranded between the lines in the first attack. During the day it was unguarded but as soon as night fell, out went a patrol to take charge of it. The first of March was quiet, only two men wounded in the morning and then silence. It was sinister it was so still. Work again that night and something happened to the soup "corvée" (carriers) for we got no food. The morning of the second arrived. At 6 A. M. they started in with 210's and 380's. Down in the village and on the first line trenches they only used 105's and 77's, but they turned their big ones on us. There is absolutely no way of conveying an idea of big shells to a man who has not been there. But in this case imagine how 250 or so mice would feel crowded into a cracker tin and someone pounding that tin at the rate of five giant or ten light blows a minute. The fort was in two parts, a long glacis with a parapet, and a strongly protected pair of fair-sized casements. The parapet didn't last two blows nor the bomb shelters under it. One 380mm. shell wounded 46 and killed 12. About half way through the morning, at ten o'clock, in came the section that had been holding a line of trenches on our right. Nothing was left of their trenches and ten of them had been buried alive. That made things even pleasanter in the fort. At no time could we all find room to stretch out on the floor. Result was that for two nights and days we had had no sleep except an occasional dozing-off while sitting down. The shelling got worse and worse. We had to keep sentinels aloft on the parapet but few lasted more than half an hour; then the cry would come: "Stretcher bearers!" and "Replace the sentinel!" Every once in a while a big one would fall just in front of the outer wall of the casemates. The blast and concussions were so great that not only was the kerosene lamp blown out, but the boards wired to the iron bars of the doors were blown in, and mind you, the doors of the casemates did not coincide with the doors

of the outer wall or apron. About 1 P. M. they got the range for keeps, and the casemates rocked and shook. There was two meters of earth and three of reinforced-concrete, but every moment we expected to see daylight and have the vaulting down on us. There was one crash when we did see daylight, but it was only a huge gap in the concrete apron. I saw strong men faint from the bad air and constant shock and blast. About 4 P. M. the look-outs reported that the troops in the village were signalling for "Artillerie devant les tranchees!" Our telephone wire with the batteries was cut. Two runners were sent out. They never got there. Finally we used rockets. Five minutes, ten minutes and we could hear our machine guns in the valley with their rhythmic "wop-wop-wop-wop-wop" and for the first time we saw the Germans advancing in their famous four-deep formation. Then, just as we were going to send up more rockets, the 75's began. Never before was I so glad to hear that spiteful "blamb-blamb-blamb". The first line melted away before a veritable wave of woolly shrapnell clouds. Right in their midst! And then back and forward, left and right. At about six or half-past it grew dark, the attack had been crumpled up. At midnight we were relieved and then confusion began! Company lost contact with company, section with section, and the Germans shelling all the roads. Finally at daybreak we got on the road to Verdun, and started for a barrack just outside it, the rendezvous (meeting place) of the regiment. We met the other regiment of our brigade on the way up again. They had been relieved at the same time, but there was an "alerte" and up they must go. The same fate was in store for us, but red-tape and regulations demanded that the tired troops should march all the way down and back again. We got to the barracks and one by one the companies came straggling in. There were six Americans in the first company, and I was anxious to find out how they had come out. As they came in sight I saw D and R, but I missed the giant form of Ganz, a happy-go-lucky sailor man who had just come to us from the Legion. Then they told me that he had been killed and C wounded by the same shell. It was like a slap in the face, it made me sore clean through. I did not realize till later how we would miss him. We found some straw matresses at the caserne (barracks) but just as we were preparing to sleep, we were told to bolt our food and get ready to march. The alert had reached us at last.

At four o'clock that afternoon of the 3rd we started off. The second batallion with the other regiment of our brigade was to attack the village of D. . . . If they failed, we were to attack also. We were hurried along, (almost running) to get us into positions as first supports. Just as we arrived at the top of a hill in the Bois de H. . . . e, out of breath and puffing hard, we were greeted by a crowd of asphyxiating gas shells. We caught our breath in our respirators. Like eating a banana under water, it is difficult but can be done. We heard the attack start and soon news came back that it was successful. So we made our eats and turned in in spite of the shells bursting all through the woods. I shared a box of sardines with another man, the first thing I had eaten in 48 hours. The next day a corvée went for coffee, and had hardly returned at seven o'colck when news came that the Germans had taken the village. It was up and hike it for us. We marched through the woods with an occasional marmite dropping near us. Finally we fetched up behind the fort of Souville, just behind the village of Fleury. Here we waited until about 3 o'clock under a slight bombardment. Then we marched across the fields, leaving the shelter of the fort and got on the read leading through Fleury to the village of D. . . .nt. We were to get back to the village. The minute we appeared on the road they opened fire on us with everything they owned. We tore through those streets by sections. Everything worked like clockwork. We would make a rush, halt behind a block of buildings, get our breaths and then move on. But in the mean time the marmites were

knocking at the back-door of those houses and the shrapnell 105's were sprinkling the front yards. The place had been evacuated so suddenly that there were all sorts of livestock running round the street and cows killed so suddenly that they were lying there with all four legs sticking straight up in the air for all the world like a Noah's Ark animal knocked over. The whole affair was such a chaos that one's only feelings were of wild excitement and childish delight at the fiendish racket. I tried to tighten my straps on my sack. It slipped and before I knew it was on the ground five yards back of me. I turned and was going back for it when I saw a captain and doctor and three men killed by a shell bursting just beside it. It was just at the exit of the village and of course one of the hottest points. I decided the sack was not so necessary as I had thought and continued on my way. At the other end of the village was a little ditch, the beginning of a boyau leading to the village of D. . . . t. We lay in that till dark, being shelled and having the wounded crawl over us on their way to the rear. At nightfall we made our way by ditches knee-deep in water to a little redoubt on the outskirts of D. . . . We were to try again to attack the next night. The next morning, the fifth of March, we moved into a little valley. We learned there that in spite of the fact they had seen us coming the day before, we were to have pushed on and attacked that night at any cost, but on arriving at the fort the batallion was so cut up it was hopeless. But at the same time the Boches had started something in the village and we were ordered to make a rush through the village and bring up supports at any cost. The 5th of March all through the day we lay in the valley and the Boches proceeded to bombard what was left of us. Their aeroplanes manoeuvered without the slightest opposition from our planes or even from our batteries. This was the case right through the whole affair. Soon five or six of their Taubes were overhead and the shells began to arrive. They made excellent practice all through the day. Every time a shell burst there were shrieks and calls for stretchermen. I was crouching down in a little improvised shelter when two pieces hit me at once, one in the knee and the other on my casque (helmet). I was like a kid with a Christmas stocking, I did not know which to look at first. But when I did, my dreams of rest in an hospital were over. Just a bruise in my knee and a dent in my helmet. That night we started out to bring some soup back for the troops. The detail started out some 12 odd men from our company. It took us four hours to reach the kitchen and half the way the road was swept by shrapnell. Here and now let me explode that little story about hot soup, etc., on the first lines, that the New York Herald published. The artillery did get hot food but our regiments in our brigade were two and three days without food and then we would get our meals stiff with cold grease, and then two or three days more without food. This time we had been three days without food and were weak as we staggered along. As I said, after four hours continuous walking we found the kitchens. We wolfed the hot soup and rice, but we should have known better. You can't go three days without food, wolf a "gamelle" (billy-can) full of hot, heavy food and expect to hang on to it. I had better luck with coffee and bread, and then we started back. We had hardly got past the village when some of those silent Austrian shells got six of us, two killed and four wounded. One of the men, wounded in the hip, though he was right by a "Poste de Secour" (Emergency ambulance post) insisted upon keeping on with us for two more kilometers. Finally we got into a "feu de barrage" and had to lie in a ditch for an hour. When we finally got back into the valley where we had left the regiment, we found that they had gone up to the first line, on the left of the village of D. . . . t. All the way up to the trenches we stumbled over heaps of dead, mostly French. The next day showed us the other side of the equation. The last hundred yards of the journey was done at the double. The trenches had no boy-

aux to them; the Boches were only five yards away and might turn a machine-gun on at any moment. We got there without further loss and after the soup had been dealt out, took our turn at watching and digging. The trenches had only been started during the night before and there was work to be done. Gone were all hopes of a little rest. When dawn broke we got some idea of the importance of the position. Before our trenches, and for fifty yards beyond, was wave on wave of grey-green corpses. This was easily more than the French half of the equation. But the day showed us something else. Our section of the trench was enfiladed by the German machine-guns in the village. It was the same sensation that one feels in the back of one's neck at snowfall time. After about two hours of it, I couldn't stand it any longer so two of us collected some sand-bags. I hopped out of the trench and the other man passed me the bags as fast as I could place them. The barricade was barely in position before the Boches cut loose, but they were five minutes too late! During the day we could see them massing for an attack but the 75's and rifle-fire cooled their ambition. At midnight we were relieved, the Boches taking advantage of the occasion to shell us. We had hardly left the trenches when they attacked. This time, though, they had fresh troops against them who drove home a sharp counter attack and cleared D. . . . for the sixth time, there was no need for us, so we continued on our way once more to the Bois de H. . . . At this point I lost the column just as we were going through the valley where we had lost so many two days ago. I raced after them till I came to some marmite holes full of water. It was shiny and green and had a queer taste of powder, but it was the first drink I had had in 36 hours and I drank my fill. Just then they sent some shrapnell over the valley and I judged it time to catch the column. I spent a bad quarter of an hour floundering among barbed-wire entanglements, corpses and mud, but finally found the road and caught up to the last company.

We marched all night, lost our way once, and finally arrived at the Bois de H. . . . e at 5.30 A. M. the morning of the seventh. At 5.35, every man was sleeping oblivious of hunger and the sodden ground. But it was not to last for long. At 7 A. M. they started searching that wood with a devilish thoroughness. At 7.30 they got round to our part and the sight of eight men sailing up twenty feet into the air, not 30 yards away, persuaded us to move. D, R, and I found a little dugout on the edge of a railway cutting. We stayed there for more than two hours. But they were getting nearer and nearer. I had just remarked to D. that we were in more or less of a dead angle unless they landed one just opposite on the other bank. I had hardly finished before they landed three big ones just opposite in quick succession, the pieces cutting through the roof of branches. We moved once more. Then we learned that we had to stay there till six that night as reserves. Being shelled in a wood is worse than anywhere else. The shells seem to make more noise. They explode high in the air against trees and the falling and breaking of trees and branches adds to the chaos. Everywhere one turned there was the crash of the shells and shrieks of wounded. Boches planes would pass over and then for a while the shelling would be redoubled. Finally, at three o'clock, we started to pull out for the rear. We had fifteen miles to go that night before we could eat or sleep. But the men were only too glad to get as far away as possible from that hell on earth. We had gone about eight miles when there was a call for stretcher bearers. But when they arrived, there was little use for them. A man had dropped dead in the ranks from pure exhaustion. No one seemed to care or even be surprised, even when another dropped dead half an hour later, at midnight when we reached the little town of Bellevue, and for the first time in 12 days we slept on straw. But the day after we had to move on. It was only nine miles to where we took autos, but another man dropped dead on the way. We rode in the autos for 50 miles and then spent two days in a town we had spent six weeks in last winter. The men were in a pitiable condition, over 70 per cent. had bowel trouble and there were over 200 cases of typhoid or paratyphoid. But the third day we had to march once more. The next three days were a sort of staggering nightmare. We made our 25 kilometers a day, but how is more than I can tell. Three more died on the way from exhaustion. D. looks like a bony skeleton and the rest of us were not much better. Finally we stopped here. Our reinforcements came from the depot and have been here ever since.

A few generalities and I'm finished. I spoke casually of shelling here and shrapnell there, etc., but you can understand better what it means when I add that our brigade went into it with 5,500 rifles and we came down with 1,100. Another thing that struck me is there were no heavy columns of troops in evidence as there was in Champagne. It did not occur to me till afterwards that in our unceasing changing of sector and long forced marches from one threatened part of the line to another we were doing the work of three, two at least, regiments. At the time we all swore and grumbled, but on looking back the cleverness of the French Staff shows up in their ability to stop such an attack with so few troops at hand. But with no other troops in the world could they have done the same. No other troops could have stood the exposure to rain and the bitter cold, lack of sleep and the marching and attacks on empty stomachs. Perhaps the success of the French staff lies in the fact that they know to a nicety how much the long suffering "fantassin" (French infantryman) can stand. It is all over now and being human we forget the rough spot and only remember that we stopped them with only half the men that was really needed for the work.

There, that is about my limit, excepting that I forgot to mention that hundreds of men made the last marches with frost-bitten feet.

David W. King.

Mr. Sunday on College Men

AVE you heard "Billy" Sunday? I mean *You,* not your friends, not your newspaper, not you clergyman—not even your room-mate. For Mr. Sunday is a concentrated mass of intensified personality, only to be judged after direct contact.

I met the famous revivalist at the close of his afternoon sermon. The crowd was slowly filing out of the Tabernacle—very slowly indeed — very slowly indeed — with a halting, limping movement. A smaller crowd of potential converts eddied about the platform, craning their necks to catch one last glance of Mr. Sunday. He stood there smiling at them, an erect, well-proportioned man, dressed in a dark grey suit, patent leather shoes, and a sombre cravat. As he same down the pulpit stairs, I stopped him and explained my mission.

"Certainly", he said. "Surely I'll talk with you. Let's get out of this mob first, though. My car is right outside, and we can talk on the way home."

Before I could reply to this proposal, he seized my shoulder, whisked me about, and proceeded to alternately guide and shove me towards a side entrance. Our progress was constantly interrupted. White-haired women, stooped by toil, tottered forward and tremblingly held out their hands. One of these, with tears streaming down her face and a breath strongly reminiscent of the liquor interests, tottered perceptibly as she whispered "God bless you, sor." Men of widely varying ages and states of prosperity greeted the recipient of this blessing, some with a slap on the back, others with a more sedate pressure on his arm. Mr. Sunday returned every salutation with a brief, hearty clasp of the hand.

At last we reached our promised land — Mr. Sunday's car. We were hardly in the car when a small sized mob collected itself, seemingly from nowhere, and formed in a rough ring about us. The chauffeur, however, finally manoeuvered his way through the crowd to the street entrance. Mr. Sunday took out a large handkerchief and with a sweeping motion rubbed away the perspiration which glistened on his face. Then he leaned back with a quizzical look in his steel grey eyes. "Now, then, what can I do for you?"

"I want to get some of your views on college men and college problems."

"I like college men very, very much", said Mr. Sunday in low, slightly rasping voice, emphasizing his remarks with quick, darting gestures of his forefinger. "They are so finely responsive, so intelligent, that they follow every question through all its intricacies. I can preach to them rationally; for religion, you know, is, after all, rational."

"Yes", I interposed timidly, "but I didn't know you believed in a rational religion."

"I believe religion is rational, but I don't believe in what you call a rational religion—that is, any religion founded on a scientific or philosophical basis. No sane man would question that God provides ears to hear with, mouth to taste with, and so on. Well, what are we going to do about our souls. I take care of the physical 'me' carefully, I wash its face, I bathe it, I give it three meals a day, I give it exercise and distraction and sleep. If I didn't give sufficient attention to my physical body, I would expect it to become warped and diseased. Yet how can men who never go to church, who never pray, who never read the Bible, how can men like these believe their souls will keep strong and pure? Won't their souls become warped and diseased and puny?"

"What do you think about the spirituality of the Harvard men and about religion as we regard it, with non-compulsory chapel and freedom of belief?"

Mr. Sunday gently rubbed his forehead with his thumb, absent-mindedly tugging at his hair. "I think", he began with a genial smile, "that the college man is distinctly above the average in religious personality. Practically all you fellows are going to blaze trails after graduation. You are going to do the most important part of the world's work along political, scientific, and business lines. I wonder if the average college man realizes how much influence he can exert for good work. Other people are watching him; he is generally a community leader, and his example can have a far-reaching effect. I don't know exactly what to say about non-compulsory chapel. It has its good points, but I believe there is a reaction setting in against it."

"Then you think a return to compulsory chapel a future tendency?"

"Yes, I do. Take college men fifty or sixty years ago when chapel attendance was required. Of course they sinned then to some extent as they sin now—but there wasn't the 'boozing', the gambling, the white-light 'frolics that the undergraduates of today indulge in. I think our mature men are looking on this tendency of the college man with increasing alarm, and that they will use every means in their power to curb the evil. A return to compulsory chapel will probably be one of the means of correction."

"How then, Mr. Sunday, would you account for the fact that so many college 'boozers' reform after graduation?"

"That's easy enough! When a man is in college, Father pays the bills. If he gets drunk once in a while, he doesn't worry about it, because he hasn't cultivated any sense of responsibility. But when he gets out into the business world and has to pay for his drinking—not only for his drinks but also for his decreased efficiency, he soon learns that he is up against a losing proposition."

"Do you reach college women with your revivals more easily than college men? I mean, do the women give a better reaction, so to speak?"

Mr. Sunday, with a sly twinkle in his eye, hesitated almost imperceptibly before replying. "No! You see, nearly all college women are Christians already — so there is far less reason for their having any reaction. Men offer a less developed and more profitable field

for my work. Personally, I prefer to preach to men, but that"—here he laughed heartily—"is probably because I am a man and can get more trail-hitters from among men. And anyway — I don't care what any one says, men are the leaders in the community, and I've got to get them!"

Yet Mr. Sunday is a believer in women's suffrage.

All this while I had been listening carefully for a trace of the much-vaunted Sunday vulgarity. Not even a slang word had escaped from his lips. He talked with extreme rapidity, earnestly, in a low, almost passionate voice, often putting his hands on my shoulders or clenching his fists by way of emphasis. His smile was peculiarly expressive — it was so flexible that it mirrored all his emotions instantaneously. Judging from the reports of his sermons, I had expected to meet a noisy, slangy individual with "snap-judgment" decisions on any questions asked him. Instead I found an alert, super-active gentleman, who spoke quietly and thoughtfully, who by his innate forcefulness seemed to radiate sincerity to the finger tips.

One could see there was no forced energy about him. It is as natural for Mr. Sunday to be in action as for a kitten to chase a ball of yarn. He simply exudes vitality; he has such a superfluity of energy that he is never still for a second.

"Ma" Sunday, a dignified matron, watched him anxiously the while. "I'm so afraid he will hurt himself", she explained apologetically, a tired smile flickering in her large brown eyes. "Daddy will insist on overworking. And Boston has given us such an unexpectedly generous reception that I'm afraid he won't get any rest."

"What did you mean, Mr. Sunday, by your statement to the Unitarians that you did not believe in a bastard form of evolution. Don't you think a man who believes in evolution can still be a good Christian?"

The evangelist gazed at me solemnly. "Do you believe in evolution?"

"Certainly", I replied, "what's wrong with the theory?"

Mr. Sunday cast a sad and reproachful look

at me. Evidently he was too courteous to forecast in brutal English my destination during some future life. But I could feel that he regarded me as a brand doomed to destruction. Finally he broke the silence.

"If evolution means development—Yes! I am with you. If evolution means changing species — No! Burbank has immensely improved the potato, but it was always the potato he was working with. If you ask me to believe that man as a type has improved since the creation, I'm with you; but if you say my great-grandfather was a gorilla—No! No! No!"

"Do you believe in salvation by works?"

"No", was the reflective answer, "God judges the motive, not the act. God has always manifested His supreme mercy towards mankind. First there was Adam who sinned when he and Eve broke God's covenant by eating the apple. Then, although God turned them out of Eden, he gave them another chance and showed them a way to Heaven. But when Cain tried to get into God's good graces by bringing presents of fruit instead of the appointed lamb, God said: 'Cain, I'm not going to do business in fruits. You've got to do as I tell you.' Then when the Jews began to worship graven images, God gave them the Mosaic law, and finally, he gave them Christ as his supreme gift. He has given people no other way to Heaven since then."

"Now", continued Mr. Sunday, not even pausing for breath, "only man can be saved and only through Christ. There is no salvation for the devil and his host. They are fallen angels. Angels do not reproduce; they have no sex — each is peculiar unto himself. To save the devils, Christ would have to take the form of each individual devil and die for him. But man is a species, a type — and when Christ died, he died for all men."

The automobile glided up to the door of Mr. Sunday's house and stopped with a jerk. The chauffeur sprang out to open the door, but Mr. Sunday had anticipated him and had already swung the door open. Not to be outdone, the chauffeur ran up the stoop to open the heavy storm door. Mr. Sunday tore after him, two steps at a time, and they arrived at the top simultaneously. Thereupon "Billy" swung his fist with feigned viciousness at the chauffeur's head. "Thougth you could beat me — huh", then they both chuckled like schoolboys.

As the maid opened the door, Mr. Sunday's thoughts returned to Harvard again. "By the way", he said, "how is that game with Brown coming out? I saw the Princeton game and cheered myself hoarse. My sermon is over at three o'clock tomorrow. I ought to be able to get out in time to see half the game, don't you think? Sometime when I have a day off, I'm coming out to Cambridge and see what your plant is really like. I've passed through once or twice but I've never had an opportunity to get a really good idea of the place.

"How about speaking out at Harvard?"

Mrs. Sunday took it upon herself to reply. "I think it would be a fine thing for 'Daddy' to speak out at Harvard. Of course we wouldn't come without an invitation, and we needn't hunt for one — for, goodness knows, we are busy enough. But it would seem too bad for Mr. Sunday to be in Boston ten weeks, so near to a great college, and not speak to the students."

I turned to Mr. Sunday for corroboration. "When you come out to Harvard, Mr. Sunday, you should attend a chapel service at Appleton and see what it is like. I think you would be very much interested."

Mr. Sunday grinned a Rooseveltian grin. "If I get an 'invite', I'll be there."

Lowell Brentano '18

To a Dilettante Killed at Vimy

Years of small sorrows and of small endeavor;
Years of great plans, and mental cowardice;
And we that hoped they would not last forever:—
That's all. To cut the whole thing short, came this.

And yet the petty muddle you made of it;
The pose; the brave dreams foundered in a sea
Of idle talk, now seem to us resolved
Into clean metal by catastrophe.

M. Cowley '18

A Theme With Variations

I.

*As Written by Miss Edna St. Vincent
Millay on Her Typewriter.*

My thoughts had festered in the heat
Three months; I could not do a thing.
The pavement boiled beneath my feet
Three months; I could not even sing
And wondered what the fall would bring.

But yesterday at dusk, the lost
North wind sprang up after a rain,
And when I woke, I saw the frost
Had patterned lacework on the pane,
And on my lips were songs again.

II.

As It Appeared in 'The Pagan'.

Three months summer held me like malaria.
A fever drove me up and down the streets;
Underfoot the pavement
Was soft and viscous with heat.
About garbage cans flies came into being
And buzzed their enjoyment of the world
And died.
Children played about like flies
And died.
I fled to the wild places
But there in the solitude my thoughts festered
And to forget their foulness
I fled among people.
Yesterday.
A wind sprang up after a rain
And this morning there was a delicate tracery of frost on
    the window.
I have been praising the beauty of men all day.
I am a god in a new creation.

III.

With Apologies to Mr. William Carlos Williams.

I wish I could pass out
lie with my toes towards the daisies
it must be cool even now
down there.
                   Next autumn
there'll be wind, frost,
biting rain.
             I'll be peppy.
August is like last night's
Stale Pilsener.

IV.

*As Rendered by a Member of the Spectric School
with Appropriate Overtones.*

Crawling infinities of atoms. Death. Sweat and the livid perfume of surheated asphalt. Thing unmentionable floating down sewers. All humanity is floating down a sewer into the cleansing sea.

A Brahmin once, performing his ninth pilgrimage to the waters of the sacred Ganges, observed a maize field drying up in the sun. "May the seven seas and the thirteen rivers of Paradise shed their healing moisture on that field." And the sun beat down, and the maize turned from yellow to brown, and the people starved. But that winter came the rains, and all those that survived blessed the words of the prophet.

My soul is a larva, a fat grub that feeds on flies.

Crack . . . crack . . . crack. The leaves are snapping off in the frost and falling one by one. On my window is the forest of Arden.

A young man in a silk hat runs down the street like a little boy Someone asks him why, but he only stares. Paradise looms behind swinging doors.

The wind is my breath and the sea is my spittle. I shall overthrow a hundred Brahmas and gods greater than Vishnu shall I raise up.

Malcolm Cowley '19

COLLEGE DORMITORIES

By STEPHEN LEACOCK

Professor of Political Economy, McGill University

WHEN I was a student at the University of Toronto thirty years ago, I lived, from start to finish, in seventeen different boarding houses. As far as I am aware these houses have not, or not yet, been marked with tablets. But they are all still to be found in the vicinity of McCaul and Darcy, and St. Patrick Streets. Anyone who doubts the truth of what I have to say may go and look at them.

I was not alone in the nomadic life that I led. There were several of us drifting about in this fashion from one melancholy habitation to another. We lived as a rule two or three in a house, sometimes alone. We dined in the basement. We always had beef, done up in some way after it was dead, and there were always soda biscuits on the table. They used to have a brand of soda biscuit in those days in the Toronto boarding houses that I have not seen since. They were better than dog biscuits but with not so much snap. My contemporaries will all remember them A great many of the leading barristers and professional men of Toronto were fed on them.

In the life we led we had practically no opportunities for association on a large scale—no common rooms, no reading rooms, nothing. We never saw the magazines—personally I didn't even know the names of them. The only interchange of ideas we ever got was by going over to the Caer Howell Hotel on University Avenue and interchanging them there.

I mention these melancholy details not for their own sake but merely to emphasize the point that when I speak of students' dormitories, and the larger life which they offer, I speak of what I know.

If we had had at Toronto, when I was a student, the kind of dormitories and dormitory life that they have at Harvard, I don't think I would ever have graduated. I'd have been there still.

The trouble is that the universities on our continent are only just waking up to the idea of what a university should mean. They were, very largely, instituted and organized with the idea that a university was a place where young men were sent to absorb the contents of books and to listen to lectures in the classrooms. The student was pictured as a pallid creature, burning what was called the "midnight oil," his wan face bent over his desk. If you wanted to do something for him you gave him a book: if you wanted to do something really large on his behalf you gave him a whole basketful of them. If you wanted to go still further and be a real benefactor to the college at large, you endowed a competitive scholarship and set two or more pallid students working themselves to death to get it.

That, as I see it, was about the idea and theory of the Canadian universities as they used to be. In the course of time and through the plain teaching of circumstances, we have been getting away from that idea. We are beginning to see that the textbook and the classroom are but a part of the student's life. If they are taken by themselves, in undiluted doses, they probably do more harm than good. They not only injure the student's health but they impair his mind. True education cannot be achieved after this fashion, by shoveling in information. The most that

this can ever give is erudition and pedantry, never capacity and genuine acquirement. The typical product of it is the college pedant possessed of a stomach-full of fact, but with a mind the size of a peanut and the outlook of a child.

The real process of education consists (as the derivation of the word implies) in bringing out of the mind the inborn capacity than is in it. I think that Horace said something of this sort before. But there is no harm in saying it over again.

Since the melancholy days of which I speak, I have had the experience of nearly a quarter of a century of post-graduate work and of university teaching. It is a noble profession, and, with the continued aid of the governors of McGill University, I hope to have another quarter of a century of it at least before I hang up my mortar board and sink into the arms of the trustees of the Carnegie Pension Fund. But as a college teacher I have long since realized that the most that the teacher, as such, can do for the student is a very limited matter. The real thing for the student is the life and environment that surrounds him. All that he really learns, he learns, in a sense, by the active operation of his own intellect and not as the passive recipient of lectures. And for this active operation what he needs most is the continued and intimate contact with his fellows. Students must live together and eat together, talk and smoke together. Experience shows that that is how their minds really grow. And they must live together in a rational and comfortable way. They must eat in a big dining room or hall, with oak beams across the ceiling, and the stained glass in the windows and with a shield or tablet here and there upon the wall, to remind them between times of the men who went before them and left a name worthy of the memory of the college. If a student is to get from his college what it ought to give him, a college dormitory with the life in common that it brings, is his absolute right. A university that fails to give it to him is cheating him.

If I were founding a university—and I say it with all the seriousness of which I am capable (just think of that!)—I would found first a smoking room; then when I had a little more money in hand I would found a dormitory; then after that, or more properly with that, a decent reading room and a library. After that, if I still had money over that I couldn't use, I would hire a professor and get some text-books.

To my mind the greatest of all the needs of a modern university is the building of college dormitories to supply to our students a wider college life than we can give them now. There is no nobler object of benefaction than this. There is no better way to perpetuate an honored name or to cherish the memory of one who is lost than that the name and memory should be inscribed, cut deep in stone, over the gateway of a college dormitory.

A CHARLES RIVER ANTHOLOGY

I. NAPOLEON
1912

For years I pulled the ice-wagon,
And I got so expert that I could go to sleep
As soon as the nose-bag was off of me
And never wake up till it was on again.
I wondered why people wanted ice
In their ice-boxes even in winter,
And thinking of this, once, I woke up
And I fell down, and the driver
Said I was old. The next day
I was taken to the abattoir, and now,
Part of me is down here, and part
Knows all about ice-boxes and mutton,
And I wish I'd minded my own business.

II. WANNUCHECOMECUT
1643

For years I bought fire-water
From the white men, then one day,
I bought some from a young man
At the college.

III.   JOSIAS SMITE–THEM–HIP–AND–THIGH SMITH
1632

Ebenezer Howey laughed on Sunday.
I planned to accuse him, and have him burned
Because anyone who can laugh here on Sunday
Is a sorcerer, or a Quaker. And I then
Should get this plot of land by the river.
And so, I was looking it over

With a proprietary air, and he, the jester,
Pushed me into the river, and before he could
Pull me out again, the Indians came, so I
Drowned. A while ago the city decided
To build a bridge here, and they bought
The land from Ebenezer's heirs
For a fabulous sum. And one of my
Great, great, great, great, great, great,
Great grandsons was foreman of the gang
That sunk this pile right on top
Of me. And every time the subway goes over,
I feel it, and know that more dimes are going
Into stocks that the Howards bought with their
Money, and I am losing my confidence
In Jehovah. Perhaps young Josias will turn
Bolshevist and blow up the bridge. Then
I shall come to the top, and laugh
Horribly.

IV.   ROVER
1876

It's nicer down here than it was up there.
My master used to kick me, and the big
Dogs all picked on me. Here
I play with the mud-puppies and dog-fish,
And we chase the cat-fish
All over the place.
I think, that if someone would cross
One of those Boston Bulls and one
Of these mud-puppies, the result
Would be interesting.

Dgr L. Mstrs.

BOOK REVIEWING IN THE UNITED STATES

STEDMAN BUTTRICK

1. In the manner of the Harvard Crimson

"LUST" is an interesting and well-written novel by Mrs. Jennie Ginsberg. It holds the interest throughout and is replete with sparkling dialogue and natural characters. Mrs. Ginsburg whose "Passion-seekers" made a "hit" last year tells an interesting story about a married couple, Albert and Irma Krantz, who live in New York City. He works at a candy factory where he is employed and she at a fashionable dressmaker's "on the Avenue." It seems that Albert falls in love with one of the factory girls and Irma, in turn, falls in love with a young student who goes to Columbia. Mrs. Ginsberg develops this interesting plot in clever fashion showing cleverly how the thwarted desires of husband and wife have brought about the unhappy situation. But Selma Jacobs, however, a young girl who shows promise of being a world-famous violinist discovers how affairs stand between husband and wife and brings about a reconciliation and is adopted by the Krantzes. But Selma, however, falls in love with Amory Thorndike, the young student who Irma Krantz had been in love with and Irma, jealous, tries to win back young Thorndike. In a powerful scene that is realistic without being sordid Irma injures Selma's hand so that she will never be able to play her violin again. But Irma, however, touched by Selma's goodness and beauty begs forgiveness and young Thorndike promises to marry Selma, her injury turning out to her advantage because young Thorndike had always said he would not marry Selma if she went on the concert stage. Thus a story that seems to be consistently gloomy is relieved by Mrs. Ginsberg's light touch and the story ends happily. The story is a little too long and some of the descriptions are rather elaborate but on the whole, however, it is an interesting and well-written story.

2. In the manner of H. L. Mencken

A YEAR or so ago in the columns of America's family magazine, "The Smart Set," I denounced "Passion-Seekers" by Jennie Ginsberg, the East-side Messiah, as being as witless and unlovely a yokel-yanker as had ever set a-whooping the congregation of Woodmen of the World, Baptists, Lime and Cement Dealers, United Daughters of the Confederacy, Congressmen and Comstocks that constitutes the reading public of these States. This Ginsberg confection by Laura Jean Libbey out of the Chatauqua was a direct and bumptious assault on the intelligence of anyone who did not hold Maurice Maeterlinck to be one of the great thinkers of the Age and Cotton Mather superior to Johann Sebastian Bach and I dismissed it as such, for which offense I was visited by a posse of agents of justice who accused me of being in league with the Black Beast of Potsdam.

Today, a new opus by the Ginsberg hight "Lust" again makes lamentably clear that the lady author fits in snugly with our literary bagmen and yahoos. What she has to offer is, in essence, no more than a dramatization of current sociological rumble-bumble — a dramatization based on the thesis that one Knight of Pythias is more desirable than ten John D. Rockefellers. Yet for all its wowing and clapper-clawing in the name of New Thought, "Lust" remains at bottom a ripe and carnal specimen of the tin-horn romanticism that came out of the puff-sleeve period. Even a college professor should detect that under the vast moraines of pish-posh thrown up to bemuse Uplifters and Inspired Dreamers is the solid foundation tried and true hokum, that under the arpeggios on the harp is the unison singing of the First Methodist choir, that under the bogus appeal aimed at the suburban intelligentsia is the appeal aimed at the gizzard of the typical American, the tenth-rate oaf, the product of fifty years of Christian Endeavour and Right-Thinking. In the face of opposition of this flashy and hollow sort is it strange that fellows of such high purpose and dignity as Dreiser and Cabell find the going hard, the way beset with snares.

3. *In the manner of Dr. Frank Crane.*

THE greatest book of these times. Written not by a propagandist or a crank or a poet but by a mother.

Written not by a fashionable lady who moves in an artificial set but by a frank, honest worker who has come face to face with the great realities, who has in a word such practical knowledge of the conditions she sets forth that if she does not know what she is talking about who does?

"Lust," it is by Jennie Ginsberg.

It is a book of cold, scientific facts beautifully warmed and humanized by Love, in the best sense.

If I had one hundred million dollars I would see that every man, woman and little one in the United States owned this volume.

I would have it taught in every public school.

Like you, I have read many novels and am callous. But this book staggers my imagination. It grips my heart and sweeps my brain clear.

If you buy no other book and read no other this year, buy and read "Lust."

Unreservedly I place it as the best book in the world to read right now for every man, woman and little one in America including the President and others who guide human destinies.

Clear, dispassionate, yet living, it is as shattering as any great masterpiece of the English language save perhaps the Bible.

Take it home. Read it. Talk to your friends about it. Get your wife to read it. Get the point of view of everyone.

You will find in it, as I found, a great hopefulness for the future of America. It has a message for your home that will give you new faith and courage.

4. *In the manner of Robert Benchley.*

"LUST" is one of those frothy little things about Birth, Life, Marriage and Death that Jennie Ginsberg tosses off every now and then for a *jeu d'esprit*. Just the sort of thing for Christmas reading when the lights are low and the yule logs are blazing merrily, and you hear in the chamber above you the patter of little feet. You must know by this time how Mrs. Ginsberg does it — how, just when you're willing to swear that Irma Krantz, née Ackermann, is going to leave the flat with a Columbia student for a nasty evening at the Hippodrome, little Selma Jacobs who supports a blind father, a paralytic mother, three invalid sisters, and two brothers with the rickets by playing "Humoresque" at the picture house round the corner loops in and wises up to the tense drama that is being enacted and appeals with childish insouciance to the student to clear out for the honor of Columbia. Then in a jiffy she fixes up the nicest supper you ever ate, while Mrs. Krantz tears at the wall-paper, and when Albert Krantz comes home from work tired out after six hours of dipping great, heavy chocolate creams he never suspects in his man-like way what has been going on.

Well, you've guessed the rest. Personally this department got a great deal of satisfaction out of the scene toward the end where poor old Irma Krantz cracks little Selma over the right hand with the meat-axe.

Vol. CVII, No. 7

THE·HARVARD ADVOCATE

THE ATLANTIC MONTHLY

APRIL   1921

THREE POEMS

BY O. O. GOINGS

LOVE POEM

i

I

!

PLAIN POEM

beneath the whither-cock
the   funny   little

God!

ain't-he-the-cutie-Mazie?
Steeple Jack
       sings Hee and Haw!
if i had been ther i would should could
Christ kid how many ten
       s
        e
        s
        are there in this
goddam language
cut
       the ropes
of the little swinging monkeyshineseat

Then Mister Sidewalk
       whatwouldyerdo
         withyer
Blue-eyed
       Puddle?

A POEM

and i said

                                        snuggling down into

the electric chair

     tell me why O intrusive handkerchief they chose

     the six suppressed poems from a hat

                                a derby hat

     and why this newspaper i read should be with us

     inevitably shouting, screeching the small lousy

     news of the day in our highly Florentine faces

and my soul

                            turning on the current

answered me

     for the same reason that your lap goes there when you

     SuDdEnLy s,t,a,n,d uP   that in brief and no more

     sense   while behind the merry masks of the angels

     there is much weeping and Gnashing of teeth

gracious

                                   said i

snickering

     am i that clever is this little spinningball an

     important part of the great walloping solar

     sys;tems   if i am doomed thus)as a fly to(walk the

     noisy cracked ceilings of infinity why at least not this stark-

     ness and umbrellas with which neW yorK is afflicted

     and the world

                              grieved

with which

                             my soul

admitted

     i don't know do you

so   i

     got out of the chair and

went   home

     it was the end of the line

                           anyway

PORTRAIT OF AN EX-LADY

BY T. S. TELLALOT

This lady uses brilliantine
but where I ask you not to ask me;
peacocks by her fountain preen:
I use clericals to masque me.

Tea as casual as you please;
Holy Church and Babylon
balance teacups on their knees
till the candles are their sun.

He in Gothic vault and fanning,
naked of his bowler hat;
she conjectures what unmanning
process made a man like that.

Till reluctance fills her vowels
where desire lisped before;
long parade with spades and trowels:
twenty gardeners pass the door.

"Ah! So soon? Come in next Sunday."
China winks upon the shelves.
Somewhere in the Bay of Funday
twenty gardeners drown themselves.

WINKELMANN AMONG THE TEACUPS

T. S. TELLALOT

(Having loved passionately
We drank our tea;
Having donned our clothes,
We crushed a rose.)
Arma virumque cano . . .

Love is noble, love is fine,
   Down on the mud-flats.
It's like a draught of ancient wine
   To fall through the bed-slats.
Omnis Gallia . . . tres . . .

Isn't·it dark here, Ming,
   Among these pebbles;
Come, let us sing
   Atrocious trebles.
Μῆνιν ἀείδε θέα . . .

Mr. Schmilkraut is a funny chap
   With a face like a moon;
He wears a dipper instead of a cap;
   He'll die soon.
Tarantara tarantara!

CAPTAIN TOM AND MOTHER CAREY'S CHICKENS

OLIVER LA FARGE

IF neither you nor yet any of your ancestors have ever dug for clams, if there is in you no blood of men who have piloted fishing-sloop or schooner or dancing brig on a murky night into some New England harbour, with the taste and smell of the bottom on your lead for a guide, nay more, if you have never sailed in Rhode Island harbours and your ear is not attuned to Rhode Island speech, this story is not for you. If you are not one of the elect, you will read it and smile, because you will not know how to believe it. Then hastily forget, or else eschew the sea, for sure as the passage of the black duck over Wesquague Pond in April, the stormy petrel will haunt you for your unbelief.

This tale should be told only in one place, and under special circumstances; so if I, cheating, tell it to you, you must promise faithfully to remember all the time that you are sitting in the forecastle of an old, full-breasted two-master, anchored just off Austin's Hollow in the Western passage of Narragansett Bay. You are in here finding a partial haven from a smoky sou'easter. This is the easiest place to drop anchor on your way down to the Eastward, and the only shelter this side Sakonnet Harbour that does not take you way off your course.

The wind howls in the rigging, and great, low-flying clouds scud overhead. The moon peeps through for wan moments, lighting up the sheltering ridge of bleak Conanicut Island, showing for a second your main-topmast wagging crazily at the clouds, and gleaming faintly on the froth of jumbled waters between you and the shore.

The ground for the story has been prepared by the mate — come forward to avoid the wrath of the skipper, involved in intricate mathematical calculations concerning the wages of another hand, the cost of a fore top-mast and the profit of speed gained thereby. The mate, sitting in the forecastle doorway, has just ended.

"And so he jumped right off the cliff, and the last Block Island seen of him he was sailing off to sea in the burning ship, with one of the fiery horses on each side of him, and he was never seen by mortal men again."

The forecastle lamp swings in great circles from the ceiling, casting irregular, jumping splashes of light and shadow on the bunks and ceiling. Now it brings out clearly the dark, keen face of the Portugee cook, now hides him in the shadow till all you see are the glints of light on his earrings and the flash of his white teeth.

There is a general scraping of boots and shifting of warm, lazy bodies as the story ends. The hand, from East Greenwich, reputed talkative, true to his form remarks,

"Wa-all, wa-all, wa-all."

The rest say nothing.

There is a moment's pause, and in the comfortable, warm, damp atmosphere you can feel heavy thoughts and opinions being brought into order. Then the Oldest Sailorman coughs, and all are still. Slowly and solemnly the Oldest Sailorman extracts from the cavernous recesses of his pockets a black, shapeless hunk and a broken, ancient jacknife. With razor-keen stump of blade he hews himself a morsel of "dark B.L." and stows it neatly under his brown mustache.

The two hands, knowing that the great tale is coming, crumble sticky strips of "Driver's Cut Plug" into their battered pipes. The mate does even as the Oldest Sailorman, save that his plug is a light brown — "light B.L." The Portugee shoves forward the tin full of his gingerbread, so that its odor may take pleasant place with the other forecastle smells, rich tobacco, salt water, tar, and humanity. You hastily suppress your desire for a cigarette, and fill your pipe from your pouch, conscious of a polite interest in your actions, and polite contempt of the chopped hay you call tobacco.

Then, in the comfort and friendship of the cabin, the low voice of the Oldest Sailorman, with its genial accent of the born clam digger, takes up the tale, while the faintly heard storm outside seems to keep a running commentary thereon. I cannot reproduce his speech nor give word for word his story, but as nearly as I can remember it, I pass it on to you.

The credit for the whole thing lies between the Alonzo Gorgee that then was, and the Mother Carey's chickens. Ever since anyone can remember there's been an Alonzo here, just like the fellow that come out past us in that cat-boat this evening setting traps. They ain't never changed, they all walk bow-legged and shuffling, they all talk like they had potatoes in their mouths, and all have shapeless, fuzzy mustaches. And this one, like the rest, spent his time on shore drinking, and on the water doing things no other man could have done. He was town drunkard — used even to get drunk with the Indians — and could catch fish when all others came home empty-handed, and foretell the weather when all others were wrong.

In those days everybody had a hand in running the rum. They ran it in where the old breakwater is below South Ferry, and hid it up by the Johnson house back of the marsh. But that wasn't a proper harbour, the land being too low to break the wind from the westward, and it was right open to winds from the south and east. There wasn't any Bonnet Cliff there then, and where we be was a big, rocky, treacherous headland sticking out.

But the real trouble was Alonzo's mortal enemy, Captain Tom Pearse. He was the worst man ever was in Rhode Island. He had a smart little brig that was supposed to be a revenue cutter, and a crew of rapscallions that were supposed to be the King's men. And he used to catch us running in and take our rum, and nary a drop the King saw. Nothing riled old Gorgee so much as having his rum taken, excepting when Captain Tom took his fish.

And that wasn't the worst of it, neither. You seen Wesquague Beach as you come in this evening, how it lies all open to the ocean, and how in this southerly blow the great waves go a-roaring in, hell bent for leather. No holding ground, just a long, smooth bottom of sand for the waves to pile up on, and not being any Bonnet Cliffs, just low land to Northwest of it, it was as bad in a northeaster, and a westerly storm coming down over the open marsh and dunes would carry the misguided vessel that anchored in that slipping sand right out again to break to bits on Joneses Ledge. Well, Captain Tom built him a house back of Wesquague south of the marsh, and raised him a light on the dunes, and let the weather do the rest.

A fine barquentine called the Lizzie Smith out of Charlestown went ashore there one night, and when we found her in the morning — Captain Tom was the only soul who lived in sight of the beach — she'd been stripped right down to the copper rivets.

No one darst cross him, because he was so strong. He used to could take a mainmast in his hand the way you'd take a marling spike and drop it into its hole and step it just as easy! No, no one darst cross him.

Then one foggy day when no one else would have put out, Alonzo was down in his sloop fishing off the Old Man. And the first thing he sees floating on the water is one of Mother Carey's chickens that's been shot. And he broke right down and cried. Then he whistled, and a couple more chickens came and perched on his gunwale.

"How come," says Alonzo, "How come George's been killed?"

"Captain Tom Pearse did it," says one of the birds. "And we're a-going to get him. There'll be no wind and no lifting of the fog 'till he's starved to death off Brenton Reef." There wasn't any lightship there in those days.

"That ain't right nor hardly fair," says Alonzo. "What about us, that you like?"

The birds scratched their heads and allowed that that was right.

"Now you listen to me," says Alonzo, "you get a-hold of Peter"— Peter's the big wave that lives just under Whale Rock —"and all the birds, and you figure out how to block up Wesquague beach so's to make us a harbour that his big boat can't follow us into and other boats can't get wrecked in, and he'll lose all his business and go away. Then ye can becalm him somewhere else."

Before the fog lifted there was a great confabulation of birds, with Peter as moderator and Alonzo listening and suggesting. There were chickens, clever and sharp, and great gulls, wiser and more dependable but not so quick, and terns, and coots making no sense at all, all talking at once. Finally they decided to put it up to Mother Carey herself, and the oldest of her chickens went flying northward to tell her all about it.

As for Alonzo, he put back into Willettville with a hold full of Bluefish when no one else was getting anything but tautog.

When Mother Carey heard about it she went on knitting for a while — she was busy turning out some extra fine Northern lights on account of a man she liked being up in Baffin Bay — and then she sent her fastest gull down to the Great Grandfather of all the waves who lies under the Sargasso sea, ready to go north or south as the case may be. He comes up in the very biggest storms, roaring and raging mountains-high all across the Atlantic, with littler waves big enough to sink an ordinary vessel swirling in the wake of his great, smooth, green back. The fringes of his right flank beat all along the French coast and go swashing up the Channel, and the fringes of his left flank throw the ships around off Hatteras like a man tossing salted cod. All the way up to the great ice-fields he sweeps, then comes a-roaring and a-crashing down on them, and there's your next season's crop of icebergs all ready made. After which he'll slip under the floes and lie there, talking to Mother Carey as man to man, until it's time for him to go south again.

But this time, being its all calm, he just slithered north as quiet as he knew, and

strange sight he must have been towering over quiet seas.

When he got to the ice he slid up on top, and set there scratching his white head with one big, green, flipper forty fathom wide, and says, "Well, Mother, here I be."

And the tide sunk a foot all round the world.

Mother Carey explained everything to him, and they sat and planned and talked for it might be two days. Then he slipped back into the ocean, the tide everywhere rose a foot, and a lot of people all over the world got their feet wet.

That night off Rhode Island there was a tempest out of the southeast that would make this gale look a flat calm. The clouds came a-scudding by overhead so low you could almost hear them a-swishing, and the great breakers went a-roaring and a-shouting into Wesquague Beach and a-rushing up on the dunes, with their long, green fingers curling around the bones of the Lizzie Smith as if they wanted to feel their work and be sure it was thorough.

Then Alonzo puts out in his little boat, and there off Whale Rock he meets Peter and the Great Grandfather of all the waves, and the chickens and the gulls. When the big waves gets inside the bay the water rises about a fathom, and Mrs. Yardley's cellar is flooded and her cat drowned. Barring that, there was no harm done save to Old Daddy Briggses dory. Old Daddy Briggs was too mean to get him a proper anchor-line, and he had her moored so short that at high tide there wasn't no scope at all. When the extra fathom hit her, her bow went right straight under, and all you could see was her stem sticking out, with the rudder kind of thumbing itself at Daddy jumping up and down on Willettville dock when he found her in the early morning.

Meantime Alonzo and the waves and the gulls were a-working like all get out. They took rocks from over by Beaver-Tail and down by Narragansett Pier up by Narragansett and piled them up in a great line from the tip of the Wesquague crescent to Northward — where the Bonnet is now — clear across to Joneses

Ledge. The Mummies are the remnants of them. Then they got more rocks and built them out from Watson's Pier to the Southward, until they had as nice a breakwater and harbour for small craft as ever you can see to Sakonnet or down to Point Judith Point. Inside it was all sweet and calm, too shallow for a revenue cutter to follow, with the sand beach to land on and the marsh behind to drop things in if you were in a hurry.

By that time it was late in the morning, so Peter and the big wave quit, letting Narragansett Bay get back to normal again. The storm moderated so that fishermen could go out. Then the chickens told Alonzo that the rocks weren't sot yet, and so for one more night they must be watched. He's to come down the next night and anchor off of them and then all would be fine.

But Captain Tom was no fool, and as soon as ever he saw what had been done, he fell a-thinking. Not so much for any good reason as just because it seemed a good idea, off he went and put a hole as big as your fist in Alonzo's sloop. Put a sail-maker's palm on his hand, he did, and then punched a marling-spike in and out like he was putting stitches in a worn out studding-sail.

Alonzo didn't figure out how it happened; he just cussed a lot, got him another jug of rum, and went that night to keep his watch on land. And on land Alonzo was just a drink-sodden old coot, which Captain Tom well knew.

By the time it was dark the storm had risen again to the last night's violence. You could see the breakers rearing up on the breakwater, and hear them thundering curses at being kept out. By the middle of the dog watch Alonzo was fast asleep, dead drunk, and Captain Tom had carried him a mile inland, out of the way.

Then Captain Tom walked out to the rocks over Joneses Ledge, and began heaving them away. He worked 'till he was down to the reef itself, and there he planted his feet and got set for the real labour. No one saw him, but you know what it must have been like. This great man, tall as his own cross-jack yard and broad as the two flukes of the Bower anchor

on a ship, with great legs wide apart straddling the rock, the water now hissing out in white foam round the ankles of his cowhide boots, now thundering past his shoulder in a black wall, and he reaching out to right, and left, picking up rocks as big as whaleboats and throwing them through the smother of spume onto either shore. The moon didn't get a chance to look out at all that night, all the sign there was of a moon's being there at all was the succession of pale-grey lines along the fringes of the clouds as they passed under.

When Alonzo had waked up in the morning and got back to Wesquague, there were the high Bonnet Cliffs to Northward, and the nasty rocks of Watson's pier — that the *Lulu Epps* was wrecked on last March — just as Captain Tom had built them. The waves, were running clear into the beach again slapping the dunes on the back sort of, as if to say,

"Wall, wall, here we be back again. And haow's Lizzie Smith this morning?"

Alonzo sat right down on the top of the Bonnet with his legs stuck out in front of him and his fist in his eye, and began to bawl and blubber like a kid. Bye and bye the petrel came round and they give it to him good and proper. When after awhile he felt better and had got around to cutting himself a plug of tobacco, the oldest gull said to him,

"Wall, Alonzo, looks like you'd got the lines perty wall snarled up this time. Ain't no use crying 'bout it, the big wave's gone back, and Mother Carey won't take all that trouble over ye again. But we're with ye, Alonzo, and we'll see what we can do. Next time Captain Tom's down to Block Island or perty well out to sea you just stick a knife in your mast and whistle up a westerly wind, then maybe we can do something."

So four or five days passed with Alonzo keeping by himself and not even drinking more than enough to wash down his johnnie-cakes. Come one day, however, Captain Tom's gone out beyond Block Island trying to get some swordfish. When the birds tell this to Alonzo where he's anchored off Beevar-Tail he takes his old knife and runs it into the mast. Then he whistles and whistles until he has as nasty a wind blowing out of the northwest as you could meet from here to the Bay of Fundy.

Captain Tom hadn't seen hide nor hair of swordfish nor any other fish since he killed the petrel, and every day he come home with empty hold he got madder and madder. So coming back from Block Island he was pretty well set for trouble.

Every wave that broke on the brig sent a splash of spray on his lips. The salt clung to him, and the wind blew wisps of froth into his mouth when he opened it to bellow a command. He got thirstier and thirstier, and so did all the crew. So he had up some of the rum he took off of Alonzo the last time. But the more they drank the more the spray flew at them, and the more they wanted to drink.

By the time they got into Narragansett Bay it was dark, black dark, so's you couldn't see your hand before your face. The boat was leaping and shaking with the big seas, every rope aboard of her was singing and screaming with the wind that rolled her down, and skipper and crew were boiling, howling drunk.

Captain Tom sees his false light over Wesquague, and he grins wickedly. Then he looks over to the pile of rocks in Conanicut, and on them he sees two lights, a-waving and a-dancing like anchor-lights on ships in the lee of the wind but not in still water. He starts cursing something awful, and crying out that someone's trying to spoil his trade, and by God he'll teach them.

"By God," he sings out, "if I can tear down one pile of rocks I can sail over another. And I'll take my vessel through that there point if it's the last damned thing I do on earth!"

Then he swings her head round and comes a-boiling down at those lights. No one sees it save Alonzo, and he tells afterward how she tore along, the wind a-whooping and a-screeching in the rigging and the crew a-yelling and a-cursing below. A leak of moonlight through the clouds, or maybe it was some kind of hell-fire, picks out every rope and spar of her in dim, wavy light, standing out against the purple-black sky; the white water under her foot and her whirling wake is all a-gleam, and greenish white fire is pouring out of the binnacle lamp onto Captain Tom's face where he stands at the wheel. She strikes the shore and never trembles, but goes on pitching through the rocks, crashing and grinding, and the land sinking beneath the seas that shoulder along under her dolphin-striker. Suddenly, as she somes to the middle of the island, she's gone, and the wind drops, and the moon comes out lighting up Austin's Hollow, ready-made refuge in a southerly blow.

And that's why, if ye'd looked out the starboard port-hole as I did a minute or two ago, ye'd have seen a shining brig with a northwesterly gale of her own behind, and black clouds wreathing her top gallant-masts, go gliding past us, and running in over the shoal water 'till she diaappeared just as the land's edge.

REMEMBER THE ROSE

JAMES GOULD COZZENS

THE afternoon sunlight fell in shafts between the elms; hollyhocks along the brick wall stood like trophies and standards of August, bathed in golden glory. Above, the hills were settling into cool shadows and heights of sunny trees. A sky like unrippled blue silk came down to them and steep white clouds appeared with slow, adventurous intent along the crest.

There were cedars in one corner. The grass, a thick green tapestry reaching down from the wall by the road, hesitated, and gave way to warm, needle-soft openness about them, there was a faint perfume of cedars in the sun. A tea table was set here in the shadows with the tremble of breeze stirred linen, the sheen of silver, and the fineness of pale porcelain.

Mrs. Bakewell, a contrast in her black silk and snowy hair, looked half smiling at a friend who had finished tea. The friend was a boy. He regarded abstractedly the cigarette between his fingers and its slim straight column of smoke. You noticed first that he had that casual tan which comes from mornings on the links and the blaze of the tennis court. Afterwards you saw his hair was the color of old gold.

He broke the intimate silence at last, rousing himself and smiling a little; "I was in town this morning," he said, "I managed to get hold of that old book of Monsieur Hardy's." He produced a dingy volume from his pocket and laid it on the table beside her. "I thought you'd like it," he said.

"How very nice of you, Blair!" Mrs. Bakewell's smile carried you back to the days when she had been Nancy English and Joseph Ames had done her in oils, astounding the old Philadelphia Academy and making his own reputation. She looked at the battered gold lettering: *Un Faineant dans la Roseraie.*

"I looked to see if this was the one in which he told about his work on the Damask roses,"

remarked the boy, "it's got a whole chapter on the Amanda Patenotte."

"It's been out of print for thirty years at least," Mrs. Bakewell turned the pages thoughtfully, "The love of roses, except for fanatics like you and me, died even longer ago. This had five editions in its day, and now it can't be bought."

Blair dropped the cigarette in the ash tray on his chair arm.

"Aren't the Duchess of Southerlands blooming yet, Mrs. Bakewell?"

"Oh, Blair, they are. I almost forgot. Shall we go and look at them?"

He arose and drew the chair away. Still bearing the book she led him through the round arch where the brick was lost under the green of the ramblers. It opened into a second walled garden with spacious gravel paths radiating from the steps and stone work of a sun dial in the center. They went down to the glossy leaved bed where the fresh buds of the Duchess of Southerlands had broken gently into crimson.

"It's really a triumph to have them blooming now," said Mrs. Bakewell, "it's because I pruned them so hard this spring. Thomas protested a great deal, but he found he couldn't do anything with me. He is really a good gardener in the sense that he keeps the paths so neat, but he will not learn about roses. I shall never forget his chagrin when he came that morning to tell me they had budded after all."

She and Blair passed down to the dial. The stone was softly grey and graceful, the old bronze clear cut for all the long exposure, the rain and snow.

"I've always meant to look at that inscription," said Blair, bending before the metal plate set in the side. He read aloud the fine swash-letter script; 'Remember the Rose, how it doth fall.'

"Yes," smiled Mrs. Bakewell, "that dial

was set up by my father and he had those lines put on it. A rebuke to youth, he called them. I can remember him so well on summer evenings walking the paths here in a yellow linen suit with a long cigar that trailed a delicious aroma, holding my brother's hand on one side and mine on the other. He would walk about and look at the roses and grumble over his problem of the moment — Verdier had sent him cuttings of his Souvenir de Malmaison, I remember one year, and he was trying to make them grow, refused to believe they were dead long after they really were — he would always end his stroll before the dial and read the words solemnly,—'Lines to take note of . . . .' he would say, and thump off leaving us there to look at them. My brother used to make little parodies and father would be annoyed when we came out of the garden squealing with laughter."

They walked down toward the back. Those were the Phaloes, dusky over a faint flush of rose. So would Cleopatra's cheek have been, thought Blair. The Eugenie Jovins were like tinted foam. What could one call the Barbots? Blair thought of Watteau's fawns in a painted park.

Here were Eliza Sauvages, yellow like aged silk, and as thin and fine.

"You know," he said after a moment, "one can't say much of anything. I hate people who whisper 'ah, beautiful!' at everything from roses to Walter Pater."

"Some people can't say anything else, and they do mean it."

"I should think if they meant it they could say something else. They've spoiled a good word."

He paused among the musk roses. The Princess of Nassaus were in bud, golden.

"They are very white when they open," said Mrs. Bakewell, "its like magic."

Beyond were the Eponines, true Persian roses, white as milk; Eponines, the show drift of whose petals wise Omar hoped would soothe him in his grave. They stood in the gate presently.

"Such roses!" said Blair at last. "It's a dream, it really doesn't exist at all. You step through this gate into a dream garden which vanishes when your back is turned."

"Yes, but it always comes back, when, like Peter Ibbetson, you dream true."

After he had left and a dusk was settling on the garden, dulling the rambling lines of the old white house, Mrs. Bakewell sat in the candle light at her desk waiting for dinner to be announced. She penned a fine script in a black bound book.

'My sixty-ninth birthday,' she wrote, 'I had a delightful tea with Blair and we looked at the roses afterwards. He and I, are I think, the last of the rosiéristes . . . .'

Her eye wandered to the book he had brought and from there the albums in the bottom of the book cases.

When Parke entered to tell Mrs. Bakewell dinner was served, he found her looking at the pages of faded letters; good wishes, congratulations and advice, written long ago by Vibert and Laffay and Hardy; the notes in the great Rivers' angular characters, the neat little lines from old Wood. Mr. English had known them all.

"Blair," said Mrs. Bakewell one afternoon as they left the garden, "would you care to come over for dinner Thursday night? My niece Millicent is going to spend a few weeks with me, and I would like very much to have you meet her."

"I'd love to," said Blair.

He rode John Halifax down to the village to get the mail the next afternoon. The train was in, dark and compact along the open gravel platforms. He saw Mrs. Bakewell's carriage with the team of chestnuts waiting. John Halifax objected to trains, and pawing the air refused to go nearer. A girl appeared, laughing, followed by Mrs. Bakewell's man carrying bags. The train gathered strength with a tremendous burst of steam and iron roar, John Halifax backed away with desperate vigor, Mrs. Bakewell's carriage turned about. Blair went over to the post office steps and swung out of the saddle. As he lit a cigarette he saw the carriage disappear up the long maple arch of the road.

On the evening Blair was to come to dinner Millicent English had appeared in Mrs. Bakewell's rooms clad in heavenly blue over laid with silver, accepted Mrs. Bakewell's admiration with a happy smile, and gone downstairs. Mrs. Bakewell still stood by a window looking out over the gardens in the gathering twilight. The sound of Millicent at the piano reached her faintly and seemed to bring with it years very long ago. Late afternoons were perhaps more golden then, or better, a gold more soft. A certain magnificence had given way to cool efficiency; you saw it in the summer dusk, you saw it — Mrs. Bakewell half smiled — in Millicent's dress. She thought of the flowing gowns of those days, the billows and gorgeous mounds of lovely cloth. The evening clothes of today had none of the leisurely grace.

The pace of life had quickened. Men no longer wore such beautiful linen; their gloves and hats, the cut of their clothes, had sacrificed pleasant dignity and beauty. She thought of her husband with his curling mustachios, his graceful capes, the glitter of quiet gold, the cambrics no longer made, the rich folds of black satin. Such things had been relegated to a past which seemed now subtlely better bred.

Her attention was taken by the appearance of Millicent and Blair strolling on the garden path. She saw thoughtfully the white of his shirt front, the cigarette in his hand. A gauze veil Millicent had slipped about her shoulders detached itself a little and floated after her in the light breeze. Across the sounds of summer evening her laugh came low and clear. Mrs. Bakewell turned away, went out of the room and down the wide cool stairs pensively.

The sound of horses hoofs died away on the road beyond the wall. The long shadows had sunk the tea table in coolness and quiet, and Mrs. Bakewell sat alone.

I'm glad they like each other so much, she thought. Blair and Millicent were always together, riding, or playing tennis, or paddling on the river. Only yesterday Millicent had brought home an armful of water lilies, wanly fragrant. There had been a dance or two in the village, dead dances, Blair had said, but they went none the less, laughing, and came back quite late still laughing.

Young people did things differently now. Millicent would come down in' boyish riding clothes, flit into the breakfast room where the morning coolness yet remained, urge Parke to hurry and be out on horseback to ride away with Blair into the nine o'clock shadows, under breezy elms, up sunny slopes, untold miles into the summer country before she appeared dusty and breathless, late for lunch.

They had left now to ride over the hill road and see the sunset. Up there the long fields were yellow with golden rod; cardinal flowers and gentians grew in the hollows about the brooks, the asters, blue beneath the dust, thronged along the road. So Millicent said.

She had told Blair when they had finished tea a little while before that the Moirés were blooming at last. Once, she thought a little wistfully, he would have wanted to see them. Millicent had got up and gone toward the stables and he had followed, unreluctant.

It was late in September when Millicent left. The next afternoon Blair came in. He was very hurried.

"Thank you," he said, "I can't stay to tea, I've got lots of packing to do to get back to the University tomorrow."

"I'm sorry you're going, I haven't seen you at all lately, Blair; you and Millicent were so busy."

"She's very nice."

Mrs. Bakewell walked to the gate with him.

"The roses will soon be gone," she said.

"There will be more roses next spring," said Blair, and he smiled and turned down into the glory of the afternoon sunlight.

THE HOBGOBLIN DEFEATED

JOHN FINLEY, JR.

JOHN TUCKER, having been brought up by three unmarried aunts whose varient natures contained strong character as the single common element, had early opportunity to learn the social tactics and manœuvres used in a congregate life. For each of these intractable females, whose erect spines were visible symbols of erect lives, when appropriately cajoled, became not alone well disposed but dotingly tender and indulgent to young John. It was, therefore, not wonderful that he should learn from the tuition of his comfort to treat each aunt in a fashion to please her and to profit himself, which he did, discovering the combination of word and action to open the animated safes, nearly related to him, which, though apparently impregnable, yielded without reserve to the proper twirls and stops of manner. Only his own clumsiness kept shut the vaults of his aunts' benevolence. If he did not confuse the combination or overtwirl the customary marks through carelessness, he gained without variation his desires. But if he retained before Aunt Margaret, whose suspicious charity always heard ill of the world, the subversive sharpness of the young intellectual, which Aunt Caroline liked, he must expect the failure which he received. Conversely if he relied with Aunt Caroline on his innocent smile and yellow hair, which, if presented to Aunt Margaret with nothing said to spoil the impression proved quite devastating, the former quick-minded and acidulous spinster found him dull and was accordingly of no spiritual or practical use. And since both capacities, those, namely, of providing companionship and trips to the theatre were necessary to him in an aunt, John learned that he must not overstep the clear, infallible rules. With Aunt Lizzie, too, he must assume his particular habit, which was that of a helpless but brilliant boy who must be fed and clothed well and picked up after. If he arrogated any

domestic knowledge, Aunt Lizzie found him fractious; for he would leave the broom in a convenient but strange place, and strangeness in the house was as an intimation of her death to Aunt Lizzie. Thus John, prompted by his comfort which was gravely unsettled during the irritation of any of the three strong-minded females, learned the narrow but infallible ways to materterine honor, a task as arduous as Ali Baba's, if that forgetful Persian had had to say "open sesame" before several doors, each time with a nicely varied articulation.

While John was a boy, he pursued his various courses with his aunts unconsciously with a natural wheedling common to children. When, however, he came to be conscious and analytical of himself, which for every civilized young man like John is the stage following youth and can be described variously as the first wall of the prison house, the first flight of the butterfly, or the first hop of the tadpole, he observed what he had been doing in innocence and drew therefrom the moral principle, which was later to cause him so much trouble. He observed, so he thought, that the success of his conduct with his aunts had in each case been the result of the unexpected. "I do," he said to himself, "what they fear I shall not do. Aunt Margaret fears that all good is dead in the world, until the unexpected candour of my face convinces her that she is wrong." Here he looked in the mirror to see if he resembled the boy Goethe and if the world was better, containing such youth, hope and the like, and being disappointed in both speculations, resumed. "Aunt Caroline suspects that people are grown stupid and read Shakespeare for the sentiments and not for the words, until I say something good, which surprises us both. Then we are both happy and she especially, all by the unexpected." And since the success of this reflection was surprising, he thought himself a bright young man and continued. "Aunt

Lizzie secretly thinks herself and others too domestic and fears I shall be. Thus when I do not drink milk for breakfast, she is startled by the unexpected, and pleased, or solicitous, which is the same thing with many women."

"Now, of course," he went on hurriedly in some suspicion of the logic in the previous informal syllogism, "everybody cannot spend their time doing unexpected things. Certainly, few people do. Most people live in the peace of the somnolent majority.

> Qui somno partem maiorem conteris aeri
> et vigilans stertis nec somnia cernero cessas.

He quoted the Lucretius he had learned and went on.

"The fact that they do not surprise themselves and others is probably the reason for their being of the majority, which is a stupid body. In fact, now that I think of it, the greater a man is, the more surprising he is. Emerson says a great man is like the wind, and a common man like the grass. 'When the wind blows, the grass bends.' But doubtless, the grass did not have it in mind to bend, but slept in the vague dream of a perpendicular activity. The wind wakes things, at least. Grass more likely grows better for being deflected a little and for a short time from the zenith." This thought pleased him, since he had a philanthropic heart. If he was to assume the character of the wind, as appeared allegorically obvious, and could improve people by surprising them, his life would be at once useful and congenial, which was as it should be.

"Now that I think of it, every one needs contrast. That is what great people are for." He was now in the full course of the complacent, yet lively, thought, which he pursued with innocent gratulation. "Aunt Lizzie can never be anything but domestic. She is most useful as she is. But it is good for her to see some one who is different, to make her reflect. It does her more credit as a human being to choose her position after thought. It is the same with Aunt Caroline. She would be gloomy, but intelligent, if she were not surprised by me. As it is, she is cheerful and still intelligent. Lincoln," he added, "was probably most upsetting to Nancy Hanks, and she, doubtless, loved him the better." He paused for a moment; then, boldly struck out his conclusion.

"That is my work, then, to surprise people agreeably."

Here he stopped, having come to a resolution, a noble principle of life. There was stillness about him on the porch where he stood; the trees stood silent, gilded by the sunset. Then Aunt Lizzie called to him, interrupting the antiphonous flutes of wood thrushes.

"John, supper is ready."

Though he was hungry, he replied with some nobility for his principle's sake:

"I think I can eat very little, Aunt Lizzie."

"Ah, John, you are so impractical," she sighed, unconsciously made happy by her solicitude. He followed her into the dining room, thinking.

"What beatitude for her. The mere statement that I should neglect potato salad makes her think me the poet Shelley." He then consumed great amounts of that widely used but unpalatable foodstuff, neglecting his previous assertion. But Aunt Lizzie was so concerned with a fancifully detected pallor in him that she did not notice his defalcation from idealism. This he observed, saying to himself between mouthfuls.

"One can frequently do the unexpected without a subsequent personal inconvenience. This comes from the *idée fixe* in Aunt Lizzie and almost every one else."

He leaned towards Aunt Caroline who sat next him about the shiny table, symmetrically set for the four, and nodding toward Aunt Lizzie, preoccupied behind the glancing tea tray, said, "She thinks I am ill, though I have eaten two helpings. Voluntary blindness is very wonderful." Aunt Caroline, pleased by the unexpected confidence of their kind jokes at Aunt Lizzie, smiled. Aunt Margaret smiled, too, since John looked singularly unworldly in the candlelight and she had not heard the previous remark. Thus, all were happy at the prim supper, the nutritive conclusion of another day, they, in the joy of their delusions always unexpectedly fostered, and he in the delight of his new and practical principle of life.

Through the next week John continued the assiduous practice of his theory and found it in general much after his heart. Only occasionally did he observe it to fail. When it did, he displayed the strong character common to the family and pursued his course, like Hudibras, plying the single spur of his resolution. He was disturbed, however, at his failures, since people when unsettled not pleasantly, as he had planned, but painfully, as from a steadying faith shaken, became not only irritated with him but menacingly hostile. He became to them, he reflected, a sort of domestic anti-Christ; for they had previously rested in a secure expectation of dinner for the next day and heaven for the next life and when unfixed from these or ancillary beliefs, blamed him, as most people blame the long-haired modern Sampsons, often not muscular, who shake the pillars that uphold the ceiling, their firmament, and cover the dinner-table. "A surprise, when well administered," he thought uneasily, "is a gentle apocalypse which shows the possibilities of daily life, but when mishandled, is an intellectual earthquake. This latter use I must avoid except when strictly necessary," he concluded, feeling much like Zeus, terpsikeraunos, and fast in resolution to improve in dexterity not abandoning the theory.

His signal success with Mrs. Jackson, moreover, coming at the end of several half-successes with the gardner and neighboring farmers, at best poor soil for his sowing, rooted him in his intention. That good lady, the mother of Mary Jackson, and therefore to be secured as a supporter if possible by dignified means, had never regarded him with much favor. The reason for this, he thought, was because she never could understand him. She, like Aunt Margaret, would have been content because of his light hair to regard him sentimentally as a noble young man giving faith to his elders if he had not insisted on spoiling by talk each ideal that she successively made of him. He could not stop talking when he was

with her daughter; that much was certain. The exhilaration of a lively minded young man must have this outlet. It was apparent, therefore, that he must make other and distinct manœuvres for Mrs. Jackson's good opinion. Being logical, he planned the matter carefully. In himself, he thought, perhaps mistakenly, his light hair and peaceful face to be his most appealing qualities; in her, the motherly instinct to be her most vulnerable. Having agreed upon this, not without some hollow suggestion of fear, he chose his time and prepared himself spiritually for the attempt. The success was instant and devastating.

Mrs. Jackson was sitting on her porch in her best gallinaceous manner, her hands busy with charitable linen, when John walked up feebly out of the sunlight. Her daughter, Mary, was away by John's ascertaining.

"Good afternoon, John," said Mrs. Jackson, the asperity of incomprehension in her voice. She never could understand that boy; he was nice, but liable to mock one. He had no heart. "Mary is not at home."

"I know, Mrs. Jackson. But—" Here he fell with suspicious grace to the porch. "It must be the sun," he sighed, and to appearances expired. His light hair, for plausibility and advantage uncovered by a hat, stirred and glanced in the afternoon air. Mrs. Jackson rose in the triumphant glow of a legitimately exercised pity and rushed transformed from a hen to a benevolent vulture on the elegantly supine John. "My poor boy," she cried repeatedly in a tender agitation, discovering an affection for him thus momentarily silent and for the first time comprehensible to her. Her concern and kind promptitude with restoratives made John, now just moving as if in return from what he had read were the undiscovered, misty regions of unconsciousness, sorry to deceive her. But denying himself this emotion, he reflected logically that if she was to have him for a son-in-law, as seemed desirable, she would be happier with some understanding love for him. And since he had decided that fainting was the only means to that end, or at least the most certain, he must not now spoil the effect or his own peace of mind by regret.

"To be genuine, you must be innocent-minded," he reflected, still on the ground with Mrs. Jackson hovering over him like a rising sea-bird. "Once you know your own virtues and defects, you cannot be genuine. Then your actions are prompted by your mind more than by your instinct and people distrust your mind as a root of acts. They think it cannot go with a good heart. They are wrong," and he added by way of a literary reference to himself, "Sir Galahad knew his heart to be pure. I know mine to be at least right." Having got the strength of three or four, if not of ten, by his comparison of himself to that eminent and insipid Knight, he rose and was supported to a chair by Mrs. Jackson, now happy that she could love in John a weakness that she understood. But Mary came home at that moment and John left, feeling motionally guilty in allowing her to be deceived, though he knew it for the best. Even she might charge guilt where none was intended. Her eyes followed him skeptically, as he walked across the pasture to his house, and he, knowing that she looked at him, had increasing trouble with his conscience, proving, thereby, that perhaps he did not know himself perfectly.

"Any way," he replied, pulling the dead tops from some steeple bush, "I made Mrs. Jackson happy. One should be enough for an afternoon — and I did faint well."

During the succeeding days, John forgot his uneasiness in the peace which came from his own pleasure in an apparent success of his theory and from Mrs. Jackson's new countenancing of him. That good lady, having gained at last a tenable impression of John, that, namely, of a young man ostensibly proud but in secret weak and dependent, refused to be shaken from it. Had she preserved this opinion in a cloistered heart, all would have been well, but passivity held no share in Mrs. Jackson's maternally embracing nature. Indeed, so practical was her solicitude that she insisted upon sending her daughter Mary to John's house with gifts of junket

and other aqueously nutritive matter to inquire after the poor young man from whom, so thought Mrs. Jackson, no one observed the haughty strength seeping. Mary, unfortunately, lacked her mother's singleness of heart. John to her mind provoked other abstractions than those of pallor and a gallantly faltering power. She was, moreover, suspicious of John, as of one for whom she was much concerned but a little uneasy. And she had no wish to foster in him a doubtful infirmity by junkets. But finding her mother impervious to nugatory estimates of his health, she perforce continued daily to carry this food, though with a black heart. John, however, was pleased with the visits and his aunts enraptured, especially when they had learned the cause. Aunt Lizzie thought it proper for young poets to faint, Aunt Caroline for wits, and Aunt Margaret for seraphs.

Mary's irritation, however, in spite of the so-general complacency with the fainting John, increased. This, too, would have been well, since she would soon have forgotten it, if she had not inherited her mother's active nature. As it was, being denied comment on John, as on something divine, both at home and at his home, she unwisely told her suspicions to Charles Gilley, a suitor of hers, very hostile to John who was quite incomprehensible to him. And this was a grave mistake, as she herself realized; for the stupid but tenacious Charles laid up in his heart John's apprehended villainy to be used later, as shall appear. Mary regretted her giving out of secrets, and would have told John, if she could have decided whether he had fainted or not. But, hovering in alternate resolution, she waited, until in a few days the matter was remembered by none but Mrs. Jackson and Aunt Lizzie.

As the autumn replaced the summer with insensibly freshening days, the town where the Tucker and Jackson families lived heaved with the presidential election. The two families, leavened intellectually by Aunt Caroline, Mary, and John stood firm for Davis, the intelligent, though Democratic nominee. Unregenerate families, like the Gilleys, whose comprehension of the campaign was cabined in observation of newspaper photographs of Coolidge mildly in the hay field, supported that great statesman, the Republican David from the hills, who had no sling, only a hay rake, to slay the Philistines in the Senate. Every one wore buttons and other insignia of their spiritual choice, and added his breath to blow up the windy contention. Mary and John, being increasingly taken with each other, spent their consequent enthusiasm in the election and were not a little effective, she with her naturally charming ways and he with his theory, now marvelously efficient through practice. To each man with whom he spoke, he said the unexpected, never repeating himself, lest he lose his power of invention, and never by any chance telling any man what he might have heard before. After considering an interlocutor carefully, like a physician, he decided what the man expected to hear and told him something different. John Davis, in John's mouth, was as changeable as the sea. To Mary, who now shared knowledge of the great method, he called him the involuntary old man of the sea and quoted the Odyssey to her.

πάντα δὲ γιγνόμενος πειρήσεται, ὅσσ' ἐπὶ γαῖαν
ἑρπετὰ γίγνονται, καὶ ὕδωρ καὶ θεσπιδαὲς πῦρ.

With the country people, he made great headway; for they cared little what he said and followed him because of his transparent honesty, which not the most arrant falsehood in speech could alter. He thought, however, that they fell into his traps, his springes to catch wood cocks.

"Yes, sir," he would say, to a farmer obviously prepared to believe Davis a handsome but useless member of high society. "Do you know that for the first thirty years of his life John W. Davis did nothing but work his way up in the railroad business? He couldn't read a word until he was thirty and in seven years he was the greatest lawyer in the United States. That fact is not generally known," he would add, though why so bold a fact should be concealed none could guess. The farmer would go away, thus violently shaken into belief.

To many Scotchmen about the town, John always said, "He was crippled until he was fifteen years old, so that he could scarcely move. He was much like Walter Scott. He collected the West Virginia border lays and read Spenser before he was ten. How like the two men's foreheads are!"

But to white-haired farmers canny, like old wood chucks, from much experience with men, he would say, "Of course, there is little difference between the men and the parties. But if one party is dishonest, is it not a duty for the sake of precedent to put it out of office?"

So gradually by his assiduity in the unexpected, John's influence grew great, until partly through him Davis moved like a rushing wind through the town. The reason for men's votes displayed small congruity, and John was quoted with alarming variations, but since the confusion of tongues is naturally great at such a time John had small fear. He had no moral qualms, since he felt it best for the voters' souls to have a violent, though incorrect, belief than a sapless one, however rational. As he passed, men's faces flushed with a generous, mistaken warmth.

"We can know little with certainty in the world," said John to himself. "It is best to feel strongly about what we think we know." And so fortified, he would tell a proudly genealogical spinster that Davis was a direct Plantagenet. And continuing in this way, he would have had no obstacle. But with Charles Gilley, that hard-headed young man, he had not reckoned.

The final fanfare and ultimate tucket blast for Davis was set for a night shortly preceding the election. At that time it was the common feeling that the town vote, which was the keystone of the county vote, in turn the very crux of the state vote, which was, as all knew, the entering wedge of the national vote, would give no uncertain Democratic promise. The election being so near, enthusiasm was the condition to any success; logic had done its best, all agreed. At this time, impulse, swifter than thought and much more compulsive, must sweep the jubilant forces to the polls. And this galvanic mission John was chosen to perform. There lacked not, of course, more sober heads, which advised against him as being too inflammable for safe employment, but their croaking, like that of timorous crows before a storm, was unheard in the gathering winds of the popular support. The old politicians, wise ditchers of the swollen courses of suffrage, farmers of the modern Nile, on whose annually deposited silt they lived richly, trusted John's essential good sense, and encouraged the murmur of the crowd. No one would hear what he said any way, they thought, and his figure would be decorative in the torch light. So John accepted the best opportunities to try his theory, and rested without worry (he was naturally of surpassing coolness) until the night.

The parade passed off in tumultuous success. Men ran and hallooed as they had not since they were children shrilly pursuing the Cleveland and Blaine processions, and women, too, raised their voices as in a pæan to their unfettered political strength. They passed through the chief streets of the town and resting at the grassy common, became nearly still. Fervor quenched even the gossip of chance-met friends. John rose between four torches and beneath the autumnal glitter of stars, and thus romantically illuminated, began his speech.

"Friends and citizens, O Quirites." So much Latin he thought would be put down to bad hearing by the ignorant. "For what do you think John W. Davis, that noble statesman, gentleman, and patriot, stands?" His voice hung upon the still air, as he paused for effect, while his listeners kept stupid silence, apparently saying severely to themselves, "I can't imagine." He made ready to resume.

"Lies, like you do." The voice of the tenacious and ungrammatical Charles Gilley broke startlingly from the crowd, like an animal running across a lantern path at night. John stood in suspension of thought, a momentary intellectual limbo, and Charles, leaping to a barrel top, addressed the faces newly turned to him.

"Lies, I tell you. Lies, lies. To one of you he says Davis is like Scott; to another like Ty Cobb." Here an irritated hoot-mon from the crowd might have been heard by the observant. Charles continued in the frenzy of a nearly grasped success. "To one he says Davis taught school till he was twenty, to another that he couldn't read till he was thirty-two. He fools you all every minute. A farmer, whose horny hands provide bread by honest toil for such as him," he indicated John with his head, too busy with rhetoric for appropriate digital exhibition, "is tricked out of his vote by lies. John Tucker would talk a cuckoo clock into believing it was a victrola. Citizens, do not believe him." He spoke now with arresting impetuosity. "Why, that fellow even fooled our dear friend and neighbor Mrs. Jackson by pretending to faint, on her front porch last summer. Tucker, can you deny it?" Charles came to a sounding but injudicious close, since John had always been able to deny anything. In the silence that followed before the collected John replied Aunt Caroline doubting him said, "How stupid to pretend fainting."

Aunt Margaret said, "How unChristian."

Aunt Lizzie, "How unpoetical.

Mrs. Jackson, "How disrespectful."

And Mary, "Oh, dear."

"Do you think I would pretend such a thing?" asked John, hesitating now before the proof of his theory. Should he surprise them? Or should he rest on a denial? Would Emerson's hobgoblin, a petty consistency, unseat him now? Or would the unexpected prove still his recourse? With a swift resolution to hold his theory, he went on. "Of course, I'd pretend such a thing. So would John W. Davis and the Democratic party. That's why it is better than the Republican party. We pretend to think the price of wheat important and nominate Bryan for vice-president. Really we don't care at all. We pretend that the country will go to pieces on the Ku Klux Klan. We talk much about it. Really all we want is to elect Davis. But we use our imaginations to do it. The Republicans are too respectable, too stupid to invent as nice issues as we have." The crowd was visibly amused, though puzzled.

He went on. "Take me, for instance, as an example. I am fond of Mrs. Jackson. She did not understand me. I decided to faint, to become pathetic to her, so that she could find something to pity in me. After this simple pretense, she is fond of me and I of her. We are both more happy than we were before." The crowd beginning to understand the un- expected, recovered a little and was amused. "It is the same with John W. Davis. We all know he is the best man. We might as well say that he is like Scott, it makes him much more personally interesting to Mr. McGregor." Here he drew a twisted smile from that good man. And simultaneously, Aunt Caroline cried, "How witty."

Aunt Margaret, "How kindly."

Aunt Lizzie, "How fanciful."

Mrs. Jackson, "How appealing."

And Mary, "Oh, dear," but with a different inflection from before.

"Of course," John went on now with swelling favor, "it is not best for all men to alter the truth. But when your heart is right, you might as well make yourself as interesting as possible to other people. Then small pre- tenses like Bryan or a fainting fit make little difference. For my heart is right, I think. And I know John W. Davis's is."

When the cheering had stopped, the next speaker rose and said. "In the words of a great Democrat, 'It is a condition that con- fronts us, not a theory.'" But John sitting beside Mary, Mrs. Jackson and his three aunts shook his head, murmuring cryptically, "Only for the unintelligent. If you are bright, life is a theory not a condition."

SONNETS TO MUSSOLINI

LLOYD McKIM GARRISON PRIZE POEM

I

Hushed was every bird throughout the land
Of Italy, and Stygian darkness clung
Like mourning-veils let down by God's own Hand.
And in the darkness, cries of pain had rung,
Slow quavering out, stilled by that Red Beast
Whose hydra heads were tearing at the throats
Of Power, Justice, Faith. And towards the East
The tramp of Mongol feet in Soviet boats . . .
But then a blaze of light appeared, for one
Had seen the torch of Cavour, ashed in shame,
Half-buried, smouldering yet, and had begun
With love-impassioned breath, to fan aflame
The paling embers, and with it alight
Kindled a million others, conquering Night.

II

The flag of order raised, then he whose sight
Had saved the land from utter darkness, sowed
The dragon's teeth. Armed soldiers rose to fight,
Ardent, ordered, marching on the road
Which Caesar's legions trod. The hills of Rome
Resounded to the stirring cry of "Youth!"
These modern Argonauts left hearth and home,
They won the fight against the beast uncouth,
And homeward bore the Fleece. The crown was seized
From Pelias, and a better rule began,
The Court well-cleaned of men with minds diseased.
The new King proved a sober, thoughtful man,
His lion heart oft leaping from its lair
To combat vice or drive away despair.

III

A man with deep eyes, and a deeper soul;
Limpid as Lethe, ruffled by no keel,
But angered, like the phosphorescent hole
Where fiery Phlegethon plunges. Hands of steel
To rein that furious steed, Fascismo. Mind
Like iron, unyielding, molded while aglow,
Then cooled by time. His eyes are never blind,
His heart is warm, his reason cold as snow.
A blacksmith's son, his task is bending souls
As in his youth he formed the gleaming bars,
Saving them from the spell of red-hot coals.
Intensely earnest, striving towards the stars,
In Italy his all; snatching her name
From dust, he won himself eternal fame.

IV

Forlian, continue to bestride
Thy eagle, seek no higher power of state,
Thy force by straight-backed youth is fortified,—
Ambitious, do not seek to alter Fate.
Crushed by thy strength, the Socialist crystal ball
Lies shattered; but beware a treacherous cut!
Bind not thy faith to sticks and stones, nor fall
By forcing thy winged feet along a rut.
King and Pope from thee must seek advice
As Age perceived its brittle power ashake
So, with the cry of "Giovannezza!" rise
Till once again the land of Vergil take
Its place in world concern. Then shalt thou be
Honored through Italy; Italy through thee.

Ralph W. Daffine.

TWO TRANSLATIONS IN SONNET FORM

I

Tristè si veniens patruelis diceret umbra
Eja lugete, omnes! abscissit Maria crines. . . .
— Novum Mariale. (11.921, 930)

If from Elysion the inebriate ghost
   Of my great-great-granduncle Phineas
   Had come to me and said " Ah, woe is us!
The Earth is flat, composed of buttered toast
And balanced in the heav'ns amid an host
   Of pies and hot cross buns stelliferous —"
   I'd have been shocked, no doubt; but even thus
I'd have observed " Well, fancy that!" at most.

But had he said to me, a week ago,
" Mary's just gone and bobbed her hair, you know,"
   Then I'd have cried " Phantom, you utter lies!
Consociation with postmortem bliss
Has addled your perceptive sense: to Dis
   Return, and treat your astigmatic eyes."

II

I diss'n: " Lo palvro catto della vuostra quéra xia
Hat relitto chesta vita." et jò diss', " In pace sia!"
— Carmen dè Mariâ Calvulâ

They said to me: " Your Aunt Priscilla's cat
   Is dead"; and I responded " *Requiem!*"
   They said: " By evil chance your Uncle Lem
Has caught the mumps." I sighed and said " That's that!"
They said: " Whilst dining in the Automat
   A misplaced bean cut off your Cousin Em."
   I dropped a silent tear and answered them:
" As God wills, be it done; Amen; *fiat!*"

They said: " Your house has burned down to the ground;
Your bank account has been attached"; no sound
   Of dole greeted this news with dolor rife.
They said: " Mary has bobbed her hair"; the cord
Of my endurance snapped; I cried " O Lord,
   It is enough — now take away my life."

Dudley Fitts, Jr.

THE HARVARD
ADVOCATE

March 1939   35 Cents $1.50 a Year

The Anatomy of the Debutante
Flamineo Bosola

The Call of Fellow Worker
Robert Clurman

BOOKS   CINEMA   MUSIC   ON THE RECORD

1929–1943

The years between the beginning of the Depression and the Second World War seem almost a golden age in the *Advocate*'s history. Never before had the magazine shown such steady strength and influence.

It would be easy to attribute this vitality to the famous men who contributed in these years. For the first time, great writers, and not merely future great writers, began to submit pieces to the magazine. Some, like Dudley Fitts, had been *Advocate* editors; others, like Archibald MacLeish and Lincoln Kirstein, had been Harvard men at least. But why would Henry Miller or Ezra Pound publish with the *Advocate*?

One might hazard a guess that they were interested in the problem of educating the young, as Pound's pieces suggest: one can imagine him at Rapallo, contemplating the "dithering timidity in the Eastern cities" and hoping to set at least a few students free of it. But we should also remember the poet's friendship with *Advocate* editor James Laughlin IV, later the founder of *New Directions*. It was Laughlin, through his acquaintance with Pound and Henry Miller, who caused "Ignite! Ignite!" and "Glittering Pie" to be published in the magazine.

But it would be wrong to attribute the high quality of the *Advocate* of those years merely to the contributions of the famous and the great. Undergraduate work also prospered. Reviews of the fine arts began to be published, like Wayne Andrews' essay on Surrealism, and John Dodge's study of the Orozco murals at Dartmouth, complete with plates. And literature flourished. James Agee and Robert Fitzgerald came first, in the early thirties. Agee's power and versatility marked him as the finest talent to come from Harvard since the days of cummings or Cowley, whereas Fitzgerald's verse—"White Valley," for example—shows not only technical skill but an intensity and intimacy new to *Advocate* readers in those days.

Scandal again hit the *Advocate* in 1935. James Laughlin's "A Natural History," along with "Glittering Pie," succeeded in having the freshman issue of 1935 banned. The Cambridge district attorney said that he did not want to send "these young writers with their allusions of grandeur" to jail, but he did force them to resign. Yet, on the whole, the *Advocate* no longer wanted outrage. The attitude of the magazine was becoming more serious and more attentive to the world outside Harvard. As an undergraduate, Arthur Schlesinger, Jr. analyzed the state of the 1936 Republican party in "The Republicans Come Back"; forty years' distance proves his judgments surprisingly accurate.

Harry Brown, '40, the cleverest writer of the late thirties, restored to the magazine some of its former flippancy: his "Anatomy of the Debutante," pseudonymously published, is a model of cool malice.

December 1938 saw the first special issue. This series, which usually commemorates great modern authors, began in honor of T. S. Eliot. The Eliot number contained short critical pieces, homages by other writers, and personal remembrances ("T. S. Eliot, '10: An Advocate Friendship"); it also reprinted Eliot's student verse. The prestige of this tribute required a successor, which came two years later. It was dedicated to Wallace Stevens, and contained several new poems by Stevens himself as well as Delmore Schwartz's "Ultimate Plato with Picasso's Guitar." The tradition of the special issue, intermittently maintained, has not ceased. The most recent of this series, which appeared in January 1977, honored Schwartz himself.

The eruption of the Second World War caused the *Advocate,* safe in a neutral country, no immediate difficulties. The editors even amused themselves by running surveys on war opinion at Harvard (5 percent of all students wanted to enter the war immediately on the side of Great Britain: this in March 1941) and by printing reports from occupied France and Norway. Fiction and verse persisted in high quality: Howard Nemerov's "The Native in the World" and "Inventory and Statement: A Declamation," and Norman Mailer's "The Greatest Thing in the World," all date from this time.

Even after Pearl Harbor the magazine went on. But issues appeared less frequently, and interest was weaker. Many men had entered the service, and Harvard classes shrank by half after 1942. The problems of a literary magazine perhaps seemed rather trifling at the time. Finances grew worse for the *Advocate*. Its creditors began to dun the university, and the trustees thought it politic to close the magazine in 1943, to be reopened after the war. The break lasted four years. It was the only interruption in *Advocate* history.

Some Notes on Moscow

E. J. Simmons

THE train, which had behaved like a consumptive all the way from Riga, finally coughed and gasped its last in the Baltic Station of Moscow. It was a bright August morning, and I hastened outside, not a little interested to find myself in the Russian capital, the citadel of revolutions, civil wars, communism, and the rule of the proletariat. Immediately I was surrounded by a host of picturesquely bearded, dirty, and ragged individuals who set upon me and my luggage with all the gusto of Ali Baba's Forty Thieves. These are the izvoshiki, an indispensable part of Moscow's local color. For the uninitiated, the carriage of an izvoshik is a tiny four-wheeled vehicle made to carry precisely one-and-a-half people and all the light freightage of the city. They are as frequent on the streets as taxicabs in New York. All a foreigner needs to know about them is that he must never give the original fare demanded. The procedure is something as follows. You hail, "Izvoshik!" One will amble up to the curb and you shout your destination and then counter, "How much?" He may say, "Two rubles." This is your cue to snort back, "A ruble!"; and you continue on your way with an air of unconcern. "A rouble and a half," he concedes sauntering along behind you. "A rouble, not a kopek more." "But citizen, how do you think I can feed this horse?" "A rouble," you yawn. "All right, we poor izvoshiki must live." He draws up and you take your place in the carriage, pleased with your bargaining, while the izvoshik smiles at you good-naturedly, wondering perhaps how you have learned the trick.

Down Pervy Meshanskaya the izvoshik drove and I got my first glimpse of the city. Moscow is different from anything you have seen before. Your first impression is that of a glorified East Side of New York at rush hours. The rough cobblestone streets and sandy boulevards with uncut grass swarmed with people,— Russians in their embroidered blouses and knee-high boots, Tatars in their vari-colored native robes, Mongolians with drooping moustaches and curious little velvet skull caps, stalwart Caucasians dressed exactly as we see them pictured in the Ringling Brothers' posters with their huge sheepskin hats, surcoats, imitation cartridges and silver daggers, and a sprinkling of swarthy-skinned gypsies shrieking in patch-quilt colors and shiny metal ornaments. Many finely uniformed soldiers mingled with the throng, and from an adjacent street I could hear the stirring revolutionary songs of troops on the march. Everybody seemed to be eating, tearing chunks out of loaves of bread, sucking at slices of watermelon, pears, or apples, or interminably cracking and swallowing sunflower seeds. And those who did not eat, smoked Russian cigarettes. At a street corner by a newspaper booth a mother unconcernedly suckled her child, and another woman held a little boy over the gutter while he performed the functions of nature, whereas more bashful grownups were forced to the walls. Filthy-looking pedlers were everywhere, selling everything imaginable, books, shoestrings, crockery, fruits, candy, cigarettes and socks. A long-haired, long-gowned priest stood outside a church door begging for money. Indeed, beggars were numerous, garbed in the poorest rags, with burlap tied about their feet for shoes. Not infrequently I saw drunken men lying motionless in the gutter or prone across the sidewalk, their faces smeared in their own vomit, and no one paying the slightest attention to them. On the boulevards crowds formed circles within which a trained bear went through his antics or a blandly-smiling Mongolian mystified his audience with tricks of legerdemain. There was much loud talking, gesticulation, and scolding, and over all pervaded an indefinable, remorseless odor.

In its architecture, too, Moscow is different. There is nothing of the Gothic wonders of London and Paris, of the neat, stony stoginess of Berlin, or the modern mammoths of New York. The general aspect of the buildings, like that of the people, is shabby and heterogeneous; but often a jewel of comparatively modern structure or hoary age will stand out, just as beautiful Russian women or tall, handsome, bearded patriarchs lend contrast to the motley throngs on the streets. There are the traditional forty times forty churches with their quaintly-rounded, golden-domed cupolas gleaming in the sun; crumbling fort-like monasteries of pure Russian and pseudo-Russian style dating from the 15th and 16th centuries; and the old China and Kremlin walls still well preserved, and the marvellous group of churches and palaces within the Kremlin itself. Oddly contrasted with these ancient glories is the recently built Lenin Institute symbolizing communism, a blackened, concrete, factory-like structure, ominous in its somber simplicity. Along the boulevards a number of futuristic statues have been erected, the pleasant effect in the distance of their sharp angles and sweeping curves becoming distinctly unpleasant the

closer you approach. On street after street one sees miserable little wooden hovels crouching beside respectable five-story office buildings and apartments. As for skyscrapers, these do not exist in Moscow.

Through the archway by the famous Iversky Chapel, my izvoshik drove into Red Square, the central point of the city and rich in historic blood. In the Middle Ages it was the great market place of all the Russias; the golden Tatar horde streamed over it to storm the Kremlin walls; and during the October Revolution, many of the Red Guard fell here from the machine gun and rifle fire of the Whites. The square is bound on three sides by the Kremlin Wall, the Church of St. Basil, and the Historic Museum. This fantastic Church of St. Basil was built in the 16th century by the command of Ivan the Terrible. Its spiraled cupolas, huge center tower, innumerable details, and the whole grotesquely painted lend credence to the legend that Ivan had the architect blinded in order that he might never build elsewhere anything comparable to this finest example of old Russian style. In the center of the square is a stone execution place; and legend also has it that the terrible Czar sat high up in the church tower and watched his victims put to death. Now the Church of St. Basil has been declared a museum by the Soviet Government.

In this same Red Square before the Kremlin Wall, and near the Brotherhood Grave of five hundred fallen revolutionists, is the mausoleum of Lenin, a black majesty of bolts and beams rising in simple graduating terraces. It is impressive, and its newness is in striking contrast to the old brick walls of the Kremlin. As I entered the square the guard at the tomb was being changed. A squadron of soldiers maneuvered in front of the mausoleum, and at the same moment two dray teams lumbered slowly across the open space. They were loaded with what looked like sturgeons, and the dirty, stiff fish stuck grotesquely out of the sides like so many logs of wood on which the drivers sat. The soldiers drew up and made the Soviet salute. The first teamster drew himself up also and saluted, and called back to his comrade to do likewise. But the latter, busy fumbling with some papers, yelled, "Don't bother me!" The new guards took their posts, the squadron marched away, and the reverent and irreverent drivers passed slowly through the Iversky arch.

My izvoshik finally halted outside a dirty-looking apartment house in the Arbat district, which was to be my home in Moscow. Of course there are hotels in the city, several very fine ones run by the government. At these foreigners stop and pay handsomely, go on government-conducted tours for a week or a month, and then return home to write authoritative articles or books about Russia and the new order of things. Being a poor traveller, I had to seek lodgings elsewhere. But the world knows at least one genuine fact about Moscow (and many other large Russian cities), namely that they are extremely overcrowded. Since the revolution, Moscow has grown from slightly more than a million to some two millions and a half of inhabitants, and the impoverished government has not been able to supply accommodations to cope with this tremendous increase. One can apply to the Commissioner of Dwellings and he will graciously assign you a few meters of space in some small room which has been adjudged too large for a single occupant. There is an obvious element of risk, however, in submitting to such an assignation,

for no method of selection obtains. Russian roommates, like all roommates, are of unequal qualities. Having accepted the good graces of a friend who offered to find me a room, I jumped, so to speak, from the frying pan into the fire, although no doubt things could have been worse. A certain Aksina, aged forty, had given up living with her husband and was willing to share her room in a platonic fashion with anyone white or black for a munificent sum which was small, nevertheless, compared to that charged by the hotels. With becoming bashfulness I accepted on the condition that Aksina would sleep in the community kitchen, a dingy hole somewhere in the misty region of Weir. Having got me nicely settled, Aksina, after two weeks, suddenly decided that it was infringing upon the culinary privileges of the other members of the apartment to sleep in the kitchen, and accordingly she moved back into her or our room. She conceded me one side, and on the opposite constructed a makeshift bed and a tiny screen behind which she coyly concealed her nightly toilet. She could understand no objections to this arrangement, for after all it was the way most people in Moscow lived. I had no other recourse than to become a Roman in Moscow.

In all there were three rooms in the apartment. One was occupied by a man and his wife, their two sisters-in-law, and the wife's eternally crying babies. The second room, a windowless affair, was commanded by a prostitute and her numerous callers. The third belonged to the good Aksina and myself, while the janitor of the apartment and his wife lived in a walled-off space under the stairs.

It is not always easy to love one's neighbors under such conditions of propinquity, yet the Russians happily adapt themselves to the situation, indulging their predilection for wrangling, but never coming to blows over the common electric bill or priority in the common kitchen. A young scholar friend and his wife had a little room whose splendid exposure they never tired of praising, whereas they accounted it no great drawback that the only access to their room was via the bathroom which was used by three other families in the same apartment. This absolute premium on space in Moscow was sadly emphasized by a married couple I knew. They eventually got divorced, the *causa belli* being that the husband was jealous of his wife's going to parties with other men and arriving home at three or four o'clock in the morning. But up to date this severed couple has not been able to find separate rooms. Accordingly, something like the *status quo* obtains, since the injured husband must still crawl out of his celibate bed to open the door for his sometime wife in the early hours of the morning. What would a Dostoevsky do with these ready-to-hand situations in which various types are brought into close contract in the average Russian apartment? Indeed, something has already been made of the humor if not the tragedy of this manner of living in the Russian theater. One especially clever play is still being produced in the Studio of the Moscow Art Theater. The plot works out the tangle of two roommates who get married, and with their young wives are all forced to live in the same room. The many opportunities of enforced intimacy convince them all that they are mismated, so they obtain a simple Russian divorce and happily remarry.

But what of this new civilization, the doctrine of communism, and the rule of the proletariat? These are the magnets that draw the foreigner to Russia, and at first one naïvely searches for visible manifestations of a great change among the people. Walk up Kuznezky Most, the Broadway of Moscow, to Tverskoi Boulevard, the Fifth Avenue. The stores, fly-ridden restaurants, theaters, and movie houses are always crowded. An endless throng of business men, shopkeepers, workers, prostitutes, peasants fresh from the country, soldiers, and students go about their business with stern or happy faces and much talking. Listen to their conversations or talk with them and you hear nothing of revolutions and civil wars, of the Right and the Left, or of Marxism and Leninism. They will tell you their domestic troubles, that they are tired of waiting outside the government co-operatives for their portion of bread and tea, that work is scarce, that the paper shortage is a nuisance. Or they may even comment on recent literature, saying that Maijakovsky has stooped to poetic advertising, or that Biedny's stuff is mere drivel, or that Shoxolov's "Quite Don" is a good book but not always easy to understand. But of the possibilities of Trotsky's return or a split in the Stalin forces you hear never a word. This is the patient Russian people who laugh today and cry tomorrow. They are now much as they were before the fall of the Czar. However, twelve years is perhaps too short a time to transform a people into the eager enthusiasts of a new civilization—a people that waited some three hundred years to overthrow a wretched tyranny.

But if the average Russian you meet on the street has not yet been metamorphosed into a preaching apostle of the new order of things, it is not the fault of his Soviet Government. The Russian public has ever been indifferent (until some great crisis arrives), and the present government is striving with might and main to overcome this indifference, to arouse the people to a full appreciation of their declared position as the

the leaders in the new material and intellectual growth of the world. No greater propagandist exists than the Russian government. This whole land of 150 millions of people is literally drenched in propaganda. Every conceivable agency is employed to further the doctrines of Marxism and uphold the rule of the Soviets. In Moscow we find this propaganda in newspapers, journals, posters, books, in short, in every form of printed material; in the theaters and movies, and in every manner of public entertainment; in workers' clubs, factories, mills, schools, and universities; and among organizations such as the Komsomol, the Pioneers, and the unions. The shadow of Lenin darkens the land. His statues, miniature busts, and portraits are everywhere, in all public buildings, clubs, mills, factories; and in store windows among sausages, women's lingerie, and men's haberdashery displays. In Russia God has been ousted and Lenin elevated to His throne.

A curious kind of idealism is broadcasted in Moscow and over the rest of the country. Numerous campaigns are carried on against drunkenness, vice, religion, illiteracy, laziness, profiteering, haltura (the prostitution of artistic talents for selfish ends). Members of the Communist Party must not weep at adversities, must not get drunk, and must be willing to sacrifice their all for the principles of the organization. The moral, physical, and intellectual betterment of the ruling workers and peasants are the professed aims of this ceaseless propaganda.

Conversely, bourgeoisie civilization is criticised and ridiculed through all the agencies that preach and enforce the new order of things. Any news that goes out or comes into the country is strictly censored, and no real opposition to the government or its policies is tolerated. The system of education has been entirely changed. It favors a practical education above everything else. The past and its traditions have no place in this system. Quarrels between humanists and romanticists, the glories of Greece and the grandeur of Rome, scholasticism and mediævalism, all the petty quibblings of rule and line are banned. The dead past must bury the dead. History begins with the October Revolution and is pointed towards the future. Culture has become dynamic. It must have technical and economic progress as its aims. Science and not the humanities is the basis of this new culture, and all instruction is frankly materialistic. Art likewise must adapt itself to the new culture, seeking subject-matter and forms that will express a materialistic concept of the future.

This future defies prophecy, however, for a decade is too short a time for working out infallibly the destiny of so great an experiment. Communists demand some hundreds of years for the tree to bear fruit, pointing out that it took several centuries for the feudal and bourgeoisie civilizations to mature fully. Yet despite the shortness of the period which the Soviet Government has existed, one sensibly feels the new impetus and élan that pervades the country. Of course, there have been many failures, much compromising, and a great deal of discontent exists among the people, due primarily to the poor economic conditions. But we find everywhere evidence of amazing material progress. Russia has shaken off the chains that bind it to the past, and is starting out with new hope on a career of self-betterment and world proselytizing.

The Truce

J. R. AGEE

When, in such anguish of our love
As naught can temper or remove,
We lie beyond the hope of speech
And breathe our sorrow each to each,
One passion stands within my breast
Annihilating all the rest:
Lip and hand and flesh and bone
Are one large pity; pity alone
Is all my body can devise,
And pity gazes through my eyes.

Pitying, I seek your own,
And there, as still as any stone,
Pure as water wrung from flame,
Dwells a pity much the same.
While we look, those pities swell
Wide from double-sourced hell;
Deep and wide within that pool
Shines the pity of a fool;
Closer pressing, gazing, we
Know the idiot pity we.

So we look, and so love passes:
Take two flat quicksilvered glasses,
Press each to each the mirroring planes,
You naught can see, but much remains:
Bound in those flat and fragile walls
Stretch two bright and spaceless halls;
Beyond the glass, beyond the dull
Sponge of brain and box of skull
That straight and empty hall extends
And binds infinity's curved ends.

So much can our love attain,
Just so much, and that with pain;
Though we die to change the score,
Just so much, and nothing more.
Pity need not be the passion,
Though it be our private fashion:
Any single joy or grief
Turns the trick that cracks belief;
And the body's left behind
Whispering to the abandoned mind:

"So they look, and so Time passes
Withering o'er the glorious grasses:
Time shall ravel us asunder:
Mind's delight and body's wonder
And our shrewd-contrivéd lust,
Time shall wither into dust.
Where two pities stand displayed,
Shade shall mirror endless shade,
And they that have themselves forgot
Shall find no joy where self is not."

And the quiet mind makes reply:
"Many a time, before they die,
They shall hear out mutterings
And return to earthly things:
Try once more each sly device
We invent; none shall suffice.
Since much joy, but much more sorrow
Stands before their sunless morrow,
Vex not their unperplexity;
It cannot last as long as we."

Good Friday

J. R. AGEE

High in Dodona's swaying groves,
High in the grey, the glimmering oaks,
Dodona's cauldrons, convolute,
Groan on the wind strange prophecies.

Among the whispering laurel roves
Great Pan, and on the tall sky, smokes
Of Delphi write; and now are mute
The graded reeds of Pan: he sees

Across the grey, the glimmering seas,
A leafless tree take barren root
On Golgotha; he hears the strokes
Of iron on iron, and his own hooves

The iron strikes through. Against two trees
Are driven his outstretched hands. Strange fruit
Hangs in the grey, the glimmering oaks,
Hangs in Dodona's swaying groves.

They that Sow in Sorrow shall Reap

J. R. AGEE

THE house, which was on a main street, near the tracks, and convenient to work, was painted a remote white; barrenly fronted the street, but possessed along one side a comfortable ledge of porch sparsely trellised with morning-glories; appeared to be small, but was rangy and subdivided into many small rooms. The floor of each room was covered by linoleum of one restless pattern; and each lodger's room contained a bed, a bureau, a shallow closet, a straight chair, and, upon request, a table. Throughout the house there was a flat smell of linoleum made warm, this first evening, by the sun. In every bedroom there were clean curtains; a rhomboid of light was projected upon each opposite wall, and across this the sun had stencilled a shifting lace of shadow. As I waited in my bedroom, the sun, descending, cramped the rhomboid of light, and urged the plaque of shadow and light toward the ceiling. The house was extremely clean. I lay across the clean counterpane, very tired, but lying tensely, in the hope that I might not print the counterpane with uncleanliness. I was slippery with rust and clay. I lay on my back and watched the sunlight tilt upward through the pane, and with vague impatience heard a tired man making himself clean in the one bathroom; and knew that other tired people were impatient and were waiting; and breathed the clean odor germinated on the warm linoleum; and saw a sharp gable shoulder out the sunlight.

This place was so clean; in one corner which the sun never struck I could see traces of a mop; and the linoleum was not ridged through by boards beneath; its checker pattern was everywhere sharp; and shifty, because my eyes were tired; but clean, and pleasant; and altogether the house was far better than the Eagle Hotel. I got up and looked resentfully at the bed, which I had creased with red dirt. It was my turn to wash. I took a bath, shaved with unusual care, and tried to free my hair of rust and clay; and went downstairs feeling very clean and complacently tired, like a patient ready for the operating table.

In the parlor, the boarders sat in a circle, patient but unrelaxed, and silent. The room was ornamented with pampas-plumes, and with nodular vessels of iridescent glass. There was a piano, carefully dusted, and with open music, and with an air of long disuetude. The room was quiet, except for a clock and the irregular ticking of wicker chairs. Between the next room and the next was a hurry of footsteps, and the clash and arrangement of tableware; but here, silence, and people, most of them still unrelaxed, still in poise like birds about to take wing. There were two men; the laborer looked down at his linked hands, which resembled scrubbed roots; the other, younger, a man of forty, furtively ran his nails one beneath another, while he sat self-consciously beneath his thinning hair. The two older women leaned back, now, with knees unflexed; the younger woman maintained an air of anxiety; she sat straight, with knees snapped crosswise like a closed purse. The people were tired, and without emotion they received once more the deliberate edge of evening.

Mrs. Stevens came to the door to say, supper is ready, and with abrupt commotion the six of us filed in to the table, where already an old man was standing guard.

The food was abundant and pridefully cooked. Large bowls of it, consumed, were removed, and came again replenished. The woman who carried them said to each boarder, "Good evening," (then calling him by name); "This has been a beautiful day." And she would say no more. The old man her husband, who sat with the meat pie at the head of the table, would add, "Yes, a beautiful day. A handsome day. Can't I help you to something, Miss Silk?" She, who had sat primly as a closed purse, would with difficulty reply, "No. Thank you." And in her silence a blush would thicken across her forehead. The old gentleman said, next, "Nor you, Mrs. Bixby?" at the same time nodding inquiry toward the third woman. After this, whatever the result, he would smile with embarrassment, and restore his attention to his own food.

He was a handsome old gentleman. His features were aquiline and finely regular; his cleft lower lip and chin were opulent and weak, and the whole face was drawn into a sort of perfection by a recently combed and waxed moustache. There was in his face a flicker of forgotten arrogance; and in his appearance was a suggestion of continued vanity; for his hair, shining white and fine as a child's, was most carefully set back from his shield-like forehead; and he wore the sort of "sport" shirt that boys wear; a shirt whose collar flared buttonless away from his strong youthful throat. His hands were abnormally small and veinless; as much as possible he kept them folded in his lap. As I have remarked, he spoke very little, but he smiled continually, as if at his own happiness, and he seemed unduly eager to resolve all uncertainties with his own calm.

I found this beauty, this unexpected youthfulness, somehow sinister. As I watched him, however, this repellence vanished, for he showed only gentleness and kindliness, and embarrassing humility, and shortly, I was aware of his remarkable serenity. For, each time his wife was in the room he smiled and watched her as she moved about, and his eyes blazed with peace.

He was especially anxious for Miss Silk's ease, and this, though futile, was praiseworthy. For Mr. Harbison, oblivious of his thinning hair, was brimming over with good fun and pleasant quips. The fun, much of it at Miss Silk's expense, was delivered to the table at large, as were the pleasant quips. A few of the better-turned quips were repeated so that Mother Stevens, in the kitchen, might hear them. They were carelessly deflected by six at the table, but each one struck Miss Silk solidly and with fine effect. A miserably shy woman of twenty-five, she looked straight into her plate and, for fear of her own voice, said nothing. When she was forced to reply to Mr. Stevens, or to a kind question from Mrs. Bixby, she grew red with mortification as she contemplated the rude brusqueness in her voice.

As the boarders, soothed by good food and by a coolness expanding on the air, became more talkative, it was easier to remark their various interrelations. Mr. Harbison, I understood quickly enough, had appropriated the role of star boarder; this he was granted without jealousy and without recognition. He sat op-posite Mr. Stevens at the foot of the table, and fought a routine battle of wits best comparable to shadow boxing. The two older women worked in the office of the canning factory, and were friends of long standing. From time to time Mrs. Bixby, the more gregarious of the two, made casual efforts to engage Miss Silk in conversation; she weathered each failure far more happily than did the young woman. The laborer said very little and paid much attention to his manners, furtively watching Mr. Harbison's use of knife, fork and toothpick. There were, too, certain unchanging group attitudes: mild hostility toward Harbison, tolerance toward the laborer, and a rather disturbing disregard of Mr. Stevens. I felt a faint curiosity concentrated on me, and a gathering apathetic distrust as Mr. Harbison subtly drew me out. Mr. Harbison gathered, from my replies, that I was the scion of a wealthy house, a student in Harvard, working for my health, trying to live down my education, rather a snob, and possibly about town for no good purpose. It was a good thing, he informed me, for a young man to get out and see the world a bit, to mix with all sorts; it would convince me that life wasn't all silver spoons and things. The only way to rise in the world was to start at the bottom and get to know your fellow man. I would find that there were very fine traits even in those poor souls bruised by fortune and left by the side of the road.

(The laborer took his spoon from his cup and looked ashamed.) I made no effort to reinform him or anyone else. Harbison sailed on, inexorably misinterpreting and advising and, I could see, preparing a lecture on his philosophy of life. But even when most drunk with vast ideas, he did not allow himself to forget his duty to his disciples. After every particularly memorable statement he glanced away from me, and asked Miss Silk if that was not so.

Meanwhile, Mr. Stevens, sensing as much guile as sincerity in Harbison's conversation, pitied me in my bewilderment; a number of times he smiled encouragement toward me. As we left the table and moved toward the porch, Mr. Harbison fell into step beside me, asking for my criticism of Mother Stevens' cooking; and Mr. Stevens followed.

There was no safe answer to such a question, and I grew cold in the shadow of Harbison's tall surmise, so I hung back a little and allowed him to overtake Miss Silk. This act, I could see, crystallized various suspicions he had unwillingly entertained. I was glad enough of that; with only a sharp feeling of pity for Miss Silk, I leaned against a porch post and lighted a cigarette.

"This has been a handsome day."

"Yes. Fine."

It was Mr. Stevens who spoke.

"We don't get many days like it."

"No, you're right."

"Most of this summer has been very rainy, very unpleasant."

"It has been pretty lousy."

He smiled brightly. "Yes, it has been very unpleasant, exceedingly unpleasant. But today has been splendid."

"Yes, it's been a lovely day. We don't get many like it."

"I have a feeling we are in for a good spell, now, though. Not a cloud in the sky, all day."

"It has been, very clear, today."

He was anxious, for some reason, to talk; but some sixth sense told us that the weather was a delicate subject, and had best be spoken of no more.

"Do you care for a cigarette?"

"No, thank you; I have never touched tobacco in any form." He smiled apologetically and added, "But thank you very much, just the same."

"Surely."

"I don't in the least frown upon smoking, you understand. And I don't take faith in this stuff and nonsense about its doing any physical harm. Only, I don't like to form habits, as one is likely to with smoking, don't you think?"

"Yes, I think you're right. I know it's a habit with me."

He was very liberal, for several minutes, on the whole matter of smoking and other habitual vices. I liked the old man but, because I preferred to be alone, I said as little as I politely could in reply. Just when the subject ran encouragingly dry, and I was getting ready to take my leave, he said, "You are satisfied with everything here?"

I assured him that I was. He was very glad: he and his wife tried to make everything as clean and attractive as could be, as much like home as could be. They were particularly anxious that the young folks should be happy. It was hard, he knew, being young and a long way from home. He had been young himself once, and it had been a great comfort to him when older people were nice, and tried to make everything, although there was no place like home, like home.

"Young people should appreciate it," I said, without mentioning any names. Mr. Stevens' eyes showed more understanding than I had bargained for and, genuinely ashamed, I added that I most certainly did.

Immediately reassured, he said with eagerness that I was to feel just like one of the family. We exchanged appreciations and wore through a discourse on loneliness, during which his concentration upon speech gave way before a crescent eagerness. Across his left cheek, I saw the flutter of some irrelevant sinew, and the nicely curled moustache was wry and twitching. At the same time a ticklish, cold weakness rilled through the roots of my spine.

"It's been a fine day," he said, "but very hot."

"Not so bad."

"It must have been very hot working."

"Not so bad."

"Is your work pretty heavy?"

"Digging a ditch and handling iron, today."

"That *must* have been hot, on a day like this. Are you used to such work?"

"Not very. But it wasn't bad."

"Not bad, eh? Ah, my boy, when you're young you can stand up to any sort of work."

I said nothing.

"A fine, strapping young fellow like you. You can stand up to anything, can't you?"

His shaky small hand closed upon my arm. "Let me feel your biceps. Ah, what a fine, strapping young fellow. See, I can't reach half around it." He slipped one arm across my shoulders, and his own shoulder, hard and hot, clenched against my chest. For a moment pretense was lost to him, and his eyes, narrowed, brilliant with lust, asked me: "Is everything understood?"

Everything was quite well understood. I smiled back like one of the family a bit embarrassed at such demonstrativeness, freed myself without too much obviousness, lighted a cigarette, and said: "I guess it's about time I went in town, I promised to meet some friends."

I went in through the dining-room and upstairs for matches. I could hear Mrs. Stevens washing the dishes. I hurried out the front door. As I passed the porch, the old gentleman smiled and waved; I pretended not to see him. When, in spite of myself, I looked back again, he had gone in.

2

The mind is rarely audience to experience in perfection; rarely is it granted the joy of emotions and realities which, first reduced to their essential qualities, are then so juxtaposed in harmony and discord, in sharp accentuation and fluent change, in thematic statement, development, restatement and recapitulation, as to achieve in progress a continuous, and in consummation, an ultimate beauty. As a rule, experience is broken upon innumerable sharp irrelevancies; emotion and reality, obscurely fused and inexplicably tarnished, are irreducible, and the tarnish is ineradicable; their rhythms are so subtly involved, so misgoverned by chance, as to be beyond analysis; and the living mind, that must endure and take part, is soon fugitive before, or else, however brave, falls to pieces beneath this broad unbeautiful pour of chaos.

The experience referred to is objective; the same difficulties hold in the case of subjective experience. The true sum of experience is, as a rule, an inconceivably complex interpenetration of subjective and objective experience. And the true sum and whole of experience is doubly chaotic.

It is therefore fortunate that most minds are constructed to float. However rigorous the weave of currents, however huge the plunge of waves, they are forever near the surface. And it is fortunate, God knows, that minds which would anatomize experience are given the mercy of a million moods: these complement and relieve one another, and those which are not wholly proof against pain at least shift the weight of experience to a fresh area of the mind. That mood of sustained callousness and irony which I thought one desert afternoon had perpetuated in me, still serves me well. Although it has achieved a few complexities of perception which may perhaps enrich it, it remains my habitual state of mind, it dilutes experience to a fairly palatable beverage of dubious concoction. But, when I attempt to make real use of these instruments of perception, I realize two things: my own weakness and diffuseness of mind, and the fearful unarrangement of life realized with such completeness and sincerity as my mind may be capable of.

But certain moods, if kept as clear as possible of deflecting intellect, reflect a selection and arrangement of experience which approaches beauty: beauty of form, of emotion, of shadowy idea. The experience during my first meal here, and just after, seemed casual enough as they occurred; Mr. Stevens' revelation struck away that mood, and, after long modulation of moods in my mind, the whole thing, as it occurred, emerged with symmetry and beauty.

But my relation to this progress of experience is broken, is never sure.

In the first place, I work nine hours a day, and that violently different life seems severed from this. Then, even when I am here, so much that happens is utterly without direct significance. For instance, I talk with old Stevens every night. All our conversation, because of my avoidance, is oblique to the essential in his mind. In fragments, and by implication, I have been able to recreate his life; and I find the man as a whole pathetic, and appealing, and somehow very important. The mere unfortunate fact of his perversion is, or should be, beside the point. The important things are, the complete frustration of a mind that wished to be fine and could have been good, the dwindling, for many years, of his life as an entity, his still persistent eagerness for knowledge, for the company of educated people, and this incredible tranquillity that has come with his old age. As a preacher in Maine, as a fugitive from misunderstanding, as a miserably unsuccessful grocer in this town, he can scarcely have known tranquillity. But now, as he says, he finds time once more for reading, and for music. He reads vastly and without discrimination, and he plays the piano with two fingers. Now, permitted, at last, complete nonentity, he is happy. He sits at table quiet and meek, and says little, like a good child. Apparently, he worships his wife, though they have little to say to each other. He seems to have discovered some private formula for complete contentment: yet (discounting his wooer's flattery) he is genuinely grateful for my company, for the chance to talk about books, any books, for the chance to hear music played, however badly, with ten fingers instead of two. I scarcely know whether to be glad for this, or sorry to have wrought as I have upon his ancient illness.

His wife has had a strange life. In the parlor, their wedding picture is hung. In many ways, the old man still resembles the young one there, with curled mouth, and brave moustache, and arrogant Websterian posture. But the girl who stands beside him in full pride of her beauty, intelligence and aggressiveness are frozen in her eyes, and all beauty has departed the body and the grey pebble of a face; and the woman who has time, now, only for swift patience and for thorough housecleaning, for a proper but minimum politeness; and time never for a friend, or for any glint of affection—what bitterness and what unswerving loyalty have wrought this unaccountable change? Can any memory lie behind that unequivocal mask?

What resurgencies may engulf them both, when, each Sunday, they drive away into Maine? Or, is there mutual calm delicately adjusted beyond unbalancing?

I am far from my beginning. I wonder how, or if, I can return to it.

* * * *

There is no return, and no use returning. I have tried to work out to my own satisfaction, some aspects of the mind's reaction to experience. I have tried to match this reaction with the patterns of music; the idea is incongruous; I should be kicked for trying it. My mind is hopelessly weak and tangential; time and again, as above, I fail to carry one idea through; before I realize it, I am whirled along the rim of another— and so on—ad nauseam.

Yet, from time to time, I *am* aware of a definite form and rhythm and melody of existence: however fluctuate and intermittent its progress may be, it *is* a progress; out of long contrapuntal passages of tantalizing and irreconcilable elements there emerges sometimes an enormous clear chord. And at that moment—or, rather, through its reverberations in our brain, the whole commonplaceness of existence is transfigured—becomes monstrously powerful, and beautiful, and significant—assuming these qualities validly but unanswerably—, and descends through tangled discords, once more into commonplaceness, with nothing answered, nothing gained, and heaven undisturbed.

I suppose the essentials of which this music is compounded are, the facts as they are, tempered by sternness and pity and calm. We are eight people in this house; we are endowed with as many different minds, or souls, and with as many different machines for attacking existence, and defending ourselves against it. The full vision of existence is forever denied us. We live dimly in the center of being, and thence we perform most ordinary duties, and avoid others; to some extent we guide our lives, to some extent are guided by them; and the whole object of life, whatever it may or should be, is hidden beyond a profound and inescapable confusion of egoism and of altruism and of evil and of good. And so, when these myopic people, concentrated upon their daily tasks, upon their food, or upon their rest, or upon their little loves, their little cruelties, their little aspirations; when, caught in these flimsy inescapable cogs, they are contemplated in their unrealized relation to the timeless severance of the vast radiance of life, and the enormous shadow of death, they become magnificent, and tragic, and beautiful.

* * * *

I read carefully what I had written; carefully, and slowly, tried to clarify the ideas, to give them some proper connection, to discover any single coherent thought. When I finished I was sick with exhaustion and self-contempt; I wanted to beat my face to bits. I crumpled the sheets into a fistful and looked for a match; and stopped. It was the only attempt I'd ever made to get at the bottom of anything. It was a horrible failure—but in another mood something might come of it, something might be clear in it.

I lay down and read the second act of *The Cherry Orchard*, and realized once more that here, that melody was caught, and that great drama had been made of it. How, I could not tell.

Although it was very late, and I had to get up at six, I felt it necessary to walk. It was a fine night. After two miles of walking, my brain still felt like a shooting gallery. I returned to my room and went to sleep.

3

The morning was very hot and blue, the blue fading as the heat and light increased. Heat rilled above each fragment and long spine of metal, and shimmered like clear smoke over the grass and dusty streets. The gravel showed cool and dark as our shovels turned it; but almost immediately it was white. The white light grew so wide that it was painful to look into the sky.

To my right, as I turned for each new shovel-load, I saw the half-bushel scoop slicing deep into the gravel, moving in no slower rhythm than my own square-nosed shovel. Before the second truck was loaded, the new man had struck bottom. I turned toward him and together we cleared out solid footing. The truck moved out, and we all rested in the band of shade to one side of the car, drank the already tepid water, and smoked.

Of the many jobs laborers were assigned, this was by all odds the best. Digging a ditch, or screening sand, you took your time, but worked continuously, with one eye on the foreman or his suspected direction of appearance; here, you worked furiously for a few minutes, in the surety of ten minutes of solid loafing. There was much talking during these ten minutes, and ordinarily, I joined in it and enjoyed it. Today, however, I lay flat on my back and said little. It had been nearly two when I returned from my walk; the need for sleep and the extreme heat were like tightening bolts in my temples; they persuaded me to a black and painful concentration upon the problems which had arisen the evening before. I could no longer fix upon any one idea or fragment of idea. A few words burred so constantly in my brain that they spun themselves free of all meaning; and problems, words, phrases, the uncertain nature of my own mind, the lives and the ruling moods of the people in the house, froze clear of verbal thought, assumed various geometric forms; and these in their turn underwent change, and emerged as long silver arches, thin as rods; none touched, but a current quickened each, and flickered on the intermediary darkness, and they sent forth a low and hideous multitone.

Not one arch was complete.

Despite this resonant pattern I could see and hear a little. I heard voices as one does beneath fathoms of ether; and I saw the man new on the job, prostrate on the cinders, one knee angled against the sky, head resting in a flexile sling of joined hands and bent arms. He was long and heavy and hugely powerful, and his head seemed fashioned of great plates and ridges of iron, strongly joined. When we heard the truck coming he opened his clear unintelligent eyes, smiled by drawing his mouth into a line, and towered into a magnificent repatterning of strength.

He showed some concern over my lack of skill and economy in handling my shovel. During the next rest he offered me a cigarette, and I learned that he came from Lebanon. During the next he asked me, without that leering which is apology, whether I knew any women in town. A little Canuck made the question funny for himself; the new man saw no humor in it; he said: "Do you know any?" "My women are in Manchester," said the Canuck, among other things. "Then you'd better pipe down," said the new man. The Canuck piped down.

"I've got a Chevrolet," the new man said. I told him that women were hard to find in this lousy town. He replied "I'll find them."

He said very little; he even swore little. He never suspected the existence of humor; he suspected the existence of nothing, I think, except women, work, food and rest.

He was staying, he said, at the Eagle Hotel. He agreed with me that it was a bad place. During the next rest, he asked me whether I knew of a cheaper place that was any good. I replied that I was staying at a cheaper place, that was very good, and that I believed there was room there. It was quite near the tracks; if he liked, we could go over and see.

And as I spoke, I felt my bowels turn to ice; but I continued to speak.

At noon, therefore, after eating lunch, we went over. We stood at the side door, on the porch.

"What's your name?"

"Grafton."

I stepped inside. From the hall I could see the long table. Only Harbison, the cobbler, Miss Silk the keeper of records, and the old gentleman, were here, at noon. They were broadly separated, at their regular places. As Mrs. Stevens came in from the kitchen I caught her eye and nodded. She smiled faintly, set down the food, and came to the hall.

"Fellow out here wants to board," I said, "if there's room."

As she crossed to the door, I could see beyond the fine white hair, swept by sunlight.

"Mr. Grafton," I said.

She looked at him through the opening screen. For an instant her face lost its quietude, and I was staring at merciless pain and fear. Then, with composure, she slowly said: "How do you do, Mr. Grafton. Yes, I am sure there will be room. I hope you will be comfortable."

"That's good," said Mr. Grafton.

"Shall I show you your room?"

"Don't bother," I said. "We'll get his stuff after work."

"The end of the hall, on the second floor," she said to both of us. And to me, "Thank you."

I watched her as she turned and closed the door and went into the dining-room.

"Sure," I said.

I said to Grafton: "Supper isn't till six. We'll have time to move your stuff then."

"Sure," he said.

By mid-afternoon we had the car cleared, and were back on the big job. I wheeled gravel to the mixer; he was at work digging a ditch in tough clay. Even late in the afternoon it was hot, but the coldness inside me persisted in spasms, and throughout spaces of rest, I was shivering; and watching the town clock, the hands cutting slowly their wheels on the sunlight.

At five I met Grafton, and we drove to the Eagle Hotel in his Chevrolet. As we came downstairs the younger clerk spoke to me:

"How do you like it, up on Water Street?"

"It's O.K."

He grinned doggishly. "How do you like the old gent?"

As we drove through the town, among the stores, among the houses, I wondered how spotted those square miles were with knowledge of the old man and his secret.

We lugged Grafton's meager baggage to the room at the far end of the hall. The room was smaller than mine, but like mine, very clean.

"I guess the can is empty," I said. "We'd better hurry up and wash." As I walked to my room, Miss Silk was going downstairs; she looked up and quickly down; and her reddening face disappeared.

My mail was on the bureau; a letter from my mother, and a card from August. My mother wrote that the sea had been lovely all day, and that my sister found life very dull this summer. She was going dancing tonight, though. It would be so good to have me home. August wrote that during one week there were five Chaplins and three Garbos in Berlin, and much rain.

I got my razor and soap and towel, and went into the bathroom. Grafton, standing in his work shoes and Sunday pants, was noisily washing. His head and his naked back and shoulders were a great keystone of corded muscle.

It was late, so after washing I shaved also from the bathtub spigot.

"How old are you?" said Grafton, mowing his cheek.

"Twenty."

He snorted. "I'm twenty myself. I'd have to shave twice a day, to keep down my beard.

"Who's the woman went downstairs?"

"Oh, she's no good. Silk's the name."

"Silk, huh?" He was puzzled. After a minute he said, "That's a funny name."

"Yeah."

We got dressed, and walked downstairs and into the parlor. Everyone was clean in the clean parlor, and waiting for supper, sitting patiently but unrelaxed; with labor past, with hands unbusied, with minds unmolested, they sat very tired waiting for their food and for their few hours of quiet and for their few hours of sleep; and for the next morning, and for the next evening, and for a Sunday, and for another week and Sunday; for autumn and for winter, for spring and for summer; for another year, for another ten; for the slow chemistry of change and age; for the loss of fluids and pigments and tissues, of senses and of wits, of faculties and of perceptions; for the silencing of all clamor and for the sealing of all sight; for the final levelling of all desire, of all despair, of all joy, of all tribulation; for the final quelling of all fear and pride and love and disaffection; for the final dissolution of the flesh and of all that flesh must suffer, sickness of soul and body, fast-withering delight and clouded love, unkindness and grief and wrong beyond reckoning; for the final resolution of all the good they had wrought, and all the ill; they sat resting after battle, resting before battle, with quiet hands and unperceiving eyes, without emotion to receive once more the deliberate edge of evening.

Mr. Stevens sat with the roast beef at the head of the table; Mrs. Stevens served food, and was busy between two rooms. She greeted each boarder briefly, and the old gentleman added, "A handsome day, but very hot," and asked Miss Silk if he could help her to anything. Miss Silk was sick with mortification, and stared at the center of her plate. Mr. Harbison was pleasant to Miss Silk, and quite the life of the party. Mrs. Bixby and Mrs. Thompson her friend of long standing, talked quietly and frequently dabbed their mouths with their napkins. Mrs. Stevens came in with more food, and glanced at me and at Grafton, and went out with an empty dish. Mr. Stevens watched her as she moved about the room, and his eyes were bright with serenity. The laborer, Frank Woods, scraped butter from his clean shirt, and was more deliberate in his eating. Mr. Harbison asked Miss Silk for an appointment in some sequestered grove. Miss Silk grew fiery red and said nothing. Grafton ate quickly and with thoroughness, glancing up as he bit, like a dog. I could scarcely

eat; a cold weight was in my belly, the fork was cold to my touch, my temples were numb.

I was watching Mr. Stevens. He sat at the head of the table like a good child, meek, happy and silent. As much as possible, he kept his hands in his lap. His silky white hair and white face, and the white sport collar, were bright across the dimming air. From time to time he glanced toward me, and smiled; and he smiled at Grafton.

Supper was over; we all strolled toward the porch.

"Play something," Mr. Stevens said. "Play the pyano."

I was blind with suspicion and fear, and anxious to counter such schemes as he might have. I replied that Grafton and I were going straight into town.

We stood, therefore, at the back of the porch. Nearer the street, the others sat to talk.

"Let's go," I said.

"Let's have a cigarette," said Grafton, and offered one to Mr. Stevens.

The old gentleman refused politely, and added that he had never touched tobacco in any form. To Grafton's silence he replied that it had been a hot day, but a handsome one.

That was true, I said. I was watching the sky: the sunset was unusual: night was rising from east and south and north, like an immense black hood; its edge was apparent against the day. Across the world from us there was an edge of dawn and freshness; there Greece shivered into light; but over a broadness of sea and plain, sharp mountains and the thistled light of cities, enormous shadow prevailed, and over us the shadow hung.

This is an instant I saw, and pitied the nine gathered in this house.

The old gentleman's arm slipped round my shoulder, and as he openly fondled me, he said that we were all one big family, and that Grafton must feel perfectly at home, perfectly at home.

I did nothing and said nothing. There was nothing to do or to say. Grafton stood a little away from us, and I saw amazement piercing his stupidity; and scorn, and incredulity. The old man babbled on, and I watched them both, and waited.

His cheek was twitching like a snake killed before sundown; his eyes were glassy and bright with lust; I felt his body trembling, and saw the trembling as, chattering inanely, he swung me toward Grafton, slid an arm about him, and called us his fine boys, his fine boys. And I saw the fine boy stand quietly, the eyes narrowing, the jaw muscles shifting and freezing; while a vein grew full and hard, and sprawled crooked on the old gentleman's forehead, Grafton stood in quiet; then drew away, and with flat palm struck across the mouth the old man, who, mouth flashing blood, for an instant assumed in all amazement the Jeffries sparring stance, with amazement gone raised supplicating tiny hands like a Moslem mole, while, face all blood and streaming tears, he shrank among the sorrowing flowers of morning bitterly crying, and with dependent hands fluttering before head;

while boarders rose from their chairs and looked in amaze and impended to interfere, then drew back and quickly, but staring back, removed from the porch and roomward made kind haste;

and two across the street stopped to stare;

and a second time the boy raised lowered arm through an arc and with flat palm struck through hands the old man's mouth; who, bawling abominable brat, splayed evening with weeping;

while with crashed plate and rushing footsteps

—murderous anger moving me with all strength I struck the boy, behind the ear; he turned and dealt upon my cheekbone his fist and power, that with split skin and shrouded purpose I sank against wall and floor, Defender of What?—

—the old woman his wife ran toward him, nothing saying, seeing none but him, and in her face revealed unfathomable sorrow fear and love, and two lives, broken late in this their day, that otherwise had closed in tranquillity—

—while in tallness and dignity around the corner stalked Grafton—

and five stared from across the street,

and the old woman haled the old gentleman into the kitchen,

and six stared from across the street,

and I recollecting complete consciousness, was frozen in a pratt fall, with face bleeding, watched curiously in my sudden aloneness by six people.

I got to my feet and, through the nearest door and the parlor of books, music and strange wedding picture, upstairs to my room, but straightway to the bathrooms with towel and handkerchief, to wash the cut across my cheek. It was not deep, and after a short time I stanched the blood. In the mirror I saw one with swollen temple and battered cheek, with dark stupid eyes which shone with no zeal for living. I started for my room. As I opened the bathroom door, another door opened, at the far end of the hall. Grafton, with his baggage, walked slowly toward me, and I toward him. We looked fully at each other, and, as we met in the middle of the hall, paused, as if in delicate balance, still looking at each other, without animosity, without regret, without emotion of any sort; then, after the instant's pause, walked on, I into my room, he down the stairs and out of my future existence.

I changed my shirt and sat down, weak, on a chair in the center of the room. I was within a hollow cube. It seemed to me that from five sides of this cube came excited whispering; and from the sixth, beneath me, came two sounds: the sound of dishes being washed in haste; and the sound of quiet but profound weeping.

It was beyond my endurance, at the time. I left the house and the town, and walked out to a high hill, from which I watched other hills, and fields heavy with crops, and wooded land, and the distant town, as they lay beneath the night. I was unable to think, and after a little while I did not try to. I stayed on the hilltop for a long while, and returned with mind quiet because unoccupied by thought; and, after packing, went to sleep.

I was early at the table, conspicuous because I was not in my work clothes. Mrs. Stevens said nothing. She did not speak to any of the boarders as, one by one, they came in. Nor did the boarders speak, either to her, or to each other. They carefully avoided looking directly at any-one, and methodically ate what was set before them. Covertly, Mr. Harbison watched me; he said nothing. Mr. Stevens was not at the table; nor was a place set for him. From the kitchen, from time to time, came the sound of a hoarse whisper.

While everyone was still at table, Harbison rose and beckoned to Mrs. Stevens, and they withdrew to the parlor. Their conversation was not audible, but the tone and intention of Harbison's voice, and the tinkle of money withdrawn from a pocket, were quite well understood by all of us.

For the spark of pleasure her liberation would give me, I was watching Miss Silk. I think we all were. Her eyes were quiet and comprehending; her face was without expression, as we heard him ascend and descend the stairs. When the front door closed, however, and his footsteps were no longer audible, there was change: in her face, which lost calm and became in some ways like a leaf in late autumn; and in her eyes, which grew large and alarming to look upon, and dark with tears. As she lost all control of her emotions, she rose, gnawing at her hand, and hurried from the room. The two women looked at each other, and in silence followed her. The laborer and I continued to eat, he because of a good appetite, I because of his presence. Finally he rose, looked at me with curiosity and kind-ness, and set out for work.

I stood up and waited for Mrs. Stevens. She came to the door, stopped, and waited for me to speak.

I had nothing to say, and I began to speak words which had no process from my mind:

"I've heard there's very good work near Manchester. They pay fifty an hour there."

Mrs. Stevens looked at me.

"It's road work."

Mrs. Stevens looked at me.

After a few moments I paid her nine dollars, the price for a week's board and lodging. She pulled open a cupboard drawer, opened a cigar-box, and fumbled for change.

"That is right for a week, isn't it," I said.

She counted all the change in the box. "You haven't been here a week," she said. "Your week is up tonight." She gave me a bill. "Have you a quarter?"

I had only a dime in change. "Don't mind it," I said. "Never mind it, please."

"You shall have the breakfast, then," she said. "Free." In the kitchen I heard an old man, trying to cry quietly. She let her hands fall.

I put the dollar and the dime into my pocket. The weeping was suddenly very loud. There was a scuffle across linoleum, and Mr. Stevens burst through the door. Half the fine mustache had been shaved off, and there were strips of plaster on his lips. He took my right hand in both his, and, with no further attempt to control his sobbing, he spoke rapidly through his tears.

It was a burst of mangled oratory, a sort of ex-sermon, ornamented with quotations from the Bible and with misquotations from Victorian poetry; a much prepared and half-forgotten sermon, upon kindliness, and brotherly love, upon the Christian virtues. This it ceased to be, and became lamentation for his own great sins, and loud praise of me and of all my actions. As he became more violent in self-abomination, and more florid in his praise of me, the whole was tinged with involuntary salaciousness, and with the sort of flattery supposedly employed by those whose love is hopeless.

Meanwhile, he looked earnestly into my eyes; and his wife watched us both.

I do not think my expression changed, during the several minutes he talked on. He found no encouragement, and no hope of encouragement, and at last he stopped, and, still clutching my hand, merely looked at me, his tears in balance.

Both of them looked at me. They were waiting for me to speak. Anything I might have said would have been better than silence; I knew that then; but there was nothing to say. There was nothing. I merely stood and looked back at them, and as I looked, I saw understanding come to fulness in their minds.

I saw that the old man understood this: although you could not do as I wished, you were kind to me. I was happy in your company, and in talking to you. But you were not truly kind, you did not truly understand. You deceived me with your kindness. You really despised me in secret, as openly you despise me now. Nobody, nobody on earth has ever understood it, has ever been kind, and nobody ever will.

I saw that the old woman understood this: you despise my husband. The only feeling you have for the whole thing is hatred and disgust. I can't blame you, you are like the whole world in that: but since you hate my husband, I hate you.

The old man, with this understanding to cherish, burst into new wild weeping, and retired to the kitchen. His wife waited, until, after a moment, I turned, and walked into the parlor. I heard her go into the kitchen.

I stopped for a minute, and looked at their brave wedding photograph; then took my baggage and walked northward from the town.

On the farms, people had been at work for hours. At about nine I climbed to the hill I had visited the night before, left the road, and came to the crest. The sun was high enough, now, to be free of hills and of the tall clouds along the east. The blue was slowly paling into intense light. On a farm to my right, they were cutting a little patch of wheat. Slowly the machine breasted the standing grain, and left a new band of flatness behind it.

Between sky and countryside the sunlight glanced, like a broad sheet of glass; all that I saw lay stunned beneath its clarity, save only the nearer woodlands and the grain, which swarmed and shifted with devious breezes. The sunlight, elsewhere pure and calm, was shrill upon small twisting streams, and upon far-scattered weathervanes, and upon the town clock and steeples in the town, and upon the track tangential to the town. I saw the town hall, where Miss Silk would be busy with county records; I saw the canning factory, where the two older women were at work. Beyond the town, a road was torn up, for a little space; there, the laborer was at work. In some side street, Harbison was mending shoes. Beyond that grove, the new grade-school was rising by degrees; there, Grafton was finishing his ditch. On Water Street, near the tracks, the old woman would be about her housework, by now.

The header had made a full round, now; it was turning the corner to go around again. A few more rounds, and the entire patch would be cut.

Winter Eclogue

R. S. Fitzgerald

The wound is stiffened in the chest, and the equerries
Shut their blue fists in their trouser pockets.
Smoke falls in the early morning by the door.
A packet of excellent spices is come from India
To be preserved for His Grace's funeral,
The seventh duke, and to his heirs forever
Recipients of these arms. The lady is twice bereft.
Over the stairs the armoured light, drifting
Moves the hours, the absent voices, and the dark
Shepherds, the color of their eyes like leaves.

Yesterday Mr. Hamilton is reported to have spoken
About new hangings for the east hall. His sword.
And mention of an old league broken in the Low Countries. Years ago
When the child died the prior rode from the abbey
A wet mare, and in he came, blowing his hands.
Tonight we'll have snow. Do you remember Cockrell?
They were all in there singing by the fire
And the window all of a sudden smashed in, and those bastards . . .

That was the autumn. Nothing from the queen
Whose business is muffled up in Austria
Spain, Flanders, the south sailings and the west.
My friend
Lacing his leather on with surgeon's hands
Pale as Jesus he was, the groveling toad
Through ice-rime after the lanterns, lurching
Pikes, mattocks, the whole country crossed with light.
Here are the stones and ossuaries, graves,
Memorials of mice that scratch and perish,
The elegiacs cut with considered pride.
Pain on the right side when you turn, cough badly,
Find no record of service. The old nurse in the park
Visits me sometimes but I'm lonely here.
If you like, the little man who brings wood in the evening,
He would know: he says it was a fine cortege.

Park Avenue

R. S. Fitzgerald

Between dinner and death the crowds shadow the loom of steel.
Engines dwell among the races; the tragic phrase
Falls soundless in the tune and tremble of them.
Spun beyond the sign of the virgin and bloomed with light
The globe leans into spring.
The daughter from the dead land returns.
Between the edges of her thighs desire and cruelty
Make their twin temples, whereof the columns sunder
In the reverberations of time past and to come.
A pestilence among us gives us life.
Sparks shot to the cylinders explode softly
Sheathing speed in sleep.

White Valley

Robert Fitzgerald, 1933

COMING down fast
          the snow burns on my wrist
Speed leaning from the glittering
          height, swept to the hollow
The intent two-legged dot
          jerks out, kicks far below &
Granite ten miles away is
          peace, the air is sunlight

That winter at Davos my young brother died
Of formal logic. Glaciers were his friends.

I dreamed I found him
          alone in a dark room
Many years after, I
          dreamed this: the boy still
Lying there quite still
          through frostpurple evening
Bearded & warm, breathing

          "Try not to pass out"

The goddammed motor stalled: can we reach the field?

I curse the bleeding suntanned Swiss
          who shouts back "Pardon?"
My groin aching, armpits steaming
          sweat under woolens
A long way up & hard, setting
          each ski in the fine snow

Panem Et Circenses

CYRUS L. SULZBERGER

Being but a cycle we recur
To each and all the things that were,
Pagan gods patrol their beats,
And Priapos hides in rumble seats.

TIME

The Weekly Newsmagazine

By the HARVARD ADVOCATE

PHLEETPHOOT PHEIDIPPEDES

Tersely: *"Why I ran every step of the way . . ."*

(See NATIONAL AFFAIRS)

Volume CXVIII   Number 6

IGNITE!   IGNITE!

(A perhaps too personal statement;

"Nevertheless, I will sign it".)

Ezra Pound

THERE is, if not a time-spirit, at any rate a TIME-FOETOR that reeks through the whole of an infected period, stinking from each prominent vent-hole. No man who lived in power through the Harding-to-Hoover epoch smirking and unprotesting is fit to instruct the next generation. For 25 years I have see the un-dignity, whether it were Lorimer pouring out hooey by the week to the million, floated on the "buy-more-this-that-&-the-other"; whether it were Dunkus, Wukkus, or Flobbor presiding over this or that beanery; or Coolidge setting the ALL TIME record for pusillanimity, but drawing his salary: all emit the identical pustulence.

Whatever department of "learning" general thought can pervade becomes of one flaccidity, a treacherous morass on which no building can rise.

The college presidents of America dare not read either HOW TO READ or my ABC of ECONOMICS. The cretinism of their era has left them no shred of decency. Their age did not face the facts. Lippman does not face the facts. The editors of the commercial "literary" weeklies are still unaware of their grease paint.

The economists ignore simple facts of history. The degree of sensitivity in the "clercs" could only be represented by an ideogram comprised of the portraits of all the members of our so-called Academy. From this "BODY", as Henry James called it with an intonation, no member has ever resigned, any more than a hand or a finger could resign from any somatic agglomerate at any downtown mortician's.

At the election of Nick Butler as president, no member resigned.

F.D.R. is so busy investigating Wiggins & banks that he has had no time to investigate "Foundations". It is as difficult to get an American to think evil of a "Foundation" as it wld. have been in 1860 to get a Russian peasant to spit on an ikon. A "Foundation" in the American language means a milch-cow.

I defy the assembled American college presidents to read the terms of Carnegie's donation to his Foundation for Peace, to consider what has been done during the past years with the half million dollars which the American people are condemned annually to pay to that otiose institution, and THEN to say whether this be or be not malversation of funds and an atrocious betrayal of trust.

The CAUSES of war have received NO attention. The Foundation's funds have gone into the pockets of alleged researchers, etc., who have done nothing to fulfill the terms of the endowment.

Count Mensdorf years ago wrote to the Washington office, pointing out that there *are* ECONOMIC CAUSES of war. The effect of this message has been, I think, nil; though I will cheerfully correct this statement if it contains any component of error.

At any rate, the secretary *answered* Mensdorf's letter, which is all one cld. have expected during that phase of American government.

When Lorimer's rag told the American people by the million that Kreuger was "more than a financial titan", no voice from subsidized professordom was lifted in rectification.

The inflation in business, the blah in economics, the assinine instruction in literature, are all of a perfume, a whorefume, a skunkery, of one smell, of one root at bottom.

Harvard has been spared Butler; Cross has risen to political eminence; Harvey, who didn't correct the lies in his paper, has passed into oblivion. Eliot, picked as a safe man, perhaps the only safe man among educated writers under fifty, was not on speaking terms with the late Pres. Lowell; and dear ole Binyon has been called to correct the too advanced and dangerous daring of Eliot. My gorrrd wotter country . . . whatter nedderkashun . . .

American publishers deserve the obvious distortion of their title.

In 1917 I handed American publishing the chance to take over the lead from London. The old rotting Capital by the Thames guttered down into the garbage. For ten years England did nothing. New York had the chance to take over, to lead, to bring out live books before Europe knew them or printed them.

Did she do it? She Did Not!

Even Paris is staggering up again; a faint stirring shows under the ashes. London is up again—a year, two years, ten years, 15, ahead of America. My gorrr wotter Kountry . . . My Gorrrd wotter COUNTRY . . .

Dithering ignorance in the wilds; dithering timidity in the Eastern cities.   There is not a contemporary newspaper in the Union.

Rapallo, November, 1933

A PROBLEM OF (SPECIFICALLY) STYLE

The Sage of Rapallo Discusses Among Other Things the Nature of Religion

Ezra Pound

EVEN THE death of the last survivors of the clogging and war-causing generation that preceded us, will not bring a new and illumined era unless at least the élite of ours or (that being unlikely) the next, make some effort to understand the function of language, and to understand why a tolerance for slipshod expression in whatever department of writing gradually leads to chaos, munitions-profiteers, the maintenance of wholly unnecessary misery, omnipresent obfuscation of mind, and a progressive rottenness of spirit.

Mr. Eliot in advocating a species of Christianity has, so far as I am aware, neglected to define religion. His readers are befogged as to whether he wants a return to the Christian Church (as it was in the year Sixteen Hundred in Chiswick) or whether he wants us to turn religious, or in what order.

There *is* a distinct difference in Anschauung between men who believe that the world needs religion and those who believe it needs some particular brand or flavour of religion.

Among professionals, that is, men who get their board and keep by religion, it is today almost impossible to find any professional competence in theology. I have yet to find a professor or religious writer who has bothered to formulate a definition of "religion" before touting his own particular brand. George Washington, refusing to be cornered and driven into profession of belief in an undefined something or other, commended the "beneficent influence of the Christian Religion."

Given an effect, even the most agnostic and merely logical mind will admit a cause.

Given the necessity of volition, the freest thinker might admit the necessity or advisability of a direction of that volition.

Given an increasing awareness that there exists circumvolving us a vast criminal class that never infringes any "law" on the statue books or breaks an enforceable police regulation, the more perceptive tend in some cases to believe in the usefulness of a "general disposition", you might even say they incline toward a belief in the *need* of a general disposition, toward the Whole, the cosmos, and even toward the consciousness inherent in that cosmos.

No man is aware of that consciousness save by way of his own, but believing in a great telephone central or not, or in minor centrals or not, no scientist can deny at least fragmentary portions of consciousness which have a sum, a totality, whether or no they have coherent inter-organization.

The minute a man takes into consideration the totality of this universe, or the sum of this consciousness, he has, whether he wants it or not, a religion. And some phase of that consciousness in his *theos*: whether coherent or non-coherent, labile, intermittent or whatever.

And into his thought and action there enters a component influence affecting, in all degrees from the infinitestimal up to 100%, his volition, and his specific acts or the general tone of his action.

Religion in humanist terms would be valuable in the degree in which it directed a man toward the welfare of humanity (judged not necessarily in mere terms of eating, but also in terms of mental condition, peace of mind, mental vitality).

Granting that mankind may need a religion; that, in concrete instances, many men will—so long as they lack one—do nothing that is of the faintest use or of the faintest possible interest, I should have to have some evidence that the given professional had reason for touting his own particular brand in preference to any three dozen others; and such evidence would have to come to me, either from a greater efficiency in good action or a greater mental clarity and honesty as displayed in his manifest thought. Thought to be manifest would have to be so, either by verbal expression or by demonstration in some other sensible medium.

A manifest funking of straight thought or honest action in any specific field falling under one's examination, would obviously throw out the fakers, i. e., it would obviously bring any brand of religion into disrepute with thoughtful observers, whether this applied to an individual exponent or to an "organization".

The Medieval Church in its wisdom placed excessive sloth among sins. In no field has the sloth of our time been more foul and oppressive than in the search for clear terminology. In no field have the English-speaking nations been more damned than in failing to dissociate ideas.

In all fields this muddiness is so great that any field serves as repulsive example; and among all morasses the economic morass is the dankest.

Experts representing their nations in international congresses are no better than timorous instructors holding their jobs on sufferance and fearing for the good of their offspring.

Lacking a religion or a decent ethical base, there is no reason why Bug'ush and Co. shouldn't be content in creating confusion. Lacking an ethical basis there is no argument against the perpetual (as I see it) infamy or dragging discussion continually onto the unessential, and continually away from the search after truth and knowledge.

If scientists are not always free from a personal vanity, we have at least proof that in the laboratories a great number of men do search after biological and chemical knowledge without being continually led off into personal bickerings petty struggles for precedence. Medical science does and a number of medical scientists do set an example, however, many fools may have on dramatic occasions tried to obstruct a medical hero.

In no science can truth go forward when men are more anxious to show up another man's minor error, or to prove his failure of fool-proof formulation, than to use his perception of truth (however fragmentary) for a greater perception and for the formulation of valid equations.

We were, manifestly, drug up analphabetic in economics. We are manifestly surrounded by an ignorance of economic history which sheds infamy on every college and university and shows up the whole congeries of economic professors as apes with the rarest possible exception.

ADONIC LITURGY

After Bion

Dudley Fitts, Harvard Advocate, 1925

I weep for Adonis: he is dead the fair Adonis
Dead the fair Adonis: the Loves echo my weeping

No more in dusky mantle lay thee down
Kypris no more: but awake O thou desolate
rouse thee and wailing beat on the breast and cry to all
He is dead the fair Adonis!

I weep for Adonis: the Loves echo my weeping
Low is he fallen the fair Adonis
low on the hills: piercèd the snowy thigh
(so white his thigh so white the tusk that smote him!)
and pale is Kypris and wretched
heavy-hearted forsaken
(so white his flesh so black the oozing blood!)
and his eyes are sightless beneath his brow
dark: fixed: his stiffening eyes: and the rose
fades from his lips as fades
the kiss that Kypris never may return
(even in death her kiss is upon his lips
though he lives no longer
nor knows that Kypris kissed him as he passed)

I weep for Adonis: the Loves echo my weeping
Deep deep the wound in the flesh Adonis:
a deeper wound Kythéreia wears in her heart:
around him now
mournfully baying his lovèd hounds lament:
and leafy Oreads shrill his dirge: but she wanders
wailing: the bright Aphroditè: with loosened tresses sorrowing
strays through the spikèd coppice ungirt unsandal'd
and brambles ravish her as she goes
and spilt in the long glades is her holy blood:
often and often she calls his name: her dearest
her Syrian lord her longing
(but from about his navel the darkening blood
flows black on his breast the blood: the snow
beneath his paps is stain'd with the blood of Adonis)

Ah Kythéreia: the Loves echo my weeping
For she has lost her loveliest lord
and her beauty has perished with him:

lovely while Adon lived was Aphrodite
but her glory died for ever with Adonis:
Ah Kythéreia! rings from the uplands
and all the hills give answer *Alas for Adonis!*
The rivers wail their sorrow: the
mountain streams weep for her: weep
for Adonis: and every flower
crimsons with her anguish as still she cries
through thicket and sad highland valley *Adonis!*
Ah Kythéreia! he is dead the fair Adonis!
and Echo mourns *He is dead the fair Adonis.*

And who would not lament the heavy love of Kypris?
for when she saw
when she saw the wound of Adonis flowing ever
his fair thigh fouled in his blood
casting up her hands she cried 'Ah stay
'ill-fated Adonis stay. I would overtake thee
'clasp thee embrace thee mingling lip with cold lip:
'awake but for a little time Adonis
'but for a kiss
'a last kiss
'but for a kiss brief as the life of a kiss:
'and through my mouth
'into my heart from thy innermost soul thy ghost shall glide
'and I will drink to the full the draught of thy sweetness
'and I will cherish thy kiss as it were Adonis:
'for thou leavest me Adonis thou leavest
'me ill-starred Adonis and passest
'to Acheron the sullen King:
'and I live on
'I live on: for I am a god and may not
'follow thee. . .

'Receive O Persephoné my lord
'for thou art stronger than I and all lovely things
'go down to thee:

'(Hapless all-hapless!)

'and weep for Adonis who has forsaken me
'and I fear thee. . .

'O thrice desired O belovèd Dead!
'like a wingèd dream is my longing sped: like a whisper:
'desolate desolate Kythéreia:
'idle the Loves in their halls. . .
'. . . too hardy! and needest thou strive in the chase?

'. . . so fair! and needest thou battle the raging boar?'
Thus complained Kythéreia and the Loves echoed her weepin

Ah Kythéreia: he is dead the fair Adonis
(fast fall the Paphian's tears
fast fall the blood of Adonis
and tears and blood are flowers where they fall:
his blood engenders roses
her tears anemonè)

I weep for Adonis: he is dead the fair Adonis
No more O Kythereía bemoan thy love in the forest
not for Adonis is the couch of straw
not for Adonis the lonely couch of leaves:
but let him have thy bed the fair Adonis
in thy bed O Kythéreia
(fair is he in death: in death so fair: as one sleeping)
tenderly
lay him to rest
in the coverlets where the long long night he tarried
slumbering deep with thee on the golden pile
that longs for Adonis Adonis:

Bring blossoms also and garlands
(his are they in death
as he died let every flower wither)
sprinkle him with Syrian oils with balsam
(let every perfume fade
Adonis hath lost his sweetness)

I weep for Adonis: he is dead the fair Adonis
In his web of purple he lies the delicate Adonis
and all about him the little Loves lament:
they have shorn their locks for Adonis
and one shatters his bow
and one his feathered shafts
and one has loosed his sandal's latch
and one has trampled his own greywingèd quiver
and one in a chalice of gold brings silver-plashing water
and one laves with all tenderness the cruel gash in his thigh
and one from behind him with his drooping winglets is fanning him
Adonis

Ah Kythéreia: the Loves echo my weeping
This day O Kythéreia grieve no more:
the years revolve
and often hereafter mayest thou mourn Adonis
and in thy loneliness
remember him

SURREALISM 1924-34

Wayne Andrews

> "Surrealism will admit you to death, which
> is a secret society."—André Breton

AMERICANS know the congenial side of modern French literature so well that they half forget that certain poets still resent the Citroën sign on the Eiffel Tower. For not every French writer reacted to the war like Paul Valéry. Not every writer had said that "stupidity was not his strong point;" not every writer welcomed Marshall Pétain under the cupola of the Academy. There were even some artists who thought poetry was essentially October. Those were the surrealists. They it is who have saved French poetry since the war from banquets.

Very unpleasant and impolite they are: they will never enter any academy; they will never praise any general. They are such frienzied foes of the monotonous that they would gladly change the color of the sky of Paris. They are communists (although for the most part outside the party) because they are furious that an armament magnate like François de Wendel can walk the same streets as Pablo Picasso. And naturally enough, relations between the French Communist Party and such passionate admirers of that hermetical painter are sometimes strained.

As surrealism enlisted almost the same adherents as dadaism, it has been referred to as a mere continuation of dada. Yet surrealism is an essentially different intellectual manifestation from dada, that grim humour that fascinated Europe in the early twenties. For the ideal of dada was to create nothing; the ideal of dada was to have no ideal. And as some dadaists were creative, they had to carry on their revolt in surrealism.

What is surrealism? As defined by its leader André Breton, it is "pure psychic automatism, by which it is intended to express verbally, in writing, or by any other means, the real process of thought. It is the dictation of thought, all exercise of reason and every aesthetic and moral preoccupation being absent." But then, what is a definition? To a surrealist a definition might be "a live man mounted on a live horse meeting a live woman leading a live dog."

A less offensive question would be: What are the surrealists? To that their proud painter Dalí replies: "There are existing already in the world a number of incommensurable 'living madmen' who profess to revive 'the same prerogatives for dream and delirium, the same fetichist credit, as usually accorded reality,' who extend at each moment the 'most demoralizing discredit to the rational-logical-practical world,' who exchange the substance and the shadow of objects, the substance and shadow of love, who affront aesthetes and highbrows with the perverse mechanism of erotic imagination, and who emerge at sundown to watch, with infinite cannibal nostalgia, the distant and sparkling sewing machines cut in blocks of ruby: such are the *surrealists*."

So perverse is surrealist influence today that it extends from Belgrade even to New York, where Julien Levy has exhibited those hysterical annihilations of modern painting: the tremulous poached eggs of Salvador Dalí and the gothick monsters of Max Ernst. Even after Breton had said that "we shall not allow the fear of going mad to make us keep the banner of imagination at half-mast," Julien Levy showed Louis Bunuel's surrealist film, "L'Age d'Or." "L'Age d'Or" had already wrought chaos in Paris where it elicited the following eligible comment from the critics of the "Figaro":

"The surrealist film 'L'Age d'Or' in which I defy any recognized expert to find the least artistic value, parades on the public stage the most obscene, repugnant, and wretched episodes. Our country, the family, and religion, are smeared with filth."

Although surrealism has imperiled so many arts, it has profaned none more than literature. How feared they have been, those three feverish writers, Breton, Eluard, and Aragon!

It is even rumored that if a friend of André Breton speaks at all politely to a policeman when he asks the direction, he is no longer a friend of André Breton. That shows how uncompromising the dictator of the movement is, and why certain former surrealists are now journalists.

During the war, he was a young doctor who haunted psychopathic wards. In a neurological center he met the future dada hero Jacques Vaché, who appreciated the comic side of despair. Before he committed suicide by taking an overdose of opium, Vaché used to invite his friends to call upon his mistress and gaze upon her in silent adoration. His chaotic contempt for society was a decisive influence on a young man who was not amused.

During those years when a generation was so bitterly disappointing, Breton was searching. He knew Valéry, he knew Picasso's friend Apollinaire. He was as furious as Gide when Paul Claudel tried to make Rimbaud a posthumous Catholic. But by 1918 the writer who really amazed Breton was Isidore Duvasse, Comte de Lautréamont, a genius clouded in obscurity from the time of his death, shortly before the end of the Second Empire, until the end of the World War. In those prose poems of unbearable beauty, 'Les Chants de Maldoror," Lautréamont had denied society and literature.

Duvasse died in 1870, a few months before the commune set fire to Paris and the last crinoline. Yet so inspired is his imagery that he must have foreseen the angry flames licking the Tuileries. How else could he have seen an image "beautiful as the chance meeting on a dissection table of a sewing machine and an umbrella"? How else could he have issued that splendid warning against compromise: "All the water of the ocean would not be enough to wash out a stain of intellectual blood"?

Breton knew that "Les Chants de Maldoror" were the product of automatic writing. And by 1924, steeped as he was in Freud, he was ready to plunge into the unconscious. He wrote the "Manifeste du Surréalisme" and the vice which Aragon defined as the "wild and passionate use of stupefying imagery" was already recognized.

Breton soon wrote a novel so abrupt that the timid atmosphere of the Ile de France almost forgot to be a pearly gray. That was "Nadja," which told in haunting and shocking dreams the adventures of a demented heroine. The book was especially surrealist in its attitude toward those guardians of society, alienists. The author commented:

"I still don't see how they can deprive a human being of liberty. They locked up Sade, they locked up Nietzsche; they locked up Baudelaire. The process that consists of coming to surprise you at night, putting a strait jacket on you, or doing anything else to control you, is worthy of that of the police, which consists of slipping a revolver in your pocket. I know if I were crazy, and confined for a few days, I would take advantage of a *remission* of my delirium to murder coldly one of those who would fall into my hands, preferably the doctor. At least I would secure solitary confinement like the raving maniacs. Perhaps they would leave me alone then."

One morning when an amiable inmate offered his doctor a blue-penciled copy of the work, French psychiatrists were slightly disturbed.

Giorgio de Chirico, who still believes in ghosts, should have painted the eerie first meeting of André Breton and Paul Eulard. One night when Breton was talking to Picasso at a performance of Appollinaire's "Couleur du Temps," a young man approached him, stammered a few words and finally admitted he had mistaken him for one of his friends who was thought dead at the front. Later on, when Breton came to know Eulard in dada days, he discovered he was the young man of the night of the "Couleur du Temps."

If Breton is the theorist of the movement, Eulard is the artist. His poems have the unproverbial delicacy of the line drawings of Picasso. When he speaks in his most successful book "La Vie Immédiate" of the "height where their breasts' dawn rises to unclothe night," he evokes all the mystery of Picasso's fierce maidens.

"The proletariat alone can sweep God from the face of the earth," stated a manifesto the surrealists all hopefully signed to fire the burning of more Catholic churches by Republican Spain. But of all the signers Louis Aragon was the most hopeful. Until he abandoned surrealism for the communist party he was the most gasping of the group. His anger flamed as high as that of Ravachol, the murderous anarchist of the nineties. How he had enjoyed showing the futility of all bourgeois literature in his "Traité du Style!" When he was not raving he was vicious:

"At news of a revolution, Kant interrupts his walk. Goethe doesn't. What pretention on both sides!"
And at the last he damned the French army in words worthy of Lenin.

Until two years ago, Aragon was famous for the dreamy promenades of "Le Paysan de Paris" which recalled the work of Gérard de Nerval, that beautiful and crazed poet of a hundred years ago. Then came the first number of the French edition of "Literature of the World Revolution." It contained "Front Rouge." The communism in that poem (now available in Cummings' translation) was dangerous enough for Chiappe to be cautious. The magazine was seized. Indicted for inciting to murder and for provoking insubordination in the army, Aragon was only saved from five years in prison by a petition signed by sixty thousand members of the International Red Aid in France. He understood the time had come to choose. He repudiated surrealism, and joined the communists in earnest, although Breton considered complete submission to party discipline a betrayal of the heroes of the poetic drama.

Even though Aragon was the most annoying member of the group, surrealism today is hardly moribund. There is no decadence in the description of New York Dalí wrote for his exposition there.

"To me New York is only a great silent plain of yellow alabaster, where fearsome dry grasshoppers, a few straw watches, and some raisins carried by the wind have just caught on the sticky surface of one year old children entirely covered with a thick coat of white enamel. What immense solitude! It is true (but it only accentuates so much horizontal melancholy) that in the exact center of the plain, rising to a colossal height, are two well known anguished silhouettes, antique statues, representing the celebrated and tragic couple of Millet's *Angelus*. The figure of the man is myself: I am represented as blind, with a golden mouth splashed with excrement, very beautiful feminine breasts, a whip in my hand, and crowned with roses: the female figure is made flesh by Sacher Masoch, her eyes look into mine with infinite sadness, she is dressed in furs and wears an immense lamb chop on her head. At sunset these two silhouettes acquire an irresistible and hallucinating melancholy. The cumulus clouds that rise from the horizon towards the end of day invariably adopt the vague but radiant and golden outlines of Napoleon at the head of his cavalcade. At night—the furs of Sacher Masoch become phosphorescent and one sometimes hears from a distance, tired and monstrous, the agonized bellow of the antediluvian monsters of the exhibition at Chicago.

"New York: why did you erect my statue long ago, long before I was born, higher than another, more desperate than another?"

For Breton has said: "Beauty will be CONVULSIVE or will not exist."

THE HOUND & HORN, 1927-1934

WITH A LETTER FROM VARIAN FRY AS A NOTE

Lincoln Kirstein, 1929

IT'S HARD to remember exactly why The HOUND & HORN was started. I was a freshman in Gore Hall and on the same entry, a floor above, lived Varian Fry. I had some idea of getting on the *Advocate*, but the editor at that time when inspecting candidates gave me the impression that there was not much use in trying. I got two pieces in however; a longish poem about Boston going to pieces, and a parody of Philip Hale's Symphony program books. If I remember correctly, it was coming up on the train from New York, returning from the Christmas vacation in January 1927, that Fry and myself had the idea of a Harvard quarterly. The name came from a poem of Ezra Pound's *The White Stag* ("'Tis the white stag Fame we're hunting, bid the world's hounds come to horn"). We spent a lot of time thinking about it, worrying about format, and rather little as to what was going into it. Consciously or not, it was to be a kind of Harvard *American Mercury* and *London Criterion* and *North American Review* all in one. I'd been reading Henry Adams' *Education* and still think he's said everything one can say about Harvard. We wrote to Rockwell Kent, who very kindly gave us 'children's prices', as he wrote, and did our decorations, cover and colophon for us. Fry and I were very much interested in fine printing and book production at the time and he was our idea of everything 'modern'. Incidentally, the format of the magazine changed five times in seven years, from conservative modernism to a bolder style, and back to conservative modernism and a nice looking book. Presentation was a big worry with us always. The rest of 1927 up to the summer is pretty vague. We did get out an advance issue, or rather, Fry did. I went to England armed with letters to T. S. Eliot. I didn't see him then, but did later, and he was extremely kind, interested, wrote for us and sent us his "Triumphal March". We were ashamed of the advance issue but had a steel die cut with Kent's colophon on it to use on invitations to various functions

the Editors would organize. Die cutting was cheap in England and Fry had very formal ideas about the tone we should keep, because the magazine was only going to be one facet of our activity. We were going to affect the whole cultural life of the University. This we never even made a dent on. There are a lot of details which would only be interesting if they were documented and made precise, which it is impossible to do now. We had a "consultative committee" consisting of Conrad Aiken, Judge Julian Mack, Mr. Martin Mower, the teacher at Harvard whom I owe whatever taste and information about the Fine Arts and many other things that I have, President Neilson of Smith, and Mr. Winship of the Widener. As our sponsors I think we treated them rather ungratefully. When we dropped the name of "A Harvard Miscellany", we dropped them, too. I think there was some talk of whether or not we should thank them. Whether we did or not I don't recall. Often we were thought very rude because we had to make certain compromises in accepting material from graduates for one reason or another, which we didn't want, and then took it out on them for doing it.

The first number appeared in September, 1927 Mr. Anthoenson of The Southworth Press in Portland, Maine, was our midwife and a great help and distinguished craftsman. Fry and I used to make the dummy of the magazine with quantities of paste and those blue examination blank-books. We would drive up to Portland, see the issue through the press, stay the night, and come back without cutting a class. The first number headed off with a quotation from Plato in the original; and the Horn call in Brahms' Quartet Op. 40. We had heard this at a concert at Mrs. Kingsley Porter's house. The horn part was played by a viola, but it made no difference. It was our favorite piece of music. The Crimson made some crack about "Let Mr. Joyce rejoice, let Mr. Pound resound, At the safe arrival of the Horn and Hound". We were also referred to as the Bitch and Bugle.

Even up to seven years later confused people would send us advertisements of prize beagles and airdales, thinking we were a hunting magazine. Newton Arvin, one of the most lucid writers in this country, wrote a fake Journal of one Henry Marston, editing it himself. It still can be read with interest. Henry Russell Hitchcock contributed the opening of his big book on architecture. This was generally considered to be unintelligible on account of its first sentence. It was not. *The New York Times* and *The Herald Tribune* had editorials about our classical quotation which was taken to be a step in the right direction. We had so intended it. We were combining the best traditional elements with the distinction of the present.

The rest of Volume I was distinguished chiefly by R. P. Blackmur's long study of T. S. Eliot, and a note on Strawinsky's "Oedipus Rex", by Roger Sessions, who in his day (1914) had edited the far superior *Harvard Musical Quarterly*. Blackmur did a great deal of good writing for the *Hound & Horn*. It was one of the best reasons for the existence of the magazine. He is not only one of America's best (in book form) unpublished poets. He is also emerging as one of its most respected critics, as his edition of the James' novel prefaces this year testify: his introduction came out originally in our Homage to Henry James (Spring 1934) issue. Blackmur did studies of Eliot, Cummings, Wallace Stevens, Pound, and many book reviews. People used to say the book reviews were the best part of the magazine. That and the chronicles of painting, architecture, etc.

The second volume opened with that marvelous story *Fugue*, by Sèan O'Faolain, since become one of the most splendid Irish writers. He was in Cambridge teaching at Boston College and editing a book of Celtic lyrics. Maybe it wasn't the fault of the College, but I think it was, that inside of two years it let Foster Damon, Conrad Aiken and O'Faolain slip through their by no means rich fingers—rich, that is, as far as practicing men of letters go. Foster Damon's essay on Melville in the Winter issue, and on "Ulysses" in the Fall issue of 1929, were merely examples of his brilliant, intuitive, and genuinely creative critical intelligence.

In the spring of 1929 Blackmur and Bernard Bandler II became editors too. Blackmur was working in the Dunster House Bookshop. He had not been

to College himself, and perhaps that was why he was so amazingly well-educated. His influence on the boys of his time who bought books suggested by him is inestimable. Bandler had himself just graduated. He had a mind that was so fluent, so much the master of intellectual and philosophical abstractions, so deeply involved with the real business of the spirit, that when he first talked to me at any length I was exhausted for two days. He wrote an essay on W. C. Brownell, and others on Charles du Bos and Irving Babbitt. He might have been a rabbi or a priest, and is now doctor of medicine. His influence on the *Hound & Horn*, at least from a critical point of view, was its formulating one. This influence lasted in full strength for four years. Then he became too fully occupied reading and teaching to spend his time on it.

Jim Agee was a freshman living in the Smith Halls. I take great pleasure in remembering we printed his "Ann Garner" in April, 1929, and last week I reviewed his collected verse for The New Republic. His talents are the most considerable of any one that has left Harvard in the last five years, with the exception of George Weller. Malcolm Cowley sent us some poems; Eliot his "Second Thoughts About Humanism". There was far too much about Humanism in the *Hound & Horn*. That was Bandler's interest: not mine. It was all very real to him and remote to me. By the end of the second year the magazine was much less like a weak echo of *The Criterion*.

By the winter of 1930 it had become crystalized pretty well into the form it would be known by. It ceased being purely Harvard for all time. It became what one of our harassed business managers loved to comfort himself by saying: National in scope. But it didn't. We hoped it was going to take the place of *The Dial*, which after its long and valuable existence had recently died, but it didn't. We had, all in all, very little money—even to lose. But now A. Hyatt Mayor and Francis Fergusson became two of the magazine's chief props. They both were then involved with the American Laboratory Theatre. Their essays on the drama, on style, on literature are as good as anyone has written in our time. Mayor is now in the Print Room of the Metropolitan Museum. His time in Greece and Italy, his knowledge of classical literature, his sense and soundness made him one of the best educated, stimulating and creative people who ever wrote for us. His essay on "Translation" (October 1931) is a masterpiece.

We branched out. Herbert Read and Montgomery Belgion of *The Criterion* were writing for us; and at home, Wallace Stevens, Kenneth Burke (Declamations), Allen Tate and Louis Zukofsky, and Ezra Pound. We made a fine alliance with Pound for advice, help, and contributions. We printed nearly everything he sent us, but finally, in spite of his lovely poems and his marvelous letters, we couldn't face the attendant coterie of lame duck discoveries he was always capriciously harboring, and we were relieved to let him be obscene about us in other "little" magazines. (We never considered we were a 'little' magazine, though others may have.)

The magazine was now about 168 pages an issue. We published from four to eight plates an issue, increasingly documentary photos as they reproduced more faithfully than anything else. I got to know and admire Walker Evans, who is perhaps the cruellest and most careful artist photographer of the day. His documents are more telling than any written report, and we printed many of his plates. Kay Boyle's early and good story "Episode in the Life of an Ancestor" came out in the Fall of 1930; Erskine Caldwell's story in the same number wasn't nearly as good as his remarkable "Illuminations" which my co-editors didn't like. I regret not printing that more than anything else in my editorial life, with the exception of one thing. I refused on my own hook Hart Crane's "The Tunnel". This I have never ceased blaming myself for. Why I refused it printing as I did so much bad verse, or at least verse a tenth as distinguished as Crane's, I don't know. Probably some personal, stupid prejudice against the diction. Hester Pickman did some fine, maybe the finest translations of Rainer Maria Rilke that have appeared in English, with a serious study of this great poet, in two parts. We published Paul Valery's essay on Leonardo, and afterwards decided not to run any more foreign work for a while. Our preoccupation should be more strictly American. In the winter of 1930 the magazine had moved to New York. It had a small office at 10 East 43rd Street. Out of self-protection I have literally forgotten the painful incidents attendant upon the removal. Largely through misunderstanding, but not without stupidity, I had almost involved myself in a law suit with the editors of *The Symposium*, with whom we thought we'd like to merge. The matter was settled amicably however. *The Symposium* and *The Hound & Horn* were on excellent terms, exchanged material, and the editors Burnham and Wheelwright became our good friends.

If we ever had any editorial policy it was something like this: one or two long essays in each number, either in series as Blackmur's were, or whatever accidentally interested us. One, or rarely, two good stories by writers *not previously published*, separated each from each by verses, and followed by running comments on the events of the quarter in music (Theodore Chanler, now replacing Philip Hale on *The Boston Herald*), Architecture, Fine Arts, the Drama, Dancing (by myself) and the Film. We had no political orientation at this time (1930-32). The influence of humanism was passing, thank God. Bandler insisted our greatest function was to serve as an independent organ to publish material of excellence not otherwise publishable, to be as far as criticism goes, a magazine of technical literary information for writers and laymen: as far as 'creative' writing, verse or prose, the best in the most talented of unpublished or advance-guard writers. We made some attempts at designing each issue, except for verse and stories, and indeed increasingly refused to accept unsolicited critical material, preferring to assign even the long articles to our growing staff of collaborators, the same as book reviews. As for book reviews, we made no attempt at completeness, but only reviewed books not otherwise taken care of, or books not otherwise reviewed in such an exhaustive way.

I am still proud of a few of our short stories: first of all Katherine Anne Porter's "Flowering Judas" (Spring 1930); "Apology for my Health" (Summer 1930) by Gerald Sykes; Samuel Yellen's "Death of a Girl" (October 1931) and Alvah Bessie's "Only We Are Barren" (Winter 1931). Each had a particular irreducible minimum of excellence. None of them could have been printed in the *Atlantic, Scribner's* or *Harper's*.

New York radically changed the tenor of *The Hound & Horn*. There were less eyes on Europe. We met all the people we had any curiosity about and soon discovered that neither the *Nation, The New Republic* or any other held much hope for us. We used to lunch at an Italian speakeasy at 908 Second Avenue and hope for a clique of writers as influential and as closely bound as those that made the *Nouvelle Revue Française* the best magazine of its type in the world. We wanted to come out monthly, but we were neither sure of the money nor whether or not we would get enough good material.

Typical of this time was the July 1932 issue, which contained contributions by James Joyce, Etienne Gilson, Lawrence Leighton (which prompted Ernest Hemingway's funny reply), H. B. Parkes (whose "Puritan Heresy" was one of our chief claims to fame), Gertrude Stein, Allen Tate (on Hart Crane's suicide), Yvor Winters (his excellent story of horror), and drawings by Gaston Lachaise. Perhaps I take too much credit in saying so, but from then on till its demise three years later, and the credit God knows is to the writers, not to the editor, *The Hound & Horn* was the most interesting young magazine in America, of its nature. We never sold many more than four thousand copies of an issue, but we had nearly seven hundred libraries all over the world on our list. Our circulation was a terrible problem. Ultimately, nothing much was done about it. Our adventures with business managers were more expensive and crushing than our tiny circulation. We refused to go to literary teas, not because we had any prejudice against the literati, but only because we soon saw the people whom they could affect would never read *The Hound & Horn*. It cost fifty cents a copy. I think it cost around forty to print. We lost about eight thousand dollars a year. If we had ever twenty-five thousand dollars a year to spend we could have made it pay for itself in two and a half or three years, I'm pretty sure. We paid very badly for our contributions, but we did pay, not very promptly I'm afraid. But the paying made a lot of difference in any number of specific cases.

The last two years of the magazine's existence was by far the most interesting from every point of view. We were well installed in New York and wholly acclimatized. We had rid ourselves of everything but the vestigial influences of Harvard (we hoped). The mechanics of printing, etc. were admirably handled by Doris Levine, who knows more about the real *Hound & Horn* than anyone ever will. The Editors were now Bandler, Hyatt Mayor, and myself. Our campaign for nationalization had made Allen Tate and Yvor Winters regional editors: They sent material from the neo-agrarians around Nashville and the neo-classicists of Leland Stanford, and were a great help. Particularly to me personally Winters was of great aid—in all matters relating to verse. Himself a fine poet, poetry; as he used to rail at me —he felt "as a life and death matter." My editorial taste was constantly in a state of burning shame from his explicit and explosive letters.

The next idea that preoccupied *The Hound & Horn* came from Tate and the southern regionalists. Donald Davidson's important analysis of "Sectionalism in the United States" appeared and provided subjects for our political conversations for a year. It was to have been followed by pieces on Calhoun, Ruffin and Rhett, and the Dialectic of Secession, the origins of the Civil War. These articles were not written. I had come in contact with an ex-anarchist who now called himself Max Nomad. He interested me in the idea of revolutionary principle and his articles on Marx and Bakunin, on Nechayev, gave a fine background of revolutionary history in the nineteenth century. Back in 1929 we had published Jere Abbott's "Soviet Diary". Eisenstein had sent us one of his explosive pieces on film theory. And now Harry Potamkin became our film critic. Harry was a wholly charming, gentle and indignant person. He was the first practicing communist I had ever met and affected the later *Hound & Horn* a good deal. He was encyclopedically informed about the movies. He used to take me to prevues and his criticism of Pabst, René Clair, Pudovkin and Eisenstein are permanent history and will be reprinted. Harry was one of the good reasons for our existence. Articles we paid him to write could not have come into print any other way. When he was dying, Walker Evans offered his blood in transfusion, but it was no use. Harry Potamkin was a rare and very fine person. He burned, literally burned with his ideas of social abuse and exploitation. Since then I have met other communists who have this consuming fire and there is nothing more impressive to see as a personal characteristic. Politically we were always pretty vague, except to have nothing much to do with politics. I remember at the beginning of our last volume in the fall of 1933, Bandler suddenly appearing in *The Hound & Horn* office at 545 Fifth Avenue. He counselled me to stay clear of politics. That the next decade was to be so full of them, if the magazine was to exist its only function was to be a repository of the accidental good, neither with leanings left or right. He gave me good reasons for this (as always), stayed an hour and left. I had not seen him then for over a year and have not seen him since. As usual the impact of his authority influenced me, although I realize now that had the magazine continued it would have been definitely left. My two painter friends, Philip Reisman and Ben Shahn (of the Sacco and Vanzetti murals), and Harry Potamkin had shown me the great richness in revolutionary subject matter. *The Hound & Horn*, up even to its end, was pretty consciously, isolatedly artistic, and I don't think it was a bad thing at all. It was primarily a magazine of techniques, how to write, paint, photograph and film, although what do with the technique after you got it, seemed increasingly more clear.

In the summer of 1933 I went to Europe for the first time in four years. I realized then there was little of interest either on the continent or in England for an American. Any ideas of an extended stay abroad, with the exception of Russia, seemed pointless for an American artist or writer. Mr. A. R. Orage to whom I had once been too shy about showing *The Hound & Horn*, gave me a lot of good advice, as he has done to so many others. Through him I met his friends of *The New English Weekly*, which though nearly entirely devoted to the cause of Social Credit, reflected his admirable tact and suggestiveness. I also got to know Stephen Spender with whom I'd previously corresponded since I'd admired his verse so much. We made many plans for internationalizing the magazine as an agency against reaction in every form. We talked a great deal about war and watched Mosley's fascists walk in threes to Trafalgar Square, because they didn't have enough to make four in a line, though I daresay now they can have five, if they want. Spender hoped to have something in every successive number of *The Hound & Horn,* and except for the October 1933, he did. His remarkable story, "The Burning Cactus" had come out in a small Oxford magazine the year before. We printed it in January 1934. It was agreeable to hear again the protests of numerous people at our unpleasantness, our perversity, our bad taste. *The Hound & Horn* was full of bad taste, and that is really a boast, considering all the good taste we had crammed into our eyes and ears for four years at Harvard. We also had good taste, but it was rapidly waning by the time the magazine closed. It always filled us with joy to see other magazines like *Harpers, Scribner's* and the *Atlantic,* print stories we had rejected.

Many of our authors, by "our" I mean people whom we were the first to publish, have of course had books published. I got to be friendly with publishers in New York, first on the hope they'd give us an ad, then when I knew that was hopeless, so I could have ready access to them in recommending books. Janet Lewis (The Invasion), Katherine Anne Porter (Flowering Judas), Josephine Johnson (Now in November), George Tichenor (Glibson), David de-Jong (Belly Fulla Straw), Hazel Hawthorne (Salt House), were some of "our" later writers whom we can't take entire credit for, but still. Robert Smith, whose "Love Story" is perhaps the best "short" story we ever printed (April 1933) has been having stories in *Esquire,* etc. His novel about the Bonus Army will be something to read. He came into the office one day. I'd never seen him before. His name was Smith. He had a story and his wife was having a baby and if I liked the story it would be easier. I did, very much, paid him in advance (which I was not supposed to do). He promised to name the child after me, which

I've not forgiven him for failing to do, although he named a character in a detective story after me.

The Henry James number (April 1934) was definitely our masterpiece. Bandler had bought his unpublished manuscript project for The Ambassadors, at the auction of George Harvey's effects three years before and had given it to Hyatt Mayor as a wedding present. This was the great focus of the issue, but there were also articles by Marianne Moore, Lawrence Leighton, Edmund Wilson, Francis Fergusson, Stephen Spender, Newton Arvin, R. P. Blackmur, Edna Kenton (the greatest Jacobite in America), H. R. Hays, Glenway Wescott and Robert Cantwell. It sold very well, for a dollar a copy. We had plans for similar ones on Herman Melville and Walt Whitman. The idea came from the Hommage à Proust, Rimbaud, Mallarmé, etc. numbers of the *Nouvelle Revue Française*. Gertrude Stein did not finish her piece in time for inclusion, and Eliot, after two refusals, finally decided he had nothing to say.

The magazine died because it cost too much. It could never pay for itself, and because it seemed less important than other things I was doing. All the other editors had for the past two years been otherwise occupied. Personally I was an editor by a chance, and always a weak one. I had little interest in publishing anything I did not myself like. I never thought of our "public". I always assumed the only people who read *The Hound & Horn* were the people who wrote for it. My father who unhesitatingly put up with it for seven years, used to complain no one could ever understand what we printed, and I always said he and they never took the trouble to read it. I used to write far too long reviews of books, which meant a lot to me (and I'm afraid to few others). When we finally shut up Malcolm Cowley wrote a singularly ungracious piece about us in *The New Republic*, the idea being, well, well: so what. Maybe he was right. I did get some touching and generous letters from subscribers and contributors regretting it. There were at least four schemes on hand to resurrect it, one of which had a kind of advanced insanity which attracted me strongly. I knew it was nuts, but I loved that scheme. It all blew up when some (I was never quite sure what, how, or why) British bonds depreciated in value between Arizona and New York.

Yvor Winters had been interested in *The Magazine*, which was being nicely printed in California. We more or less bequeathed our mantle to them. I'm not sorry we did now, although Winters and myself have both ceased to care much for *The Magazine*. It's too scrappy and salad-like. Any efforts to revive *The Hound & Horn* would receive little help from me. No publishing house would take it over and indeed, it reached far too few people. I always thought there were 25,000 people in the country who would have liked to have read it, if we could have afforded them two dollars a year to pay them for their trouble.

The Hound & Horn provided a lot of miscellaneous pleasure, pain, surprise and tedium for those involved. I think it is likely to be the last of its kind of paper. Or am I too hopeful? The future of young journalism will certainly not be as inefficient or as ignorant of possibility. We were just learning when we stopped. The future of young journalism must certainly lie somewhere near pamphleteering, the staff-written magazine like *Fortune*, or *The New Masses*. As the track coach used to tell my brother when he was running in Harvard and had lost his race: "That's all right sweetheart, it's not so much the races you win (snarl) as the friends you make."

*   *   *   *   *

A Note by Varian Fry

Dear Lincoln,

Thanks for sending me the manuscript and asking for my comments on it. It was interesting to see how you remember the early days of the *Hound & Horn*, and how much your account of its beginnings differs what I should have written about it. Perhaps it is because you are writing for the *Advocate* that you say so little about the part that magazine played in bringing the *H & H* to birth. But you don't mention the equally important, and far less negative, part of the *Harvard Monthly*—I can't quite make out why.

As I remember it, you and I decided to publish a magazine—a Harvard magazine—because we thought the *Advocate* was very, very bad indeed. It was so schoolboyish, and we were so self-consciously aware of Not Being Schoolboys Any Longer. We knew about the *Monthly,* had looked over the files of it in the Widener, and had lamented its untimely death.* We thought that Harvard deserved a mature magazine like the *Monthly,* one that would command the respect of our more discerning elders and make a place for itself in the history of literary magazines. We despaired of ever lifting the *Advocate* to that plane . . . in the first place because it is so much easier to begin afresh than to rebuild what others have made, and also because, whether rightly or wrongly, we believed that neither of us could ever "make" the *Advocate* board: it seemed so much more a club in those days than a magazine. I suspect that in this we were rationalizing an ambition to make a sensation, but at the time the social obstacle seemed very real to us.

And so we thought we'd publish a magazine of our own. Our early ideas, worked over in the winter of 1926-'27, were very simple. In fact, I am sure that we began by thinking of it as a *multigraphed* publication: though that notion was soon abandoned in favor of laid paper, Caslon Old Style type, and deckle-edged cover stock. But we never, in those cold winter days on the Charles, lost sight of the fact that it was to be a *Harvard* magazine, "A Harvard Miscellany," as we called it. Do you remember that one of our first projects was a series of critical articles about Harvard men: T. S. Eliot, Henry James, George Santayana, Henry Adams, and others? Each article was to be accompanied by a bibliography, for in addition to being bright the *Hound & Horn* was to be scholarly—we were much influenced by Eliot's *Criterion,* as you say. We published the article on Eliot (by Blackmur), and with it a bibliography, but after that the project went astray (though we continued to announce it in our editorials). Yet your final issue, on Henry James, was only the realization of an idea we talked about over seven years ago.

With these schemes we had also another, to bring to the consciousness of Harvard the recent developments, in art and literature, it seemed to us to be ignoring, to its own cost. I was an admirer of Joyce,

* It was cut off by the war. Ed.

you of Eliot. We had both read Gertrude Stein, looked at Picasso, listened to Strawinski. They seemed to us important, and we felt that Harvard undergraduates ought to know more about them than they did. It was to hail the new and glittering world they and their influences were creating, and to bid farewell to the stodgy in the nineteenth century and its heavy hand on the twentieth, that I chose the "Plato" distich and wrote that first editorial. Unfortunately, the reviewers thought that by them we had meant to turn our backs on America and join the expatriates, and some of them took us to task for a fault of which we were really not guilty at all.

As the *H & H* became established we gradually lost sight of our original aims, unwisely, I think. In our effort to be mature we came to scorn not only schoolboyishness but collegeboyishness, and much of what we published was certainly above the heads of our intended audience, as it was sometimes above our own. Even then I felt vaguely that we were going off the track, but I wasn't sure enough of myself to say exactly how or where. It seems to me now that in that transition period the *H & H* was floundering between Harvard and the "national (if not international) scope," and that it suffered for it. But at the time I was too immersed in detail to know. We used to go at our task with spirit, as you say, get paste and scraps of paper all over the room, read galley proof with extraordinary devotion, and then at the last minute practically climb into the presses to see that nothing went wrong: during its first two years, I insisted on seeing press proof of every page before the *H & H* was finally run. The result was more rewarding in the reproductions than in the letter-press.

But when Bandler came in, bringing with him Humanism, I *knew* that we were wrong. There is no point, I suppose, in dwelling on what was a family quarrel. Still unable to formulate my own ideas, I found myself carrying out perfunctorily the very arduous duties of a managing editor, and so I quit, not very graciously or politely, I am afraid. After that the *H & H* went to New York, and I lost sight of it for some time. I had wanted it to be a Harvard magazine, to reflect the best of Harvard past and present, and to bring to Harvard the best outside: those were aims I could understand and sympathize with. But with an international review I could not cope, and I knew it. From that time on the magazine was yours and Bandler's, and I can add nothing to its history that is not apparent to any reader.

But as I glance over the "statements of purpose" with which we filled the editorial pages of the earliest issues, I feel that the modest beginnings of the *Hound & Horn* ought to be brought out more clearly than they are in what you have written. It was to have been "an attempt," we said, rather pompously, "to provide a great university with a medium of expression worthy of the most imaginative, creative work that university fosters or influences." That in its later life it became something wholly different ought not, I think, to be allowed to obscure the fact that in the beginning it was just a Harvard Miscellany.

As ever,

VARIAN

New York, November 26, 1934

FRAGMENT OF A CHORUS FROM "PANIC"

A VERSE PLAY BY ARCHIBALD MacLEISH

The play is a play of the bank panic in February and March 1933. Its protagonist (McGafferty) is the great industrialist of his time and his time's greatest banker. The theme is the conflict between this man and the sense of fatality and inescapable destruction which is now familiar in our civilization. The choruses are spoken from a street crowd gathered at night before an electric news announcer of the Times Square type. The chorus swings through the moods of belief in the Great Man to doubt of his greatness to desire to escape from his shadow. The present fragment is from a chorus of the first type.

A MAN: Overthrowing McGafferty!
Even fools would have laughed at it!

A MAN: Name known in the foreign
Mountains: spoken in wars:
Spoken in all men's tongues—
Like the words for salt and for hunger!

A MAN: Spoken by signs and among the
Nakedest men and in cities and
Over the water pits in the
Wild plains and at fords:
At the camel halts on the borders!

A Man: Over the zinc bars and
Over the glass!

A Man: And in harbors and
Far at sea—the stokers
Clanging the coal in!

A Man: Spoken by
Mouths: stamped on the steel—
Lettered on ocean keels on the
Cold plates—the water
Washing the weeds on it!

A Man: Taught from the
Grip of a gang boss' gun to the
Niggers naked in sunlight!

A Man: Dug out of wounds—splinters of
Shrapnel showing it!

A Man: Printed on
Fifty gallon cans on the
Saddled mules by the shanties!

A Man: Overthrowing McGafferty!
Overthrowing the half of the
Common world—if they could!

GLITTERING PIE

Henry V. Miller

DEAR FRED:

I will probably take the Champlain, the boat I arrived on, because it is French and because it leaves a day earlier than necessary. I will bring the stockings for Maggy—and anything else I can think of. Don't know yet about going to the Villa Seurat, but Hotel des Terrasses suits me down to the ground—because it's 13th Arondissement and no ecologues. Make sure my bike is there. I am going to use it! And where is my phono? I am bringing back some of the famous jazz hits, the crooning, swooning lullabys sung by the guys without —. (The popular favorite is: "I Believe in Miracles." *Miracles!* How American! Well —, I'll explain all this in detail when I see you, and have a fine bottle of wine handy, a mellow one, a costly one. Here nothing but California vintages, or dago red, which is vile stuff. One must "alkalize" every day . . . . I'll explain that too, later.)

So, Joey, what are we going to do for a living, hein? Search me! But I feel that we're going to live just the same. Anyway, I come . . . . The Jew who published my notes on N. Y. C. in that revolutionary Dance Program got back at me by entitling it: "I came, I saw, *I fled.*" The expatriates are anathema to the Americans, particularly to the Communists. I have made myself heartily disliked everywhere, except among the dumb Gentiles who live in the suburbs and guzzle it over the weekends. With those blokes I sing, dance, whistle, make merry the whole night long. I have nothing in common with them aside from the desire to enjoy myself. To know how to enjoy oneself is something unknown here. Usually it consists in making a loud noise. At Manhasset one night Emil and I did the cakewalk so strenuously that Emil dislocated — — — —. It was a marvellous night in which we drank ourselves sober. Towards the end I sat down and, striking every wrong note on the piano, I played as only Paderewski himself could play, *if he were drunk.* I broke a few keys and every nail on my fingers. Went to bed with a Mexican hat three feet broad. It lay on my stomach like a huge sun-flower. In the morning I found myself in the child's bedroom and

beside me a little typewriter made of hard rubber which I couldn't write on, drunk as I was. I also found a rosary and crucifix awarded by the Society of the Miraculous Medal, Germantown, Pa. It was *"indulgenced for a Happy Death and the Way of the Cross."*

I have had a lot of funny experiences, but few gay ones. When I get back to Paris I shall remember the evenings spent sitting on couches in studios with everybody talking pompously and callously about social-economic conditions—with cruel lapses of Proust and Cocteau. (To talk of Proust or Joyce today in America is to be quite up to the minute! Some one will ask you blandly—"What is all this crap about *Surrealisme?* What *is* it? Whereupon I usually explain that *Surrealisme* is when you — — your friend's beer and he drinks it by mistake.)

Met William Carlos Williams the other night and had a rousing time with him at Hiler's place. Holty arrived with two dopey brother-in-laws, one of whom played the piano. Everybody crocked, including Lisette. Just before all hands passed out some one yelled—"all art is local"—which precipitated a riot. After that nothing is clear. Hiler sits in his drawers, with legs crossed, and plays "Believe it Beloved," another hit of the season. The janitor comes and raises hell—he was an aviator for Mussolini. Then come the Dockstadter Sisters who write for the pulps. After that Monsieur Bruine who has been in America 39 years and looks exactly like a Frenchman. He is in love with a dizzy blonde from the Vanities. Unfortunately she got so drunk that she puked all over him while sitting on his lap. He's cured of her now.

I mention these little details because without them the American scene is not complete. Everywhere it is drunkenness and vomiting, or breaking of windows and smashing heads. Twice recently I narrowly missed being cracked over the head. People walk the streets at night lit up and looking for trouble. They come on you unexpectedly and invite you to fight—for the fun of it! It must be the climate—*and the machine.* The machines are driving them screwy. Nothing is done by hand any more. Even the doors open magically: as you approach the door you step on a treadle and the door springs open for you. It's hallucinating. And then there are the patent medicines. Ex-lax for constipation—everybody has constipation!—and Alka-Seltzer for hang-overs.

Everybody wakes up with a headache. For breakfast it's a Bromo-Seltzer—with orange juice and toasted corn muffins, of course. To start the day right you must *alkalize*. It says so in all the subway trains. High-pressure talks, quick action, money down, mortgaged to the eyes, prosperity around the corner (it's always around the corner!), don't worry, keep smiling, believe it beloved, etc. etc.

The songs are marvellous, especially as to words. They betray the incurable melancholy and optimism of the American race. I wish I were a foreigner and getting it from scratch. A good one just now is: "The Object of my Affection can change my Complexion . . . ." I'll bring this along too.

At the burlesk Sunday afternoon I heard Gypsy Rose Lee sing "Give Me a Lei!" She had a Hawaiian lei in her hand and she was telling how it felt to get a good lei, how even mother would be grateful for a lei once in a while. She said she'd take a lei on the piano, or on the floor. An old-fashioned lei, too, if needs be. The funny part of it is the house was almost empty. After the first half-hour every one gets up nonchalantly and moves down front to the good seats. The strippers talk to their customers as they do their stunt. The *coup de grace* comes when, after having divested themselves of every stitch of clothing, there is left only a spangled girdle with a fig leaf dangling in front—sometimes a little monkey beard, which is quite ravishing. As they draw towards the wings they stick their bottoms out and slip the girdle off. Sometimes they darken the stage and give a belly dance in radium paint. It's good to see the belly button glowing like a glow worm, or like a bright half-dollar. It's better still to see them — — —, — — — — — — — —. Then there is the loud speaker through which some idiotic jake roars: "Give the little ladies a hand please!" Or else— "now, ladies and gentlemen, we are going to present you that most charming personality fresh from Hollywood—Miss Chlorine Duval of the Casino de Paris." Said Chlorine Duval is generally streamlined, with the face of an angel and a thin squeaky voice that barely carries across the footlights. When she opens her trap you see that she is a half-wit; when she dances you see that she is a nymphomaniac; when you go to bed with her you see that she is syphilitic.

Last night I went to the Hollywood Restaurant, one of those colossal cabaret entertainments that cost a dollar and a half, sans vin, sans pourboires. Cold sober you watch a string of dazzling ponies, fifty or more, the finest wenches in the land and empty as a cracked peanut shell. The place is like a huge dance hall, thousands of people eating at once, guzzling it, socking it away. Most of them stone sober and their eyes jumping out of their sockets. Most of them middle-aged, bald, addle-pated. They come to hear "torch songs" sung by middle-aged sirens. Sophie Tucker, the principal event of the evening, sings about a fairy whom she married by mistake. When she says "Nuts to you!" he answers—"Oh swish!" She is very fat now, Sophie, and has blue veins relieved by 36 carat rocks. She is advertised as "the last of the hot mommers." America isn't breeding any more of this variety. The new ones are perfect—tall, long-waisted, full-busted and rattle-headed. They all sing through the microphone, though one could hear just as well without it. There is a deafening roar which, without any wine under your belt, makes you sick and dizzy. They all know how to shout. They love it. They develop whiskey voices—hard, sour, brassy. It goes well with the baby face, the automatic gestures, the broken-hearted lullabys. A colossal show that must cost a fortune and yet leaves you absolutely unmoved—despite the fine busts I mentioned a while back. I do honestly believe that a poor, skinny, misshapen French woman with just an ounce of personality would stop the show. She would have what the Americans are always talking about but never achieve. She would have *it*. America is minus *it*. *You* think maybe I'm sour on my own country, but so help me God, that's what's the matter with America—*IT*. "They" and "it" go together—follow me?

And now, Joey, I'm going to tell you a little more about my lonely nights in New York, how I walk up and down Broadway, turning in and out of the side streets, looking into windows and doorways, wondering always when the miracle will happen, and if. And nothing ever happens. The other night I dropped into a lunch counter, a cheesy looking joint on West 45th Street, across the way from the Blue Grotto. A good setting for "The Killers." I met some pretty tough eggs, all dressed immaculately, all sallow complexioned and bushy eye-browed. Faces like sunken craters. The eyes mad and piercing, eyes that pierce right through you and appraise you as so much horse meat. There were a few whores from Sixth Avenue together with some of the most astonishingly beautiful chorus girls I ever laid eyes on. One of these sat next to me. She was so beautiful, so lovely, so fresh, so virginal, so outrageously Palm Olive in every respect that I was ashamed to look her straight in the eye. I looked only at her gloves which were porous and made of fine silk. She had long hair, loose-flowing tresses which hung down almost to her waist. She sat on the high stool and ordered a tiny little sandwich and a container of coffee which she took to her room to nibble at with great delicacy. All the yegg men seemed to know her; they greeted her familiarly but respectfully. She could be "Miss America, 1935." She was a dream, I'm telling you. I looked at her furtively through the mirror. I couldn't imagine any one — — — — — — —. I couldn't imagine her hoofing it either. I couldn't imagine her eating a big juicy steak with mushrooms and onions. I couldn't imagine her going to the bathroom, unless to clear her throat. I couldn't imagine her having a private life. I can only imagine her posing for a magazine cover, standing perpetually in her Palm Olive skin and never perspiring. I like the gangsters best. These boys go everywhere and by aeroplane and stream-lined platinum, lighter than air, air-conditioned trains. They are the only ones in America who are enjoying life, while it lasts. I envy them. I like the shirts they wear, and the bright ties, and the flashy hair-cuts. They come fresh from the laundry and kill in their best clothes.

The opposite to this is the suburban life. Manhasset, for instance. The idea is—how to kill the week-end. Those who don't play bridge invent other forms of amusement, such as the peep-show. They like to get undressed and dance over the week-ends. To change wives. They don't know what to do with themselves after a hard week at the office. *Donc*, the car, the whiskey bottle, some strange —, an artist if possible. (I, for example, made a hit because "I was so unconventional." Sometimes, when you are regarded as being so unconventional, it is embarrassing to be obliged to refuse — — — — ——your host's wife, let us say, size 59 and round as a tub. Larry's wife, for example, is a miniature hippopotamus who gets jealous if you dance with any of the good-looking wenches. She goes off and sulks.)

And now let me tell you what one brilliant man in the suburbs thought of last week-end to regale us. When we were all good and crocked he got out an old talking record of the Prince of Wales. We had to listen to that high and mighty potentate (then about nineteen years of age) tell us what the *idealllll* of the Englishman was. I don't have to tell you, Joey, that it was our old friend "fair play." An Englishman never *twists* you. It went on for three records— it must have been a golden jubilee or something. In the midst of it I got hysterical and began to laugh. I laughed and laughed and laughed. Everybody began to laugh, even the host, who, I discovered later, was highly insulted. No sir, an Englishman never *twists* you! He just falls asleep on you . . . .

A NATURAL HISTORY

James Laughlin, 1936

WELL THEY were real tracks this time, not like the ones Hank and Gussy had made the week before to fool Helena, and we followed them up the beach and found the turtle high in the dry sand, where the warmth of the sun hatches the eggs, already popping them. It was a big old bitch and she was half backed down into the hole she'd dug, dropping about two eggs a minute as near as I could time it. Helena started giggling, she hadn't ever seen one laying before, and we'd come out a week before, too early, because she was so het up about it and wanted to see one before she had to go up back north again, and there hadn't been any, they hardly ever start coming up out of the sea before the end of May, so Gussy and Hank faked up a flipper track with their elbows while I kept Helena busy up the beach, and then they came running up the beach shouting that they'd just seen a big one going back into the water, the idea was to try to get Helena to dig for the eggs where there weren't any, but it didn't work because she caught on because Gussy had put his foot down a couple of times when they were making the track and the pattern of the sole showed on the sand, but Helena hadn't had to go north so soon after all because her old man, who is drunk almost all the time, had the d-t's just the night before they were going to start driving back to Illinois, and they'd had to take him down to Miama to the hospital to get over them, so she could stay on longer and we'd come out again when the moon got full because the old nigger who cuts the lawn for Senator Blossom says that's what gives the turtles the signal to come up out of the sea. Helena started giggling, and Hank slapped her fanny and said something I didn't catch that made her awful sore. "That ain't one bit funny, Hank," said Georgia. I could see, with the big moon, that Georgia wasn't liking it much, but Elsy was eating it right up. She got down in the sand to look into the hole. You could hear the eggs landing as they fell, plip . . . plep . . . plip, like that, like the slow drip of a faucet into a drain tub. "Wouldya lookit the way they bounce!" said Elsy. Georgia was looking like she was going to be sick any minute and Gussy said, "Isn't that cute the way nature makes them sorta soft so they can bounce like that and not get broke?"

Georgia sat down in the sand and looked the other way; "Come on be a sport," said Helena, "You knowya wanted to come 'n you said how you came last year 'n what a laugh it was." Georgia didn't say anything. Plip . . . plep . . . plip . . . I was wondering how that poor goddam turtle must feel. She knew we were there all right, she'd pulled in her head under the shell, but once they get started laying they can't get themselves stopped, and there she had to go on with it knowing all the time that we'd cop the eggs just as soon as she got them dropped. Gussy was starting to fish some of them out of the hole already while she was still working. He gave one to Elsy and she turned it over in her fingers, fascinated with the way the air dent rolled around the shell as she moved it. "Look Gussy," I said, "Why don't you just put the basket down inside the hole? Save a lot of work." He tried it, scooping away some sand to get it down, but trying to work it under the turtle he must have scraped her behind because she struck out at him, quick as lightning, with her back foot and ripped a long bloody scratch down his wrist and hand. He swore at the turtle and gave it a kick which only hurt his toe. His hand was bleeding some and the girls clustered round. He was starting to suck at the cut but Helena said not to. Elsy asked him if it hurt bad, Georgia couldn't take her eyes off it. "Wash it in the salt water," said Helena, "Salt's just as good as iodine." They went down to the water and I stood watching the turtle. Hank fetched back the basket that Gussy had slung away in his anger. Plip . . . plep . . . plip, the hole was nearly full now and the eggs seemed to be coming a little quicker. The turtle edged her head out cautiously from under the shell and jerked it back in again when she saw me. "How would you be feeling if you was this turtle?" I asked Hank. "I don' getcha," said Hank. "Well, having all your eggs swiped from you after you'd worked so damn hard to lay 'em." "Oh," said Hank, "Oh yeah, well I guess I'd be perty sore, I guess . . . hell, I didn't never think nothin, about it, I ain't no damn turtle." Gussy and the girls came back up the beach from the water, they'd tied a couple of handkerchiefs around his wrist. "Hey look," said Elsy, "She's going to fill up the hole." The turtle had finished laying and was turned around pushing sand into the hole with her flippers. Whether or not we were there waiting to steal her eggs she was going to finish up her job the way her instinct made her. She filled up her hole to the level of the beach and then hit right out for the water. And turtles aren't so slow either, she went right along with a quick jerking movement, the flippers pulling in front and the feet pushing from behind. Hank picked up Elsy to put her on the turtle's back, we'd filled the girls up with stories about how you could ride on the turtles' backs, how on real hot nights they ran a regular taxi service up and down the beach, how you could have races on them, but Elsy'd seen what that turtle had done to Gussy and she wasn't going to get herself within reach of it. Hank was carrying her along behind the turtle, trying to sit her down on its back, but she grabbed hold of his hair, he has long hair, when he combs it down the wrong way he can chew the ends of it, and pulled until he had to dump her or lose two handfuls of it. I followed the turtle as she scrambled down the beach, and the way she was going it looked as though once she got back in the water she'd never more come out again. A big wave hit her as she went into the surf, it rolled her on her side, but she flopped down again and pushed on out into deep water. For a little while I could see her swimming along the surface but then she dove under and disappeared. I watched for a while to see if she would come up again further out but she didn't. The moon on the water was something marvellous, like some sort of silver fire if there ever was such a thing. I stood there just watching it, it was so wonderful, and Helena came up behind me and leaned against me, rubbing her chin against my shoulder. "What'you think of that?" I said, "Ever see anything like that up in Illinois?" She rubbed her chin on the side of my neck and put a hand on my arm, I could feel her breath on my cheek and the softness of her pressing against my back. "Y'know I wish I weren't never going back home at all, I wish I was just always going to stay here with . . ." "Sure," I said quickly, "That'd be great, Hel, but y'know it get's awful hot down here in summer, it get's terrible hot, I think you'd pretty soon get fed with it down here in summer." She moved away from me and kicked at something in the sand. "Come on," I said "We've got to tote those eggs up to the car." She followed me up the beach without speaking.

Well, we got this stuff from a guy with a truck who'd killed a big turtle and couldn't get it up from the beach to the road it was so heavy. It's against the law to kill them but bootlegging them is worthwhile because the niggers love the meat, they eat everything but the shell, and one of those big ones, two or three hundred pounds of turtle, will feed a lot of niggers. This guy had come down from Stuart with his truck, and he'd located a whopping big turtle and been able to kill it by getting it turned over on its back with a crowbar and then taking an axe to it, but even at that it wasn't clean dead, a turtle is such a tough old bastard that you can't really call it dead till you've cut it in pieces, because as long as two pieces are still together they can manage to wiggle, I know because Hank tried to kill one one day, just a small one, and it took him over an hour with a meat knife and a hammer and screwdriver, its legs kept twitching after he had all the insides cut out of the shell, and the heart went on beating for about two hours after he'd cut it out and there wasn't any blood left in it, it just seemed to be beating on air, and when you'd poke it with a finger it would take on a spurt and beat faster for a while and then gradually quiet down again. Well we found this guy sitting on the fender of Gussy's car when we got back to the road with the eggs in a basket, and he asked would we give him a hand with his turtle. We had quite a job dragging it up to the road even though there were four of us because it was so big around there was no way you could get ahold of it, you couldn't get a grip on the smooth edge of the shell and nobody wanted to grab it by the feet because they were still jerking in spite of how its head was all mashed to hell and blood dripping over the sand. Finally Gussy got an idea, he remembered he had an old pair of chains under the seat of his car left over from the time when it was new and he used to drive people from the Beach out into the Glades to shoot. We got a hitch around the shell with the chains and that gave us something to haul on. Just the same it was some job to get it up that bank to the road, and while we were resting in the middle this guy brought down a big jug of this stuff from his truck and passed it around. And then when we'd gotten the turtle into the truck he'd brought along planks for that so it wasn't so hard, we had another round from the jug and he filled a quart bottle from it and give it to us to take along home. I don't know whatever this stuff could have been, it tasted something godawful, but it went down like a hurricane and hit like a landslide. It did the job all right, and by the time we got back to the beginning of West Palm we were feeling just fine and dandy and plenty left over to spare. Gussy had the old wreck wide open, you could have heard it a mile away, and we went down the boulevard like an itchy snake trying to scratch its back on both sides of the street at once. We were all feeling happy, hollering and singing and almost falling out of the car, and Elsy started throwing eggs at the cars parked along the sidewalk. Georgia tried to stop her, she hadn't kept up with the rest of us, but we all pretty soon forgot that we'd gotten the eggs to eat when we saw the way they splattered all over the cars as they broke. That was some ride I can tell you, and I guess there weren't two cars in twenty blocks that didn't get messed up the way we were slinging those turtle eggs. Then somebody thought of niggertown and it caught like a light, we were all yelling "Get those goddam niggers!" as we bumped over the tracks into Blackland. It was Saturday night and they were all still outside standing under the streetlights and sitting in front of their shacks. Gussy slowed down the car and we stood up and let 'em have it, all of us firing at once except Georgia who was sore and getting scared. We went down that old street like a mowing machine potting those damn niggers on both sides and you shoulda heard them swear and holler. A couple of them ran out and tried to hop our running board but Hank and I had a wrench and jack-handle ready and we let 'em have it right in the snoot. The rest of them all beat it back into their shacks but we went up and down a couple more times just decorating their windows. Then we heard a siren across the tracks, some nigger must have telephoned to the cops, so we scrammed out the back end of the street and beat it for home. When we pulled into Gussy's garage we were just too drunk tired to get out and go home so we lay there in the car, all but Georgia who went off by herself and left us. I was lying in the back seat, looking at the dark while the inside of my head rolled round and round in my skull, and Helena rolled over on top of me and started sucking my ear with her teeth the way she does. She was all set for it I could tell but I didn't try to get anywhere at all, I was so marvellously sleepy with the likker slowly wearing off, and we just lay there tight together feeling real hot and sleepy and good.

THE REPUBLICANS COME BACK

A. M. Schlesinger, Jr., 1938

THE REVIVAL of the Republicans has probably not embarrassed the writers who in 1933 retired them to the history books. Political observers have always been careless in distinguishing between sleep and death. The reading of funeral rites over a badly beaten party is a favorite diversion of American history; but too often, the corpse, like Aaron Burr in Mark Twain's sketch, sits up and talks with the coachman. In 1798 Noah Webster reported that the flood of Federalist votes had washed away all remnants of Jeffersonian power: two years later Jefferson became president. And in 1928 Silas Bent, examining the gaping hole in the Democratic Party where the Solid South had been, pronounced the wound fatal: in the next election the Republicans were overwhelmed.

But so many parties have disappeared in American history that these amateur prophets can not be altogether disregarded. Their predictions, however, have rarely taken into account the economic bases of politics which underlie and breed the emotional attainments. As a rule, political parties begin when men come together whose economic interests will be furthered by the same policies; they always go to pieces when personal rivalries or clashing economic interests strain the party lines to the breaking point. Even then, the continuity of economic life — the fact that most people do the same thing from day to day — prevents parties from utterly disintegrating. They break into large fragments, which are re-aligned to strengthen old parties and form new ones. The Federalist Party disappeared soon after the common man had turned from a subject into a citizen; but, though the party had gone, the Federalists still remained. The Whigs, when split by conflicting economic programs, soon found themselves more at home in the Democratic and Republican parties of the day. The Democrats would have faded away in 1928 only if the public had been convinced that what was good for Andrew Mellon was good for it. And so long as a large minority of the United States believes in rugged individualism, the Republican Party will survive. It is, of course, easy to reject prophecies after the fact; but it is also difficult to escape the conclusion that the prophets used the methods of Evangeline Adams rather than those of the Brookings Institute.

Certainly the clairvoyants of 1933, who could not see how the Republicans were to recover from their drubbing, were guilty of some very wishful thinking. The number of Roosevelt's enemies is growing daily: Wall Street operators who find brokerage tame after years of speculation; industrialists aghast at the Wagner Labor Bill; the large number of people who see communism in government for the community, and the very small number who have moral or philosophical objections to public management; those who want to brain the brain trust; those who think that one of the alphabetical agencies has discriminated against them; those who look on the Constitution as something akin to divine revelation — in general, the capitalists, the conservatives and the large portion of the middle class which pays attention to them. It is this growing opposition that is waking the Republican Party to action. The economic basis for this line-up? Generally speaking (and all historical analyses in terms of economics are general), the vested interests, their hangers-on and their would-be sharers are facing the under-privileged and their defenders.

A corps of shrewd commentators daily attack the administration from this capitalist-conservative viewpoint. The New Deal, of course, has its champions; but to the unseeing reader the frothy trivialities of Paul Mallon must seem petty beside the stern warnings of David Lawrence. Columnists have

been very important in the revival of Republicanism; the case against Roosevelt is most effectively advanced by Lawrence, Frank Kent and Mark Sullivan, though they have their imitators in the local political experts of every Republican paper in the country.

Lawrence is talented chiefly in his ability to write as if he were taking his stand only after careful and impartial thought. He seems the most informed of the three; but his combination of *ex cathedra* judgments with a blanket disapproval of the New Deal gives him a flavor of insincerity. If Lawrence writes like a pope, Kent hands down his opinions like a Justice of the Supreme Court. Under this camouflage of judicial review, he is able to make quite unscrupulous insinuations about people. For this reason he is the most unfair and annoying of the columnists. To adapt an epigram of Constant Lambert's: if Roosevelt were to go up in a balloon, Kent would call him an exhibitionist; if he were to refuse to go up, Kent would call him a coward. Where Lawrence is a predisposed interpreter of issues, and Kent of men, Sullivan is a good-natured and rather bewildered dissenter to the vagaries of the New Deal. He has a clear and ingratiating style which reconstructs complex problems to make the conservative solution seem the only one. If his influence is not so great as the others, it is because he does not try to play God. Each in his own manner, these three men were probably most instrumental in the Republican recovery. The power to come back was there, but Lawrence, Kent and Sullivan had to throw on the switch.

Party leaders have not been much behind the commentators in painting the New Deal red. Magazine articles and books, signed if not written by prominent Tories, have scorched the insidious tendencies of the present government in terms as vague as the phrase "insidious tendencies." Hoover's amazing *The Challenge to Liberty* which revealed his political philosophy in 250 dull pages, reached, according to the publisher, over sixty thousand homes.

These doses of profundity have probably affected the mass of voters far less than the press attacks of stupefied Republicans and disappointed Democrats. A recent example is the series by James P. Warburg. This eminent economic thinker assailed the New Deal with great vigor and a fine air of: what a patriot am I to tell all these truths about Washington. The series borrowed liberally, especially from David Lawrence and William Randolph Hearst; but it confirmed the misgivings of the lower middle class as to Roosevelt's destination and was fearless in calling the administration "socialistic." It ended with a bitter personal attack on the President in which Warburg turned the qualities in Roosevelt that had most appealed to liberals into defects of character. What had seemed receptivity to new ideas is really, says Warburg, the vacillations of a weak mind, swayed always by the latest adviser; his frank acknowledgment of error shows nothing more than incompetence.

The effect on the very uncritical of articles like these, written allegedly from the inside, can hardly be overestimated. To the pseudo-intelligent, the attacks on the New Deal by conservative economists must seem almost as convincing. Closer examination usually reveals that those of the attacking economists who are not kept by Wall Street are voices from some academic grove where people still believe that America is an open market and the profit system is self-regulatory. But the ones who read them do not know this: the accusation that the New Deal is economically unsound damns it in the eyes of the suburban intelligentsia, no matter who the accusers may be.

The American Liberty League is the most imposing of the conservative press gangs. The nobility and patriotism in this band of corporation lawyers and millionaires fighting for the liberty which permits the rich as well as the poor to sleep in Central Park is not, however, very obvious. It is an irony of history that the American Liberty League of 1935 should be headed by men who would have led the Loyalist exodus to Nova Scotia in the days when people fought about American liberty.

The Republican Party has popular support. It has excellent men for the newspaper skirmishes which precede the battle. A constructive program would be pleasant but unnecessary; for empty catchwords about Liberty or the Constitution, reinforced by platform phrases which require neither to be understood now nor heeded after election, can bring victory. Roosevelt did not win in 1932 because of the Democratic platform. . . . In fact, the Republicans have everything a minority party needs to put up a fight, except a good candidate.

Herbert Hoover perhaps thinks of himself as another Grover Cleveland, but most of his party prefers to think of him as another Taft. To the nation, his name still means the depression; to his party, it means defeat. And he has no strong personal following to work for his nomination out of devotion to the man. Hoover undoubtedly feels that he ought to have a chance to vindicate his conduct as president. In recent months he has certainly been acting as if he were looking ahead to the nomination. The heat of the battle has begun even to melt his personal coldness; the Hoover of today is a Hoover whose speeches contain funny stories and picturesque phrases. "Joyriding to destruction"—this sounds more like General Johnson than like the man who could think of no sprightlier sentence to arouse America in the midst of the depression than, "We have weathered the worst of the storm." Hoover must be considered seriously. If he is not himself nominated, he will do his best to dictate the choice. And, if he is as effective in hypnotizing the Republicans as he was in relieving the Belgians, he will bring into the convention enough votes to hold the balance of power.

The contributors to the campaign fund would accept Hoover only under bared bayonets; his name spells disaster. One man alone is less welcome to them — Senator Borah. Frank Kent and David Lawrence write that Borah is too old to be considered; but Borah evidently has not been convinced. In the last month he has been amazingly active and amazingly noncommittal for a man who is not busy looking over the eggs before they hatch. As a nominee, he would recover the Middle West for the Republicans; the farmers, preferring the AAA to Hoover's farm relief, which had relieved them only of their savings, are Democrats today. But Borah's resolute isolationism will offend, I suspect, a rather large group in the East; and his rash endorsement of inflation has ruined him with the New York financiers. Borah's votes, moreover, depend on his personal influence rather than on a well-articulated organization of the type Hoover has been trying to build. He may go into the convention as the popular favorite — a recent poll among young Republicans proves his popularity — but the gentlemen pulling the strings will see that he is not chosen.

The rise of Governor Alf Landon shows how a democracy is at the mercy of its press agents. A year ago no one beyond the Kansas borders had heard of him; now he is mentioned as the next president of the United States. To thinking people, one term as governor of Kansas seems hardly a qualification for the White House; but to the newspapermen who discovered Landon and named him the Kansas Coolidge, inexperience is a minor consideration. This is not a nickname to fill the intelligent minority with enthusiasm, but to the mass of voters it brings memories of thrift, shrewdness and prosperity.

Landon's chances have been damaged most by the decision of Hearst to back him. The *New Masses* is inclined, I think, to overestimate Hearst's power in molding public opinion. The Hearst papers differ from others serving the same audience, not so much in their views, as in their way of expressing them. Instead of hiding his ideas on a forbidding inner page, Hearst sets up his editorials in large type and runs them on the back page. The size of his chain makes him only the best known of those who publish for the city slums. If Hearst bewitched the masses as effectively as the Communists think, he would not have such a long record of defeat on political issues. With all the support of his papers, he himself could get nowhere in politics. His papers were pro-German in the first years of the war, and the country became steadily pro-Ally. He championed Garner for the Democratic nomination in 1932, and Garner ended up as vice-president. On national questions, Hearst frightens away more backing than he attracts; the biography which ran recently in the *Boston American* is a serious blow to Landon's chances. But for most of the country, Landon has yet to show that he is more than an Alfalfa Bill Murray in a business suit.

Neither party has dared to nominate a senator since Harding. This year Vandenberg of Michigan, a fluent debater and a wary politician, has been frequently mentioned. The self-styled "discriminating critic" of the President, he stands between the New Deal and the Old, between the Progressives and the Old Guard. His chief drawback as the perfect compromise candidate is his spurts of independent thinking. The Party would prefer some political hack whom it could direct more easily. And in Senator Dickinson of Iowa it may have him. Dickinson is conservative, sober, silent and tractable; he has been a party regular of the most depressing kind. . . Vandenberg would be, prospectively, the best Republican president since Taft; Dickinson, the worst since Hoover.

Political hacks outside the Middle West will not stand much chance in 1936. Though the Party would protest the suspicion of choosing a candidate because he brings votes, it would doubtless bring itself to choose one from a region where votes lie; and the Middle West is a great deal more doubtful in the eyes of the Republican National Committee than the East. This is one cause of James Wadsworth's disappearance from public view. In 1933 he was everywhere mentioned as the Republican nominee for 1936; two years later his name appears in the papers only as a member of the American Liberty League. Ogden Mills has likewise seen his chances diminish. A slashing speaker and a master of invective, he could be perhaps the most effective critic of the New Deal in the Republican Party. Fortunately he has remained in his country estate, a New York Achilles; and Roosevelt is spared the addition of his philippics to the admonitions of David Lawrence and the bludgeonings of William Randolph Hearst. Mills has too many enemies for him to get the nomination; Wadsworth hasn't enough friends. And Hamilton Fish thinks the nomination so remote that he is trying to make himself a tail to Borah's kite.

Not all the contenders will be politicians. Several patriots have offered to sacrifice their business and personal comfort in order to save the country. These persons range all the way from lunatics under delusions of grandeur to Colonel Frank Knox. New England has already started Knox-for-President clubs; but his own section of the country knows him (when it knows him at all) as the owner of the *Chicago Daily News*. It is rather hard to see how his newspaper experience fits him for the presidency, though fitness, of course, plays little part in politics. Harding was the last newspaper owner in the White House. Knox is an immovable conservative; he can not be moved nor can he move anything. The Republican convention will watch him, not as Col.

Frank Knox, but as the close political friend of Herbert Hoover. He may well be the beneficiary of Hoover's defeat; this likelihood has already put him high in the betting.

Though this about exhausts the list of Republican possibilities for the nomination, it does not exhaust the list of possibilities for the Republican nomination. Hearst, before he took up the Kansas Coolidge, urged the organization of the conservatives to oppose Roosevelt's "Socialist Party." And many prominent Republicans, who happen themselves to have no hope for the nomination, cry out for a coalition ticket with a conservative Democrat in one place. The main obstacle to this plan is that most conservative Democrats are conservative in political behavior as well as in politics; and they prize, above all, regularity. It is inconceivable that Byrd of Virginia, Ritchie of Maryland, Ely of Massachusetts should desert the Democratic Party. As for Al Smith, he would not leave it save to head the ticket. The chance of this is slight, though the same people who were horrified in 1928 by Smith's accent and his wife's jewelry now look to him as a possible savior from the urbane aristocrat of Hyde Park.

Not to be omitted in any survey of the field is the *Atlantic Monthly's* candidate for president, Lewis Douglas. He is popularly regarded as a financial genius, the Gallatin to Mellon's Hamilton. As a matter of fact, his writing and speaking show him to be sincere and well-meaning, with a naivete of approach to economic problems in the Godkin lectures which shocked the Harvard economists last year, and a naivete of outlook on society which makes him a political kinsman of Herbert Agar. Douglas, moreover, is probably too honest a man to court the interests whose support would be necessary for the nomination; and he is probably too strong a man to tempt the interests' support in the hope that they might control him later.

Political prediction is a game any one can play but no one can play well. Nine-tenths of the forces which rule the convention are under the surface. It is easy to talk about string-pulling, but hard to name the men pulling the strings. In the long view, the Republican nominee for 1936 will probably not matter, for Roosevelt's re-election is likely. What will matter is that there will be a Republican nominee.

Republicanism is far from dead. Its economic bases are shrinking, but they are shrinking slowly. The Old Guard has its back to the wall, but it is not yet faced by a firing squad.

T. S. Eliot, '10

An Advocate Friendship

W. G. TINCKOM-FERNANDEZ, 1910

ON this occasion when the ADVOCATE gives accolade to T. S. Eliot she celebrates, so far as I know, the first occasion when one of her sons has acquired international renown before reaching middle-age, not only as a poet, dramatist and critic but as the spokesman of intellectual youth on both sides of the Atlantic.

My assignment is to present Eliot as an AD-VOCATE editor. Because the privilege of friendship with a choice personality befell me, I find myself reviving memories of an ADVOCATE friendship instead of the casual relations of editorial activities. In doing so, however, I realize that I raise hopes of a vivid personal portrait such as that undergraduate friendship justifies; whereas I find myself facing a problem which Eliot, the literary critic, has often encountered.

To look back over more than a quarter of a century and try to recapture a personality from a remote and limited period, especially of one who was then as shy and reticent as he is probably still, is a difficult task. This is not to say that this necessarily brief friendship was not intimate and rewarding, nor that Eliot was

wholly different as an undergraduate from the personality which he has since revealed in his poems, plays and critical opinions. Let me say, however, that while he was then no less concerned with literature than he is today, to flush the undergraduate writer as one who was even then conscious of literary destiny among his fellow editors of the ADVOCATE is to do him an injustice.

Small wonder that in retrospect those episodes, conversations and ideas of our undergraduate days became hopelessly kaleidoscopic. What we were like then and what we wanted to do and become are things which elude us who are now armed with experience and chastened by realities. Having to readjust our lives after two major crises like a world war and a world depression, the poets of our troubled generation are indeed "world-losers and world-forsakers."

Thus the ambitions and desires of our youth have long since made their quaint compacts with necessity. In our twenty-fifth anniversary class report Eliot told us of his lean years in England as a school teacher on a pittance with a dinner thrown in, and as a bank clerk with a free tea at four o'clock. Was it irony that led the poet to add that he liked banking? Recalling his sensitive nature, and the inspissated gloom of a London bank interior, that rather sounds like the sort of humor that was permitted in the last carriage of a funeral procession in the Cambridge of our day.

I am also conscious that such glimpses and memories as survive precariously today remind us that our personalities at that period of our lives did not have so much finality in them as they pretended to. Withal, there is the temptation to rationalize in our endeavor to overcome what James Huneker somewhere called "the pathos of distance."

II

It was in the old ADVOCATE sanctum under the eaves of the Harvard Union that I first met Eliot. As I was the first to be elected from our class, I was able to watch the other 1910 candidates. Eliot was the most promising of these, and as he was the next to be elected we began a friendship based upon such literary tastes and enthusiasms as we shared or induced each other to share.

But Eliot's ADVOCATE days were numbered. In his sophomore year he decided to complete his course in three years and take a master's degree. Thereafter the sanctum saw less of him; his comments in a minuscular hand on the contributions of candidates soon ceased along with his own. Only now and then did he come to initiations and punch nights to expand, in the midst of our hilarity, into his quiet, subtle humor; and we saw as little of him at the Stylus and Signet. As president, during the first half of our final year, I made a desperate effort to get editorials from him; but by then he was working harder than ever in the graduate school. To his classmates and the ADVOCATE board he became a recluse, and I used to run him to earth in his room.

But he was not lost to undergraduate life. He was always ready to lay his book aside and fill his pipe. With his analytical mind his curiosity was insatiable as to the meanings and motives in the literary and social currents of our day. He was always the commentator, never the gusty talker, and seemed to cultivate even then a scholarly detachment. And there was a lot to talk about, for the university was then peculiarly, and perhaps for the last time, a kind of national clearing-house, a laboratory, such as would delight the pedagogues of today. As the Ph. D. degree had just become a pedagogical fetish, the university attracted a host of aspirants for doctors and masters degrees from all over the country, and the college, with its elective system of study, exposed us undergraduates to a variety of stimulating contacts and experiences. I like to account for Eliot's flair for eclectic scholarship, which is revealed in his poems and which is perhaps their outstanding characteristic, by recalling the intellectual excitements in this competitive atmosphere which the swarm of graduate students from small and large colleges created in our class-rooms, for we rubbed shoulders with them in undergraduate as well as graduate courses.

I have no doubt that in Eliot's case this was a formative influence, as indeed it was in the lives of our generation at Harvard during those last years of the elective system. If the College seemed to lose its identity in this almost alien, as it were cosmopolitan, atmosphere, at least it had more of the atmosphere and fellowship of the medieval university than Harvard's cloistered undergraduates today in those replicas of Oxford and Cambridge on the banks of the Charles.

What if certain graduate courses received us with sublime toleration, even reluctance? Our barbarian airs and graces saved them from the heavy-witted Teutonism which the Ph.D. aspirants always threatened to inject. Our professors were more amused than flattered by the atmosphere of *lèse-majesté* with which these earnest souls surrounded them, and they doubtless appreciated our undergraduate anticlimaxes. How often the absurdly rapt attention of those grinds was disturbed, if not shocked, when someone of our group, after a riotous evening in Boston or Cambridge, would laboriously nod and finally pass into unabashed slumber?

The unfailing punctuality of these strangers within our gates irked instead of reproached us; we sometimes wondered if that superhuman phalanx had left the class room since the last lecture. And yet, we had all the breaks. None of them was ever late because, running to a lecture, he had almost bumped into Henry James at the corner of Linden and Massachusetts, and knocked off his hard, high-low-crowned English hat which resembled a Regency coachman's, and picked it up with breathless apologies, and politely waited on a sentence which had a beginning and a middle, but which tailed off unfinished in a despairing smile. If any of them had had this experience, it should have furnished him with a doctor's thesis on that distinguished novelist's style, since appropriate subjects for theses were uppermost in their minds.

And if these greasy grinds had their laugh when they poised their pens over their notebooks while we industriously plied ours as the "pickers-up of unconsidered trifles," it is a surprising amount of information we managed to pick up. We learned to swim by going beyond our depth. But we had our innings when these post-graduates from the sticks appeared in the ADVOCATE sanctum to submit contributions which, when published, were proudly sent back to the home town and the *alma mater*.

So much for the intra-mural influences of Eliot's day. The result was, for one of his precocious mind, a healthy sophistication, which is quite another thing from the sophistry which, a lecturer told us, Bacon ascribed to the medieval university. And since Eliot wrote some of his early poems during his last two years in college, it is worth our while to ask why they were not published until 1925 by that professional world of letters to which we aspired. The answer is that the professional world of editors and publishers reminded the young, unknown writer that the cautionary Victorian advice of being seen and not heard was still in force.

I recall the sensation caused in the ADVOCATE sanctum when the editor of the *Literary Digest* wrote asking for samples of ADVOCATE poets which he wanted for a survey of American undergraduate verse. Of the samples submitted, needless to say, none of Eliot's was used.

Today young writers, even those in college, are cultivated and encouraged by editors and publishers to submit their work. Not so in our day. As yet the young writer, especially the poet, was not supposed to have anything worth saying. Of course there were certain publishers who would gladly publish your poems at your own expense, and the custom was more common than is known. The late Edwin Arlington Robinson, whom I came to know in New York, told me that his first volume, "Captain Craig," was subsidized. And when I met Eliot's English contemporary Rupert Brooke in New York, still unknown in 1913, he said that he had paid for the publication of his first volumes in London.

In the light of these conditions and influences, within and without Harvard in our day, it is not surprising that the writers of 1910 have been, like Eliot, rebels, though not all have remained so. For that world we faced three years before the war was a smug, somnolent world: as yet the word Armageddon was only used by divinity students to scarify their first congregations. It will sound like rationalization to say that, although we entered college soon after the century opened, by the time we left we found, or rather sensed, an atmosphere of *fin-de-siècle*, even of disillusion, in the literary and political world. The note is evident in Walter Lippmann's first three books. Reading once more Eliot's essay "For Lancelot Andrewes" I have wondered in what mood he first discovered this stanza of Dryden's which he quotes in that study:

All, all of a piece throughout!
Thy Chase had a Beast in View;
Thy Wars brought nothing about;

Thy lovers were all untrue.
'Tis well an Old Age is out,
And time to begin a New.

As regards belles lettres, the field was dominated and monopolized by a coterie of pundits, a sort of superannuated, mutual admiration circle. Their prestige might have been said to rest upon an axiom like "that which is new is not true, and that which is true is not new." Some held chairs of literature and others were editors. The magazines always found room for their long colorless odes which we characterized as "spindaric." There were, however, notable exceptions, two of whom were sons of MOTHER ADVOCATE. One was that inspired poet and teacher, Professor George Woodberry '77, of Columbia, whose poems appeared too seldom, and the other was one of the founders and during its best years the editor of the original *Life*, Edward S. Martin '77, who welcomed us to his pages. Though retired, he is happily still with us, a modern survival of Chaucer's "verray parfit gentil knight."

These were formative or decisive influences for Eliot and his generation of writers. Almost too late in college we heard of the literary revolt abroad, which in time found American supporters like the poets Amy Lowell, John Gould Fletcher of the "Harvard Monthly" and our own Conrad Aiken. It was Eliot who first told me of the Vers Libre movement, of the work of Paul Fort and Francis Jammes; and he was to go over to the Sorbonne for study and to assess these literary influences which, stifled by the War, were to end in the literary and artistic nonsense which was appropriately termed Dada.

Meanwhile Eliot had found what he wanted in Paris and returned to Harvard for his Ph.D. study. I can testify to the fact that he had now already begun to shape his own technique of verse form and style, for, after leaving Cambridge to become a cub reporter on the *New York World*, I kept up a correspondence with him, and he sent me copies of these early poems. Of these I recall the "Preludes," "Cousin Nancy," "The Boston Evening Transcript" and

"Aunt Helen." There may have been others which have not since been published, and I regret that another Harvard man to whom I showed them never returned them. The point is that these poems waited until 1925 for publication, and it is surprising, even paradoxical, to find that even those of the post-war period do not as yet begin to date; each seems to have its note of universality.

Those who bring against Eliot the charge of a wilful or perverse obscurantism should remember that these poems crystalize the suppressed ideas, emotions, aspirations of a period of catastrophe, when the experiences of our stratified world, the world of Aunt Helen Slingsby and the Lady of the Portrait, were destined for limbo. It is not only that some medium was necessary for a distillation of these crowded, complex and inarticulate moods and experiences, but that Armageddon liquidated that world. By what miracle could a conventional or traditional frame-work contain and adequately convey their significance?

Thus it seems as if Eliot set himself the task of assessing, with his fastidious sincerity and scholarship, the myriad contacts and experiences of a transitional epoch. There was so much to record of this Human Comedy, whose moods, attitudes and whispers were destined to become international crises, that Eliot's elliptical mode of expression alone could perform the miracle of synthesis. In depicting this scene Eliot seems to have borrowed from the canon of classical Chinese painting, where linear perspective is modified by the tone values and shading of atmospheric perspective. It is futile to classify him as a symbolist, an imagist, an impressionist or a surrealist, since all these things are the concern of the modern creative artist. The poet, moreover, often found himself assuming the rôles of biographer and historian. Incidently, it is not surprising that Eliot has shared in the silly stricture which Oscar Wilde passed on Browning—of using poetry as a medium for writing prose.

While Eliot's meticulous classification of fugitive types, situations and motives may seem like rummaging in an intellectual attic among out-worn emotions and ideas, certainly these things have their tears and laughter. And so his types, his characters, are never ludicrous; they become prototypes instead of caricatures. J. Alfred Prufrock, Sweeney and his landlady Mrs. Turner, Aunt Helen Slingsby and the lady of the portrait, all have their dignity and their lawful occasions. If they seem like memories of our dead lives, that quality makes them the stuff of literature. And if Eliot's poetry sometimes suggests an atmosphere of *fin-de-siècle*, that is because of the curious time-lag which seems to haunt our tardy American reactions to the social, spiritual, intellectual and economic currents of the Europe towards which we so reluctantly and ruefully turn for orientation.

III

When the young and untried writer faces the compromise which he must make with the professional world, by a self-preservative instinct he chooses a milieu in which that compromise is not likely to be threatened with spiritual and literary extinction. Thus it was natural that, when his scholarly apprenticeship was over, Eliot should prefer to take his chances at making a living in London. As writers the idea had come to us in college when we discussed Ezra Pound's case. Pound, like Eliot, was a gifted poet and scholar. After teaching for a brief period at Pennsylvania, he had gone to London for literary recognition, and his first poems, which reached us in 1910, were published there. In the fall of 1913 I decided to exchange the journalism of New York for that of London, and Eliot came to see me off when I sailed on this forlorn hope from Boston. Thus the idea must have been in his mind during those last years in Cambridge when he was beginning to write with professional ambitions.

Before he left, however, I used to descend on him at his summer home in East Gloucester on my way to Maine. There I saw him in a quiet, charming family circle of parents and sisters, whose affectionate understanding of his arduous scholarship and his untried gifts must have been an inspiration for him in those lean years he faced in a foreign land. He used to take me sailing in his catboat, and he could handle a sheet with the best in Gloucester.

Although I lost touch with him when he went abroad, it is sad to relate that this friendship died when it should have been revived. A guilty conscience compels me to admit that I did not see him while I was in London in the months before and after the Armistice. And if those months were not propitious, I failed again to see him while I was working in London as a newspaper correspondent during 1924-26, and once more when I passed through in 1927. Our only excuse for such seemingly perverse omissions as these is that the world is too much with us in earning our living.

The Anatomy of the Debutante

FLAMINEO BOSOLA, 1941

*I have heard of your paintings, too, well enough; God hath
given you one face, and you make yourselves another: you jig,
you amble, and you lisp; you nickname God's creatures and make
your wantonness your ignorance: go to, I'll no more on't; it
hath made me mad.*

To begin with, a debutante is a young woman
(There are no male debutantes, in spite of what
you may think of Lucius Beebe and Maury
Paul), and she is generally a very fine figure of
a young woman, in a splendid state of preserva-
tion. She does not possess false teeth, a wig, or
artificial limbs. True, stomach ulcers sooner or
later catch up with her, but that's an internal
ailment, and as this is not a medical treatise, we
need have nothing to do with ulcers, pro or con.
No, we are concerned with the external attrib-
utes of these nice girls, and the ulcers can jolly
well take care of themselves.

—But, says little Gianciotto, who is fourteen
and promiscuous, how will I know a debutante
when I see one?

—Why, says old Malatesta, making a *cornuto*
at him, by her clothes. You can tell a debutante
by her clothes, just as you can tell a Hottentot
by his lack of them.

—As simple as that? says little Gianciotto.

—As simple as that, says the Old Roman.

And he was right; for if one should put
a debutante in a room with twenty other
women, she would always be recognized by her
clothes. Of course, if one should put a nude
debutante into a room with twenty other
women, similarly attired, —

—It would not, said little Gianciotto, be a
bad idea. Little Gianciotto is fourteen and promiscuous.

*   *   *

Now that we have fought our way through
the introduction, we should define what this
piece is concerned with, thus: A debutante is
composed of one part background, one part
Antoine de Paris, one part *Harper's Bazaar,*
five parts money, and eight parts ignorance.
Taking ten parts as a norm, you can see that
this adds up to considerably over that sum,
which should give you a pretty good idea of
what we have to deal with. She inhabits large
cities, small cities, towns, hamlets, and Los
Angeles, California. However, we are more interested, for our present needs, in the New England or Bury Me In Boston type of debutante.

There are several variations within this species,
but it is best that in the beginning we consider
the species as a whole. This, we understand, is
the usual approach, as practiced by the young
gentlemen of Harvard, Princeton, Yale, and the
Hanover Ski School.

The debutante, as a whole, spends her afternoons in charity work, her nights in polite
carouse, and her mornings in bed. She has breakfast at noon, dinner at any hour from eight to
eleven, and supper, if she can keep it down, at
two in the morning. Other than this she does
nothing, for fear of becoming an object of scandal. From the age of fourteen to eighteen she
goes to school, which, for her, is the equivalent
of doing nothing; at the age of eighteen she becomes a debutante, which is the public's idea of
doing nothing; and eventually she marries a Porcellian man, which is God's idea of doing nothing. All in all, she is, together with a housefly,
one of the most useless things on the face of
the earth. Not *the* most useless thing, mind you;
for the Democratic Party beats her out there.
But she does quite well in her way.

Well, then, here's the Littul Ole Boston Debutante, not worth a tinker's dam, and proud of it. She believes in Heaven, the Junior League, the Ritz Bar and Margaret Sanger. As far as marriage goes, she believes in (1) security, and (2) a decent amount of love. A husband, she realizes, is a necessary thing, for respectability's sake, much like the bottom part of a bathing suit. But of course, marriage is a concern of the post-debutante (a debutante becomes a post-debutante when she developes stomach-ulcers), and, as the post-debutante is the concern of a good psychoanalyist, we needn't bother with her. No, we started on the debutante, and, by Heaven, we'll stay on her.

If little Gianciotto should wander into the Ritz Bar at five o'clock in the afternoon, he would see several debutantes, of various shapes and sizes. This place, which is known familiarly as the Littul Ole Boston Watering-Hole, is where all the young ladies go to see the people they haven't seen since yesterday. Little Gianciotto (who is fourteen and promiscuous) wouldn't have much fun; but then, a fourteen year old, even if he is promiscuous, doesn't have much fun anyway.

Now, as we said before, there are several variations on the theme of the debutante, and we might as well take them up now. There is, to begin with, the Vincent Club, or Geez, I'm Duse, type, who has her artistic side but doesn't quite know what to do with it. Calling her the Vincent Club Type covers a multitude of sins, because she may be a poetess, a sculptress, or just a plain screwball; but we use that classification because we feel that the Vincent Club, together with the North Church Burying Ground, typifies the higher aspects of Boston culture. It is difficult to imagine just why the mental dry rot of Boston should produce young women with artistic leanings, but this is no more difficult than to imagine why the moral dry rot of Boston should produce young women. Yet it is necessary to admit that young women with beautiful souls do at times appear between Manchester and Cohasset, and it is also necessary to admit that these beautiful souls go the way of all flash.

Terpsichorean ability in Boston is based on an ability to tapdance, artistic ability spends itself in fashion drawings, and the less said about the poetesses the better. It should suffice to say that art, of any kind, is at present foreign to Boston, the *Transcript* and God to the contrary.

Of course, debutantes are often used as models; and it must be said for them that they take to modelling like ducks to water, evidently because the practise of modelling requires no mental power. All that is necessary is for one to exhibit oneself, like a prize dog, which is really very easy; so easy, in fact, that professional models are trembling for their laurels. But, understand, we can't accuse the Vincent Club and amalgamated organizations of this. The Vincent Club tapdances. At least, we think it tapdances. Of course, there may not be any such things as the Vincent Club. It may be just a bad dream, the kind of bad dream that you get after eating Welch rarebit, which, like the soul of Boston, is composed of cheese.

Anyway, we wash our hands of this type of debutante, and turn to the Charity, or Up The Masses, Type. This group is made up of young women who want to work, but, as they are mentally incapable of the responsibilities vested in an employee, find it necessary to work for free, usually in some charitable enterprise. They, like the Black Plague, are a sociological phenomenon.

—But what, says Little Gianciotto, is a sociological phenomenon?

—Beacon Hill, said the old *condottiere* without a quaver.

—Well, bless me, says little Gianciotto, shifting his quid to the other side of his face, I wouldn't have known.

There are all sorts of charities, most of which have been going on for years and years, like decay at Yale. The main duty of charities, it would seem, is to have projects. These projects are invariably accompanied by several cameramen, who photograph the young ladies assisting, all of which leads to the assumption that the main function of these charities is to assist the

Photographers' Guild, if there is one.

—Then what is charity? says little Gianciotto.

—Charity, replies old Malatesta, is Love.

—And what, says little Gianciotto, leaning forward eagerly, is Love?

—Love, says the Lord of Rimini, with a leer, is fun.

—I'll say, says little Gianciotto, dragging down the housemaid.

All of which brings us to the third, and most horrible, type of debutante; the Glamour Girl, or Over The Hill To The Stork Club Type. This type centers itself in Manhattan, for the simple reason that Boston girls are too ugly to be glamorous, and Philadelphia girls too prosy. Each year the soberer of New York's *bon vivants* (Fr.) gather together and elect the season's Glamour Girl, to the sound of loud cymbals, and, for no extra charge, to the sound of well-tuned cymbals. This year the Glamour Queen was Brenda Frazier (rhymes with *Asia, brazier,* etc.) who is, at the moment, in Bermuda or Zamboanga or somewhere, recovering from the effects of her debut and the possession of several million dollars.

Miss Frazier, to slip into the vernacular, is some baby. She is really a simple girl at heart, says her wise, wise mother, much preferring gingham gowns and rustic swains to the mad social whirl of Manhattan. But what can one do when one is a Glamour Girl? One must *live,* of course. It is useless to argue that some arsenic in her milk or liquidation *à la Russe* would do Miss Frazier a world of good. Even if Miss Frazier did herself in we'd still have Lucius Beebe, Miss Elsa Maxwell, and Cecil Beaton (status undetermined) to deal with.

Now, the trouble with Glamour Girls is that every debutante over fourteen (little Gianciotto's age) thinks she is one; and that adds up to an awful lot of glamour. Too, it adds up to an awful lot of stupidity. After all, if a girl spends all her time in cultivating her b-dy, for what would seem to be obvious reasons, she isn't going to have much time to cultivate her mind. As a result, we have a good, round number of nuts cluttering up the Social Register, which, we might add, is neither social nor a register.

Once, when we were younger and more foolish, we thought of saving our money and buying a Glamour Girl, but we finally rejected the plan because we realized that the upkeep on our purchase would be tremendous, while, at the same time, it would depreciate like hell. Yessir, there's no drug on the market like an old, decrepit Glamour Girl, we always say. Two or three years of parties, tossing in a child here and there, and they start to sag between ear and nostril. A Glamour Girl's face always goes first: their bodies hang on tenaciously. But that, of course, is beside the point—this is not a medical treatise.—

—That's what you think, says little Promiscuity.

Of course, America owes a lot to debutantes. When one is tired of newspaper accounts of wars and rumors of wars, one can always relax in the foolishness of the Society Page. I don't know what we'd do without Jerome Zerbe, Messrs. Billingsly and Perona, Cholly Knickerbocker, and Mrs. Harrison Williams. I don't even know what we'd do without Brenda Frazier (rhymes with *Asia* and *brazier*: see *Annals of Club Life at Harvard, 1939*). In fact, I don't even know what we'd do without debutantes in Boston.

For one thing, a lack of debutantes in Boston would mean that Harvard undergraduates would have to buy their own drinks. It would mean that the *American* and *Transcript* would have to shut down their plants. The reverberations would be felt from Eliot House to San Simeon. Of course, the main mass of the people would go its quiet way; but what do we care for the people, anyway?

The question is, now that we have the debutantes, what are we going to do with them? Certainly they can't be allowed to roam the streets night after night. No, they've got to be taken care of. But how?

—I know, says little Gianciotto, who spent a week in Berlin, a concentration camp.

—Hold your tongue, says old Malatesta, and take your hand off that maid.

—Which hand? says little Gianciotto innocently.

—The one I can't see, says old Malatesta.

But little Gianciotto has given us an idea. Why not put all the debutantes in a concentration camp? Of course, it would be a very nice concentration camp, with all sanitary facilities; and we could charge admission to the general public. We could divide the camp into three parts; a part for the artistic debutantes, a part for the charity workers, a part for the Glamour Girls. The artistic contingent could put on shows in which they could kick high and show their legs, if they have any—but we'd better go into this in detail.

Well, in the first place, the section of the camp devoted to the *artistes* would have, at one end, a huge stage, complete with a stage director, applause machines, and a noble purpose. At the other end would be thirteen microphones, a bundle of contracts to sing at the Sert Room, Ozzie Nelson, and assorted photographers. The floor would be paved with Cole Porter, Noel Coward, and Tommy Manville, the Asbestos Adonis. There would probably be no reason for Mr. Manville, save that his position on the floor would make him very happy.

The section of our camp devoted to Charity would have a floor paved with photographers and formal applications for aid. Each incumbent debutante would have a neat little desk, on which would be placed her hands and any number of cosmetics. There would be a great bustle of activity, because the girls, like the Red Queen (or maybe it's the White Queen) would have to work very hard to stay in the same place. Around the walls would be murals depicting *The Junior League Girls In Brookline,* or *Married But Willing.* (Readers are referred to my earlier books, entitled *The Junior League Girls At Rosemary Hall,* or *Thwarting the Evil Janitor,* and *The Junior League Girls At The Ritz Bar,* or *If It Ain't Dry It Ain't A Martini.*)

Finally, the section devoted to the Glamour Girls would contain, at one end, a throne on which Brenda Frazier is seated (till next season). Miss Frazier will hold in one hand a drink compounded of milk, coca-cola, and old blood; in the other she will hold a bill from the Ritz. She will be wearing a creation whipped up by Maggy Rouff, Schiaparelli, and the effects of three quarts of champagne. On her lap will repose a book by Lucius Beebe, and at her feet will repose Lucius Beebe himself, all in mauve. Photographers will be everywhere; and the place will be full of Glamour Girls, zebra stripe motifs, and sex with a vengeance. Restrooms will be provided for any spectators who feel nauseated.

Now, this camp should be placed, if we have anything to say about it, on Boston Common, between the Subway Station and the Bandstand. Admission will be nominal; say, fifteen cents. And when it's all done, we can forget the whole business and start cleaning up Massachusetts politics, an infinitely harder job.

But of course, the debutante is really not as bad as she sounds. She recovers from her debut, marries Jonathon Codpiece, (of the Boston Codpieces, her second cousin), propagates, and eventually dies. All in all, she is a nice, well-rounded girl, without a brain in her head. But, as she is a member of the upper classes (in Boston, at least), and as the upper classes have been operating on no mentality for nearly half a century, she really has nothing to fear. As long as she can afford psychoanalysts, she gets along. Unless Mr. Dies is right—

—Who, says little Gianciotto, is Mr. Dies?

—Mr. Dies, says old Malatesta, is a booger. And take your g-dd-m hand off that maid.

NARCISSUS IN WINTER

Charles Henri Ford

Shiver, then, by the faint water,
clip the ferns of ice with your teeth;
the body of the black snake falters
and flows from the palms of your feet.

The leaf curled in the snow's mouth
repeats your hand whose lines are prone,
separate as a branch the blizzard brought
to remind you of Echo's bones.

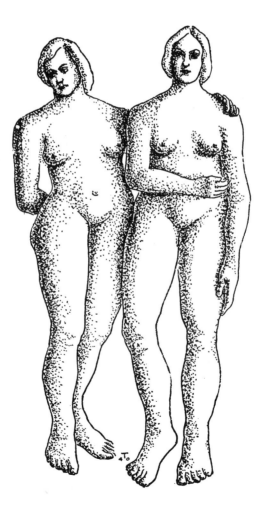

THE ULTIMATE PLATO

Delmore Schwartz

WITH PICASSO'S GUITAR

Instead of attempting a detailed study of some aspect of Stevens, I should like to try to make a rapid survey—barely more than a list—of several closely-related aspects of his work as a whole. The virtue of such a bird's-eye view is the relationship and unity it may reveal. The defects will be plain enough; one always risks being superficial in trying to cover a good deal of ground.

1. "*A Point of View*": Taken generally, Stevens' perspective is that of the man of art, the museum- and concert-goer, the student of French poetry (but not of American poetry), the intelligent tourist (but nevertheless, the tourist, not the native), the aesthete in the best sense of the word. This can be quickly illustrated merely by mentioning some of the details of his work. He summons up Mozart, Corot, Bach, Picasso, and other famous artists as witnesses and symbols. Statues, organ music, paintings, and words for paintings, French words and archaic dictionary words are important elements in the texture of his work. He mentions and uses significantly a great many places which are exotic, tropical, and foreign: Cuba, Yucatan, Mexico, Sweden. He describes Paradise as if it were a landscape garden and writes of the Carolinas as if they were exotic too. But the city of Hartford, Conn. is almost never named, though in his latest period he appears to be finding his frame of reference in some such American city, and in some of his most recent lyrics, he comes as close to Hartford as Jersey City (these exceptions, however, are signs of the profound concern about society at present which marks off his latest work from the rest).

This predominance of references derived from Art of some kind is not merely a matter of surface, but also of the way that objects are looked at, and some of the values by which they are judged. It is a vision instructed in the museums, regarding objects in the world after seeing them in paintings. So, when Stevens is writing most seriously of love in middle-age, he naturally finds such a trope as "men at forty . . . painting lakes." So too a naked body is a nude in some poems, and so it is that the predominant theme of "Harmonium" is the imagination, the source of all art,

> The magnificent cause of being,
> The imagination, the one reality
> In this imagined world.

Now the perspective of the Art-man is nothing new in the history of modern poetry. On the contrary, it has its beginnings in Gautier, Baudelaire, and Laforgue (whom Stevens must have read), and it sustains itself in various ways through many different authors. It can be seen at its worst in authors like James Branch Cabell, at its average quality in some of Verlaine, Dowson, Arthur Symons, and other poets of the nineties; and at its best in Stevens. For these writers, when their various differences have been allowed for, have in common a belief that Art is a most important source of value, perhaps the central interest of Life. Consider how in Mr. Cabell's prose it is so often insisted that the imagined world is the only one worth living in, and to write beautifully of fine things is the only sensible course for an author. Mr. Cabell is an extreme; but of all these writers it can be said that their language is profusely burdened with references and derivations from literature and art; their subjects are very often not the ordinary experiences of life, but works of art; and their most exalted moments are those in which they enjoy works of art.

This tradition, for it is continuous enough and

strong enough to be dignified with that name, has very deep roots in modern life. It springs from the separation between art and the rest of life which is due to many causes, the chief of which may be industrialism. Thus it is almost natural that writers in this tradition should be *against* Life and *for* Art, a partisanship which would have seemed inconceivable to most authors in most societies. The doctrine of Art for Art's sake and the desire to dumbfound and appall the middle class are obvious public expressions for the attitude which moves these writers. For what a good deal of their poetry actually *presents* is the experience, in modern life, of art as separated from the rest of life, so that the former is special, precious, taken as merely decorative, often misunderstood and abused; while the latter is impoverished, ignoble, vulgar and full of disorder, presided over by the business man and the Philistine (such terms as Philistine and Bohemian received their art-connotations during the 19th century). "O how quotidian Life is," wrote Laforgue, and proceeded to juxtapose the ordinariness and vulgarity of everyday experience with the beauty of Literature by rewriting classical, and medieval fables in a language in which the ironic effect is consistently gained either by speaking of the heroic and classical in cheap conversational slang; or conversely, by hailing the vulgarity of modern life in the rhetoric of the grand manner.

In such a writer as Laforgue, the result of this fundamental division is irony, pathetic irony, but irony without relief and without insight. This empty conclusion, hardly avoided by most authors of the tradition except when they turn to another basic subject, is penetrated and seen through by Stevens first, by means of the thoroughness with which he inspects his point of view, trying to look at everything from its station; secondly, by a profound "contemporaneity," an awareness of the present and the present movement of society which is almost a vigil, and which has motivated his last two volumes of verse; but above all, by a philosophical concern with the nature of things which has enabled him to generalize his experience in ways not available to other such authors. This philosophical interest is quite distinct, it should be noted, from the way in which Laforgue plays ironically with philosophical terms.

2. *Thoroughness*: "If one became sufficiently absorbed, *absolutely* involved, in one passion, then it would become the whole world for one. All things, including one's duties, would be translated into its terms. It would then present the same difficulties as any other interest or mixture of interests. For if one becomes completely interested in a thing, it becomes something else, not what it seemed to be." This may serve to describe what happens when one attempts to see the whole world from the perspective of Art. Beginning with an interest in works of art, apart from the rest of life, if one holds to that interest long enough and completely enough, the conditions of works of art, art's relationship to Life, the disorder of society in which art exists, and the ultimate questions about Nature and Life come into the foreground, within the frame of the painting. This is what has occurred in Stevens' work. When "Harmonium" was published in 1923, the critic who could have foreseen that in his third book, Stevens would be making acute observations about Basilewsky's airplane concerto, the latest Soviet réclame—without in the least giving up his style or his major interests—such a critic would have seemed fantastic and would now seem to be a veritable Joseph.

3. *The Fate of Society*: One reason for this growth of interests, within a frame, is probably simple curiosity, tenacious and continuous; but another is undoubtedly the poet's sense that something catastrophic is happening to the society in which he lives. The most explicit statement of this is to be found in "Ideas of Order," the book of verse Stevens published after a silence of eleven years:

> There is order in neither sea nor sun.
> The shapes have lost their glistening.
> There are these sudden mobs of men,
>
> These sudden clouds of faces and arms,
> An immense suppression, freed,
> These voices crying without knowing for what,

Except to be happy, without knowing how,
Imposing forms they cannot describe,
Requiring order beyond their speech . . . .

This poem is entitled, fitly enough, "Sad Strains Of A Gay Waltz," and the poet himself appears on the scene, speaking of himself, of the past, of the forms of society which are in peril:

Too many waltzes are ended. And then
There's that mountain-minded Hoon . . . .

Who found all form and order in solitude,
For whom the shapes were never shapes of men.
Now, for him, his forms have vanished.

The solitude of "that mountain-minded Hoon" (this may be a coinage from "one alone," that is, the introvert, the solitary man) is the isolation of the modern poet from the rest of society. It was an isolation accepted and used by the poet. But now it is ending, the glistening shapes of the dancers have turned into sudden mobs of men.

In "Owl's Clover," a long poem obviously to be contrasted with "The Comedian As the Letter C," the poet considers the future which may develop from the present crisis of society; brings to bear upon this subject his old machinery of high-flown blank verse, art-works as sources of value, of symbols, and of the very texture of the writing, and states his ambiguous feelings about the future in characteristic terms:

Basilewsky in the bandstand played
"Concerto for Airplane and Pianoforte,"
The newest Soviet réclame. Profound
Abortion, fit for the enchanting of basilisks . . . .

Shall you,
Then, fear a drastic community evolved
From the whirling, slowly and by trial; or fear
Men gathering for a final flight of men,
An abysmal migration into possible blue?

With final insight, the poet states the criterion which ought to prevail:

As the man the state, not as the state the man.

And the whole meditation concludes upon the poet's fixed obsession, the place and rôle of art in life, in any society.

4. *The Ultimate Plato:* Confronted by the disasters of society, what could be more characteristic of the poet than to consider with fear and trembling and some hope, the place of art in the future? So too, in "The Man with the Blue Guitar," the complicated relationships and interconnections between Art and Life, between things as they are and things as they are on the blue guitar, are meditated upon in considerable detail. The characteristic, the ability which makes all the difference is clear in these instances. His resource is meditation and philosophical generalization. It is this which makes possible an escape from the perspective of the Art-man, or rather a transformation of that perspective simply by considering its general significance. Even where society is his direct subject, he tends to regard it in terms of essences and abstractions; not in specific social terms.

In his earlier work, Stevens became explicitly philosophical on subjects like Man in Nature, or Man's belief about the final character of Nature. He wrote not only of the "the curtains in the house of the metaphysician," and the veritable *ding-an-sich,* but concerned himself in one of his finest poems, "Sunday Morning," with Christianity and supernaturalism. Here he asks if supernaturalism is not too much, in a way, and not enough, in another, for "what is divinity if it can come Only in silent shadows and in dreams?"; he compares Nature and Paradise, pointing to the beauty made possible by process and death, and presumably not available in Paradise; and then he proposes a new religion, if not a new god:

Supple and turbulent, a ring of men
Shall chant in orgy on a summer morn
Their boisterous devotion to the sun,
Not as a god, but as a god might be,
Naked among them, like a savage source . . . .

yet this naturalism which makes him say in two other poems that a person is what is around him, his dress, his house, his carriage, and that "the soul is composed of the external world," this naturalism or materialism is qualified by a radical scepticism which makes the poet admit and envisage other possibilities and thus conclude "Sunday Morning" on the note of deliberate and sublime ambiguity:

> in the isolation of the sky
> At evening, casual flocks of pigeons make
> Ambiguous undulations as they silk
> Downward to darkness on extended wings.

It is perfectly clear in the context that the poet is not merely referring to pigeons, but to talking animals.

The ability to think philosophically (and with considerable philosophical tact) enables Stevens to write successfully such long meditations as "The Comedian As The Letter C" (which is, to be summary, a search for a way and a view of life by experiments with various views of life, realism, romanticism, subjectivism). It enables him to write of Nature not merely as something to be looked at but as a rich instance of fate, so that a wintry scene, "the junipers shagged with ice. The spruces rough with the distant glitter . . . the sound of the wind, the sound of a few leaves" are heard and seen by a listener who can grasp "Nothing that is not there and the nothing that is."

The idea and the ideal, he says in one poem, are like the evening star (as elsewhere he identifies the moonlight and the imagination) and, as if of his own use of the idea and the ideal, he says that

> It is a good light, then, for those
> That know the ultimate Plato,
> Tranquillizing with this jewel
> The torments of confusion.

It is a good light, indeed, for this particular poet. It is the light which distinguishes him from every poet who has worked from his perspective. In so far as any man can take on the insights of Western thought and make them his own, the poet can thus be said to be the ultimate Plato, or at least the latest. Or rather, let us say that the poet has stared so long at a picture of Picasso's and at its blue guitar that he has seen its general significance:

> Is this picture of Picasso's this "hoard
> of destruction," a picture of ourselves?

5. *Certain Costs:* These qualities are not gained, however, without certain losses. Stevens has written neither dramatic nor narrative verse, and it is difficult to see how he could. As Howard Baker has pointed out, there are no human beings in his poems (even the lady having breakfast in "Sunday Morning" disappears by the sixth stanza). We are presented almost always with the poet, or the protagonist of the poem, in isolation before the tableaux of Nature and Society, meditating upon them. The meditation consumes the poem again and again. There is seldom a specific scene or time or action, but only the mind moving among its thoughts and impressions and responding to situations which are referred to, but not concretely presented in the poem itself. "Rocks, moss, stonecrop, iron, merds," another poet writes, "The woman keeps the kitchen, makes tea, Sneezes at evening, poking the peevish gutter." By thus placing the fact within the poem, the meditation on the fact gains a great deal of strength and relevance.

Stevens might thus be located in the Spenserian-Miltonic line of English verse as opposed to the line of Webster and Donne (but the lines cross many times, sometimes in the same poet). One might say that the difference may have had its source in the fact that Eliot read Laforgue and then read Webster and Tourneur, while Stevens, having read Laforgue or at least been moved to the same point of view, then read Milton (of course Eliot also read Milton, but disliked him). In the end, however, these two readers' difference would have to be reduced to a profound difference in temperament; for they would not have sought what they were seeking, if they had not already found it, though perhaps only in a primitive form, in themselves.

In Stevens, an abstractness is always present; everything is turned into an object of the imagination and of the poet's meditation, and the result is that he is sometimes "too poetic," which is what Eliot said of certain poems of Tennyson. This may be the source, too, of the word-play which does not always escape the adventitious frivolity for which it is always mistaken by the careless reader. The burden of the meditative center may be responsible for the faults of Stevens' blank verse, a lack of variety in going from line to line, a difficulty with overflow, and in his later work, a tendency to anapestic substitution which unsettles the sonorous period. But virtue and defect seem inseparable. The magnificence of the rhetoric and the broad philosophical concerns seem to necessitate an exclusion of narrative and drama and make possible the richness, range, and freedom of the symbols.

6. *Hints for Historians*: Other aspects of Stevens' work hardly suggested in this hurried survey are perhaps equally important; and of the related aspects I have taken up, it is plain that a great deal more remains to be said. But now I should like to suggest a few further connections and comparisons which might be fruitful. Some of them are within the scope of the literary historian and no one else.

Thus, Stevens' poems began to appear in various publications at a time when free verse and free love were once again new things, when *The Smart Set* was a leading literary magazine, James Huneker a leading literary critic, and sophistication, provincialism, and membership among the élite were concerns of the *intelligentsia;* or rather the names they gave to their concerns. This local or national context brings us back to the isolation of the modern poet to which one always returns in considering Stevens. The causal connections can only be guessed at, of course, but as soon as one remembers that to be a poet at that time was to be peculiar, one has a possible explanation of the constant self-mockery and self-depreciation and depreciation of the seriousness of the poem which marks Stevens' titles in particular: it is as if the poet were ashamed of being a poet, or extremely self-conscious about the fact, and this may explain why he calls his wonderful meditation on love, "Le Monocle de Mon Oncle," thus resorting to French (for Paris has been the capital of Western culture) and thus presenting a decora-

tive ironic surface for a poem which is as serious as human discourse can be.

Another examination which might prove illuminating would be a detailed comparison of such poems as Valéry's "Le Cimetière Marin," "Dover Beach," Yeats' "Among School Children," Eliot's "Gerontion," and Stevens' "Sunday Morning." What these poems have in common is the death of belief in Christianity; all of them, save Eliot's, make use of Nature as a source of the particular details of the poem; and all of them but Yeats' reject supernaturalism in the most explicit statements. The resemblances among the poems are striking; so are the differences; but much light might be shed by considering them in comparison with one another, and then in the context of the intellectual history of the last fifty or seventy-five years, perhaps even going far back to such authors as Darwin and Huxley, and the scientists who impressed Paul Valéry so much.

A third context for Stevens' text is Shakespeare. It may not be immediately recognized that Stevens' "Peter Quince at the Clavier" is the Peter Quince of "A Midsummer Night's Dream." But one feels that the quality of the imagination in such a play as "A Midsummer Night's Dream" is very like that of Stevens when he is most free and most fanciful. Or consider such a line in Stevens as "Death is absolute and without memorial." It may be wholly original, of course, and spring from the common language similarly used. Or it may be a development of the line in "Measure for Measure," where the Duke says to the condemned Claudio, "Be absolute for death." But these connections are matters for the scholar. The important point is the resemblance of Stevens' verbal usages to one variety of Shakespearean blank verse.

Then, there is the intermittent concern with Puritanism, as seen, let us say, in the 'twenties, and as opposed to the imagination. In poems like "Academic Discourse at Havana," and "Disillusionment of Ten O'Clock," Puritanism becomes an important element in the poem. In the latter poem, one begins with the houses in which everyone is going to sleep at ten o'clock:

> The houses are haunted
> By white night-gowns

None of the night-gowns (with the implication of sex) are green, purple, or yellow; the people dressed in them, we are told, are not going to "dream of baboons and periwinkles;" only an old sailor,

> Drunk and asleep in his boots,
> Catches tigers
> In red weather

and is thus sole representative of the imagination in the small town where everyone goes to sleep at ten o'clock. The background of Puritanism suggests a cause for the exotic character of the verse less general, more local or more American, than the separation of Art and Life I discussed at the outset.

* * * * *

Confronted by the need of conclusion or summary, one is impressed by how much more there always is to say about Stevens. No matter with what aspect one begins, one has a sense of inexhaustible richness of significance and connection. But if one returns to the personal impression—the source of the critic's sincerity, we are told by two voices with authority—then one must say that this poetry, studied during the difficult evenings of modern life, is of a very familiar strangeness (as a view of one's brain and heart might be strange), and seems to have something to do with everything important and beautiful.

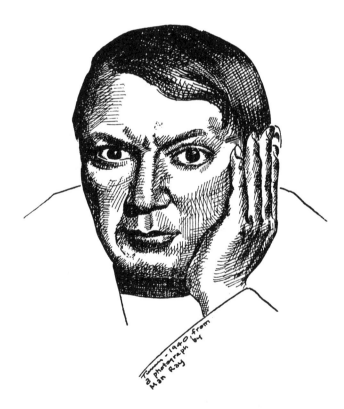

Tanawa – 1940 from a photograph by Man Ray

THE GREATEST THING IN THE WORLD

Norman Mailer

INSIDE, out of the rain, the lunch wagon was hot and sticky. Al Groot stopped in front of the doorway, and wiped his hands, and wrung his hat out, and scuffed his shoes against the dirt-brown mat. He stood there, a small, old, wrinkled boy of eighteen or nineteen with round beady eyes that seemed incapable of looking at you, unless you were in back of him. He stopped at the door, and waited, not sure of his reception, examining the place carefully, as if he might have need of this knowledge soon after. It was a little fancier than the ordinary lunchroom, with dark, old-wood booths at the left that fronted the sharp, glittering stools and counter of well polished chromium. A clock on the wall showed that it was after ten, which might have explained why the place was almost empty. There was no one at the counter, and the few truck drivers, sprawled out on two adjoining booths, to catch a late dinner, were tired, and very quiet, engrossed only in their sandwiches and hamburgers. Only one man was left behind the counter, and he was carefully cleaning the grease from the frankfurter griddle, with the slow motions of a man who has a great deal of time on his hands, and is desperately afraid of finishing his work, to face the prospect of empty tables and silent people. He looked at Al, uncertain for a moment how to take him, and then he turned back to the griddle, and gave it a last studious wipe. He spoke, without looking up, but his tone was friendly.

"Hi," he said.

Al said hello, watching the man scrape some crumblings off.

"It's a hell of a night, ain't it?" the counter man asked.

"Lousy."

"It sure is. Guess we needed it," he said. "The crops are hit bad when it don't rain enough."

"Sure," said Al. "Look, what does coffee and doughnuts cost?"

"Ten."

"Two doughnuts?"

"That's it."

"Uh-huh," said Al. "Could you let me have one doughnut, and half a cup of coffee for five cents? I ain't got but a nickel."

"I don't know," he said. "I could, but why should I?"

"I ain't had nothing to eat to-day," Al pleaded. "Come on."

The man looked up. Al sucked expertly on his cheeks, just pulling them in enough to make it look good.

"I guess you could stand it. Only, pay me now."

Al reached into his pocket, and tenderly extracted a nickel from two halves of a dollar bill. He finished over one third of the doughnut in the first bite, and realizing how extravagant he had been, he took a small begrudging sip of the coffee.

"Nice place," he said.

"I like it," the man said.

"You own it?"

"You're damn right, buddy. I worked to get this place. It's all mine. You don't find me giving anything away on it. Every cup of coffee a guy drinks feeds me too."

"Top of the world," Al said.

"Nyahr," he answered bitterly. "Lot of good it does me. You see anybody in here? You see me clicking the cash register? The hell you do."

Al was thinking of how tough his luck was that the truck drivers should be uniformed, which was as good as a 'no rider' sign. He grinned sympathetically at the owner, trying to look as wet as he could.

"Boy," he said, "I sure am stuck."

"Been hitching, huh?"

"Yeah, walked the last three miles, ever since it started to rain."

"Must be kind of tough."

"Sure, I figure I won't be able to sleep if it don't stop raining. That was my last nickel. Say, look, you wouldn't have a job for me?" he said stupidly.

"What'll I do, watch you work?"

"Then let me sleep here tonight. It won't cost you nothing."

"I don't run a flop-house."

"Skip it, forget it," Al said. "Only, let me stay here a while to dry off. When somebody comes in, maybe they'll give me a ride."

"All right, stay," he said. "I have such a fancy trade. New chromium, brass fixtures. Ahhhhr."

Al slipped off the stool, and sat down at a table in the rear, out of sight of the counterman. He slouched down against the side of the booth, and picked up a menu, supported between the salt and pepper shakers, looking at it interestedly, but past all craving or desire. He thought that it had been almost a year since he had had a steak. He tried to remember what it tasted like, but his memory failed, and to distract him from the tantalizing picture, he started examining the spelling on the sheet, guessing at a word first, then seeing how close he had been. Another company truck driver had come in, and Al shot a quick look back to see where the owner was. Finding him up front, almost out of sight, he quickly picked up the ketchup bottle, and shook large gobs of it into his mouth as fast as he could get it out. It burned and stung inside his stomach, and he kept blowing, trying to cool his mouth. Noticing a few

drops on the table, he took a paper napkin, and squeezed them over to the edge, where they hung, ready to fall. He ran his little finger along underneath, gathering them up, and catching the drops in his mouth as they dripped off.

He felt for the split dollar bill, and fingered it. This time, he thought, it was really his last. Once three months ago, he had five dollars. He thought back, and tried to remember how he had gotten it. It was very vague, and he wondered whether he had stolen it or not. The image of five separate bills, and all that he could do with them, hit him then, with all its beauty and impossibility. He thought of cigarettes, and a meal, and a clean woman in a good place, and new soles to his shoes, but most of all he thought of the soft leathery feel of money, and the tight wad it made in his pants. "By God," he said thickly, "there's nothing like it. You can't beat it. If I just had five dollars again." He withdrew his hand, taking the two pieces out, smoothing them lovingly on the table. He considered breaking the bill for another doughnut, but he knew he couldn't. It was the last thing between him and . . . . He stopped, realizing that he had passed the last thing, there was no 'and.' Still, he did not think any more of spending this last bill. Tomorrow or to-night he would be in Chicago, and he could find something to eat for a day or two. He might even pick up half a buck by mooching. In the meantime he felt hungry. He stayed in the booth, staring at the end wall, and dreaming of his one-time hoard.

Three men came in to eat. Al saw them hesitate at the door, wondering whether to eat in a booth or at the counter.

"Take a booth," one said.

Al looked at them. This might be a ride, he thought. He waited until they had started eating, and then he went over to them, hitching at his faded gray-blue dungarees.

"Hi, sports," he said.

"Hello, sweet-face," one of them said.

"They call me Al Groot."

"His father's name was Groot," said one of them turning to the others.

"I ain't asking for any dough."

They eased up a little. "Boy, you sure ain't, sweet-face," one of them said. "Sit down, sit down," he said. "My name's Cataract, account of my eye, it's no good, and this here is Pickles, and this is Cousin."

They all looked alike.

"I guess you know what I want," Al said.

"Ride?"

"Yeah, where you going?"

"Chicago."

"Start warming the seat up for me," Al said.

They grinned, and continued eating. Al watched Cataract go to work on a hamburger. He held it between thick, grease-stained fingers, that dug into it, much as they might have sunk into a woman. He swallowed a large piece, slobbering a little, and slapping his tongue noisily  against the roof of his mouth as he ate. Al watched him fascinated. Wild thoughts of seizing the hamburger, and fighting the man for it, deviled him. He moved his head, in time to Cataract's jaws, and he felt madly frustrated as Cataract dropped the last bit into his mouth. Cataract lit a cigarette, and exhaled noisily, with a little belch of content.

"Jesus Christ," Al whispered.

He turned his attention to the other two, and watched them eat each piece down to the very bitter end. He hated them, and felt sick.

"Let's go," shouted Pickles. "Come on, sweet-face."

The car was an old Auburn sedan, with a short humped-up body. Al sat in back with Cataract; Cousin was driving. Cataract took out a pack of Luckies, and passed them around. Al took the pack, and fumbled with it, acting as if he were having trouble extracting a cigarette. When he handed it back, he had a bonus of two more cuddled next to his dollar bill.

"Where you from?" Pickles asked.

"Easton," Al said. "It's in Pennsy."

Cataract rolled his tongue around. "Good town," he said, extending his arm, fist closed, twisting it in little circles at the wrist.

"Yeh," Al said. "One of the best. I ain't been there in four, no three years. Been on the road since."

"Hitching?"

"Hell, no," Al exploded with contempt. "It's a sucker's game hitching. I work the trains; you know, 'Ride the rails in comfort with Pullman'."

"Yeahr. How're the hobo camps?" Cousin asked.

It was Al's turn to extend his arm.

They all started laughing with wise, knowing, lewd laughs.

"What do you boys do?" Al asked.

They laughed again.

"We're partners in business," Cataract said.

Al looked at them, discarding one thing after

another, trying to narrow down the possibilities. He decided they were sucker players of some sort.

"You guys know of any jobs in Chicago?" Al asked.

"How much you want?"

"About twenty a week. I'm in now. Got thirty-four bucks."

Pickles whistled. "What're you mooching meals for, then?"

"Who's mooching?" Al demanded. "Did I ask you guys for anything besides a ride?"

"Noooo."

"Awright, then don't go around being a wise guy."

Pickles looked out the window, grinning. "Sorry, bud."

"Well, awright then," Al said, acting sore.

"Well, awright then, dig, dig, dig, well awright," Cousin mimicked.

Cataract laughed, trying to be friendly. "They're funny boys, you know, just smart. They wish they had your thirty-four, that's all."

It worked, Al thought. He let himself grin. "It's okay," he said.

He looked out the window. They weren't in Chicago yet, but the lights shining from the houses on the side of the road were more frequent, making a steady yellow glare against the wet windows, and he knew that they must be almost at the outskirts by now. Just then, he saw a City Limits and Welcome sign flash past. Cousin turned off the highway, and went along for a way on a dirt road that in time turned onto an old oil-stained asphalt street. They passed a few factories, and Al thought of dropping off, but he wondered if it might not pay him to stay with the men a while.

Cataract yawned. "What about a game of pool now, boys?" he asked.

So that's what they are, Al thought.

"Say," he said, "I'd like to play too. I ain't very good, but I like the game." Pickles assured him. "We're no good either, that is, I'm no good. You and me can play."

"Yeah," Al said, "it ought to be fun."

Cousin was driving up Milwaukee Avenue now. He turned left, slowing down very carefully as he did so, although there were no cars in sight.

"That Cousin drives like an old woman," Pickles commented. "I could drive faster going backwards."

Cousin jeered at him. "You couldn't drive my aunt's wheel-barrow. I'm the only guy left who hasn't lost his license," he said speaking to Al. "It's because I take it easy when I drive a car."

Al said he didn't know much about cars, but he guessed maybe Cousin was right.

The car pulled up in front of a dark gray building on the corner of a long row of old brownstone homes. It was a dark street, and the only evidence that people lived on it, were the overflowing garbage and ash cans spaced at irregular intervals in front of the houses. The poolroom itself, was down in the cellar, underneath a beauty parlor, and a secretarial school. On the steps going down, Al could see pencilled scribblings on the walls; some hasty calculations of odds, a woman's telephone number with a comment underneath it, a few bits of profanity, and one well drawn nude woman.

The foot of the stairs opened right onto the tables, which were strung out in one long narrow line of five. The place was almost dark, only the first table being used, and no lights were on in the back. Pickles stepped over to the counter, and started talking to the boss, calling him familiarly and for some reason, annoyingly, by the name Nick. Nick was a short, broad, sweaty Italian. He and Pickles looked up at Al at the same time, and Pickles motioned to him.

"Nick, this is a pal of mine. I want you to treat him nice if he ever comes in again. Tell thick Nick your name, sweet-face."

"Call me sweet-face," Al said.

"H'lo," Nick said. "Pleased to meet you."

"Where we play?" Al asked. He noticed that Cataract and Cousin had not come down yet.

"Take number four."

"Sweet-face and me on number four," Pickles said. "Got it."

He walked down turning on a few lights. He

stopped at the cue rack, and picked one at random. Al followed him, selected one carefully, sighting along it to see if there was any warp, and sprinkled some talc over it. "Should we play a rack for table?" he asked.

"Sure," said Pickles. "You mind if we play straight? I don't know any fancy stuff."

"Me neither."

They tossed a coin, and Al had to break. He shot poorly, hit the wrong ball, and scratched. Pickles overshot and splattered balls all over the table. Al sunk two, shooting as well as he could, knowing that Pickles would notice any attempts at faking. They both played sloppily, and it took fifteen minutes to clear the table. Al won, eight balls to seven.

"We're pretty close," Pickles said. "What about playing for a couple of bucks this next table?"

He watched Cataract and Cousin, who had just come in, and were starting to play.

Al could feel the sweat starting up in the small of his back, and on his thighs. I can still get out of it, he thought. At least I'll have my buck. The thought of another five dollars, however, was too strong for him. He tried to think of what would happen to him if he didn't get away with it, but he kept remembering how it felt to have money in his hands. He heard himself speaking, feeling it was not he, but some one right in back, or on top of him.

"Make it a buck," he said.

Pickles broke, again shooting too hard. Al watched him flub balls all over the table, slightly overdoing it this time. They finished the rack, Al getting a run of three at the end, to win, ten to five. Pickles handed him a dollar, and placed another on the side of the table. Al covered it with the one he had won. I wonder when he starts winning, Al thought. If I can only quit then. They played for a dollar twice more, Al winning both times. A first drop of perspiration drew together, and raced down his back. He saw Cataract watching them play, juggling two balls in his hand. They played for three dollars, Al winning, after being behind, five to two.

He straightened up, making an almost visible effort to relax.

"That makes six bucks," he said.

"Sure," said Pickles. "Let's make it five this time. I want to win my dough back."

This time Pickles won. Al handed him five dollars separating the bills with difficulty, and handing them over painfully.

"Another one for five," Pickles said.

Al looked around him desperately, wondering if he could get out. "Five," he croaked. Cataract was still juggling the balls.

It was the longest game he ever played. After every shot he stopped to wipe his hands. In the middle, he realized that this game was going to be given to him. He couldn't relax, however, because he knew the showdown would merely be delayed for another game or so.

He won, as he knew he would, but immediately the pressure was on again. They played once more for five, and he won. After it was over, he didn't trust himself to stand, and he leaned against the cue rack, trying to draw satisfaction from the money in his pocket. He dreamed of getting out, and having it all, to do with as he pleased, until he saw Pickles and Cataract looking at each other. Cataract threw a ball up, and closed his fingers too soon, missing it. It came down, with a loud shattering crack, that made Nick look up from his counter. That's the signal, Al thought.

They were the only ones in the place now.

Pickles stroked his cue, grinning. "Your luck's been too good, sweet-face. I think this is going to be my game. I got twenty bucks left. I'm laying it down."

"No," said Al. "I don't want to."

"Listen, I been losing dough. You're playing."

They all looked at him menacingly.

"I want to quit," Al said.

"I wouldn't try it," Cousin said.

Al looked about him, trapped, thoughts of fighting them, mixing with mad ideas of flight.

Cataract stepped toward him, holding a cue in his hand.

"All right," Al said, "I'll play."

Pickles broke, making a very beautiful 'safe,' leaving Al helpless. He bent over his stick to shoot. The balls wavered in front of him, and he could see the tip of the cue, shaking up and down. He wiped his face, and looked around to loosen his muscles. When he tried again, it was still useless. He laid his cue on the table, and walked to the back.

"Where you going?" asked Pickles.

"To the can. Want to come along?" He forced a laugh from the very bottom of his throat.

He passed through a small littered room, where old soda boxes were stored. The bathroom was small and filthy; the ceiling higher than the distance from wall to wall. Once inside, he bolted the door, and sank down on the floor, whimpering softly. After a while he quieted, and looked around. The only other possible exit was a window, high up on the wall facing the door. He looked at it, not realizing its significance, until a chance sound from outside made him realize where he was, and what was happening to him. He got up, and looked at the wall, examining its surface for some possible boost. He saw there was none, crouched down, and jumped. His hands just grasped the edge, clung for a fraction of a second, and then scraped off. He knelt again, as close to the wall as he could possibly get, flexed himself, and leaped up. This time his palms grasped hold. He pressed his fingers against the stone surface, and chinned up enough to work his elbows over. He rested a moment, and then squeezed his stomach in and hung there on the ledge against the window, his legs dangling behind. He inched the window open noiselessly, and forgetting he was in the cellar, looked down into blackness. For a moment he was panic-stricken, until he remembered he was in the cellar, and had to look up. He shifted his position, and raised his head. There was a grating at right angles to the window, fixed above a dump heap, much like the one beneath a subway grille. It was very dark outside, but he could make out that it opened into an alley. Overjoyed, he took his money out, almost falling off in the act, kissed it, put it back, and tried to open the grating. He placed his hands

under it and pushed up as hard as he could in his cramped position. The grille didn't move. He stuck one foot through the open window, and straddled the ledge, one foot in, one foot out. Bracing himself, he pushed calmly against the grating, trying to dislodge it from the grime imbedded in it. Finding his efforts useless, he pushed harder and harder until arms were almost pushed into his chest, and his back and crotch felt as if they would crack. Breathing heavily, he stopped and stared up past the grating. Suddenly, with a cry of desperation, he flung himself up, beating against it with his hands and arms, until the blood ran down them. Half crazy, he gripped the bars and shook, with impassioned groans. His fingers slipped against a little obstruction, on one of the end bars. His hand felt it, carressed it, hoping to find some lever point, and discovered it to be a rivet between the foundation and the grille. He sat there, huge sobs torn from him, his eyes gazing hungrily at the sky above. After a bit, he withdrew his leg, wormed his body in again, closed the window, and dropped heavily to the floor, lying in a heap as he had fallen, his face to the wall. I'll just wait till they come for me, he thought. He could hear someone coming toward the door. Pickles knocked. "Hey, kid," he yelled from the other side of the partition, "Hurry up."

Al stood up, a mad flare of hope running through him as he thought of the money he still had. He held his hand to his throat, and struggled to control his voice. "Be right out," he said, managing to hold it through to the end. He heard Pickles walk away, and felt a little stronger. He started to wash himself, to get the blood off. His hands were still bleeding dully, the blood oozing out thickly and sluggishly, but he was able to stop the flow somewhat. He backed away, glanced out the window once more, and took his money out. He held it in his hands, and let the bills slip through his fingers. Gathering them up, he kissed them feverishly, rubbing the paper against his face and arms. He folded them tenderly, let down his pants, and slipped the cash into a little secret pocket, just under the crotch. He flattened out the bump it made, and unlocked the door to go out. His heart was still pounding, but he felt calmer, and more determined.

They were waiting for him impatiently, smoking quickly and nervously.

Al took out one of Cataract's cigarettes and asked for a match. He lit it, sucking deeply and gratefully from it. They glared at him, their nerves almost as tight as his.

"Come on," said Pickles, "It's your turn to shoot."

Al picked up his cue, gripping it hard to make his hand bleed faster. He bent over, made a pretence of sighting, and then laid his cue down, exposing the place where his hand had stained it.

"What's the matter?" Cousin snapped.

"I can't hold a cue," Al said. "I cut my hand in there."

"What do you mean you can't play?" Pickles shouted. "My money's up. You got to play."

"You can't force me. I'm not going to play. It's my money, it's mine see, and you can't make me. You guys can't pull this on me; you're just trying to work a sucker game."

It was the wrong thing to say. Cataract caught him by the shirt, and shook him. "Grab ahold of that stick," he said.

Al wrenched loose. "Go to hell," he said. "I'm quitting."

He picked up his hat, and started walking down past the tables to go out. He had to pass three tables and the counter to get to the stairs. He walked slowly, hoping to bluff his way out. He knew he had no chance if he ran. He could feel the sweat starting up much faster this time. His shoulders were twitching, and he was conscious of the effort of forming each step, expecting something to hit him at every second. His face was wet, and he fought down an agonizing desire to turn and look at them. Behind him, they were silent. He could see Nick at the entrance, watching him walk toward him, his face expressionless. Fascinated, he hung onto Nick's eyes, pleading silently with him. A slight smile grew on Nick's face. It broke into a high

unnatural laugh, squeaking off abruptly. Terrified, Al threw a quick glance back, and promptly threw himself on his face. A cue whizzed by, shattering on the far wall with a terrific smash. Before he could get up, they were on him. Cataract turned him on his back, and knelt over him. He brought the heel of his hand down hard on Al's face, knocking his head on the floor. He saw them swirl around him, the pool tables mixed in somewhere, and he shook his head furiously, to keep from going out. Cataract hit him again.

Al struck out with his foot, and hit him in the shin.

"You dirty little bastard," Cataract said. "I'll teach you."

He slammed his knee down into Al's stomach. Al choked and writhed, the fight out of him for a moment. They turned him over, and stripped his pockets, looking for his money. They shook him. "Where is it, sweet-face?" Pickles asked.

Al choked for breath.

"I lost it," he said mockingly.

"It's in his pants somewhere," Cousin said. "These rats always got a secret pocket." They tried to open his pants. He fought crazily, kicking, biting, screaming, using his elbows and knees.

"Come on," Cataract commanded, "get it off him."

Al yelled as loud as he could. Nick came over. "Get him out," he said. "The cops'll be dropping in soon. I don't want trouble."

"What'll we do with him?"

"Take him out on the road where no one will hear you. After that, it's your imagination." He squealed with laughter again.

They picked him up, and forced him out. He went with them peacefully, too dazed to care. They shoved him in the car, and Cousin turned it around. Al was in front, Cataract in the back seat, holding his wrist so he couldn't break loose before they started.

Al sat there silently, his head clearing, remembering how slowly Cousin drove. He looked out, watching the ground shoot by, and thought of jumping out. Hopelessly, he looked at the speedometer. They were going around a turn, and Cousin had slowed down to less than twenty miles an hour. He had jumped off freight trains going faster than that, but there had been no door in the way, and no one had been holding him. Discouraged, he gave up the idea.

Cousin taunted him. "See that white sign, sweet-face? We turn left there, just around it, and after that it won't be long."

Anger and rebellion surged through him. They were taking away something that he had earned dangerously, and they were going to beat him up, because they had not been as smart as he. It was not fair. He wanted the money more than they did. In a fury, he decided to jump at the turn. The sign was about a hundred yards away; it would be his last chance. He figured it would take seven seconds to reach it.

He turned around to face Cataract, his left elbow resting loosely against the door handle. He had turned the way his wrist was twisted, holding it steady, so that Cataract would not realize the pressure was slackened. One, he counted to himself. "Look," he begged Cataract, "Let me off. I ain't got the money, let me off." Maybe thirty yards gone by. Cataract was talking, "Oh, you're a funny boy, sweet-face. I like you, sweet-face." Another twenty. "Yeh, sure I'm funny, I'm a scream," he said. "Oh, I'm so funny." The sign, where is it? We should have reached it. Oh please God, show me the sign, you got to, it's my money, not theirs, oh please. "Goddam you, please," he shouted. "What?" Cataract yelled. Cousin slowed down. The sign slipped by. They started to turn. Al spat full in Cataract's face, and lashed out with his wrist against the thumb. His elbow kicked the door open, and he yanked his hand loose, whirled about, and leaped out, the door just missing him in its swing back.

His feet were pumping wildly as he hit the ground. He staggered in a broken run for a few steps, before his knees crumpled under him, and he went sprawling in the dust. His face went grinding into it, the dirt mashing up into his cheeks, and hands. He lay there stunned for a very long second, and then he pushed hard

with his palms against the ground, forcing himself up. The car had continued around the turn, and in the confusion had gone at least a hundred feet before it stopped. Al threw a stone at the men scrambling out, and plunged off into a field. It had stopped raining, but the sky was black, and he knew they would never catch him. He heard them in the distance, yelling to each other, and he kept running, his legs dead, his head lolling sideways, his breath coming in long ripping bursts. He stumbled over a weed, and fell, his body spreading out on soft wet grass. Exhausted, he lay there, his ear close to the ground, but no longer hearing them, he sat up, plucking weakly at bits of grass, saying over and over again. "Oh, those suckers, those big, dumb, suckers. Oh, those dopes, those suckers . . . ."

At two-thirty, Al Groot, his stomach full, swung off a street car near Madison Street, and went into a flop-house. He gave the night man a new dollar bill, and tied the eighty-five cents change in a rag that he fastened to his wrist. He stood over his bed, and lit some matches, moving them slowly over the surface of his mattress. A few bedbugs started out of their burrows, and crept across the bed. He picked them up, and squashed them methodically. The last one he held in his hand, watching it squirm. He felt uneasy for a mement, and impulsively let it escape, whirling his wrist in a circle to throw it away from the bed. He stretched himself out, and looked off in the distance for a while, thinking of women, and hamburgers, and billiard balls, and ketchup bottles, and shoes, and most of all, of the thrill of breaking a five dollar bill. Lighting the last of Cataract's cigarettes, he thought of how different things had been, when he had first palmed them. He smoked openly, not caring if someone should see him, for it was his last. Al smoked happily, tremendously excited, letting each little ache and pain well into the bed. When the cigarette was finished he tried to fall asleep. He felt wide awake, though, and after some time he propped himself on an elbow, and thought of what he would do the next day. First he would buy a pack of cigarettes, and then he would have a breakfast, and then a clean woman; he would pay a buck if he had to, and then a dinner and perhaps if he had time he would see a movie. He stopped suddenly, unable to continue, so great was his

ecstasy. He lay over his pillow and addressed it.

"By God," Al Groot said, about to say something he had never uttered before, "By God, this is the happiest moment of my life."

Inventory and Statement:

by Howard Nemerov

A Declamation

50 beautiful girls count 'em 50, are dying,
all together and slowly. Their hearts
beat one-two-three-four, they've worked
together all their lives and given you
good entertainment: and the young clerk
with the hot pants, in the third row center,
was perhaps the least of the sinners among you.

Plato dreamed of a surpassing love
bound up beyond the moving spheres: and Ziegfeld
dreamed of fifty beautiful girls fifty,
who are dying.
                The private citizen talks Babylon,
and has a righteous tea with the pastor,
and lusts in his heart; while my landlady
threw Alice out on the street and read Paris Nights.
Plato is dead, and Ziegfeld no less dead:
for I have given you here a thread of mine own life,
or that for which I lived.

What shall you do when winter is on the world,
and time comes out of the cliff to dine among you:
and the strumpet has none to love with her legs,
and the bride goes to an empty bed,
and the lover lies in the hasty grave
the earthworms dug under him?
Why, then you will set alarm clocks,
and whisper the time in restaurants;
there will be learned discussions, there will be
symposia; and the newsreels will picture
decay in the organism, newspapers will devote column
to the death of a leaf.

Enforce the censorship: excise the merely
heterosexual: and show instead
defecation, masturbation, and a new
all-color version of Les Cent-Vingt Jours
—let the people learn the fashionable
technic from Alcibiades, and let
the newsboys peddle pictures of the Marquis
performing a subtle experiment.

For the fifty fair are dead, and godhead gone:
Brightness is dust, and through these portals pass
Plato, Ziegfeld, and all loveliness.

THE NATIVE

IN THE WORLD

by

HOWARD

NEMEROV

THE CLIMB from sleep was difficult, a struggle up a staircase of soft pillows into which he sank again and again, drowsily defeated, from which he clumsily climbed again to a sight of the room that, seen in the equivocal wisdom of sleep, seemed to him any room, or all the rooms, in which he had ever slept, or ever been at home. Perhaps (an instant afterward he could no longer remember)—perhaps the phrase 'at home' struck the first tone of clarity in his mind, for about it the room began to arrange itself, to become again the familiar fashion of his circumstance, rising and composing to his own composition of its features. One thing—the overturned chair by the desk, with his clothes crushed under it—remained obstinately unfamiliar; when had he done that? He searched his memory, but the incident had sunk under sleep; he could readily imagine himself coming in drunk and knocking the chair down in the effort to hang his clothes over it, but actually to remember doing it—that was a different thing.

He got out of bed, and as he stood up felt

pain protest harshly in his forehead, making him dizzy with the angry sleep that would not readily dissolve. The clock said ten more or less exactly and it was dark outside. That meant twenty hours sleep; since two Tuesday morning. The dizziness surged higher as he bent in a methodical stupor to set the chair right and get his clothes. Going into the next room he started the phonograph and put on the Ricercare of the Musikalisches Opfer; then settled back in the darkness of a far corner. The one voice strode through his mind with a more or less plaintive confidence that another would follow, and soon another did, then one more and another, and the rest were sunken in the ensemble and the scratch of the needle. He closed his eyes, and as if his consciousness rested on quicksand he was irresistibly sucked back toward sleep, his eyelids grew heavy in a sort of undertow that he could feel heavily about his head. A dream, some frightening and fast forgotten dream, jarred him out of sleep; he had a vague impression of fear, something was being thrown at him. He turned on the light, changed over the record and picked up a book that was lying on the couch: *Alcohol the Friend of Man*. It was a reassuring volume by a doctor of unspecified repute; one must, he thought, turning over the pages, combine theory with practice. It seemed to him, as he had so often said, that there was a way to drink seriously, and a way not to drink seriously. Of three years at Harvard he had spent the last two learning the former, and was glad to distinguish himself from many of his acquaintances whose drinking was of the rowdy-up-and-puke sort. If a man wish to drink himself into insensibility, he phrased it pedantically, that is his own business; but equally he should not become a charge on his fellow-beings, and there is no excuse for forgetting manners one instant before passing out.

The record was over, and he walked across the room to change it, a strange figure in white pajamas, barefoot, head slightly too large for his excessively small frail body. He already had on his silver-rimmed reading glasses; he must have picked them up from the desk without thinking. He came from the Middle West, but one would unhesitatingly have called him a Yankee, judging by his pedantic contemptuous manner, his manners so civil as to be rude whenever he gave a cutting edge to his voice. His own estimate of himself was quite accurate: that his aloofness was respected, also his enormous and casual erudition; that even full professors were chary of a too great freedom with him or with his papers; that it was generally said of him that he would go far it he did not drink himself to death; that his paper on Augustinianism in the 17th century would no doubt put him in line for a fellowship; and at last, that he was drinking himself to death, or near to it—a state which he conceived of dubiously as a slight chill in his personal weather, as though a cloud should slide over a hill on which he was sunning himself. As to his reasons—if a man wish to drink himself into insensibility, he thought again · · · and perhaps it is not even his own business, or perhaps it is a shady transaction in that business, into which he does well not to inquire too far; look what happened to Oedipus.

He had put on the Ricercare again, but now he turned it off in the middle and called Rico's number. He listened apprehensively to the empty buzz of the phone, three, four, five times: he could hear it as if he were in the room, but as if the room were still empty, the lonely stupid ringing. Damn Rico, he thought, letting the phone ring again and again. Damn Rico, damn the twisted little Cuban Jesuit gone wrong, and damn, he said, and damn with the ring of the phone, and damn again and hung up. The receiver clattered into its cradle, and he felt again how painfully slow it was to wake up, how fiercely he must fight to stay above the surface, so to speak, to force every last ache and hurt in body and mind to the service of wakefulness, to a nagging insistence on belief in being awake. Rico was probably out with Alan; Alan, he thought angrily, the little blond jew-boy who's trying to get me out of the way by advising me seriously to go see a psychiatrist. And Rico is helping him too.

He shuddered slightly, envisioning conspiracy and betrayal: the swift, sure honest-eyed kiss of treachery, the bright, the clear, the trustworthy Judas; and the appalling thing was that it took place on such a pitifully small scale, the love life of a colony of worms. The disgust, and the hate, were waking him, slowly, as one fever will fight another and overcome it.

He took up the phone again and called Rhys. One could always talk to Rhys, no matter how far they had gone apart. Long ago, before the drinking, as he thought, they had been close friends, working furiously together, reading two and three books in an evening and listening to Bach from two to four in the morning. And then— there had been no break, not even a coolness; but they went their ways and saw rather less of each other. When he was drunk and wanted to talk out of turn, he often still climbed to Rhys' room, and he would talk wildly for fifteen minutes, often incoherently, and then Rhys would deliberate heavily, and say at last, "Well, John, it's difficult . . . . " which in itself would be somewhat reassuring; and then they would exhaust a small stock of polite and cynically erudite remarks about obscure poets, or faculty members, and it would be over.

"Hello, Rhys? This is John—Bradshaw . . . . I hope I didn't disturb you?"

"Not at all," said Rhys, in the coldly amiable tones that meant he was disturbed.

"Look, Rhys, . . . you mustn't mind me; I'm not drunk, but I took twelve grains of amytal last night when I was. I've just managed to get out of bed and I'm a little—woozy." He was, in fact, woozier than he had thought; there was that dull weight on his forehead that was worse than pain, more unknown and more fearful therefore.

"What I wanted to know was could you meet me for a drink, about fifteen minutes from now?"

"No, I can't," said Rhys. "You sound troubled. I don't know medicine, but isn't twelve grains rather much?"

"The prescribed adult dose is a grain and a half. I wish you'd come out for a drink. I want

to talk to you. Really, you know, it gets to be too much, sometimes . . . everywhere you go people are such bitches . . . . "

"What the hell is wrong, John?"

"Oh,—look, I'm liable to ramble a bit—I'm not very awake and the drug is still pretty strong—Oh goddam it Rhys, I've been betrayed, I—"

"Again?" A politely skeptical coolness.

Steady, he thought to himself; he was weak and falling again, and before answering he bit his lower lip hard, till the blood ran, to save himself from sleep.

"I mean it," he said stubbornly.

"Yes," said Rhys; and John recognized the tone Rhys used to nice drunks. "Yes, people are . . . difficult sometimes."

"Rhys, I'm not drunk. I want to talk to you. Why won't you have a drink with me?"

"Because I don't feel like it, John."

"Rhys, you think I'm drunk. I'm not, Rhys. It's the amytal. I couldn't be drunk, Rhys, I just got up, I've slept since two this morning."

"I know you're not drunk, John," said Rhys coldly. "I'm busy, and I think you ought to go back to bed. You don't sound very well."

"I only want to talk to you about Rico. You think I'm drunk."

"What's Rico done now?"

"I want to talk to you, Rhys."

"Well . . . . ?"

"Not on the phone."

"All right then, good night."

"Rhys—"

"Goodnight."

He waited for the dead click at the other end, and then placed the receiver carefully down. That had been a shameful performance; he was not drunk, but he could not have been more maudlin in any case. Rhys would be nodding his head sagely at this very moment: poor John Bradshaw. Oh, Damn Rhys. It was unfair of him. He might have had the common courtesy to listen to me, Rhys the careful, Rhys the undrunk, the dullard so proud of his dullness; one could summon up at will that favorite image of Rhys the damned, sitting deep in his armchair after a peculiarly bitter confessional period, sitting like a tolerant father-confessor, saying slowly between puffs at a cigarette, "Gawd, all you people live such exciting lives—it must be so difficult for you—you come and tell me about drinking and drugs and your homosexual experiences—and I sit here on my can, taking it all in, living my dull life . . . . " And he would sit there on his can, looking as old as he could, and staring into the fire, saying "they also serve," or some such. Poor Rhys! And so anxious, too, for you to know that he was only pretending dullness (which God knows he was not) and that he was a man of deep spiritual crises; as he would say, and so smugly, "My blowups all take place inside." All right. Let Rhys take that attitude. He wasn't required.

He got to his feet and walked slowly about the room, still thinking about Rhys, beating one little fist determinedly into the other hand and thinking with melancholy savagery, 'cut away the non-essentials, cut them out.' Rhys was a non-essential, Rhys always worrying about his writing, his piddling poetry, his painful anxiety that you read his newest work, that you pat him on the head, that you say nice things . . . . As for himself, he thought, there would be a book one day . . . a book after this long silence, after the non-essentials had been cut away and meditation had burned some great stone to form inside him, a book that would say all these things that had to be said, against the lying time, against the lying treacherous people, against Rhys, against Rico, against Alan, against (he sneered) all these smilers with their dull knives. One voice in this wilderness would not waste time crying out for help, for cries would only bring the wolves along faster. And through this, beneath the pain and the hate and the disgust and still half-prevailing sleep, he knew that he was crying out.

He went into the bathroom and looked at the bottle of amytal. There were at least twenty-five grains left; he smiled a little to remember the time when one grain could give him a solid night's sleep, the rapid necessity to step up the dose, the doctor at the hygiene building telling him pedagogically that he was by definition a drug-addict, his crazily epigrammatic crypticism to the doctor ("Jonathan Swift was by definition not a well man, and a neurotic to boot"), his cheerful announcement to Rhys (Rhys again): "You may call me De Quincey, I'm depraved." It was the precipitous, the plunging rapidity with which it had happened, this drug business, that astounded him and started slight inadmissible fears from their careful rest. How one thing led to another! in such seemingly inconsequential succession of one pettiness on the next, until, looking back from the most extravagantly fantastic heights of improbability, from the most unwarranted excesses and distortions, one was surprised and shocked to note how accurately and how unerringly every smallest act, word and gesture quietly conspired to build such a wildly rococo and out-of-the-way edifice,—such a goblin's architecture that at one moment one shuddered to think how it drove one on to the end, and at the next dismissed the whole structure with a smile for its implausibility. He stared fixedly at the bottle, imagined himself reaching out for it, tried to imagine himself refusing, and could only get a more or less chromo reproduction of a man in a magazine advertisement with his head turned disaffectedly away from a cup of coffee, saying: "Nope, I keep away from it. Keeps me up nights." This did not seem to him a satisfactory image of moral grandeur; with a smile he took up the bottle and locked it away in the filing cabinet on his desk. Then, puzzled, he looked at the key to the cabinet; what to do with that? He took it with him into the living room. He stood in the very center of the carpet, shut his eyes and turned around thrice, as though he were absurdly playing some children's game of blind man's buff; with his eyes still tightly closed, he threw the key straight before him, heard it tinkle in landing, then turned around twice more before opening his eyes. A glance about the room satisfied him that the key was not in evidence, not obviously anyhow. It might be days before he came across it. Unless the chamber-maid picked it up in the morning. He could imagine that she might hand it to him, asking whether he had lost it, and imagine himself saying no, I wonder how it could have got here . . . but one couldn't do that; all one's correspondence was in the filing cabinet, and notes for a couple of essays as well. Anyhow, it would be easy to find the key again, when it was really required. Meanwhile, one could . . . imagine it lost.

He decided to give Rico one more chance, and dialled his number again. The equivocal ringing—does it ring if you're not there to hear it?—angered him: he thought it possible that Rico and Alan were in the room, refusing to answer. he could hear them guessing who it might be, smiling complacently, drifting from smiles into their moonings and caressings, their adolescent, ill-informed lecheries—but no, neither one of them would have the strength to let the phone ring and keep on ringing; across each ugly infirm purpose would flash thoughts of importance, of some great person, some missed opportunity, the thought especially: it might be something better. And they would answer the phone. Rico particularly would answer the phone, compliant opportunist, affection's whore . . . had he ever done differently, or been anything else? Rico? who told (with pride) how he had been seduced by the house-maid when he was fifteen, and how three weeks later he had gone to his mother and got the girl discharged on some pretext.

No, they would answer the phone, he knew, and since they had not . . . . Perhaps they weren't even together; he cut the call short and dialled Alan's room. Alan's roommate answered:

"Hello."

"Hello, is Alan there?"

"No, he went out half an hour ago."

"Was Rico with him?"

"I think he was going to meet Rico. Is there any message I can give him?"

"No thanks."

"Your name . . . . ?"

"No thanks," he said coldly and replaced the receiver. He thought desperately for a moment that he might call Rhys again, then rejected the idea. There was no sense in begging. He felt tired again; the weight in his forehead had turned into a headache, and his eyes tended to water. The slight exertion of walking about the room made him want to go to bed, but he refused, and to clinch his refusal, began to get dressed. A drink was probably what was needed, he thought. A drink, and an hour out of this room. There was the mood he had been in all too often lately: his room depressed him, almost as much as did a library, for example; and the best things in the room,—the Matisse over the victrola, for example—they were so recognized, so much the very breath of his tepid climate that they became unbearable, and music was unbearable, and work as well, and it all seemed to him the ugly and ready-to-hand diversion afforded a man sentenced to life imprisonment. Not the ugly, but the commonplace disgusts, he thought. If they put Matisses in the street-cars, one would counter by hanging advertisements on one's walls. Yet he felt unsatisfied outside his room, again like a prisoner so acclimated as to shun freedom; a walk, however short, tired him inordinately, and climbing two flights to the room made his head throb as if the blood would burst out. He felt now that he required a drink; he would go to St. Clair's, nor did he disguise from himself the fact that half his motive was to find Rico, and that if Rico were not at St. Clair's he might be at Bella Vista, or McBrides, or the Stag Club; or he might be in town at the Napoleon or the Ritz or the Lincolnshire.

By the time he had finished dressing he found himself nearly exhausted. He had to sit down on the couch and turn out the light, and it was then that he began to think about the key to the filing-cabinet. He felt that he had perhaps been foolish, with his infantile stratagem. He might need the key in a hurry, for his notes, or to answer a letter, or—no need to disguise the fact from himself—to get the amytal when he came in drunk; it had to be conveniently to hand, or he would get no sleep. He must recognize the fact by now, he argued: he required the amytal, he was a mature individual, still sane, heaven knows, more sane than most of his dull acquaintances, he would not over-dose. And anyhow, the test was in the will to stay off the stuff, not in locking it away, there was no help in that. To be able to keep it before his eyes, that bottle, to look at it steadily, and steadfastly not to take it—at least not more than was absolutely necessary—there was the thing. Besides, suppose he needed it in a hurry, sometime, and the key had got lost—there were any number of ways that could have happened: it might have fallen into a crack in the floor, might have slid under the carpet, might even have landed down the radiator gratings, irretrievable short of large-scale operations that would require the janitor.

Hastily he turned on the light, began to look around. It was not that he wanted any now, or would take any tonight; but this was the saner thing to do, he must know.

The key was discovered with ridiculous ease, under the bookcase. He picked it up and laid it carefully in the middle drawer of his desk. And unformed to speech or even to clear thought, but present in his mind, was that justification, that ritual against reason, of a postulated higher power, of unspecified nature, watching over the episode, the feeling, carefully swathed in obscurity: Providence didn't want me to hide the key, or I wouldn't have found it so easily.

Put vaguely at ease, he began to get on his overcoat, and then decided to call Rhys again, buoyed up by this same vague assurance that he would, by however narrow a margin, do the thing which was to be done, that the thing would be right because he did it. But there was no answer, and for some reason, he was more infuriated at this than at Rico's absence—a little relieved, too, for Rhys would have been annoyed; but angry, angry that Rhys should not be there, should have gone out after making some excuse to him. Betrayal, he thought, furiously and without power. Rhys too. Although loneliness was his habitual way, it was by preference, because it suited him to be alone, but this, the loneliness by compulsion, was a new thing. He felt a terrible isolation, the phone seemed to him now only an instrument of the Inquisition, to teach him his loneliness as it were by rote, and he had the sudden sense that whatever number he called, it would be closed to him by that instrument. In fact, he thought in satiric anger—in fact this whole room is given only to people who want to be left alone. It is made to teach them the measure—that is, the unmeasurable quality—of isolation, of being absolutely alone. Harvard College built it that way—they get a lot of lonely ones around here.

The brief walk in the cold, up Dunster street and across the Square to St. Clair's, fatigued him excessively; he recognized that last night's dose had not nearly worn off, and that the cold had the unusual effect of making him want to lie down and go to sleep just wherever he was, in the street even. It was almost like being drunk, that disgusting soddenness with drink that made it Nirvana just to stop moving, anyhow, anywhere. He kept up his heart to a degree by repeating his little catechism of betrayal, his interdict on Rico and on Rhys, all the fictions of his misery forming into churches for his martyred self: here was a first station, where one knelt to beg forgiveness for being rude to Bradshaw; and here a second, where one knelt to do penance for being out when Bradshaw called, here another for thinking Bradshaw drunk when he wasn't, here another for the general sin of offending Bradshaw; and a last, where one prayed for the grace of Bradshaw: Oh Bradshaw, we do beseech thee . . . and a return for the petty humiliations, and a hundredfold paid back each error, and he knew it for pitiful, but nevertheless went on, in a rage of cynical benevolence, to forgive Rico, to forgive Rhys, to forgive them and cut them away from his side, and to go on in the thorough lonely discretion of his anger.

When he entered St. Clair's the first person he saw was Rhys, big, rather stout, and darkly dressed as usual, sitting by himself at a corner table. Rhys waved and beckoned to the chair opposite, and John sat down there.

"You're avoiding me," he said without thinking; his anger came to a head and he wanted a fight.

"If I were avoiding you, would I come and sit in a bar?" asked Rhys politely, and it was like being hit across the face.

"Then why did you tell me you couldn't go out?"

"I didn't say I couldn't go out. I said I didn't feel like going out." Rhys was nettled, and showed it by getting more and more polite.

"If you don't want to see me, I won't sit here."

"Don't be silly. Sit around and have a drink."

Rhys, he thought, was playing for a dull peace and it was not to be allowed; he must be disturbed, made to give himself away. He ordered, and got, a large martini, and sipped it in an uneasy silence.

"You should have gone to bed. You look as if you were trying to kill yourself." Rhys gave in and said something.

"What the hell would you care?" he asked rhetorically, hoping at the same time that Rhys would say something friendly and reassuring.

"How is it possible for anyone to care? You're not very responsive to care, you know."

"Oh, some have managed." He lit a cigarette. It tasted very bad, but it was against the sleep that even the drink seemed to drive him at. The place where he had bit his lip was still tender, it hurt when he spoke.

"You alienate even those," said Rhys. It was for him as though he had said 'where are you, John?' and reached out a hand in the darkness; it was such an unwelcome thing to be forced to find people when ordinarily they came and disclosed themselves.

They finished their drinks in silence and ordered more.

"Now what's this about Rico?" said Rhys at last.

John emptied his glass again, slowly, before answering. "It's only that from now on," he said, "I'm going to play dirty too. If you don't what chance have you got?"

"I always thought of Rico as more or less irresponsible said Rhys, "but—"

"It's not only Rico, God knows. He can be excused, if you were bounced out of a parochial school in Cuba and landed at Harvard with the prospect of eight million bucks when you came out—alors. Not alone Rico, no. It's everyone. And you too, sir. Don't you understand: I'm playing your way now, the safe way you all play, don't give anything with one hand that you can't get back with both, any time. And if I can't beat these Jesuits at their own game— well, what the hell . . . " he shrugged his thin shoulders, deliberately blew smoke across the table between them.

Rhys determined to show no annoyance, to maintain objectivity. So he sat with hands out equally on the table, looking like the balance-pans of the blind goddess.

"Essentially stupid attitude to take," he said.

"I mean— granting that people do present . . . difficulties at times—still, just how much have you got hurt?"

"Got hurt, hell. That's not—"

"You don't need to answer me," continued Rhys with a show of calm. "I'm just suggesting the question as something for you to **worry** about."

"Don't go on; you had it right the first time, when you said something about responsibility. You just make an ass of yourself when you put it on the piddling level of 'getting hurt.' It's only a question of how the essential non-pirate is to live in a world of pirates."

Rhys had no immediate reply to this, so they ordered more drinks and John continued:

"Romans and Orthodox Jews make the best pirates because even if they do put pretty far out to sea after plunder, they've both got a sailor's snug harbor to get to again. The Catholic can drop anchor in a church, the Jew carries his absolution along on shipboard. But they aren't the only ones, not by a long shot. It applies to everyone you know . . . piracy isn't so safe a game for them, but if you think for a minute—"

"I wish you wouldn't pretend to sit in judgment when you're looking so pitifully ill. You remind me not so much of the Christian Way as of Nietzsche."

And suddenly John felt the fatigue again, the wish to give it up; what was the use in arguing with Rhys. The drink was having an inordinate effect because of the amytal. He knew it would be difficult to get up, next to impossible to walk home.

"Hell," he said. "It's only an argument for you. Forget the whole thing." and then: "will you take me home?"

"What's wrong? Not feeling well?"

"I'm sick to death of sitting here with you, listening to your well-fed brain. I want to leave and I can't do it by myself. I'm asking you: as one last favor, would you see me home? Let me assure you, sir; it will be the last. I shan't disturb you and your values again."

"Please don't be melodramatic with me, John," said Rhys in a quiet rage.

"Can't you see that's not the question?"

"Don't you think you'd feel better if you

sat here without drinking for a few minutes?"

"Oh for heaven's sake, Sir, don't be reasonable with me. I've asked you a question, will you—"

He felt a draught on his back from the opened door. Shivering extravagantly, with the hope that Rhys would think him ill, he turned and saw Rico and Alan standing beside his chair.

"Wha's wrong, little one," asked Rico, slightly drunk, smiling with his beautiful teeth.

"Rico!" he held out his hand, forgetting Rhys, forgetting Alan. "Rico"——and more softly, as though drawing the other into conspiracy—"will you take me home? I can't go myself."

"Sure, little one. I can take you home. Come, give me your hand." Rico laughed, his laugh and his glance taking in the whole room, stranger and intimate alike, as though to disclaim all embarrassment and responsibility, as though to enlist their sympathy not for John but for self-sacrificing Rico who had to take him home.

"Come," he said. "Up on your feet."

He got to his feet slowly enough, his eyes half fading from their focus. The floor seemed to rock beneath him, his ears filled with noise, and it was as if he stood on a separate planet that rocked backwards and over in space, out of sight of Rhys who sat there with an embarrassed expression on his face. Then suddenly he knew he was heavily in Rico's arms, and in one instant synapse of sobriety he heard himself saying to Rhys "I hate you more . . . " and Rico saying roughly "Come on," pulling at his arm. Then the two little voices were again swept away in a wave of sound against his brain, formless sound at first, that resolved itself into a rhythm and at length into words spoken from far away: "Drink and drugs that done him in," or some such; and then—drink and drugs—he could no longer hear for noise, but the enormous voice of Rico was in his head saying "Come on, come on," and all at once they were in the street and the cold stung his eyes and the sweat on his cheeks.

Rico and Alan had taken him by the arms, close to the shoulder, and were dragging him along. Whenever he stumbled they set him right with a jerk that lifted his feet off the ground.

"Wait," he said. "Sick."

And while they stood silently by holding him, Rico holding his head forward, he was sick, with a horrible violence, in a little alley off Dunster street. His stomach, almost empty to start with, twisted painfully at the finish, and he lost consciousness.

When he came to he was alone in his room with Rico. He could not see Alan anywhere. He rested on his bed and Rico was taking his clothes off. There was no longer any rest, or desire to sleep; there was only pain in his stomach and an actively hurtful weariness.

Rico finished stripping him, folded him in between the sheets. "You'll be OK in the morning," he said. "You were sick as a bitch. How d'you feel now?"

"Rico," he whispered. "Don't go away, Rico." He felt distantly that he was a child, in his child's bed at home; he had done a wrong thing, and Rico would be angry, with the efficient necessary anger of a mother.

"Kiss me, Rico," he said. "Kiss me good night." and then, as Rico made no move to comply, he said: "you're mad at me . . . ?" with a pathetic dubious note of shame in his voice, and Rico stooped and quickly kissed him on the cheek.

"Now good night, little one."

"Don't go, Rico. Stay here tonight."

"I can't. You'll be all right now."

"But I won't, Rico. I won't. I'll be sick again." He grew panicky with new fear. "I swear I'll be sick again," he said. "The minute you leave. Don't leave, Rico."

Then, in a tone of malicious invalid craft, he said accusingly: "You gave Alan the key to your room, didn't you?" Breathless, he went on: "You told him to wait in your room, didn't you."

Rico's face gave him away; it was true, it could only be true. "That's why you want to leave," he went on. "I know why." Quietly he began to whimper, and the tears rolled down his face. Then in a desperate martyrdom he said in a choked voice: "I'll kill myself if you go. I'll kill myself the minute you go out that door."

"Nonsense, what would you do it with, little one." Rico was not very good at situations like this; he felt vaguely that he should comfort, should sacrifice himself a little and help; but he had no intelligent means of doing it, being frightened not by a lie, but by a lie that would involve him later.

"I'd take all the amytal. I would. It would be enough. You'd see it would be enough. Rico, don't be a bastard. Don't go away."

"You mustn't do that, John. You mustn't think of it."

"And you can't find the amytal either. I hid it." There was a terrible cunning in his voice, he was determined to have the drug. It did not at that time matter to him whether it was a lethal dose or not; it was to spite Rico, to hurt him, to say to him: 'see what might have happened. The guilt would have been yours, you would have murdered me.'

Rico went to the bathroom to look for the amytal.

"You can't find it, you can't," he mocked in a thin voice cracked with approaching hysteria. "Go away, damn you. Go away."

Rico came back into the room.

"You won't do it, John."

"Get out."

"Promise me you won't do it."

"Get out."

"If you don't promise I can't do anything."

"I said get out."

Rico was faced with something beyond his comprehension, and he took the only way he understood.

"All right," he said sullenly. "I guess it's your life." And having thus washed himself clean in his own eyes, he walked out.

There was no question of decision, now he was alone. It was again that unfaced trust in a higher power, in some back world watching. With unnecessary stealth he got out of bed and, entirely naked, went to the desk, got the key and opened the filing cabinet. He took the bottle into the bathroom and poured all the pills into a highball glass, which he filled with warm water. This decoction he took back into the living room, where he sat down on the couch by the phone and began to drink. When the glass was empty there remained a considerable residue of damp powder at the bottom, so he refilled the glass and started again, more slowly,

from time to time stirring the mixture with a pencil. At last he had finished. From experience, he knew there would be about fifteen minutes to wait.

He turned on all the lights, not feeling like getting into bed again. As he stood naked in the corner by the light-switch he was taken suddenly with a frenzy. The thing was done, it was done. Was it right? was it so at all? The indecision after the event frightened him, he imagined the maid finding him in the morning and with a certain sense of abject shame rushed to put his bathrobe about him. How to know? He questioned if he should be saved, and then, as he became somewhat more calm, there occurred to him another of those tests of providence, another cryptic question to which the oracle might smilingly equivocate over his special case.

He took up the phone and dialled Rhys' number. If Rhys answered he would explain and have him get a doctor. If there were no answer . . . and as he listened to the ring he felt certain there must be. It was not so much the test of fate, but the thought that he must speak again to Rhys, apologize, absolve, ask forgiveness.

There was no answer. Unwilling to believe, he put the phone down on the table and let it ring. The answer was given, but unsatisfactorily only more or less given, with the smiling ambiguity of power. He went to the window and opened it, then sat back on the couch. It is doubtful that he thought any more of death, of the probability or the certainty. He listened to the dried icy branches of the trees scratch together in the wind, down in the courtyard; and it is doubtful that he thought of leaving anything behind, of regret, of the irrevocability of death.

For his room, warm with the lights full on, seemed to him some tall citadel of the sun, with a certain congenial ease of sunlight upon it, and when the sleep came down, it drifted in like the cool sudden shadow of a cloud, that only made him shudder slightly.

THE YEAR THE RAIN

CAME TO DEAUVILLE

Or Why France Fell

EDITOR'S NOTE: *In the midst of lengthy articles and dull books on the collapse of France it is refreshing to find a new point of view. Mr. Thomas in the article below gives a graphic picture of the international smart set which was so symptomatic of the interbellum period. In these paragraphs the cause of the fall of more than one European nationalism is implied by an anecdotal sociology which carries behind it the weight of actual experience. It has an interest and vitality that dogmatic or dialectical statement rarely attains.*

SINCE few of us Americans, I hope and fear, will spend the summer in France, it might give us a reminiscent pleasure to look back upon the mid-years of the Golden Twenties, to that summer the rain came to Deauville when the international set jolted out of the rut prescribed for the Followers-of-the-Sun and whoopee took on its brightest overtones. It is soothing to recall that the sun followed in the Twenties was a sun becoming to champagne and lipstick, it was a sun that baked out the hangover you had carefully laid in the night before. It was, in short, the sun that was so good for you that, so long as you kept in it, you could do everything that was bad for you. Unlike the everyday sun, it rose in Egypt toward Christmas, got to the Côte d'Azur for spring, blazed over Deauville and the Lido in high summertime and set into the Atlantic off Biarritz, come autumn. There was no rain in the schedule.

It was just after the running of the Grand Prix that the rain came to Deauville in the first momentum of the season. The least nuptial though most prosperous of the Marrying Mdivanis had just broken the first collar-bone of the season at polo. For the first two or three days the rain was accepted grudgingly, like any other act of God, but it made one wonder just how good Deauville was after all. It forced one to admit that Deauville smacked more of nature than its competitors. Even in fine weather you ran the risk of being asked on picnics to look at a view, Mont-Saint-Michel was dangerously near, and not much further were the Bretons being quaint. People at Deauville were given to asking friends on cruises and, if you weren't careful, you found yourself pulling a rope. Of course, Deauville was further north than most of the sun spots and it brought out the Viking in one. There were menaces like Betty Carstairs—just when you'd made up your

 Curtis Thomas

mind to let yourself be kidnapped on a Round-Africa cruise, you'd find yourself whisked right past the yacht into a speed-boat and your remnants would be lifted onto a Cow Island by an undamaged sailor.

And then there was the Deauville sand. At the best of times, the Casino and the Hotel Normandie and the villas dumped you into it; sand sprinkled out of your hair into the cocktails and filed sharply at the bosom under a boiled shirt—or a string of last year's emeralds. It was all one could do to keep from falling straight into the Channel as he came away from losing that third thousand at baccarat—that is, dollars— the franc was too low for calculating Deauville p r i c e s. Like Egypt, Deauville was frightening expensive. Not that everyone wasn't stinking

rich (or knew people who were) but somehow you or your friends stank even more richly in Biarritz or along the Côte d'Azur.

Anyway that was how Deauville seemed after two or three days of rain—and that was only the start. We sat on through the week in damp hotels and villas, pickling without respite. If you lost at the Casino, it got on your nerves; if you won, there was nothing to do with the winnings but lose them again as usual, and that got on your nerves even more. Without sun for vitamins, *Fernet-Brancas à l'eau* had to be substituted for champagne cocktails as eye-openers. Perhaps the worst of it was that the women dressed in clothes instead of bathing suits. Tubular women were in their prime, skirt-hems clung half way up from the knee just below the dropped waist-line, dutch cuts with side bangs and shaved points on the neck were stuck into *cloches,* and necklaces moved round from front to back and bashed you in the face

on the dance-floor as the next couple whirled into a Black-bottom. Like the necklaces, female contours moved from front to back. Breasts retreated and shoulder-blades protruded. For all the *tout ce qu'il-y-a de pius chic,* many a man suspected that woman as a biological tradition and a decoration was not at her best. By the tenth day of the rain, the women themselves were beginning to suspect this home truth and consequently something happened—something big! The circuit of the sun was broken—and the great hejira was on!

Buggattis, M e r c e d e s, Rolls-Royces, Panhard-Levassors, Hispano-Suizas and Maybachs roared f r o m damp garages; packed and glittering they swelled geysers of mud back at the clouds, h e a d i n g south through Normandy, o n through the Midi, across to the rainbow valley of the Rhône; onward, southward, eastward into Provence they streamed by night with relays at the wheel till the sun (the famous sun!) rose upon the scarlet Estérel above a peacock sea, and Cannes lay just ahead.

That morning, the Croisette woke to the cries and fanfare of the sun-bound. In astonishment, the Regent dropped its shutters and sprouted heads at every window. Hotel after hotel stood to the shock and the half-furnished Miramar filled like a balloon. The overflow spread on to St. Paul, to Nice, to Beaulieu and Monte and, in the excitement, two or three over-enthusiastic carloads found themselves bedded down in Menton. The hitherto individualistic adherents of Antibes, and the new summer colony at Juan-les-Pins nodded with fresh aplomb at the *brou-haha* and said 'I told you so.' That is, all except Somerset Maugham who considered the influx no act-of-God but a deliberate invasion of his privacy. He was busy at the time producing his most successful drama—the one about the bitter recluse withdrawn from the world in a house packed to suffocation with permanent week-end guests. Even in the Twenties, he'd been playing the leading rôle for some time. And then there were the inveterates at Monte who just went on watching their wheels and wondered why there was more money stacked on the tables than usual.

The relief at finding sun again was so great that all social coherence was lost the first week. Organized entertainment strained to the breaking point, and broke. (Though it must be admitted that wherever you looked appeared Peggy Hopkins Joyce in three yards of assorted jewelry.) People who had avoided each other for years slept together and even exchanged remarks on the weather when they met in the street, denying the pronouncement attributed to Lady Diana Manners that intercourse did not constitute grounds for social introduction. It was a care-free, happy throng, back to nature, plastered to the gills, that discovered, overnight, what a Riviera summer could be. They even went so far as to tolerate amateur entertainment at the night-spots for *Café Society* was at that time only a gleam in Elsa Maxwell's eye—and they were rewarded for their tolerance with a Pied Piper who, a moment before, had been only an officer and a gentleman. Where Tutin had come in, no one ever found out, so many people laid claim to him after that night at the Château-de-Madrid. But there of a sudden he was singing outrageous French couplets to any tune, to anybody he could outrage, and then he would clap his hands and then he would dance curiously, insinuatingly, and people would catch the rhythm of his clapping and the rhythm of

his dance and get up from their tables and follow him in follow-the-leader fashion round the dance floor, over chairs and tables, round the floor and into the bar. Tutin vanished in the riot, and then, after a while he would be back insulting people with the peculiar frankness of a French gentleman—and so on, and on. But you never got enough of Tutin. It seemed that Tutin was dying; he would collapse once in a while even before he was ready to slip away. His so magical a mountain gaiety had been mined in the war, but so far as anyone knew, he didn't die that summer. He was young and had a turned-up nose.

Of course, the bloom of *pastorale* got a little blistered after the first week but the arrival of the Midlands Cicisbeo rather tended to keep things going. Somebody may have told him what was happening, but I'm inclined to think he just blundered into Cannes like a fly against a closed window.

In spite of all the people, there was always a nucleus somewhere in Cannes that marked storm-centre, determined by no particular person nor even group. It formed of a morning at an undetermined point along the beach for cocktails before second breakfast—it gathered sufficient momentum by degrees to carry itself through the next eighteen hours. This phenomenon appeared round noon among the early risers. On a certain day at the end of the first week, the nucleus got the shock of the season when Osewald, the Midlands Cicisbeo, came strolling along by the water. Since Deauville, no man but the Duca de' Medici had been seen in anything but a polo-shirt and slacks— Medici was the sort of person who could get away with a dinner-jacket the morning after and not look strained. But even he could not have overpowered tweeds in that time and place (jacket, plus-fours and cap to match) with tassels to the stockings and flaps to the shoes. But that's how Osewald appeared to the nucleus that effulgent noon, and a hush fell upon them as Osewald strode by, pale, cool and nineteen, staring at a little cloud. It was a matter of conjecture whether Osewald were good-looking. I believe it was Olga who collapsed, and by the time she'd been brought around, Osewald was gone for the day. Olga had learned a lot of Hollywood technique playing opposite Valentino and was competent at holding her share of attention.

It wasn't till that evening, during one of Tutin's lapses at the Château-de-Madrid that Osewald reappeared and in 'flawless evening attire,' all the way to pearl studs and gardenia. He sat down at a table near the orchestra, alone, and looked out a window at the moon. "He woad luke preety on a French pustcart," said Olga who was famous for her four letter words in twenty-two languages.

"Did I tell you, dear," said Julie to distract Olga's attention, "the last time I was crossing the Place de la Concorde, a man tried to sell me some of your 'stills' through a taxi-window. I couldn't make out who was playing opposite you." Julie was on the dance floor with me before Olga got her languages sufficiently disentangled to be comprehensible.

All I could hear of her retort which convulsed the party was, "So's your old man!" a phrase redolent with the smartest connotations of the moment.

There was no one who could dance better than Julie but she led when she had something on her mind. As she whirled me over the floor, Osewald was christened—Julie always had a name for everything—and there we were, idling by his table. Osewald looked round from the window and the moon—Julie was like that, too. He looked up, got up and before I could get my hand out from under her shoulder-strap, Julie dipped and swung, then glided away with Osewald in a series of pitches that would have downed any but an inveterate yachtswoman. I stepped into the wake, floundered among the dancers as a pedestrian must and was spewed forth at my table.

But Julie was back as quickly as she'd gone. One heave round the floor and she washed up beside me with a toss that put her hair on end. Cool and white Osewald glared at me for an astonishing moment, clicked his heels and walked away. "I'm not expecting to be believed," Julie explained, "but Osewald asked me where I'd been all his life and wanted a serious answer. It's a difficult question to answer seriously."

"Yo cood have sade 'in bed'," Olga suggested.

"I did, dear—"

"And than?"

"He asked for the number of my hotel room—"

"But you vare it on your sleeve, no?"

"Osewald's not quick at figures—anyway it slipped out before I could stop myself," Julie explained.

"Habeet," said Olga understandingly and went on to say what other people only thought—and, after all, how was she to know that Julie had changed her room at the hotel that very afternoon? She was skeptical even when Julie explained that she'd given Osewald the wrong number. Olga believed things when she saw them, and not always then.

Back at the hotel, in the dead hush of the twilit corridor as I set my door ajar, I heard faint murmurs and saw little shafts of sunlight streak across the long floor. As Osewald came up the stairs there was nothing to be heard, however, but the seven-o'clock birds outside and the faint fall of his slippers. He stood in black smock pyjamas and scarlet dressing-gown with a black crested eagle clutching its pocket. He looked at numbers, stepped to the assigned door and opened it, went straight in and closed the door after him. At once, the corridor was filled with eager heads exchanging glances of anticipation. We waited in the morning silence and, finally when nothing happened, went our various ways as discretely and silently as the circumstances allowed. Julie told me quite frankly that she thought Osewald had proved a rather shallow sort of young man.

Next day, there was as much interest in what would come out of that door as in what had entered it. There was loitering in the corridor, a great running back and forth and exchange of neighbourly calls among those who were well past the unscrambling hour. Julie and I were on our way to see Olga when the revelation occured —the door opened and filled with many hundreds of pounds of woman in a Patou tent, showing penants of paradise feather. From all sides there was a cry of 'Timmie!' (Everybody recognized Timmie, the wonder-woman cockney who'd snared a startling American fortune in her slenderer days.) The hand kissers miscalculated her rings—at a glance, you couldn't gauge how big the stones were. Those who were in the know removed an eye-glass before approaching them. The rush of mysterious popularity (Timmie was a little on the bias in her social niche) went to her head on the spot. She asked the whole floor to stop with her at whatever villa she could find that day.

We all moved in with Osewald that afternoon and everything went well for a week till Timmie's husband showed up. He was a difficult man

any way you looked at him but he was particularly trying over Osewald. Since he paid the bills, he felt, in his mercenary way, that it was up to Timmie to supply the home with intimates of unimpeachable background. Since their long forgotten honeymoon, Timmie's husband had fought to pull her up socially by the shoulder-straps. Bogged down in the struggle, he'd acquired a shockingly distorted, worm's-eye view of society, understandable but not particularly sympathetic. Timmie had put up with a lot from him, but that time he went too far, and on the very night of his arrival.

After dinner, it seems, he found out everything about Osewald that the rest of us already knew. Osewald was ingenuous to say the least. Everybody had learned that his father made millions with knives in Sheffield and that he ate peas with them. They knew that Osewald had run away from his tutor while on holiday, determined to gipsy about on his own with three trunks but not a shilling to his name. Like his well-known contemporary, Richard Halliburton, and with similar tactics, Osewald had taken 'The Royal Road to Romance' but more intensively and less extensively. He had read Dumas for a course in Greek tragedy at one of the Universities and, with a practicality beyond most scholars, had discovered a working principle for his life that, joined with an Horatio Alger technique, was solemn to the point of grimness. It was not his solemnity that annoyed Timmie's husband, however, nor Osewald's status as *cicisbeo* that rankled—Timmie's husband had never been selfish about his wife—it was Osewald's type of Midlands background that riled his sense of propriety. Timmie's husband had provided her, once upon a time, with a recognizable American name. He had expected her to be a credit to that name and couple it in the gossip columns with nothing but the best out of *Debrett* and the *Almanach de Gotha*. As her charms had diminished in indirect ratio to their profusion, he had subsidized them increasingly, failing utterly to take into account the warm feminine heart that throbbed so deep within, nor had he allowed her little personal preferences to enjoy so much as a well-earned sabbatical, without being spiteful.

She had done particularly well by her husband that evening with a small, and as things went with Timmie, select dinner-party for fifty to celebrate his arrival. By dawn, not a few of us were tired enough to want to go to bed and sleep. At Timmie's parties one was apt to fight his way to solitude behind locked doors, seeking the eccentric luxuries of a recluse. There were times, even in the Twenties, when one wanted to be alone. I remember that I had the lamé suite next to Timmie and was quietly passing out when roused by a crash of pottery and a set of *style-moderne* lounging chairs. The pottery landed on the other side of the wall behind me and the chairs went out the adjacent window which, I believe, had been closed for the express purpose since it was a warm morning. Her husband's sarcasms on Osewald had roused all the woman in Timmie—which was a great deal. Having stripped their room of ammunition, Timmie followed her husband afield with the thoroughness of reveille. Since sleep was out of the question for the next hour, I joined the indignation meeting in the bar off the drawing-room and finally cast my vote with those in favour of mass exodus. Timmie had got to the kitchen by then and was going through the copper-ware and cleavers.

The hotel was so full we all had to triple-up, willie-nillie, and there was an undercurrent of disgust. Sympathetic as we were with Timmie, we felt that her pent-up reflexes had carried her too far—and Timmie paid for it! Next day, when there was little left of the villa to break but the lease, she broke that and went to New York for the rest of the summer! There were many who believed that she was the first woman to have gone there at such a season. Having lost all sense of proportion, Timmie ended up on the front pages of the tabloids with a remunerative divorce, and with a 'cinderella man' in his early twenties and a pair of trunks. It may have been an exaggeration, but I heard they were married at a prize-fight, in the ring, just after the bridegroom had lost the Carnarsie Silver Cup to a

dusky contender. But that was another year.

Meanwhile, in Cannes, we rather expected to lose Osewald, but he was of sterner stuff than we had supposed. 'Do and Dare,' 'Fight and Win'—it's surprising how successful those catch-words can be at nineteen even in plus-fours and a crested dressing-gown. But fate also lent a hand to youthful endeavor in the accredited fashion of all true Alger heroes.

Within a fortnight after the memorable flight from Deauville and directly after Timmie's dearly bought victory, many people who hadn't already sublet their villas began to fill out the customary lines of Cannes. Notable was the double advent of Janet, Dowager Ranee of J_____, and Mr. Fothergill. The obvious must be pointed out, that Janet had not started life as a Dowager Ranee. According to Olga she hadn't started out as anything—she'd been too young—but her mother had been a tinner of kippers in Glasgow. On the other hand, which was not so obvious till you saw him, Mr. Fothergill hadn't started life as Mr. Fothergill. Mr. Fothergill was stubby, dark, nearer-Eastern than anyone usually is with a name like Fothergill, and he was out of Hollywood by Grand Street. Janet, by way of contrast, had lovely red hair and a figure that the Wife of Bath might have enjoyed in her earlier thirties.

Now it must not be thought that there was any sort of scandal implied in the coupling of their names—far from it. Janet and Mr. Fothergill were deadly rivals in the field of philanthropy. They both realized that, even in the most prosperous of times, there are any number of worthy and needy young men who would starve if not fed. Between them, they contrived to put the Salvation Army in the shade. No crowded cots and bread-lines for *their* strays! Dormitories weren't moveable, and yachts were—bread-lines were colourless and niggardly when there was enough champagne and caviar for everybody. Like all collectors, Janet and Mr. Fothergill were somewhat on the cut-throat side, and if their groups overlapped and there were frequent displacements and snatchings, and the social amenities became a little strained, everyone laughed good-humouredly at squabbles that were occasioned by philanthropic zeal.

The important thing was, as we all foresaw, that fate had elected to temper the wind to a lamb shorn of Timmie, and we were all glad to feel that Osewald's youth must not be crushed back into the mould of a Midlands summer, Osewald's one fear being discovery by his knife-magnate father and irrevocable orders to bring his three trunks home.

Janet and Mr. Fothergill arrived the same day and it was clear to all those who trooped out to the yachts that Janet had enjoyed a far more successful season of philanthropy than Mr. Fothergill. She had been at the Lido and recruited not only her guests but a good share of her crew from the many unfortunates who had miscalculated their bills at the Excelsior. The Dowager Ranee was Scotch, after all, and the crew of a three-hundred foot yacht can be expensive unless you know how. Mr. Fothergill, on the other hand, though thrifty in his own way, had come straight from Hollywood by train, picking up his yacht in New York, already staffed and under steam, with no time for rearrangements.

There was a surface intimacy between the two and Mr. Fothergill took most unfair advantage of this by asking Janet and her entire collection to a housewarming at 'Fothergill-super-Cannes.' The game of snatch was on. Mr. Fothergill, at heart a simple peasant and he didn't care who knew it, put the party on an informal basis at once by making himself handy round the house. Scattering staff in all directions, he took his place behind the bar with Janet safely across the counter and proceeded to manufacture his dynamite special. Mr. Fothergill was not a drinking man, but if there was anything that Janet liked as well as philanthropy it was a cocktail. She knew she was playing fly to his spider—it had happened before—but Janet let herself in for it. Perhaps it was the wonderful cobwebs with which Mr. Fothergill's quaint Elizabethan bar was festooned. He had brought over a rubber-blowing machine from Hollywood to blow

fresh cobwebs each morning after guests had been cleared away with the other debris. Janet eyed him, took a deep breath and a long drink, and swayed round on her stool as Olga brought Osewald up to the bar. He was in tennis clothes with a red scarf knotted round his pale neck. "Yo mast now dees pore yong deer," said Olga and set him down by Janet, opposite Mr. Fothergill. Mr. Fothergill filled Janet's glass as quickly as she had emptied it. As she took Osewald's hand, Janet poured the refill into her campaign décolletage—a favourite trick of hers. She said it always cleared her head in a crisis. She took a thoughtful look at Osewald as he watched the cocktail drain slowly away.

Olga, like most women, had never been very fond of Janet, and she began to play up Mr. Fothergill. After all, it was he who had got Olga her lead opposite Valentino. She had always had a warm regard for his philanthropic tendencies and a quiet friendship had sprung up between them. To the interested observers, it soon became clear that the issue was decided and most of them got away.

Janet had been well organized when she started on the dynamite specials. Before an hour was over, she began to look glassy. It was rather becoming to her—lent her a brilliant patine. She swayed on her stool, then steadied herself with the ease of long practice for the plunge. She laid a hand on Osewald's arm. "If you will just see me home," she began then added, "pot-luck, you know—"

Mr. Fothergill made it clear that Osewald was engaged for the evening and Olga began to disentangle Osewald from Janet, reminiscing pointedly of Valentino. But Janet managed an interruption. "And I want to hear all about your *dear* father!" Osewald froze to attention. "My late husband, the Rajah you know," Janet went on, "always so counted on your papa's knives for those restless moments at the Khyber Pass—" Her eyes lidded and she caught herself on the verge of slumber. "You must tell me what to write him. Perhaps you'd rather I—"

"Oh, no!" cried Osewald. "I say, you really mustn't! The pater is— Well— That is—" And then Janet pitched dreamlessly forward into his arms.

Of course, Osewald stayed on for a little in Cannes. He wasn't very bright but he was good-hearted underneath—he owed his father something after all the distress his disappearance from the tutor had caused. He got on famously with Janet's dusky little son (the incumbent Rajah) and it may be remembered how ably the British Empire held its own at the Khyber Pass, next season, with an astonishing array of cutlery bought, they say, at a thumping figure from Osewald *père*.

It was not all sport along those sunny shores— no indeed! If the Empire held the Khyber Pass, Olga did not play the *femme fatale* to Valentino's Scaramouch—these serious affairs of cinema and colonial policy as well as social questions, like the painless disposal of war-worn veterans and the keeping of unemployed young men out of pool parlours, were dealt with skillfully if informally. It was by no means all play and no work, and there was never a dull moment for all the talk there was of boredom and futility. At least no one stopped long enough to take the matter of boredom seriously—it was apt to prove fatal.

THE HARVARD ADVOCATE

COMMENCEMENT ISSUE 25c

1947–1960

The main feature of the postwar *Advocate* was its retreat from university issues, and indeed all activities outside literature. This decision hurt the magazine, not only by narrowing its sphere of influence but by imposing financial difficulties as well.

The restoration of the magazine seemed an encouraging start. Early in 1947, *Advocate* trustees decided that it was time to reestablish the undergraduate board and resume publication, lest any new periodical supplant it. The choice of editors fell to them, and early issues proved that they had chosen wisely. The years from 1947 to 1950 saw a strong magazine, for the energy and maturity of the postwar classes made up for the disabilities caused by four years' silence. Poetry was particularly good: John Ashbery, John Hawkes, Donald Hall, Robert Bly, and Frank O'Hara supplied the *Advocate* with a new kind of poetic style, distinguished by reticence and intimacy of expression, that would soon change the state of American verse.

But these trends were accompanied by a growing distaste for Harvard and its wider sensibilities. Trustee influence encouraged articles of general interest like "The Jew at Harvard," but as control of editorial policy gradually returned to the student board, pieces of broad Harvard appeal disappeared. The *Advocate* of 1950 saw its task as exclusively literary, and the old interest in the university, which had given strength and support to the prewar boards, was now in neglect.

Talent itself did not fail. Even during these years of increasing limitations we find the poetry of Adrienne Rich and the drawings of Edward Gorey. In November 1951, for the first time since the war, a special issue appeared: dedicated to William Faulkner, it contained, among other tributes, Alfred Kazin's "Faulkner's Vision of Human Integrity." Items of general interest would also come in regular issues during the fifties, like I. A. Richards' "The Idea of a University," Peter Viereck's justified snarl at modern critics in "Full Cycle," and Achilles Fang's translation of Lu Chi's ancient *ars poetica*. But the number of contributors declined over the years, and the issues grew thinner. The *Advocate* editors were becoming a literary clique, the magazine their house organ. They showed little interest in student affairs.

But from time to time the *Advocate* could produce a sensation. In March 1957 the publication of a plain little love story—"Winter Term" by Sallie Bingham—caused a small stir and a literary fashion. The story appealed to the sexually bewildered students of the late fifties, and for a few years the Harvard-Radcliffe romance was a commonplace in Cambridge letters. By 1960 it had died out. "Sex: The Literary Breakthrough in Harvard Square" is the *Advocate*'s own remembrance of the fad.

But the Harvard Square sex story ended more often than not in rejection. It was usually the work of amateurs, and the *Advocate* preferred the more published efforts of its own members or the Harvard writing classes. "Creole Love Song" and "Brother Carlisle" indicate the standard of *Advocate* fiction in the fifties. Writing on the whole had never been better, but the magazine had lost a broad base of contributors and some of its readership. It was slowly suffocating from confinement to a literary club, and by the early sixties needed to escape.

The Jew at Harvard

William E. Wiggin

In his commencement address of 1922, President Lowell called for a quota against Jews in the admission of students to the University. This request provoked nation-wide discussion inasmuch as it represented one of the earliest overt recognitions of discrimination by a large and respected college. Carey McWilliams, in his authoritative study of the rise of antisemitism in the United States, *A Mask for Privilege*, notes that the University never acted upon President Lowell's suggestion. The impact upon public opinion, however, has been so great that the existence of a quota has been assumed in much of the speculation regarding Harvard's admission policy. Not only is the Jewish student's chance to get into Harvard subject to curiosity, but his status within the college, his opportunities in extra-curricular participation and leadership, and the social avenues open to him are all controversial and provocative questions. Talk on these issues has its foundation in generalization, bias, wishful thinking, good will and ill, hasty observation, and innate human nosiness. The hazarding of opinions at the college dining table, and the somewhat subjective dissemination of petty facts about big issues, within the confines of the small group, are absolutely valueless in creating a realistic picture of the Jewish student at our school. If the subject is of such general interest as common talk indicates, it would be well to have a basis of hard fact upon which to construct generalizations. In creating this statistical-interpretive study, we have seen some of our pet notions destroyed, and some partially confirmed. We recognize the multiplicity of factors which are beyond the scope of a brief article such as this one, and for that reason are most cautious and tentative about the conclusions we have drawn.

Our initial task was the definition of the Jewish student. We decided that for our purposes he was an individual adhering to some form of Jewish faith (Orthodox, Conservative, or Reformed) and declaring that adherence by the religious preference cards that are filed with Phillips Brooks House. Hillel Foundation, the local Jewish Students association, has a list of undergraduate Jews, which Rabbi Zigmond defines as 90% accurate. This was, necessarily, the basis of our lists for statistical analysis. By 90% accurate Rabbi Zigmond refers to the absence from the list, of students of originally Jewish religious adherence, who decline to list a religious preference. As we go upon the assumption that there is no anthropological foundation for the idea that Judaism has a racial entity, the religious definition seems the best. It is most reasonable to suppose that an individual no longer of Jewish religious persuasion may act in conformity with a social experience peculiar to those of Jewish faith. But in the absence of both faith and race as a basis for identification, a study would become arbitrary and subjective were it to attribute "Jewishness" or lack of it to those with "Jewish" names. It would be contrary to the scientific spirit of our approach, and it would be exceeding difficult to set a figure upon the peripheral Jewry who are unquestionably a part of the undergraduate body.

With the Hillel list as our standard, we have prepared a series of statistics which comprise the main body of the article. A passage of interpretive material concludes it.

There are 725 Jewish students in Harvard College. As of last term, the undergraduate body numbered 5458. Jews, by these figures, represent 13.3% of college students here. This figure makes a useful yardstick in measuring Jewish conformity to the group standard of undergraduate students. While the percentage may be greater by a slender proportion if we admit (unscientifically) the 10% presumably beyond the pale of Hillel, the frequently cited figure of 20% seems significantly inaccurate.

Does the smaller figure indicate the existence of a quota? If a quota system operates at Harvard University, it is liberal, or fantastically clever, or both. In a nation of 140 million people, 5 million Jews represent less than 4% of the population. Therefore, if Harvard has a quota, it is hardly discriminatory, even with the assumption of unusual Jewish intellectual prowess. Secondly, as the University and the Scholarship department both fail to inquire about religious adherence, the rigid observation of a quota must be difficult.

Perhaps the most interesting statistics derived from this study were those concerning the Jew as a scholar. The examination of last year's Freshman class academic performance in the first term is illuminating: Of Freshmen on Dean's List Jewish students represent 26.7%.

Assuming that the class of 1951 is neither disproportionately Jewish or non-Jewish, we must conclude that the percentage of Jews on Dean's List is unusually high. This finding is supported by the statistics on undergraduate membership in Phi Beta Kappa. Of its members 47% are Jewish. This statistic coupled with those of teh Dean's List for the class of 1951 may well give us the basis for a valid generalization.

A considerable amount of unfounded assertion about Harvard's Jewry involves the house system. It is frequently charged, for example, that Leverett House has a high proportion of Jewish students of Leftist political sympathies. Of course, the political assertion is a typical feature in prejudiced analysis of Jews as a group. It is recognized by students of anti-semitism, and relates to the larger problem of scapegoatism in any society. Our findings do not show Leverett House to be disproportionately Jewish. In fact, it is the average house as regards Jewish representation. We have frequently heard, moreover, that Adams House is highly Jewish. Adams has the second lowest representation of Jewish students. The following statistics are based on House membership as of the fall term of 1948: Winthrop House: 16.8% undergraduate residents Jewish

Dunster:	14.5
Kirkland:	14.2
Leverett:	12.8
Lowell:	12.1
Adams:	10.9
Eliot:	8.3

It will be noted that Eliot House has less than one half the representation of Winthrop House. However, it would be foolhardy to draw any conclusions regarding the admissions policies, or the relative anti-semitism of any house resident body. There are too many unconsidered factors such as house preference on the part of applicants, and activity interests, to make any generalization about house admission policies that would be either accurate or kindly. The figures do, however, indicate a pattern of house membership composition, and are useful in dispelling many prevalent notions about the Jewish student and his house affiliation. Jewish students, incidentally, represent 12.6% of the house dwellers, a figure close to the 13.3% that Jews represent in the undergraduate body. All told, 357 of the 725 Jewish undergraduates are House residents.

One of the major bones of contention in discussing the Jewish student is social discrimination within the University. Our every statistic on that subject seems to support the common notion that a Jew has little or no opportunity to make a final club. The A. D., D. U., and Porcellian clubs were found to harbor no Jewish students. These findings are so obvious as to make the presentation of a string of zero percents a trifle ludicrous. The Hasty Pudding, however, has some Jewish membership. The exact percentage could not be obtained, for the membership list was not available. When the nature of the project was explained to a gentleman at the Pudding office, it was asserted that less than 1% of the membership was Jewish. We have no reason to either dispute or support the statistic.

We thought it would be interesting to discover the incidence of Jewish students in crew, inasmuch as there seems to be a high correlation between crew and club. We found that letters last year were awarded to no Jewish students in Varsity, J. V., 150 lb., or Freshman Crew. This finding contrasts interestingly with the 14% Jewish representation on Varsity Football, and the 12% of Varsity Soccer. It must be re-iterated that this in no way indicates any formal discrimination. The figures merely suggest a pattern in sports and social organization.

If one feels the social opportunities for the Jew are small at Harvard, he must bear in mind that the club system admits only a small part of the student body. Moreover, in a school like Amherst or Princeton where fraternities play an important role in college life, those who are discriminated against must sense their position much more sharply than they do at Harvard. At Harvard the club system is relatively unimportant, and the Jewish student has many fellow outsiders who never see the inside of clubs. What is germane to our discussion is the opportunity for the Jew in participation and leadership in those extra-curricular activities based on talent and competition.

A great deal of interest has been manifested by the student body regarding Jewish participation in political activity. Unfortunately it has been impossible to get statistical data sufficient to make any really authoritative statement on this subject. It is frequently the contention of gentiles that Jews are "radical." Statistics on the local chapters of the AYD and of the Young Progressives would have been helpful in determining the accuracy of this charge. The AYD at the moment is in a state of confusion, and may in the near future face a sort of spontaneous disintegration because of its unpopular Communist origins. The Wallace group felt that this study we are making would be valuable, but refused to allow us to check their membership lists, inasmuch as people of the left wing are subject to considerable disapprobation, and a confidential membership list for that reason was doubly important.

We know that there are Jewish students in the Free Enterprise Society, but that group is too small to be statistically significant. Perhaps the best indication of Jewish political activity at Harvard may be found in the percentages for the Harvard Young Republican Club, and The Liberal Union. As of last fall, the HYRC had 4.2% Jewish membership (17 of 406 undergrad members) and the Liberal Union a 43.6% representation of Jewish students (41 of 94 undergrad members). Of the Liberal Union's executive board, however, only a third were Jewish. These organizations represent the position of moderateness, one slightly to the right, the other slightly to the left of center. Jewish adherence seems to be significantly to the latter position. This, however, is no indication of the radical tendencies that are frequently and loosely charged, for the Liberal Union is in pretty close harmony with popular political opinion as expressed in last November's election.

Erik Homburger Erikson in his study *Hitler's Imagery and the German Youth* analysed the foundations of anti-semitism in modern society, and his findings are appropriate to this facet of our article. He divided the Jewry into two groups: the orthodox, and the element which has lived in a multiplicity of cultures, and has been perpetually capable of easy adjustment to new social environments. This latter group, he feels, frequently functions to a significant degree as salesmen of ideas and progressive interpreters of esthetics. The Jew's easy acceptance of change makes him the target of hostilities evidenced by those who fear loss of status or security during a period of rapid social change. The McWilliams book, previously cited, describes the loss of security suffered by the middle class as industrial concentration has increased, and correlates it with the rise of anti-semitism within the middle class. The confused nature of anti-semitic charges ("Jews run Wall Street" and "Jews are communists") indicate the double pressure on the middle class today, and they should make us doubt the supposed objectivity of any sweeping statement about Jewish political allegiance.

The Jewish student seems to have excellent opportunities for self-expression in other than purely social organizations. Perhaps the most respected and demanding extra-curricular activity in the college is the Crimson. Jews represent 31% of the Crimson board. Even more significant is the 57% representation in Crimson *executive* positions, which would indicate both opportunity and talent as characterizing the Jewish student in this type of endeavor. The *Advocate* has a representation of 7% on its board,

but the total number of editors is really too small to make for a telling statistic. The Lampoon has no Jewish students on its board.

The musical organizations of the college are sufficiently large to offer meaningful figures:

Glee Club: 9%
Band: 16.4%
Orchestra: 25.8%

In other extra-curricular fields the Jewish student seems to be well represented. The Harvard Dramatic Club has a 12% Jewish membership. Signet and The Student Council are respectively 12% and 21% Jewish.

Mr. Charles Duhig, in an interview at Phillips Brooks House, informed us that the membership lists of that organization were in a state of recompilation because of the addition of second term members. He explained, however, that Jews represented a high proportion of Phillips Brooks House membership. Brooks House is non-sectarian and welcomes anybody who is interested in good works in the community. Mr. Duhig said that in the past four years there have been two Jewish and two Christian presidents. Jews, he added, are well represented on the Brooks House cabinet. His explanation of the high percentage of Jewish students in this group is the tremendous willingness to work hard in charity activities, manifested by Jews. We have no way by which to demonstrate this statistically, but respect Mr. Duhig's close observation of this type of activity.

We have examined the composition of the college and many of its subsidiary student groups. There has emerged from this study a picture of the Jewish student which we consider heartening. The University policy of admissions is enlightened (particularly when compared with Dartmouth or Princeton, which sticks rigidly to a 3% quota) and the opportunities for Jewish participation in non-scholastic activities seem ample. Clubs represent an exception to this rule, but a very minor one, considering the status of clubs as a whole. There may be tacit social discrimination, but the only formal affront to Jewry has been the anti-Zionist stand of the short-lived League for Reaction. Dr. Albert Sprague Coolidge has admitted to a Massachusetts Legislative hearing that discrimination occurs in the awarding of chemistry scholarships because of an agreement between the University and chemical companies granting these scholarships. With this exception, we find no basis for believing any other University discrimination exists. The refusal to inquire into religious backgrounds suggests that the University seriously attempts to avoid discrimination. The Jewish student at Harvard is not repeatedly made conscious of his "Jewishness" as he would be at other schools which have a tight fraternity system and admitted quotas. This is evidenced by the lack of appeal of Harvard Zionist activities for a great part of the undergraduate Jewry. Where there is no patent discrimination there is little basis for militant organization along religious lines.

A period of crisis is particularly dangerous for the Jew. In this article there has been a discussion of the causes of rampant anti-semitism in periods of disorganization and social instability. Inasmuch as we live in an era where change is both rapid and harsh, and individual emotional security is a slender thing, it is not unreasonable to believe that organized anti-semitism may reach new heights in the next few years. As the college is a part of the larger community, it must necessarily reflect trends in society. The post-war rise of Gerald L. K. Smith's following, the abortive prosecution of Mrs. Dilling et al., and the appearance of such groups as the Columbians in Georgia does not augur well for better conditions for minority groups. Despite the efforts of men of good will, and the Federal Government, the condition and the direction of our culture presages new dreadfulness unless some major social change can occur. Harvard, we agree, is pursuing an enlightened policy, and in view of this University's traditional liberalism, will no doubt continue to pursue it. Anti-semitism within the college must therefore appear within the framework of extra-curricular activities and informal social contacts. The condition of the Jew at Harvard is relevant to the very nature of the society we live in. The degree of a tolerance in a social body is closely correlated with its health. For these reasons we feel such awareness as motivates this study essential to our cultural survival.

LITTLE BEATRICE

by JOHN HAWKES, JR.

Your misery does not touch me;
Nor the flame of this burning
Assail me.

DANTE

Straight the hair, dull the little girl;
I see her hiding from the crowd, a squirrel,
Clutching to her chest the half filled bag,
Her eyes the staring chestnuts of a vender
Mad with the cold, an old Venetian faker.
She will never ride the dark gondolas.
She stops to mimic a song that she once heard,
And darts at a passing woman with a word.

Her father, a ringed gipsy, rakes the coals;
Holding his coat he curls round the fire,
Puts the folded paper inside his shoes
And hears the tambourine under the trees.
He knows her coming by the slamming door
And confident that she will watch the stove,
He retreats within the olive grove;
Mounting the stairs she contrives to be a queen
And drops her cloak, a gesture against the heat;
Then picks it up, remembering the street
Where frozen Caesars and Giuseppes meet.

TYWATER

By RICHARD WILBUR

Death of Sir Nihil, book the *nth,*
Upon the charred and clotted sward,
Lacking the lily of our Lord,
Alases of the hyacinth.

Could flicker from behind his ear
A whistling silver throwing knife
And with a holler punch the life
Out of a swallow in the air.

Behind the lariat's butterfly
Shuttled his white and gritted grin,
And cuts of sky would roll within
The noose-hole, when he spun it high.

The violent, neat and practiced skill
Was all he loved and all he learned;
When he was hit, his body turned
To clumsy dirt before it fell.

And what to say of him, God knows.
Such violence. And such repose.

POEMS

By RICHARD WILBUR

THE WALGH-VOGEL

More pleasurable to look than feed upon,
Hence unconserved in dodo-runs, the round,
Unfeathered, melancholy, more than fifty pound
Dodo is gone,

Who when incarnate wore two token wings
And dined on rocks, to mock at mockeries.
Empowered now by absence, blessed with tireless ease,
It soars and sings

Elated in our skies, wherever seen.
Absolute retractility allows
Its wings be wavy wide as heaven; silence endows
Its hoots serene

With airy spleenlessness all may unhear.
Alive the dodo strove for lack of point,
Extinct won superfluity, and can disjoint
To joy our fear.

Dive, dodo, on the earth you left forlorn,
Sit vastly on the branches of our trees,
And chant us grandly all improbabilities.

OBJECTS

Meridians are a net
Which catches nothing; that sea-scampering bird
The gull, though shores lapse every side from sight, can yet
Sense him to land, but Hanno had not heard

Hesperidean song,
Had he not gone by watchful periploi:
Chalk rocks, and isles like beasts, and mountain stains along
The water-hem, calmed him at last near-by

The clear high hidden chant
Blown from the spellbound coast, where under drifts
Of sunlight, under plated leaves, they guard the plant
By praising it. Among the wedding gifts

Of Here, were a set
Of golden McIntoshes, from the Greek
Imagination. Guard and gild what's common, and forget
Uses and prices and names; have objects speak.

There's classic and there's quaint
And then there is that devout intransitive eye
Of Pieter de Hooch: see feinting from his plot of paint
The trench of light on boards, the much-mended dry

Courtyard wall of brick,
And sun submerged in beer, and streaming in glasses,
The weave of a sleeve, the careful and undulant tile. A quick
Change of the eye and all this calmly passes

Into a day, into magic.
For is there any end to true textures, to true
Integuments; do they ever desist from tacit, tragic
Fading away? Oh maculate, cracked, askew,

Gay-pocked and potsherd world
I voyage, where in every tangible tree
I see afloat among the leaves, all calm and curled,
The Cheshire smile which sets me fearfully free.

ENTR'ACTE FOR A FREAK SHOW

THE MAN WITH THE IRON MOUTH: See how
      the light-bulb powders on my tongue:
Miraculous.

THE HUMAN FROG: No more than a mockery,
A trade you learned, as useless as a lung
Without a body. Rather gaze on me:
My shrunken body utterly depends
Not on a trick, but birth; this should delight
By making nightmare solid for you, friends,
So that, undressing in your homes tonight,
Your undeniable symmetry will mean
The terror was unreal that made you cry:
For you are you, and with your eyes have seen
The twisted proof that figures do not lie.
I am a thing of God.

THE MAN WITH THE IRON MOUTH: My
      vulgar friend
Disdains me for my intellect, but this
Alone can set you free: That I defend
Absurd perfection, happily dismiss
All other kinds of action, must console
All you good people gathered in this place
Who feel your hands go empty and your whole
Body tremble, suddenly meet the face
Of your own childhood, when sleep will not bring
Its usual peace, reminding you of love
And what you have not been; remembering
My serious diet of glass, you can remove
The vision with a smile, sane and sincere,
Clenching your fists.

THE HUMAN FROG: You speak of things that seem.

THE BEARDED LADY: Gentlemen, you both lie.
      Confess me here
The twice tormented mirror of your dream.

KENNETH KOCH

FETE GALANTE

John Ashbery

The eightieth birthday of Andrew E. Wylie! That old reprobate still alive! Imagine! In one corner of the huge foyer there is a grotto made of silver twigs, in which musicians try to rehearse a work of Telemann. In another part of the room an accompanist strikes chords, but the worried soprano does not attempt to sing. There is so much noise! Two sylph-like young men, one with an accordion, the other with a guitar, hurl themselves at the groups of guests, breaking up conversation, making bad music. Nobody can talk to the same person for long, and one begins to sense one's futility. A fortune-teller has been trying to get at Lucy for several minutes, but people are always in the way, laughing and talking rather loudly, a little sad maybe. "What sign did you say you was born under, dear?" asks the lady.

Lucy repeats the odd words which enter her head, "The sign of the flying red horse." After several seconds her companions laugh at this, turning their flushed faces on Lucy. Lucy begins to laugh a little too, wondering if she meant it as a joke. The fortune-teller doesn't seem to be offended, but she looks earnestly at Lucy and tries to clutch her dress. Lucy shrinks away. "When is your birthday?"

Lucy stammers and blushes prettily and looks into her glass of champagne. "Actually", says the sweet miss, "It's today!"

Today? But why hadn't Lucy said anything? We could have had a party! But—of course we couldn't have though for everyone is here! But—we must do *something!* Right now!

The fortune-teller has something to say to Lucy, she stretches out her withered arms. "No." says Lucy in a little voice. But people seem to be joining hands for a Paul Jones, a chain of intoxicated guests divides Lucy from the ancient hag. Maybe it's not a Paul Jones after all, but everyone seems to have changed his position. Now the two young men in their ruffled white shirts and black tights have found Lucy, now they drag her to the center of the great hall.

Silence! It is Rudy, Andrew E. Wylie's trusted old servant. "Ladies and gentlemen!" he calls from the top of the stairs. "Mr. Wylie wishes me to say that he is sorry to have missed so much of the party, but will soon be with you. Meanwhile let me remind you that it lacks but five minutes of midnight! At midnight everyone unmasks!"

But no one is wearing a mask. Evidently this is some kind of satirical joke on the part of old Andrew E. The guests snarl a little and jostle each other, as if to say, we know we're not a very pretty lot but look who invited us here, after all. Their host's absence disturbed no one, it's the sort of thing you get to expect from that old nut. His sarcasm doesn't bother anyone either, but—the fact that he should have motives for sarcasm is a little discouraging.

Lucy is tired. All the attractive people seem to have gone home early. Or perhaps getting drunk makes them look different, there are certainly more people here than ever, all shouting and laughing, but not seeming to have a very good time. Lucy makes her way to the terrace, eluding her two companions, who apparently have forgotten her anyway. It's nice out here, the light from the tall windows makes a silver checker effect on the stone flagging, also the moonlight on the coconut palms is lovely.

"Darling", somebody says, and wraps her in a pair of strong arms. His mouth descends over hers like absolute night.

"Oh stop", Lucy says presently, "You don't know how physically revolting you are to me."

"That could hardly be true in the light of certain recent events", says the man in a sulky voice. Then changing the subject, "Why didn't you let Madame Sospirio read your horoscope. She's remarkable, they all say. She predicted the atom bomb six months before it happened. She also predicted Corinne Wauchtheimer's twins."

Lucy says, twisting her long scarf, "Frank, your behavior is impossible. You must go away from here. We must not meet in public."

Why does she talk like this? Is this the way they talk in real life? Does she love this man? That's the important question. But try and get a look at him in the phoney light from the foyer, or hear him, really his voice soaring into the ultra-effeminate, or full and carefully modulated, or sinking into a bestial monotone, like drums or the sound in a sea-shell.

Then all the lights go out, all the noise and the music stops. What a funny dead silence! Not even an echo.

Something makes Lucy's fingers explore, explore, along the balcony rail to where Frank's hand last lay. Very plump and appealing in the moonlight, it seemed. Now she has found it, now they are holding hands. What a lovely sensation.

Help! It isn't Frank's hand at all! And someone is whispering very close, a velvety voice:

"YOU WILL GO ON A TRIP. A MAN WITH BROWN EYES WILL SEND A GIFT — A JEWEL. A BROADWAY STAR LENDS YOU HER FLAT. YOUR LIFE IS WOVEN OF DARK THREADS OF FORGETFULNESS AND GOLD THREADS OF JOY."

SOME TREES

JOHN ASHBERY

These are amazing; each
Joining a neighbor, as if speech
Were a still performance.
Arranging by chance

To meet as far, this morning
From the world as agreeing
With it, you and I
Are suddenly what the trees try

To tell us we are;
That our merely being here
Means something; that soon
We may touch, love, explain.

And glad not to have invented
Such comeliness, we are surrounded:
A silence already filled with noises,
A canvas on which emerges

A gathering of smiles, a summer morning.
Placed in a puzzling light, and moving,
Our days put on such reticence,
These accents seem their own defence.

WHY WE FORGET DREAMS

JOHN ASHBERY

I.

Through the half open door came a sound of April—
But I'm sad, said, the tenor, O unwisely the spring
Piles up its dangerous architecture!
Who expects wisdom from lightheaded birds
Moving through a forest of constant desires,
A world continually budding and fading,
Where only death flowers and is exact
And the season of love will never happen?
The sun went out, the noise of his crying
Fell across the year like an icy rain.
Who can make his sorrow or his happiness real,
Or make of their changing a beautiful thing?

II.

Now, he said, it is all over; only
Someday, crossing a street, or innocently
Pulling on our gloves, the will
Of an unseen lover will stare us into silence:
In the sky, palladian, or the waving
Tips of the willow, his sudden song
Will confound us, for it shall be noiseless and wordless;
The sky of his coming, dreamless, and we
The ghosts of which a dreamer takes possession.

So today, the Swans in the public gardens
Carry his sentence from shore to shore
Yet we sit in the sun with our legs dangling
And my knowledge black and cold beneath.
To move, he said, in his definition
Peaceful as swans! As in a poem
Love is forgetten, and in a dream
The poem is lost in a desert of contexts,
So motion is our cure, but till he names us
Love can be only waking to each other;
I to the blinding nowhere of your limbs,
You to the sad spring lost in my stammerings.

Recessional

DONALD A. HALL

The temperate Methodist scowls at the saloon; the Baptist
Titles his sermon: "The Efficacy of Prayer,"
While Peter, old professional, walks the waves,
Solid as a burgher on a hike.   How
Can the temperate Methodist know this rock
Of bones, built before his backwoods Christ?

But even Peter shivers with the wind.
Now fuzz-legged girls, their crucifixes
Coining the vault between their tutored breasts,
Ignore the bones, the martyred rocks, the saints
Who dance in parish halls for smiling priests.

LETTER FROM A WEDDING TRIP

ROBERT E. BLY

Travelling south, leaves overflow the farms.
Day by day we watched the leaves increase
And the trees lie tangled in each other's arms.
Still generation, and calls that never cease
And rustlings in the brush; yesterday
She asked how long we have been on the way.
So in the afternoon we changed our route
And came down to the coast; everywhere
The same: fish, and the lobster's sensual eyes.
The natives sang for harvest, gave us fruit,
At night the monkeys sat beneath the trees.
All night the cries of dancers filled the air
And last year's virgins pressed into the leaves.
Sometimes I think of your land, cold and fresh,
And try to think: what was the month we quit
Our northern land that seemed inhabited
By more than reproduction of the flesh?
I wonder, watching how the branches interknit
If monkeys gibbered by our bridal bed.

ENGLAND, 1935

L. E. SISSMAN

To those young men in the shadow of machines
Steel more exciting than cathedrals loomed:
Battersea's four gaunt towers in their dreams fumed
And overhead screaked the black dock-crane that leans

Seaward at Rotherhithe. On its gold lines
Across their nights the locomotive boomed,
Rushing to morning, where the azalea bloomed
About Vitesse Saloons in rural lanes.

Between them and the hills the gas-works hung;
Outside Olympia the only tree
Stood ringed in granite; the rarest birds had sung

To them in slums. At noon their tall aunts called
To take them to museum rooms to see
The World, a map on which destroyers crawled.

TWO POEMS

by

FRANK O'HARA

POEM

The eager note on my door said, "Call me,
call when you get in!" so I quickly threw
a few tangerines into my overnight bag,
straightened my eyelids and shoulders, and

headed straight for the door. It was autumn
by the time I got around the corner, oh all
unwilling to be either pertinent or bemused, but
the leaves were brighter than grass on the sidewalk!

Funny, I thought, that the lights are on this late
and the hall door open; still up at this hour, a
champion jai-alai player like himself? Oh fie!
for shame! What a host, so zealous! And he was

there in the hall, flat on a sheet of blood that
ran down the stairs. I did appreciate it. There are few
hosts who so thoroughly prepare to greet a guest
only casually invited, and that several months ago.

THE DRUMMER

Baraban! baraban! this is a quick
stiletto bounced tight in tin casket!
The devil you say! Wicked the way
my aunt had to tell me after uncle
rolled over and over inside the locomotive
bellowing like a walrus's guffaw!

Baraban! Tighten till it pricks through
keen as a blond feather, the saint!
the rib-tickler! oh! oh! the dromedary
sharp-tooth, swaying its all-muscle belly,
has all the luck. What a whale! it careens
over the tracks, dropping bison cakes.
That's the way it was on the prairies,
with a baraban! every two minutes and
the red men knocking us off like turkeys.

Oh uncle, you died in a roadster coupe
fighting the Pawnees and Banshees, you did,
and I'll drum you over the hill, bumpily,
my drum strongly galumphing, kangaroos
on all sides yelping baraban! for you.

THE PRISONERS

Enclosed in this disturbing mutual wood,
Wounded alike by thorns of the same tree,
We seek in hopeless war each others' blood
Though suffering in one identity.
Each to the other prey and huntsman known,
Still driven together, lonelier than alone

Strange mating of the loser and the lost!
With faces stiff as mourners, we intrude
Forever on the one we turn from most,
Each wandering in a double solitude.
The unpurged ghosts of passion bound to pride,
Who wake in isolation, side by side.

NIGHT

The motes that still disturbed her lidded calm
Were these: the tick and whisper of a shade
Against the sill; a cobweb-film that hung
Aslant a corner moulding, too elusive
For any but the gaze of straitened eyes;
The nimbus of the night-lamp, where a moth
Uneasily explored the edge of light
Through hours of fractured darkness. She alone
Knew that the room contained these things; she lay
Hearing the almost imperceptible sound
(As if a live thing shivered behind the curtains)
Watching the thread that frayed in gusts of air
More delicate than her breathing, or by night
Sharing a moth's perplexity at light
Too frail to drive out dark: minutiae
Held in the vise of sense about to die.

ADRIENNE RICH

THE HOUSE AT THE CASCADES

All changed now through neglect. The steps dismantled
By infantries of ants, by roots and storms,
The pillars tugged by vines, the porte-cochere
A passageway for winds, the solemn porches
Warped into caricatures.
                            We came at evening
After the rain, when every drunken leaf
Was straining, swelling in a riot of green.
Only the house was dying in all that life,
As if a triumph of emerald energy
Had fixed its mouth upon the walls and stones.
The tamest shrub remembered anarchy
And joined in appetite with the demagogue weed
That springs where order falls; together there
They stormed the defenseless handiwork of man
Whose empire wars against him when he turns
A moment from the yoke. So, turning back,
He sees his rooftree fall to furious green,
His yard despoiled, and out of innocent noon
The insect-cloud like thunder on the land.

FAULKNER'S VISION OF HUMAN INTEGRITY

To Hannah and Heinrich Blucher

ALFRED KAZIN

Speaking at Stockholm last December, Mr. Faulkner said, in part: "Our tragedy today is a general and universal physical fear so long sustained by now that we can even bear it. There are no longer problems of the spirit. There is only the question: When will I be blown up? Because of this, the young man or woman writing today has forgotten the problems of the human heart in conflict with itself which alone can make good writing, because only that is worth writing about, worth the agony and the sweat . . .

"He must learn them again. He must teach himself that the basest of all things is to be afraid; and teaching himself that, forget it forever, leaving no room in his workshop for anything but the old verities and truths of the heart, the old universal truths lacking which any story is ephemeral and doomed —love and honor and pity and pride and compassion and sacrifice . . .

"Until he relearns these things, he will write as though he stood among and watched the end of man.

I decline to accept the end of man. It is easy enough to say that man is immortal simply because he will endure: that when the last dingdong of doom has clanged and faded from the last worthless rock hanging tideless in the last red and dying evening, that even then there will still be one more sound: that of his puny inexhaustible voice, still talking. I refuse to accept this. I believe that man will not merely endure: he will prevail. He is immortal, not because he alone among creatures has an inexhaustible voice but because he has a soul, a spirit capable of compassion and sacrifice and endurance. The poet's, the writer's, duty is to write about these things."

We in America do not often hear such talk from our novelists—and perhaps we expect it least from a realistic novelist whose work is still identified with the sadistically meticulous account of Southern "decadence" we so often get from the fashionable new novelists. Even Faulkner's larger reputation in Europe, at least in the form in which it comes back to us, shows that if that hydra-headed monster, the twentieth-century American novelist—he whose name is simply Faulkner - Hemingway - Caldwell - Steinbeck—is still thought of as the last word in brutality and savage materialism, it is predominently Faulkner who so personifies him to the outside world.

But the thrill of pleasure I felt on reading Faulkner's Nobel Prize speech was based not only on my gratitude that such words should be spoken today at all—and how badly our frightened intellectuals need to hear them—but also on a sense of recognition. *What* Faulkner said at Stockholm is in its explicit adjunction unusual for him and even untypical. I would not have said that it is to lift our hearts that he writes. But that voice, that unashamedly eloquent voice in all its true terseness, reminding us by the very rush and edge of his sentences that all human affairs are settled first within the heart, returning back and back to those large words like love and honor and pity and pride by which, after all, we do try to live; pointing to the fear-racked man of our age in all his secret daily aloneness—it is precisely that voice, passionate and steady, that seems to hold his novels together in their fierceness, line by line. Even the most perfunctory reading of a page should intimate to us the nature of the mind we are dealing with, warn us that he is different in kind rather than in degree from our other novelists today.

Yet it is remarkable how many people seem able to read Faulkner

through, even to analyze his work on its secondary levels with the greatest shrewdness, without finding any very constructive purpose to his style. For what is the usual objection to that style? Why, that is *needlessly* involved, that it is perversely thick with parentheses, even with parentheses within parentheses; that it is a pity a man who can tell a story so well should get so heated in the telling and be so long-winded. I have just read an article in the latest number of *Partisan Review* that states his art is wholly uneven, hopelessly lost between two styles—"one is simple and full of references to nature; there is nothing to equal it in American writing today . . . In his other style, which dominates his writing, Faulkner constructs his legend of the South. It is here that all his famous traits are found: the rhetoric, the difficult, involved sentences, gratuitous and exaggerated, the tangle of meanings and motive." "So little is left of the touching simplicity and openness," Isaac Rosenfeld goes on, "it is hard to believe that the same man writes in both styles." Your thoroughly sensible man, like Bernard DeVoto, thinks he is a talented man who unfortunately tends to get lost in floods of excess sensibility; your humanist liberal, like Lionel Trilling, that he rants; I have recently heard a Marxist critic suggest that he is simply a floridly uncontrolled reactionary brooding over the decline of his class. Even one of his most sympathetic critics, Malcolm Cowley, thinks that the defects of his style can be attributed to the traditional isolation of the American writer. "His novels," Cowley says in the introduction to his brilliantly arranged Portable Faulkner, "are the books of a man who broods about literature but doesn't often discuss it with his friends; there is no ease about them, no feeling that they come from a background of taste refined by argument and of opinions held in common . . . Like Hawthorne, Faulkner is a solitary worker by choice, and he has done great things with double the pains to himself that they might

have cost if they had been produced in more genial circumstances . . . All of them are full of overblown words that he would have used with more discretion, or not at all, if he had followed Hemingway's example and served an apprenticeship to an older writer."

Now these objections—and I have contributed to them myself—spring in part from a certain false professionalism in our attitude toward style. One might call it the Hemingway influence. Hemingway's own early style, and his—a whole generation's—particular craving for simplicity and naturalness, are something else again. The Hemingway influence has now become an article of commerce. The dregs of that influence can be seen not merely in the shallow and smug language of a slick news-weekly like *Time*, but even more in the method of production that puts the magazine together on the belief that anything can be rewritten, and apparently by anyone. I have often detected in the language of editors and critics the unconscious belief that all writers have the same needs, and that all write to the same audience. They favor that "clear," because convenient, style through which one can see immediately to the bottom of any subject—and indeed, to judge from Hemmingway's recent work, the bottom is very quickly reached. I call it a falsely professional attitude—Richard Chase complains in a recent book on Melville that even he was too little the continuously professional writer! — because it stems from that morbid over-consciousness of the audience that afflicts even the most serious writers in this country. We have become so intent on getting the audience to understand quickly, rather than on encouraging the writer to have his full say, that we brutally dispose of the individual differences between writers.

Now Faulkner, as is well known, is less conscious of his audience than most novelists today. He has even written in a letter to Cowley: "I think I have written a lot and sent it off to print before I actually realized strangers might read it." Many objections to his style, I am convinced, stem from our disbelief that a writer in America *can* write without thinking of the "strangers" who might read him; that he will not sacrifice an iota of his realization to "communication" at any price. But the primary reason for our objections to Faulkner's style is our refusal to believe that what he writes about is entirely real even to him. Most of his critics show a genuine indifference to his point of view.

By point of view I mean not a writer's social opinions, which he may and usually does share with many people, especially if he is a Southerner; not those psychological interpretations by which we now so easily interpret and think we entirely reveal someone's character; not even his moral philosophy, whether on its most realistic or exalted level. I mean the angle of vision from which one recurringly sees the universe—that native disposition of mind which plants in us very early those particular words, those haunted stresses and inflections, those mysteriously echolalic repetitions, to which we most instinctively return—and which at our best we accept with joy, and sometimes even understand.

It is his point of view, his personal convictions of the shape life has, that presents any writer with that resurgent theme from which he chooses the subject of his art and even many of its devices. For a real artist never simply borrows a technique even when he may seem to, but uses it as if no one had used it before him. It is by his point of view, surely, that we *know* Dostoevsky is more than the sum of his reactionary social opinions; Proust more, even, than *his* sensibility; Melville more than his pessimistic abasement before the magnitude of the divine. It is a writer's point of view that gives us our immediate experience of his mind in all its rich particularity. It is *in* his point of view though not necessarily for his point of view, that we read him.

Yet it is amazing how many people disregard what is most im-

mediately present to their minds when they read a page of Faulkner. It is very hard for me to believe that the often tumultuous and deeply spiritual experience we have in reading something like "The Bear" adds only to another "parable of the Deep South," or the fact that he is really — the holy simplicity of literary historians! — a "romantic." (The word today apparently signifies that one romantic is just like another.) I do not think Faulkner would have been any different if he had gone to school to Ezra Pound, had learned to trim his style, to be more sparing of those "overblown" words. I think he needs those words. Hemingway may not; Faulkner does. I would suggest that he means something by them essential to his stubbornly individual vision of the world. I would guess they have been in his mind a very long time, that it was almost to see them live a life separate from his own that he began to write, that it is to rediscover their meanings through and through the whole range of his adult life that he continues to write.

For what are those words to which Faulkner constantly returns? Cowley cites "*immemorial, imponderable, immutable.*" But the more active words, actually, are *astonishment, outrage, furious, intractable, implacable, inflexible, impervious, amazed, outlast, endure, repudiate, rage, sourceless*—and less and less in the recent works, but always present, for they awoke the image of the soaring arch and of the ecstacy in retracing its height that are both so essential to his mind— *upsoar, avatar, apotheosis.* And significantly, most of these words are applied to individuals of every type and in every class—not only to his intellectuals or visionaries, like Quentin Compson, Horace Benbow, the Reverend Gail Hightower, or his tiresomely sage spokesman, Gavin Stevens; but to a Snopes as well as a Major DeSpain; to the farmers in the field and sitting Saturday afternoons in their "clean well patched overalls" around Varner's store; to the old hunter Ike McCaslin; to a criminal like Pop-

eye; to some children and most boys; to the hunted Negro in "Red Leaves" trying to escape being buried alive with his dead Indian master; to the Negro slaves and to their silently wise descendants still doing the dirty work in the kitchens after the war is over. They are used with particular force about the unscrupulous Jason Compson in *The Sound and the Fury* and the hunted and murdering Joe Christmas in *Light in August*; they are applied to houses, hills, roads, dogs, the dark and mighty figure of the bear in Faulkner's great story of that name; about doors, and at least once, by implication, about God.

These words are not merely interjections, or—as they might often seem—assertions trailing off the loose ends of his narrative. They are the very ground bass, to borrow a figure from music, above which he sets his narrative theme; in and out of which his story is composed. They are the atmosphere in which Faulkner's characters move—even God Himself in the middle section of "The Bear," that God so struck with the outrage and the horror of man's blind exploitation of the land that he was prepared to repudiate him altogether until John Brown, who was fully a man, and so astonished even Him, stayed His hand. All of them, Negro or White, Southern or Northern, old settlers or new exploiters, feel this outrage, this astonishment, this fury. It is the living state—not merely of ourselves caught for a moment above the motion of life, but of everything within our ken and which we color with the violence of our state—astonished and furious and outraged, outraged freshly over again every day and every hour, yet still trying to be impervious, to believe ourselves implacable, and by claiming our own intactness, showing that we seek to endure. And it is a state that is known to his characters and about each other not in moments of contemplation only—for that would arrest the momentum—but, like the constant echo of the ground bass that we can still hear in Bach even when it is not, immediately in use—as that particular knowledge to which they must all return.

Now it is with this word *return* that I can perhaps at last get at what is so distinctive in Faulkner's vision —the fact that, more often than not, his characers view things without surprise. It is not the happening that makes a story of Faulkner's move; it is the confirmation. Everything seems to have been known beforehand. The event itself seems to be assimilated first in brooding expectancy; then to occur as a confirmation; then requickens the familiar outrage and astonishment that it should happen at all. So that when the event does occur as expected, and the usual baleful grim glance is thrown over it, it seems to have been not so much lived as relived. Thus one feels—particularly about his most thoroughly realized characters, like Jason Compson and Joe Christmas—that their suffering and their thinking incorporate the very momentum of life. It is as if *their lives were thinking for them*. All through the greater part of *Light in August* one seems to see Joe Christmas running, constantly running ahead on the public highway, yet with his face turned to us, amazed that everything he has expected so long *should* finally be happening to him—even as he runs. All through the great monologue of Jason Compson in *The Sound and the Fury* one sees him rushing about the streets, or hunting his niece from his automobile, yet investing each terrible moment with this greater frightfulness—the fact that his whole life is present in his ordeal, and that he should have expected life to come to a crisis just so, for he has really spent his life thinking it over.

I believe it is this expectancy, this forehand knowledge they bear about with them through each moment of their lives, that gives Faulkner's people that peculiar tension of watching and listening under which he sometimes seems to stagger from page to page of his novels like a man lifting a heavy plaster cast. Surely there is no other living novelist who has lavished so much attention on the human face in its inflexible watchful concentration, who has pinned down so much of the simultaneous impact of human

events upon the eye. Each character seems to bear the whole weight of his actual and potential knowledge on his face — yet to doubt that knowledge, not out of any genuine disbelief, but out of astonishment and outrage that he must bear it. And along with it, that fiery screen of background detail, of historical causality as it pertains to his own life and the tradition-racked consciousness of the South, that enters into his mind like those background details of a dream that we take in without always knowing that we do.

In short, Faulkner burdens his characters with the integral human state; he will not let them off. This is the undergrowth of every day— sometimes unbearable in its keenness and recoil—which Joe Christmas must trample through even as he runs. This is that inflamed sense of one's whole life entirely present before one that is the real agony of Jason Compson all that terrible day, "April 6, 1928,"—and that makes him, though infinitely repellent, so giant a paradigm of man clutching at the air of this world as, assailed by every conceivable pain and anxiety, he searches for the niece who has stolen the money he had originally stolen from *her*. In *Intruder In The Dust* Faulkner calls it "that naked agony of inasthetisable nerve-ends which for lack of a better word men call being alive." In "Beyond," that beautiful little story of the responsibilities we still bear dreaming of our death, the Judge describes it as that "certain integral consistency which, whether it be right or wrong, a man must cherish because it alone will ever permit him to die."

It is this "consistency" as the very foundation of awareness, which rejoices in awareness as its most joyful and healthy end, that I see in Faulkner's conception of human integrity. It is this consistency that gives him his inner freedom as a storyteller, and as a stylist, that fierceness and openness of tone beside which the voices of our Hemingways and Fitzgeralds sound peevish.

Now obviously this integrity is not what we usually mean by the word today — that which Stuart Chase once so significantly described

as a "luxury." As one hears the word nowadays, integrity seems to represent something we should like to have, that we know—if only for our health's sake!—that we need to have, but, nevertheless, is always the paradise lost in the conflicting allegiances of our middle-class existence. And in fact, by our imperative, but still in one sense unworthy, calculations whether we dare to say this thing, to write this article, to defy that boss; by our wearing and wistful questioning of the "integrity" of our simplest relationships, the most casual things we do, we have come to feel that the tidal waves of prosperous unhappiness constantly sweeping over modern American life may represent chiefly a bad conscience. Faulkner starts beyond this point; I do not suppose he has ever written a line simply to please a magazine editor or to impress his audience. At one time, as I have noted, he didn't even know he had one. If he has a bad conscience, it is the bad conscience of the sensitive Southerner who bears in his heart the whole history of the culture he loves, and that culture Faulkner has examined over and over with paramount good faith and that necessary love for one's own people, simply because one is *of* them, without which our judgments of other people are arbitrary and usually destructive. For him integrity represents not that hoped-for state of "integration" which enables us to "function," but that which alone enables us to grasp our existence.

Ironically enough, those critics who insist on reading Faulkner exclusively as an historian of the South, "another Balzac," find it easier to think of him as a profound social thinker than to face up to his philosophical emphasis. Yet if you study carefully something so fundamental to his thoughts as the long dialogue on slavery and the land which composes the middle section of "The Bear," you find that the obscurities of his work stem not from any particular profoundity or complexity of ideas, but from the fact that his mind is so astonishingly energetic, his sensibility so vividly aroused by all the issues present to his mind, that he is always

HARVARD

ADVOCATE

Midgette '58

Commencement
Issue ~ 35¢

leaping from one to the other in excited discovery. Faulkner writes like a man thinking aloud. And quite often, indeed, like a man who has suddenly fallen into a hypnotic trance of thinking about any issue that may present itself to him in the midst of a story. Nor, despite the quiet boldness of his thinking about the South and slavery, is he particularly free—how could he be? —of the tangle of motives, self-defensive rights and wrongs, that we usually detect in Southerners reviewing the history of slavery. For every positive acceptance of its great wrong and guilt—and no other Southern novelist has gripped the subject so frankly—he will go out of his way to plead the despotic kindness of the old slaveholders. There is a particularly amusing example of this in the middle section of "The Bear," where the extraordinary crescendo of argument leading up to the imminent revelation of God's curse upon the land suddenly falls away into a crooning lullaby of the kindness the women showed the slaves when they were ill—and then is capped by the admission that these same services were performed for cattle, but not by those lower-class people, ancestors of the Snopeses, no doubt, who had to hire their horses from a livery stable! Faulkner is a Southerner; and very much a man of his class. But let us not forget that for him the guilt of slavery is tempered by the realization that the exploiter, too, is a man; that no more than the slave can he be dismissed from the other end of the relationship. Yet it is not entirely fair to him, it conventionalizes him, to assume that he sees all these things simply under the general and individual rubric of human guilt. Faulkner does not give the impression that so many Southern poets and critics do—that their highest aim as *writers* is to become good Christians again. He seems more intent on understanding the human situation than on being saved.

But here I am wandering away from my subject, for it was my intention a while back, by stressing the number of things present to his mind at once, to evoke his specific quality as an artist. It is what I have already noted as his momentum. Faulkner's imagination seems to be characterized by a velocity of memory that one finds only in writers of genius—by the ability to sustain details in so long and dynamic a single period that they finally compose a single order of progression. A characteristic example of this can be found early in *Intruder In The Dust*. It is worth quoting here not because this novel, or even the passage itself, is among his best—indeed, I would say that since *The Sound And The Fury* and *Light In August*, written about the same age that Melville was when he wrote *Moby Dick*, Faulkner has nothing so good, and lately seems suspiciously as mellow as Melville became at too early an age — but because it shows to what extent Faulkner's momentum will assert itself in a novel interpreted by our best critics as a Southerner's conventional case against President Truman's Civil Rights Bill.

It is the scene in which the boy Charles Mallison is taken, after he has fallen through the ice while hunting, to the house of the Negro Lucas Beauchamp. He knows, of course, that the man is a descendant of the old planter Carothers McCaslin, and like everyone else in town is constantly irritated by the Negro's pride, his air always "intractable and composed," his refusal of the customary servility. And now, as he trails sheepishly behind, he is more than ever aware of this elderly Negro who with calm dignity insists on taking him into his house and who humiliatingly reminds him that, like his own grandfather, "the man striding ahead was simply incapable of conceiving himself by a child contradicted and defied."

"So he didn't even check when they passed the gate, he didn't even look at it and they were in no well-used tended lane leading to tenant or servant quarters and marked by walking feet but a savage gash half gully and half road mounting a hill with an air solitary independent and intractable and then he saw the house, the cabin and remembered the rest of the story, the legend: how Edmonds' father had deeded to his Negro first cousin and his heirs in perpetuity the house and the ten acres of land it sat in—an oblong of earth set forever in the middle of the two-thousand-acre plantation like a postage stamp in the center of an envelope — the paintless wooden house, the paintless picket fence whose paintless latchless gate the man kneed open still without stopping or once looking back, and he following and Aleck Sander and Edmonds' boy following him, strode on into the yard. It would have been grassless even in summer; he could imagine it, completely bare, no weed no spring of anything, the dust each morning swept by some of Lucas' womenfolks with a broom made of willow switches bound together, into an intricate series of whorls and overlapping loops which as the day advanced would be gradually and slowly defaced by the droppings and the cryptic three-toed prints of chickens like (remembering it now at sixteen) a terrain in miniature out of the age of the great lizards, the four of them walking in what was less than walk because its surface was dirt too yet more than path, the footpacked strip running plumbline straight between two borders of tin cans and empty bottles and shards of china and earthenware set into the ground, up to the paintless steps and the paintless gallery along whose edge sat more cans but larger — empty gallon buckets which had once contained molasses or perhaps paint and wornout water or milk pails and one five-gallon can for kerosene with its top cut off and half of what had once been somebody (Edmonds' without doubt) kitchen hot water tank sliced longways like a banana —out of which flowers had grown last summer, and from which the dead stalks and the dried and brittle tendrils still leaned or drooped, and beyond this the house itself, gray and weathered and not so much paintless as independent of and intractable to paint so that the house was not only the one possible continuation of the stern untended road but was its crown too as the carven ailanthus leaves are the Greek column's capital.

"Nor did the man pause yet, up the steps and across the gallery and opened the door and entered and he and then Edmonds' boy and Aleck Sander followed: a hall dim even almost dark after the bright outdoors and already he could smell that smell which he had accepted without question all his life as being the smell always of the places where people with any trace of Negro blood live as he had that all people named Mallison are Methodists, then a bedroom: a bare worn quite clean paintless rugless floor, in one corner and spread with a bright patchwork quilt a vast shadowy tester bed which had probably come out of old Carothers McCaslin's house, and a battered cheap Grand Rapids dresser and then for the moment no more or at least little more; only later would he notice— or remember that he had seen — the cluttered mantel on which sat a kerosene lamp handpainted with flowers and a vase filled with spills of twisted newspaper and above the mantel the colored lithograph of a three-year old calendar in which Pocahontas in the quilled fringed buckskins of a Sioux or Chippewa chief stood against a balustrade of Italian marble above a garden of formal cypresses and shadowy in the corner opposite the bed a chromo portrait of two people framed heavily in gold-painted wood on a gold-painted easel. But he hadn't seen that at all yet because that was behind him and all he now saw was the fire — the clay-daubed field-stone chimney in which a half burned backlog glowed and smoldered in the gray ashes and beside it in a rocking chair something which he thought was a child until he saw the face, and then he did pause long enough to look at her because he was about to remember something else his uncle had told him about or at least in regard to Lucas Beauchamp, and looking at her he realized for the first time how old the man actually was, must be — a tiny old almost doll-sized woman much darker than the man, in a shawl and an apron, the head bound in an immaculate white cloth on top of which sat a painted straw hat bearing some kind of ornament."

I shall not dwell here on the remarkable inwoven textures of this passage, or — what for technical reasons is perhaps most interesting

to any writer of prose — on the peculiarly impelled rightness of those words which by their ecstatic repetition hold and propel the phrases so that Faulkner can release the whole scene already present to his mind. But I should like to complete my argument by defining the necessity behind the passage. For what I see and hear in the soar and thud of these details is an effort to present — not merely *to* the consciousness of a single mind but *along* the whole circuit of time and thought through which we move— that which *is* our life in all its presentness. We suddenly feel in some momentary shock to our physical being that we are being played on by history, but the forces of our own character, by that tangle of rights and wrongs, of present injustice and perhaps ultimate injustice, too, that asserts itself in every human situation. And it is only such an awareness, such a willingness to live the situation through and through with everything we are, so full an acceptance of the presentness of our lives *as finally real*, that mollifies some of the ache of being alive, the old split between our being and our knowing. For this is who we are when all entirely present *here*—"this living entity at this point at this day."

Faulkner's insistence on embracing all actuality in the moment is more than a novelist's innovation or technique. It goes far beyond the stream-of-consciousness method, with its emphasis on the underground level of man's knowing — a method that always shows man as half-asleep, and just becoming aware how much he lies to himself. It is an attempt to realize continuity with all our genesis, our "progenitors"—another of Faulkner's favorite words—with all we have touched, known, loved. *This* is why he needs those long successive parentheses, and parentheses within parentheses. They exemplify the chain of human succession. The greatest horror his characters know is to feel they have been dropped out of this stream of being, to think of themselves as "self-progenitive" or "sourceless." But no matter how many parentheses he may use, he knows how to leave them behind him, to come

out flush to the end of a sentence with a fresh, stabbing, often humorously concrete thought. We may live in our tradition, be haunted by it as Southerners are: but we are not our tradition; we are individual and alive.

With Faulkner it would seem as if the theme of the journey which is so elemental in American literature, always present to our minds because of our very history as a people, has here been contracted to display the real journey each human being makes through time—minute by minute of the universe with which we are filled. And so thoroughly is the moment lived and relived that only when it is over can we look back and see how rich our lives are. Here is one main source of Faulkner's humor, which is so often the wild grin he throws over a situation after it has been lived; it is his own amused astonishment at how much a human being can take in, how long a road he travels through in his own mind. And here, too, we approach that ultimate word which means so much to him—endurance. This endurance, or "outlasting," is not the mark simply of his favorite Negroes, like Dilsey in *The Sound And The Fury*. The Negroes are its greatest *social* example. For the Negroes, like the Jews, have the curious bitter advantage—and how often they have wished they could lose it—of having suffered an historic injustice so long that the noblest individuals among them can finally take in the whole of their situation precisely because they know it is the *human* situation, and so in some sense cannot be remedied. What endurance seems to mean to Faulkner is that if one sees one's whole life in time, only then can we realize our secret courage, our will to have endured; and only so relinquish our life to others. Only through integrity can we feel that our existence has fully been done justice to—for we have *lived* it — in all its outrageousness and astonishment.

One word more. It is often said that Faulkner owes his place in American literature to the fact that he has been fortunate in his background, which is so filled with "tradition and drama"—or perhaps simply to the fact that he has had the remarkable patience, or unusual good sense, to stay with his subject. It is implied that other writers, had they not been so rootless, had they not been open to the usual temptations, might have done as well.

And perhaps it is true that any writer — say Sinclair Lewis or Thomas Wolfe — might, if only he had stayed in his Minnesota or his North Carolina, have been able to work *his* way through and through the region he knows best, to write finally not only of what men do, but of what they mean.

But I wonder if there is not another way of putting it. Perhaps it is only the writer who knows that men are not the same everywhere, who believes that each human being is original and has a soul—perhaps it is only such a writer who will stick to his birthplace as if the whole of life were as much there as anywhere.

RHYME PROSE ON LITERATURE:

The Wen Fu of Lu Chi

ACHILLES FANG

Introduction by James Chace.

Lu Chi was killed in A.D. 303, at the age of 43. If, as Tu Fu says, the *Wen Fu* was written when its author was twenty, we may place its date at A.D. 280. But the matter is obscure. At any rate, this greatest *ars poetica* has almost completely escaped Western literary critics, and when, indeed, the present translation of it was presented to the editor of one of our principal literary reviews some time ago, it was thought to be a hoax. But Mr. Achilles Fang has accomplished his work in such a way as finally to establish both a great treatise on poetics and a great poem.

The *Wen-fu* generally includes 131 distichs, mostly parallel lines or antithetical couplets. The preface is in normal prose style, and the *fu*, as Mr. Fang translates it, may also be read as prose. As he has noted in an appendix to this translation, which first appeared in the *Harvard Journal of Asiatic Studies*, vol. 14, nos. 3 and 4., "for those critics who bifurcate all writings into rhymed and unrhymed classes, *fu* is verse; for those who posit regular rhythmic patterns as a criterion for verse, *fu* is considered prose. Pending a detailed study of *fu* rhythms we may be permitted to take it as prose."

The problem for the artist, as Lu Chi sees it, is to order thought by a penetration of the world outside himself. As Archibald MacLeish has stated in his very fine essay on the *Wen Fu* in the *Kenyon Review*, Summer 1952., "... he is attempting to think his way into the poetic phenomena with which he is concerned, using, for that purpose, poetry itself ..." Or, in Lu Chi's words, the purpose is "the embodiment of an object." If we may further quote Mr. MacLeish: "The poet undertakes to penetrate the world outside himself, the world of objective experience, the spiritually inpenetrable world of 'things out there.' Departing from no preconceptions, depending on no initial certainty, hauling himself along from find to find, from perception to perception, like an explorer on an unclimbed mountain, the artist works his way into his experience."

Here, in effect, is the *sine qua ñon* for the achieved poetic fact: the poet must work with preconceptions; his effort culminates in a complete transparency of himself. And such an action (and action it is) — for although it is self-denial, it is the best way of *coping* with things — alters, to use Eliot's phase, "all the works of art that preceded it," and in this case, all the works that have come after. Poetry becomes here "the power to order thought."

> Now he selects ideas and fixes them in their order;
> he examines words and puts them in their places.
> He traps heaven and earth in the cage of form; he
> crushes the myriad objects against the tip of
> his brush.

In other words, to order thought is to create and the perfection of the creative act results in great poetry. The beauty of great art becomes a concise statement of the relation of poetry to thought, an organic whole *under the mind that controls them.*

The *Advocate* is grateful to Mr. Achilles Fang for his translation, and readers who are interested in a fuller elucidation of the text are referred to the *Harvard Journal of Asiatic Studies*, vol. 14, nos. 3 and 4. A substantially identical but more taut version by Mr. Fang will appear in the fall issue of the New Mexico Quarterly, and Italian translation will be printed in the review, *Inventario.*

PREFACE
(IN UNRHYMED PROSE)

Each time I study the works of great writers, I flatter myself I know how their minds worked.

Certainly expression in language and the charging of words with meaning can be done in various ways.

Nevertheless we may speak of beauty and ugliness, of good and bad [in each literary work].

Whenever I write myself, I obtain greater and greater insight.

Our constant worry is that our ideas may not equal their objects and our style may fall short of our ideas.

The difficulty, then, lies not so much in knowing as in doing.

I have written this rhymeprose on literature to expatiate on the consummate artistry of writers of the past and to set forth the whence and why of good and bad writings as well.

May it be considered, some day, an exhaustive treatment.

Now, it is true, I am hewing an ax handle with an ax handle in my hand: the pattern is not far to seek.

However, the conjuring hand of the artist being what it is, I cannot possibly make my words do the trick.

Nevertheless, what I am able to say I have put down here.

TEXT
PREPARATION

Taking his position at the hub of things, [the writer] contemplates the mystery of the universe; he feeds his emotions and his mind on the great works of the past.

Moving along with the four seasons, he sighs at the passing of time: gazing at the myriad objects, he thinks of the complexity of the world.

He sorrows over the falling leaves in virile autumn; he takes joy in the delicate bud of fragrant spring.

With awe at heart, he experiences chill; his spirit solemn, he turns his gaze to the clouds.

He declaims the superb works of his predecessors; he croons the clean fragrance of past worthies.

He roams in the Forest of Literature, and praises the symmetry of great art.
Moved, he pushes his books away and takes the writing-brush, that he may express himself in letters.

PROCESS

At first he withholds his sight and turns his hearing inward; he is lost in thought, questioning everywhere.

His spirit gallops to the eight ends of the universe; his mind wanders along vast distances.

In the end, as his mood dawns clearer and clearer, objects, clean-cut now in outline, shove one another forward.

He sips the essence of letters; he rinses his mouth with the extract of the Six Arts.

Floating on the heavenly lake, he swims along; plunging into the nether spring, he immerses himself.

Thereupon, submerged words wriggle up, as when a darting fish, with the hook in its gills, leaps from a deep lake; floating beauties flutter down, as when a high-flying bird, with the harpoon-string around its wings, drops from a crest of cloud.

He gathers words never used in a hundred generations; he picks rhythms never sung in a thousand years.

He spurns the morning blossom, now full blown; he plucks the evening bud, which has yet to open.

He sees past and present in a moment; he touches the four seas in the twinkling of an eye.

WORDS, WORDS, WORDS

Now he selects ideas and fixes them in their order; he examines words and puts them in their places.

He taps at the door of all that is colorful; he chooses from among everything that rings.

Now he shakes the foliage by tugging the twig; now he follows back along the waves to the fountainhead of the stream.

Sometimes he brings out what was hidden; sometimes, looking for an easy prey, he bags a hard one.

Now, the tiger puts on new stripes, to the consternation of other beasts; now, the dragon emerges, and terrifies all the birds.

Sometimes things fit together, are easy to manage; sometimes they jar each other, are awkward to manipulate.

He empties his mind completely, to concentrate his thoughts; he collects his wits before he puts words together.

THE HARVARD ADVOCATE

winter issue   35cents

He traps heaven and earth in the cage of form; he crushes the myriad objects against the tip of his brush.

At first they hesitate upon his parched lips; finally they flow through the well-moistened brush.

Reason, supporting the matter [of the poem], stiffens the trunk; style, depending from it, spreads luxuriance around.

Emotion and expression never disagree: all changes [in his mood] are betrayed on his face.

If the thought touches on joy, a smile is inevitable; no sooner is sorrow spoken of than a sigh escapes.

Sometimes words flow easily as soon as he grasps the brush; sometimes he sits vacantly, nibbling at it.

VIRTUE

There is joy in this vocation; all sages esteem it.

We [poets] struggle with Non-being to force it to yield Being; we knock upon Silence for an answering Music.

We enclose boundless space in a square foot of paper; we pour out a deluge from the inch-space of the heart.

Language spreads wider and wider; thought probes deeper and deeper.

The fragrance of delicious flowers is diffused; exuberant profusion of green twigs is budding.

A laughing wind will fly and whirl upward; dense clouds will arise from the Forest of Writing Brushes.

DIVERSITY

(i) *The Poet's Aim*

Forms vary in a thousand ways; objects are not of one measure.

Topsy-turvy and fleeting, shapes are hard to delineate.

Words vie with words for display, but it is mind that controls them.

Confronted with bringing something into being or leaving it unsaid, he groans; between the shallow and the deep he makes his choice resolutely.

He may depart from the square and deviate from the compasses; for he is bent on exploring the shape and exhausting the reality.

Hence, he who would dazzle the eyes makes much of the gorgeous; he who intends to convince the mind values cogency.

If persuasion is your aim, do not be a stickler for details; when your discourse is lofty, you may be free and easy in your language.

(ii) *Genres*

Shih (lyric poetry) traces emotions daintily; *Fu* (rhymeprose) embodies objects brightly.

Pei (epitaph) balances substance with style; *Lei* (dirge) is tense and mournful.

Ming (inscription) is comprehensive and concise, gentle and generous; *Chen* (admonition), which praises and blames, is clear-cut and vigorous.

Sung (eulogy) is free and easy, rich and lush; *Lun* (disquisition) is rarefied and subtle, bright and smooth.

Tsou (memorial to the throne) is quiet and penetrating, genteel and decorous; *Shuo* (discourse) is dazzling bright and extravagantly bizarre.

Different as these forms are, they all forbid deviation from the straight, and interdict unbridled license.

Essentially, words must communicate, and reason must dominate; prolixity and long-windedness are not commendable.

THE MUSIC OF POETRY

As an object, literature puts on numerous shapes; as a form, it undergoes diverse changes.

Ideas should be cleverly brought together; language should be beautifully commissioned.

And the mutation of sounds and tones should be like the five colors of embroidery sustaining each other.

It is true that your moods, which come and go without notice, embarrass you by their fickleness,

But if you can rise to all emergencies and know the correct order, it will be like opening a channel from a spring of water.

If, however, proper juxtaposition is not made at the proper point, we will be putting the tail at the head.

The sequence of dark and yellow being deranged, the whole broidery will look smudged and blurred.

REVISION

Now you glance back and are constrained by an earlier passage; now you look forward and are coerced by some anticipated line.

Sometimes your words jar though your reasoning is sound, sometimes your language is smooth while your ideas make trouble;

Such collisions avoided, neither suffers; forced together, both suffer.

Weigh merit or demerit by the milligram; decide rejection or retention by a hairbreadth.

If your idea or word has not the correct weight, it has to go, however comely it may look.

KEY PASSAGES

Maybe your language is already ample and your reasoning rich, yet your ideas do not round out.

If what must go on cannot be ended, what has been said in full cannot be added to.

Put down terse phrases here and there at key positions; they will invigorate the entire piece.

Your words will acquire their proper values in the light of these phrases.
This clever trick will spare you the pain of deleting and excising.

PLAGIARISM

It may be that language and thought blend into damascened gauze—fresh, gay, and exuberantly lush;

Glowing like many-colored broidery, mournful as multiple chords;

But assuredly there is nothing novel in my writing, if it coincides with earlier masterpieces.

True, the arrow struck my heart; what a pity, then, that others were struck before me.

As plagiarism will impair my integrity and damage my probity, I must renounce the piece, however fond I am of it.

PURPLE PATCHES

It may be that one ear of the stalk buds, its tip standing prominent, solitary and exquisite.

But shadows cannot be caught; echoes are hard to bind.

Standing forlorn, your purple passage juts out conspicuously; it can't be woven into ordinary music.

Your mind, out of step, finds no mate for it; your ideas, wandering hither and thither, refuse to throw away that solitary passage.

When the rock embeds jade, the mountain glows; when the stream is impregnated with pearls, the river becomes alluring.

When the hazel and arrow-thorn bush is spared from the sickle, it will glory in its foliage.

We will weave the market ditty into the classical melody; perhaps we may thus rescue what is beautiful.

FIVE IMPERFECTIONS

(i) *In Vacuo*

Maybe you have entrusted your diction to an anemic rhythm; living in a desert, you have only yourself to talk to.

When you look down into Silence, you see no friend; when you lift your gaze to Space, you hear no echo.

It is like striking a single chord — it rings out, but there is no music.

(ii) *Discord*

Maybe you fit your words to a frazzled music; merely gaudy, your language lacks charm.

As beauty and ugliness are commingled, your good stuff suffers.

It is like the harsh note of a wind instrument below in the courtyard; there is music, but no harmony.

(iii) *Novelty for Novelty's Sake*

Maybe you forsake reason and strive for the bizarre; you are merely searching for inanity and pursuing the trivial.

Your language lacks sincerity and is poor in love; your words wash back and forth and never come to the point.

They are like a thin chord violently twanging — there is harmony, but it is not sad.

(iv) *License*

Maybe by galloping unbridled, you make your writing sound well; by using luscious tunes, you make it alluring.

Merely pleasing to the eye, it mates with vulgarity — a fine voice, but a nondescript song.

It reminds one of Fang-lu and Sang-chien,—it is sad, but not decorous.

(v) *Insipidity*

Or perhaps your writing is simple and terse, all superfluities removed—

So much so that it lacks even the lingering flavor of a sacrificial broth; it rather resembles the limpid tune of the "vermilion chord."

"One man sings, and three men do the refrain"; it is decorous, but it lacks beauty.

VARIABILITY

As to whether your work should be loose or constricted, whether you should mould it by gazing down or looking up.

You will accommodate necessary variation, if you would bring out all the overtones.

Maybe your language is simple, whereas your conceits are clever; maybe your reasoning is plain, but your words fall too lightly.

Maybe you follow the beaten track to attain greater novelty; maybe you immerse yourself in the muddy water — to reach true limpidity.

Well, perspicacity may come after closer inspection; subtlety may ensue from more polishing.

It is like dancers flinging their sleeves in harmony with the beat or singers throwing their voices in tune with the chord.

All this is what the wheelwright P'ien despaired of ever explaining; it certainly is not what mere language can describe.

MASTERPIECES

I have been paying tribute to laws of words and rules of style.

I know well what the world blames, and I am familiar with what the worthies of the past praised.

Originality is a thing often looked at askance by the fixed eye.

The *fu*-gems and jade beads, they say, are as numerous as the "pulse in the middle of the field" [which everyone can pick].

As inexhaustible as the space between heaven and earth, and growing co-eternally with heaven and earth themselves.

The world abounds with masterpieces; yet they do not fill my two hands.

THE POET'S DESPAIR

How I grieve that the bottle is often empty; how I sorry that Elevating Discourse is hard to continue.

No wonder I limp along with trivial rhythms and make indifferent music to complete the song.

I always conclude a piece with a lingering regret; can I be smug and self-satisfied?

I fear to be a drummer on an earthen jug; the jingles of jade pendants will laugh at me.

INSPIRATION

(i) *The Flow*

As for the interaction of stimulus and response, and the principle of the flowing and ebbing of inspiration,

You cannot hinder its coming or stop its going.

It vanishes like a shadow, and it comes like echoes.

When the Heavenly Arrow is at its fleetest and sharpest, what confusion is there that cannot be brought to order?

The wind of thought bursts from the heart; the stream of words rushes through the lips and teeth.

Luxuriance and magnificence wait the command of the brush and the paper.

Shining and glittering, language fills your eyes; abundant and overflowing, music drowns your ears.

(ii) *The Ebb*

When, on the other hand, the Six Emotions become sluggish and foul, the mood gone but the psyche remaining,

You will be as forlorn as a dead stump, as empty as the bed of a dry river.

You probe into the hidden depth of your soul; you rouse your spirit to search for yourself.

But your reason, darkened, is crouching lower and lower; your thought must be dragged out by force, wriggling and struggling.

So it is that you make many errors by overtaxing your emotions and commit fewer mistakes when you let your ideas run freely.

True, the thing lies in me, but it is not in my power to force it out.

And so, time and again, I beat my empty breast and groan; I really do not know the causes of the flowing and the not flowing.

Coda: Encomium

The function of style is, to be sure, to serve as a prop for your ideas.
(*Yet allow me to expatiate on the art of letters*:)

It travels over endless miles, removing all obstructions on the way; it spans innumerable years, taking the place, really, of a bridge.

Looking down, it bequeaths patterns to the future; gazing up, it contemplates the examples of the ancients.

It preserves the way of Wen and Wu, about to fall to the ground; and it propagates good ethos, never to perish.

No path is too far for it to tread; no thought is too subtle for it to comprehend.

It is a match for clouds and rain in yielding sweet moisture; it is like spirits and ghosts in bringing about metamorphoses.

It inscribes bronze and marble, to make virtue known; it breathes through flutes and strings, and is new always.

1912-1952: FULL CYCLE

PETER VIERECK

I. LOVE SONG OF PRUFROCK JUNIOR

Must all successful rebels grow
From toreador to Sacred Cow?
What cults he slew, his cult begot.
"In my beginning," said the Scot,
"My end;" and aging eagles know
That 1912 was long ago.
Today the women come and go
Talking of T. S. Eliot.

II. INSCRIBED FOR YOUR BEDSIDE
"GLOSSARY OF THE NEW CRITICISM"

Here's the eighth form of ambiguity:
The *new* philistia loves "obscurity," —
And only we still dare to hate it
Because a *texte* without a Muse in
Is but a snore and an allusion.
Well then, let's turn the tables hard:
The snobs all snubbed, the baiters baited,
The explicators explicated,
And avant-garde the new rearguard.

*Events of 1912, the key year: *New Age* starts publishing Hulme's essays; Imagist nucleus founded (Pound, H. D., Aldington); *Poetry: A Magazine Of Verse* founded by Harriet Monroe (to whom Pound in 1914 sends Eliot's "Love Song of J. Alfred Prufrock," written 1910-11); October 1912, the American-verse number of Harold Monro's *Poetry Review* (W. C. Williams, Pound); symbolic clash of the simultaneous 1912 publication of *Georgian Poetry* and Pound's *Ripostes*.

III. FROM THE SUBLIME TO THE METICULOUS
IN FOUR STAGES

DANTE: We were God's poets.

BURNS: We were the people's poets.

MALLARME: We were poet's poets.

TODAY (preening himself) : Ah, but *we* are critic's poets.

IV. EPITAPH FOR THE NOUVEAUX NEW CRITICS,
HUGH KENNER, E TUTTI QUESTI

Cliché is dead, long live cliché,
And in old fields new Georgians play.
O miglior fabbro and O mandarin,
You who skinned Georgians like a tangerine,
Two Hercules who on your natal day
Strangled these snakes of cliché-pandering,
These same that now through backstairs wander in:
Let not (while death-knells from Kinkanja ([1]) ring)
The pedant town of Alexander in.
From kitsch the nineteenth century banned her in,
You freed our Muse. For what? Was Queen Victoria
Primmer than précieux new "Prohibitoria" ([2]) ?
Loving your ART and not your fleas, we pray:

May time protect you from your protégés.
Time's up when pupils' pupils school the school.
Cow? Bad enough! But sacred — calf?
Now that the cup of insolence is full, —
By God, who'll start a brand new Nineteen Twelve?

This poem about Alexandrianism in verse, written in 1952 and copy-righted by the author, also appears in Peter Viereck's book THE FIRST MORNING, Greenwood Press, Westport, Conn., 1972.

THE IDEA OF A UNIVERSITY

I. A. RICHARDS

*Notes of a Speech given in the
Eliot House Symposium
March 11, 1953*

The man who invented the University may well have been Plato. His School, the Academy, lasted, they say—with ups and downs, more downs, I would think, than ups—longer than even the University of Paris has lasted. It kept the name. But what is a name? When I first taught in Peking there were twenty-six Universities there; now, I understand, there is, in fact, one.

We have Plato's outline, blue-print, *aperçu*, in the *Republic*. It is so familiar that we may miss its main point. This inquiry into "What is Justice?" comes down actually to an inquiry into "What would a just man be?" and "How could we produce him?" A just man (or woman) is one with all his or her bits and parts and talents and abilities in their right places, doing their own work and not getting in the way of one another. The book lays out *together* an account of the just man and an account of the just society, an organization chart for man and for society: on the ground that we can hardly have a truly just man without a just society to produce him or a just society without just men to guide and guard it.

It may freshen this up if we use "sane" along with "just". A just man is a sane man—nothing out of order or unbalanced about him. Similarly, a just society is one in which no faction, pressure group or self-interested power-seekers can push the rest of the

citizens around to serve, not the commonwealth, but their own aggrandizement.

The University is to be the supreme organ in such a society for producing men and women fit to and able to guide and guard it: to guard it from foreign enemies (insane states) and still more from its bosom enemies, self-promoting power-seekers. Plato knew all about civil war—that for him was the worst evil of all. The only man, he thinks, who may safely be given high political office is the man whose only motive in holding it is a *knowledge* that, if he does not, some worse man, worse qualified, will hold it in his place.

Now, just what does a University *do* to produce such men: capable of such knowledge and thereby fit and able to govern themselves and the state? Here is the recipe. Take the cream of the school crop, the hand-picked short-list, the most talented young men and women, the best learners, and give them a long and all-important course. A course in what? Here is the course description: "They will take the arts and sciences they have been educated in at school and put them into connection, in a comprehensive *synoptic* view of their relations, with one another and with what truly is." (*Republic*, 537.)

Most people will want to ask three questions about this astonishing program: 1. Has any University ever tried seriously and thoroughly to carry it out? 2. Just what would carrying it out be like? 3. If it could be and were carried out, what good

would it do? Would it help produce the juster, saner persons we so badly need?

1. Institutions very commonly don't pursue the ideals they are founded on. How far have Confucianism, Buddhism, Christianity—three other cultural institutions having aims comparable in scope to Plato's dream University—how far have they sought the ideals they were founded on? Very likely Plato's Academy (even in his lifetime as its Director) sought almost anything rather than the *synoptic* view. It is arguable that *his* Socrates (of whom we know so little apart from Plato), that model he set up of the ideal University teacher, has in fact only taught people how to trip one another up and catch one another out rather than how to understand one another and use that understanding cooperatively to the common advantage. It is to be feared that the Platonic dialogues and their progeny have spread chiefly the techniques and strategies of intellectual combat, while the original aim may have been to teach people not to fight but to think. There is a deep difference between a dispute about the position of a business and an auditing of its accounts, between refuting a man and converting him, that is giving him, permanently and with the consent of the whole of him, a more *synoptic* view. (We are becoming more and more terrified of other sorts of conversion as we come to know more and more about how they can be brought about.)

2. What would a course inducing and educing this *synoptic*

view be like? Would it be at all like any of the General Education programs? I doubt it. I think they mix subjects in our minds, as you mix ingredients for a dish or a drink, rather than invite us to ask: "What, deep down, has each subject to do with all the others?" and, as a result of this asking, invite us to reconceive the whole to which all subjects belong. To reconceive that whole and to reconceive the member studies too. How many whose main concern is with some branch of Science imagine that through taking a Humanities course they may have to reconceive the sciences? How many humanists taking a General Education science course can see themselves reconceiving the nature of poetry, their own nature, their very selves, as an outcome? The endeavor towards the *synoptic* view can be as radical in its consequences as that. For it attempts not only "to see all things in their relations with one another and with what truly is" but to create an organ of comprehension which can do that. "The eye altering, alters all," said Blake. We get no *synoptic* view through the routine eye.

Let me give you a minute, gem-like, lucid sample of this process of opposition and reconcilement:

One evening more than 20 years ago, Dirac, who was in Göttingen working on his quantum theory of radiation, took me (J. R. Oppenheimer) to task with characteristic gentleness. "I understand," he said, "that you are writing poetry as well as working at physics. I do not see how you can do both. In science one tries to say something that no one knew before in a way that everyone can understand. Whereas in poetry . . ."[1]

Let me fill out this superb aposiopesis: *In poetry one tries to say something which everyone knew before in a way which no one can understand.*

This I take to be (if suitably regarded) not quite what Dirac intended, but a saying profoundly and dazzlingly true: *true* in a

(1) J. R. Oppenheimer, Scientific American, "The Age of Science 1900-1950," September 1950, p. 21.

breath-taking way, but only if one realizes that—along with the mathematical switch of *no one* with *everyone*—the meanings of *know* and of *understand* undergo deep, systematic, corresponding changes. These changes can be studied. Their imaginative study is a sample—for physics and poetry—of that bringing of the subjects "into connection, in a comprehensive *synoptic* view of their relations, with one another and with what truly is" which Plato considered is what a University is for.

3. What good would all this do? Suppose the subjects, the faculties (in the individual and in the University), the studies: History, Poetry, Theology, Logic, Government, Biology, Ethics, Psychology, Physics . . . (Re-arrange them and subdivide them as you will: such *play* with collocations of these potential oppositions and alliances is all the fun. "Don't keep students at work by force but by play." *Republic* 537.) Suppose that these studies came to understand one another so well that they could give up their war?

Through how many centuries have Poetry, or Theology, or Ethics or Social Theory—backing up reverence for custom, for received ideas, for the routine line—oppressed and precluded Science? It could be so because hardly anyone, through all that time, could see that Science was a possible subject which could be precluded. Now that Science has triumphed (except in the semi-secret coigns of reactionary minds) is there a reverse action in progress? Overt oppression is not needed. Covert and unwitting stultification is enough: a drying up in the humanities, a withering away of creativeness, under the eager breath of that scholarship which is an infiltration of scientific practice. Dangerous thought, this, of course. It feels odd to suppose that the actual, incredible, everyday triumphs of methodical comparison are sucking the life blood out of everything with which man has endured and protested and endeavored in the past. It must have felt odd in the dark ages to suppose that methodical comparison was being precluded.

"In the destructive element immerse," as that butterfly collector in *Lord Jim* recommends. What if we could treat that whole struggle between the sciences, the humanities and the rest with the very same procedures ("putting into connection, in a comprehensive, *synoptic*, view") which, in specialized applications have given science its success? Suppose, through such an enlargement of our intellectual ambitions, this competition for the best brains, for the big grants, for *lebensraum*, for position and for power declined. Suppose all this were much reduced through synoptic study of, through fair auditing of, the various accounts of "their relations with one another and with what truly is"—what would we have then?

We would have *authority*: an authority which would have behind it *all* that man knows in all his modes of knowing and *all* that he would will to become through all his quests for being. It would be an authority which could wholly be respected and accepted, because it would represent the whole man, not any party or pressure group among his interests. All authority derives from the consent of those who acknowledge it. Any other government rests on coercion merely, not authority. The fears are a faction only in our minds. But the authority which Plato's *synoptic* view would try to give us could gain our complete consent, could be wholly persuasive, because it would unify us. Our minds are in analogy with the world struggle facing towards two ways of reaching unity. One is the way of force, the conquest, *by any side*, of the others, with the dreadful surgery, the blinding and maiming of the spirit, the suppressions and precludings which ensue. The other way to unity is through the task Plato wished on his University, that University to which we can so well apply Socrates' words at the end of Book Nine of the *Republic*: "Its pattern, perhaps, is already there in heaven for him to see who so desires; and, seeing it, to make himself its citizen. No matter whether it exists anywhere or ever will, this and no other is his commonwealth."

CREOLE LOVE SONG

NATHANIAL LA MAR

I USED to work for the LaBotte family. That's how I know what I'm going to tell you about Jemmie La-Botte. They lived up on Bayou Street in one of those big pink stucco houses with a wide tile porch and tall windows with fancy, yellow frosty-looking window panes.

Old man LaBotte was a doctor. He was queer in a way. I used to hear some of the white people around town say he was nothing but a "ham-fat" doctor. I never could quite get the straight of it. I do know one thing, though. He didn't go around like the other white doctors in New Orleans did. I mean he never went around to high faluting people like the kind of fine ladies his wife was always playing bridge with. As far as I know he didn't treat anybody but the Creoles down in the Quarter. Some people said it was because Dr. LaBotte was a Creole himself. They said that about Mrs. LaBotte too; but I didn't believe it. He used to come down to the Quarter whenever somebody got hurt on their job or beat up in a fight. He had a smart way about him; he could always get money out of his patients. I know of a lot of people that didn't pay their house-rent or their electric bills, but Dr. LaBotte got money out of them. He had a shiny green car, and whenever he came driving through the Quarter every-body would get in their windows and doorways and start yelling and waving at him; even old people. I'd shout just like the rest of them. "Hey! Hey! There go Doctor. Doctor! Doctor! Hey there, Doctor La-Botte!!"

That's the way we'd go on. Sometimes he'd have his son Jemmie in the car with him. That was before Jemmie went off to medical school. Jemmie was al-most grown, but he'd hang out of the car window and laugh when we'd shout.

Doctor LaBotte used to come to see my Aunt Alber-tine sometimes. My parents went to Chicago when I was little, and they didn't come back. So I lived with Aunt Albertine. She was young and pretty—had a lot of men always hanging around our house after her. She had yellow skin and long brown hair; and she had

a fine shape. She used to drink a lot. But the thing about her was that she knew it was bad for her. So she'd make me go out to a pay-station 'phone and call up Dr. LaBotte to come see her. I don't know what he'd do for her because she wasn't really sick. He talked to her; that was about all. But he could get her out of her drinking moods and she'd be all right for a while.

One day in the springtime Dr. LaBotte came to see us when Aunt Albertine was coming out of one of her moods. I was surprised, because he came to talk about me. "Why don't you let Emory come see if he'd like to work for us up at our house, 'Tine? Light work—kind of helping around the house——you know. We'd give him his breakfast and lunch and he could get his supper down here with you. He could save, maybe——go back and finish high school in a little bit."

At first Aunt Albertine didn't say anything. Finally she sized me up and said, "He fifteen. Let him do what he want to. *I* don't care. It ain't like he was going far off." She could tell I wanted to go by the way I was looking at her.

So I started working up at the LaBottes'. I think it was March when I started, and Jemmie LaBotte came home from medical school that June. He was a lot like his daddy; he laughed like him, and acted just about like him. He was glad to be back home. Sometimes he'd walk through that big house all day long, smiling in a funny way. Or sometimes in the evening he'd go **walking down in the Quarter**. People saw him down there; just walking those old, narrow grey-looking streets when it was almost dark.

I guess Dr. LaBotte was glad Jemmie was home. He laughed more than I'd heard him laugh when Jem-mie wasn't there. But then he started carrying a funny look on his face. And when he came home in the after-noon he'd go in the little room where his desk was and just sit there with the door open.

Jemmie LaBotte didn't pay me much attention. I'd pass by him in the house and he always looked like he was thinking to himself, or sometimes he'd be talking to his mother and daddy. Sometimes he sat in the living room and read all the morning. I knew they were medical books; most of them were old, and had pages as flimsy as tissue-paper—they were full of fine print. Jemmie LaBotte seemed like a fool to me, reading like that in the summertime. Especially since he was supposed to have just graduated from wherever it was he'd been. One day I asked him, "You remember all you read?"

"Yeah. I sure do." He laughed when he said it; he was a friendly somebody after all. "They make you —in a medical school."

"But you're not going back are you? Your mother says you're a doctor now."

"I want to do what Daddy's doing—doctor up people down there where you live." He looked at me like he wanted me to believe he really meant it. I could see he meant it.

I wondered why Jemmie LaBotte didn't seem to have any friends. Maybe once in a while somebody would call him on the 'phone. Answering the telephone was one of the things I was supposed to do. I'd call him to the 'phone and he'd talk a little while to whoever it was, but he never went anywhere much.

It got so Jemmie and his daddy argued. They'd sit out on the front porch late in the afternoon. I could hear them through the screen door. The old man's voice would be squeaky and high like he was afraid of something. "You sure you want to stay in New Orleans and practice?" He'd say. "You could always go back up there and study another year, if you wanted. You could be a specialist!"

They'd talk a long time, and Jemmie would get worked up and keep telling Dr. LaBotte how much he wanted to be just like him. He wanted to help people down in the Quarter just like the old man did. Jemmie LaBotte was always so serious about everything. He'd beg his daddy like I used to beg Aunt Albertine when I was little and wanted her to give me money to go to the movie or the carnival. I mean it; and he sounded queer when he begged like that. You'd have thought he was as young as I was. It didn't sound right to hear somebody who was supposed to be grown going on that way. "I don't want you to quit, Daddy. I'm not trying to make you *quit*. I just want to go down there with you."

"You don't know how they live—it's hard to get to know. I understand every one of 'em down there." Dr. LaBotte's voice sounded so old. I don't think I'd ever thought he was old before. It was almost pitiful the way he kept trying so hard to get Jemmie's mind off staying in New Orleans; like there was something in New Orleans he was ashamed of. "If you got to be a specialist you could get on at that baby hospital up in Philadelphia—I know you could."

Mrs. LaBotte took Jemmie's side. She must have thought old man LaBotte was jealous of Jemmie's being young and right out of school. Most of the time he wouldn't say anything to her when she started talking, because he knew what she was leading up to. "You know good and well you ought to let Jemmie make some of your calls for you—'specially those late calls. It'd be better for *him* to go down there in the Quarter at night. I'm always afraid somebody's going to jump in the car or something one of these nights. It's always so bad down there at night." She worried him all the time.

It got so when somebody from the Quarter called up old man LaBotte he'd get his bag and leave the house before Mrs. LaBotte and Jemmie could ask him where he was going. And when he was home he stayed shut up in the little office room. He started acting old and crabbed.

Mrs. LaBotte was the one who finally did it. I know it was her and not Jemmie because every time I heard her and Dr. LaBotte talking he'd be saying, "I'm tired of it, Juanita! I'm tired, and sick of it too!" It was what you'd call clever, the way she'd bring it up all the time about letting Jemmie stay in New Orleans and help him. She did it while they were eating, or when Jemmie was out taking one of his walks, or even when he'd just go out of the room a minute. I never did talk any of the LaBottes' business to anybody, because it didn't make a bit of difference to me what they did, but I did tell Aunt Albertine how bad the old man was looking, and how Mrs. LaBotte wouldn't lay off. Aunt Albertine said, "Well, you just make sure you don't be smelling in something you ain't got no business bothering with."

One morning Dr. LaBotte didn't come out of his bedroom early like he usually did. And Mrs. LaBotte tipped around, because she said he needed rest. That bedroom door didn't even open when the 'phone started ringing. It was an old man called David calling up from a grocery store. I knew who he was because he stayed about two blocks from where me and Aunt Albertine live. The children in the Quarter named him "that li'l man with the great big head." He wanted to tell Dr. LaBotte he had the "choky-feeling" in his chest again, and he couldn't lie down and sleep. So Mrs. LaBotte went in the bedroom. But they didn't start fussing, though. All Dr. LaBotte said was, "Tell Jemmie he can go down there—he wants to go." I think Mrs. LaBotte had worn him down to nothing. His voice sounded so tired, "Let Jemmie go down there—."

I went down to the Quarter with Jemmie LaBotte because I knew where David's house was. It's hard to find a place you're looking for in the Quarter because the house numbers are all faded off. I'm telling you the truth, it felt good riding through the Quarter in old man LaBotte's shiny car, because everybody really *did* look when they saw it was me in there. Jemmie was nervous. He kept laughing and saying, "You know, when I was little, people used to ask me what I wanted to be. As little as I was, I'd always say I wanted to be a doctor. They'd ask me why, and I'd tell them it was because Daddy was a doctor—I thought there wasn't anything else anybody *could* be but a doctor!" He laughed too much, and that childish way he had about him made me think he was foolish.

David's house was like the rest of the houses down there; the weather-boards were old and needed some paint. And it had fancy rusty iron banisters around the front porch, with iron flowers and curls. The room old David was in had the shades down and it was black-dark, except David had a little candle sitting in a piece of saucer on his chiffonier. Jemmie LaBotte didn't know what that little candle was for. He didn't pay it much attention at first; but I knew. You see old folks always burning a candle when they're afraid they're going to die, or afraid somebody in their family is going to die. Sometimes you're supposed to put pepper on the candle because everybody says it'll keep the worms from eating you after you're dead. David was propped up on a pillow. I sat down on a little stool by the door. Jemmie said, "You know good and well you ought to have some air in here, hot as it is." And then he went over to the window to let up the shade.

But old David screwed up his face at Jemmie La-Botte. "I wish you wouldn't be messin wid that window shade, 'cause that air out there got things in it bad for my feeling right here." He hit his chest with his wrin-kled-up little hand. I could see he didn't like Jemmie LaBotte.

"Air never did hurt anybody's heart trouble." Jem-mie LaBotte pulled up the shade a little.

"Your daddy don't never make me keep no air in there if I don't want none." I think that was the first thing that got Jemmie. And then old David wouldn't let Jemmie touch him with the needle. He held out those skinny old arms like he was scared to death. "Naw! Naw! You ain't going to put that thing in me. I don't want to have that thing sticking in my arm. And your daddy don't never stick me with none, either!"

I felt sorry for Jemmie LaBotte. He stood there like he didn't know what to do. Old David kept on holler-ing, "Oh Jesus! Oh Jesus! You going to stick me with that *thing*. Your daddy don't never do nothing like that!" Finally Jemmie LaBotte took a good hold on his old arm and jabbed him very quick; and you'd have thought David was having a baby by the way he was taking on. But after that I started feeling good toward Jemmie LaBotte because I liked the way he just went on and stuck the needle in anyhow. And he tried to be nice to old David after he gave him that shot: he told him to be quiet because he was through and ready to go, and he said he hoped he'd rest easier.

But old David wasn't ready for Jemmie LaBotte to go away. "You ain't going to give me nothing like

what your daddy give me when he comes?"

"What'd my daddy give you?"

"Some kind of stuff—."

"What stuff does he give you?"

"That stuff what make me sleep a lot. *You know,* Mr. Jemmie LaBotte." He kept smiling a sly, hateful smile. "Your daddy always give me a piece of paper that I can get it with at the drugstore-man's. Your daddy say it's codeine."

"My daddy didn't give you any codeine. Where'd you get that, talking about codeine? Don't you know your heart's too bad for you to be taking anything like that?"

"Well that's what your daddy say it was. Codeine. Make me sleep." He winked at Jemmie LaBotte like he expected him to understand something. "Your daddy give me that stuff instead of all that sticking me with that goddam old needle."

I don't know what made me think I had to say some-thing; because it wasn't any of my business at all. But Jemmie LaBotte had such a funny look on his face all of a sudden I said, "Don't pay attention to old man big-head David. They say he don't never tell the truth about nothing." But Jemmie looked strange. And we went out of the house with David still begging for some of the "sleepy stuff."

Jemmie LaBotte just asked me one thing while we were going back to Bayou Street. "Why'd old David have that little candle? How come he didn't have the electric light on?"

"That's the way a lot of folks do when they're scared of sickness. You smell how that candle was making that stink in there?"

"I'd have made him put it out if I'd known that was what it was."

"A lots of people keep a sick candle," I said. "I bet your daddy never did try to make anybody put out their sick candle. They wouldn't do it anyhow—for him or nobody else." He didn't say anything after that.

The day after we went down to old David's Mrs. LaBotte called me out on the porch and she tried to make me think she just wanted me to sit out there and rock back and forth in the rocker and talk to keep her company. But she kept on trying to get it out of me about what happened when we went down to the Quarter.

I didn't tell her a thing, though. It wasn't my busi-ness. But I did tell Aunt Albertine how Mrs. LaBotte tried to pick me and Aunt Albertine said, "You better be careful—that's all *I* can say." She'd seen old man David that day at the grocery up on Ogechee Street and he was telling everybody Jemmie LaBotte was a good-for-nothing doctor; and then he'd roll up his sleeve and show the little place the needle made. Aunt Albertine said he was clowning and telling everybody Jemmie LaBotte was nothing but "ca-ca."

About a week went by and old man LaBotte didn't seem to be getting better of whatever was wrong with him; at least he didn't come out of his room. And Mrs. LaBotte kept saying all he needed was rest and for people to let him alone and not worry him. There was something wrong between him and Jemmie ever since the day Jemmie went down to David's. But as far as I know Jemmie hadn't even seen him since then; so I didn't understand what it could be. Then one Sunday morning early a lady named Mrs. Clara called up the house to ask for Dr. LaBotte because her little girl was having a fit. It was so early in the morning Jemmie and Mrs. LaBotte didn't even bother about telling Dr. LaBotte. Mrs. LaBotte said she knew he wouldn't care if Jemmie went.

Jemmie LaBotte took me with him again, and we went driving fast through those grey little snaky-looking streets in the Quarter. We saw a lot of people walking the sidewalks; and some of them were still drunk from Saturday night. When we got to Mrs. Clara's house she was out in a funny kind of silk dress washing the steps to her front porch with a jar full of pepper-water. She was real fat and she had her behind turned up to us because she was down on her knees scrubbing the steps; and at first it looked funny. But she turned around and it was pitiful because her big fat face was screwed up and she was crying. The pepper-water had the front steps smelling loud like grease and vinegar. So Jemmie LaBotte asked her what that stuff was and why she wasn't in the house with her little girl. Mrs. Clara said, "I ain't in there 'cause I got to wash with this old pepper-water. Keeps off bad things from coming in the house—keep 'um way from my baby." Jemmie LaBotte told her she had no business believing in such things and he made her put down the jar with the pepper-water in it. But she kept on saying, "Your own daddy—your flesh-and-blood daddy—your daddy—he say it's fine if I want to wash off them front steps with my pepper-water!"

I sat on the porch while Jemmie LaBotte was inside. I'd seen that little girl lots of times with Mrs. Clara when they'd be walking up Ogechee Street. Her name was Monica and she was about eight years old, and she was pretty because she had a round face with a funny kind of purple eyes and light, hay-colored hair. But you could tell something was wrong with her because she walked so slow and funny, and held her head like her neck was made out of rubber.

When Mrs. Clara came to the screen door with Jemmie LaBotte she was saying, "Ain't you going to give her none of them pink pills what makes her sleep? Your daddy say them be good for her—they make her lay real quiet so she don't have no more of them fits. She don't roll her eyes or nothing if she have them pink pills."

Jemmie LaBotte kept looking at the little thing around Mrs. Clara's neck. It was hanging on a greasy string. I don't think he knew what it was, but I did, because my Aunt Albertine always has one so she'll be sure to have good luck. It was a little ball of hair; only this was a little ball of hay-colored hair. Mrs. Clara and Jemmie LaBotte were both acting all upset.

"I'm not going to give her anything to make her sleep, because it wouldn't be good for her. She had a *fit*! It's not good for her to go to sleep on medicine, I don't care *what* my daddy told you." So we left, and Mrs. Clara stood on her front porch; and she was crying and sprinkling pepper-water because she said Jemmie LaBotte must be evil and she didn't even want the smell of him around her house.

"You ain't no good kind of a man like *Doctor*," was the last thing we heard her say.

Then Jemmie Labotte told his mother. They sat in the living room on that big settee and he told her how old David asked him for codeine and said Dr. LaBotte always gave it to him. And he told her how he didn't want to believe a thing like that on his daddy; but he told her what happened with Mrs. Clara. "That little girl's name is Monica, and the whites of her eyes are all dulled over. Like she's been asleep a *long* time! She had a lot of codeine—I can tell she has."

Once Mrs. LaBotte looked up and saw me standing in the doorway, but she turned her head away. Dr. LaBotte came in the living room; I don't know whether he heard them or what. But Jemmie didn't act like he was there. "I thought my daddy was something." He said it just like the old man wasn't there at all.

And Dr. Labotte said, "They do magic down there, Juanita!" When he called her name Mrs. LaBotte put her little handkerchief up to her mouth. She made a little choking noise. Dr. LaBotte kept blaring his eyes; I thought he was going to go crazy. "Real magic," he said, "they wouldn't stop that voodoo down there for anything. They wouldn't even stop it for *me*."

"You've got them so all they want is codeine. You think codeine can do an epileptic fit any good, Daddy?"

"I told you—you don't know how they are. You think they'll take medicine, don't you?"

"You're bad as they are. You put them all to sleep. You can put them to sleep, all right!"

Dr. LaBotte said, "They love me. You get so you'll do anything for them if you can just get 'em to love you." And then he went out of the living room and left Mrs. LaBotte and Jemmie still sitting there on the settee. He walked away slow, like he was so old.

From then on some strange things started going on. Jemmie LaBotte swore he was going to be what his daddy never was. He could hardly wait until some more of the old man's patients called up so he could go back down to the Quarter. He kept saying he knew he could make them like him down there, if he could just get them to let him do them some good. It got so the main thing for Jemmie LaBotte was his big idea about how he was going to do them some good and make them like him. You should've heard the way he kept talking to his mother about it.

But Jemmie LaBotte didn't know the word had got around about him. It just takes one mouth to spread things in the Quarter, and David and Mrs. Clara ran their mouths a plenty. Everybody down there was whispering old man LaBotte was sick and going to die and his boy didn't know a thing to do for him or anybody. His boy wasn't nothing but "ca-ca," and a good-for-nothing. That's what they said about Jemmie La-Botte. David told everybody he could feel funny things crawing in his arm where Jemmie LaBotte stuck him with that needle. And Mrs. Clara said her Monica was bloody-eyed and always screaming with fits, because Jemmie LaBotte didn't give her sleepy-stuff to quiet her down.

Then one day Jemmie LaBotte got tired of waiting. He must've known what was wrong by that time. So he went down to the Quarter. That evening when I got home Aunt Albertine told me, "Jemmie LaBotte come driving down here today. Folks say he was trying to see old David and when David found out who it was he locked up his door on him. Yeah—I hear he was even begging old man David to let him talk to him."

"Begging him do any good?"

"Didn't do a bit of good!" Aunt Albertine laughed about Jemmie LaBotte because she was just like the rest of them; she didn't think he was anything.

But I give him credit. He tried hard in the Quarter. He tried to get David and Mrs. Clara to believe he wanted to do them some good. But David would always lock his door, and Mrs. Clara wouldn't even let him come up on her front porch. It got so bad people would sit in their windows and laugh whenever they'd see him coming. But he kept on going down there.

Then one day Jemmie LaBotte did get a 'phone call. It was August then, and that day was rainy. All over the house was quiet like somebody was dead or going to die. And it was so hot all the windows and doors were open and you could hear rain hitting the gardenia bushes out in the front yard. Whoever it was calling sounded like they were crying. All they said was for somebody to come down to Mama Callie's house quick. So he went down there by himself. I could see he wasn't thinking about taking me down there with him that day. But I wouldn't have gone anyhow, because I didn't like that old Mama Callie.

When I was little I used to go over to her house with Aunt Albertine. Aunt Albertine never has stopped going to Mama Callie's because Mama Callie knew her when she was just knee-high. In the first place I didn't

like Mama Callie because she was always coughing. Everybody knew she had T.B., and she was sleepy-looking and slow-talking because she stayed all doped up on codeine to ease her coughing spells. She must have been about seventy-five years old, and she had a sister named Alena who was somewhere around fifty. She and Alena spent all day making little charms and things; and they sold them around to a lot of people. Like if Mrs. Clara wanted a hair ball out of little Monica's hair she'd cut off a snip of hair and take it to Mama Callie, and Mama Callie would do things like dip it in hot chicken fat and tie it on a string and wrap it up for a week in senna leaves. Then she'd give it back to Mrs. Clara when it was ready to do some good. Sometimes on a hot day you'd walk past their house and you'd see Mama Callie and Alena sitting in the open window and Mama Callie would always be singing something in French. She said that song was a Creole song her father taught her when she was a little girl. They say she was real proud of that, because her and Alena's father was a Frenchman. Anyway, whenever she and Alena sat in the window Mama Callie would hold her old sleepy-looking face out the window to see who was walking up and down the street. Alena, who liked men, would be just sitting there beside Mama Callie brushing her hair. She had long hair that came all down her shoulders, and she always brushed it with a brush soaked in strong tea to keep it from getting grey.

When Jemmie LaBotte came back from Mama Callie's he looked discouraged, and he didn't say a thing.

But that evening Alena was going around telling everybody in the Quarter about how when Jemmie La-Botte got to Mama Callie she'd had a hemorrhage and blood was coming out of her nose and mouth all over the bed-sheets. Alena said, "He come bringing his fancy bag with them bottles in it. He thought he was going to give Callie one of them needles of his, but me and Callie wouldn't even let him get near the bed. I told him he wasn't going to touch my Callie!" Alena was bragging about how she told Jemmie LaBotte right to his face they'd just called him so he could give Mama Callie some codeine. But he wouldn't give her any, and he started telling Alena how much Mama Callie needed a hospital, or at least some medicine. Alena laughed, "That Jemmie LaBotte wanted to pay me money to let him stick Callie with one of them shiny needles—even much wanted to pay me *money!* Callie and me told him if he couldn't put her to sleep there wasn't *nothing* he could do. We fixed him. Callie, bad off as she was, she couldn't help but laugh at him. We fixed him all right!" Alena said she warmed up some pig oil with mustard seeds and went to work on Mama Callie and started rubbing her all over with it right there in front of Jemmie LaBotte. "He was just standing there looking. And he looked like he couldn't take his eyes off. He couldn't even stop looking for nothing. Like a young'un watching his daddy in the bed with his ma." Everybody laughed at Alena's saying that. "I could see he didn't like it for nothing, but there wasn't a thing he could do about me rubbing up Callie with that hog grease. Callie was warm, and shiny as she could be when I got through with her. He just stood up there like he had that hog grease on his brain—stood there just looking 'cause that's all he could do—look."

You could tell Alena liked to talk about it. Everybody she told it to sure did listen. I know it must have made Jemmie LaBotte feel beat down for Mama Callie not to let him even touch her, because even old man David, bad as he was, let Jemmie give him a shot that first time, anyway.

About a week after all that happened Jemmie LaBotte asked me if I knew Mama Callie and Alena, and I told him yes. Then he started talking about how queer they were. He talked so fast; like he couldn't tell me quick enough. I didn't see why he was acting so worried. "That old Mama Callie—you know what she did? She wouldn't even let me put a stethoscope on her. You ever see all the little baskets in there—in her bedroom? They were all full of leaves!"

I knew the little baskets he was talking about. "Yeah, They're willow leaves."

"You know what she does with them?"

"Naw," I said, "I never did know."

I knew what those willow leaves were for, but I didn't tell him because I didn't see what difference it made to him.

One evening Mama Callie called up again; Jemmie LaBotte didn't seem to want to go down there. But his mother couldn't see why. "You ought to go if they called you, Jemmie," she kept saying. She was so proud of him because she thought he was everything old man LaBotte never *had* been. "You have to go right on down there, even if that old lady won't let you attend to her—she *called* you."

Mama Callie and Alena must have known he'd come, because they told Aunt Albertine and a lot of other people to be on the look-out if they wanted to see the car when it drove up. Mama Callie was feeling weak and puny, but she was sitting in the window singing that little French song, and Alena was sitting beside her brushing her hair with that brush she kept wetting in a bowl of tea. Mama Callie told Aunt Albertine Jemmie LaBotte started worrying her to let him give her some medicine as soon as he got there. The way they talked about it you'd have thought Jemmie LaBotte was like a little dog or something they'd taken some kind of a fancy to. Alena got rid of all her men friends, and even when it made Mama Callie cough and spit up blood she burned a little basket full of dried up

willow leaves every day. Alena said, "We burn them leaves 'cause it make him get us on the brain. And pretty soon he be coming right on down here all the time."

Sure enough Jemmie LaBotte did start going down to Mama Callie's. He told Mrs. LaBotte he went down there so he could leave medicines for Mama Callie and try to make her take them. But Mrs. LaBotte noticed how much he was going down there. She even told old man LaBotte. And he used to lie in his bed and call Jemmie. "Jemmie, come tell your daddy what's going on down there at Mama Callie's. Come tell me! How come you're down to Mama Callie's so much, Jemmie?" But Jemmie stopped going in his daddy's room. Even Mrs. LaBotte couldn't make him go in anymore. And that hurt Dr. LaBotte. He began to fall off a lot. You could tell because his hands and his face got so thin. But still he'd lie in his bed and call in that nagging voice, like there was something he knew about Jemmie.

Mama Callie and Alena got so they bragged and said they were going to have Jemmie LaBotte pretty soon. Alena tied up her hair every day in a lot of silk rags because she wanted to look fine when he came. And Mama Callie claimed they could get him down to the Quarter whenever they wanted to. Alena was always telling everybody, "All I got to do is heat up that hog oil and start rubbing on Callie with it. That Jemmie LaBotte look like his eyes going to pop out. When I do that he look like he don't want to do nothing but just look at me and Callie; and he knows we ain't going to let him touch her. But he just keep on looking. Sometimes he look right pitiful."

I didn't think Jemmie still cared anything about his daddy. He did though. Because when old man LaBotte had that heart attack you could see it did something to Jemmie. They had a lot of fine specialists with Dr. LaBotte, but it didn't do him any good. He lingered, and got weaker every day. They said he was "in coma" so nobody could go in there to see him. Jemmie and Mrs. LaBotte would just sit in that big living room all day long with the shades down; and two or three nurses were always coming and going and walking soft on those big thick rugs. They made me think of white rabbits, the way they were always streaking through the house. I didn't like them because they wouldn't let Jemmie LaBotte even see his daddy, and he wanted to a lot. He kept saying there was something he wanted to tell his daddy.

Alena and Mama Callie told Aunt Albertine Jemmie LaBotte had stopped trying to make Mama Callie take his medicines. They said he came to their house just to see them and they called him sweet-boy-Jemmie. "He just like a baby," Mama Callie was always saying. "He come and just sit there and watch Alena swing them plaits around in the air. Sometime Alena hand him one of them hair-plaits and he hold it and he just laugh. Just like a young'un with a sugar-tit." Alena swore Mama Callie was telling it like it was. "Callie telling the honest-to-God truth! That Jemmie LaBotte done changed a heap." Then they'd both laugh. Mama Callie would laugh so hard she'd start coughing.

It got around that Jemmie LaBotte had started writing prescriptions for Mama Callie to get codeine with. Somebody even said they saw him go in the drugstore to get it for her one day; but I still thought it was just meanness making them all tell lies on him. All that time Dr. LaBotte was sinking. Mrs. LaBotte couldn't understand why Jemmie was staying away more and more. She didn't think it hurt him that his daddy was dying, but she was wrong. He never did mention Dr. LaBotte much, but you could see he cared about the old man, just by some of the other things he'd say. Like one day he told me, "Mama loves this house, but I want to get out of here. I can't stand it anymore."

My Aunt Albertine was there at Mama Callie's one day when Jemmie LaBotte came to see her. She said Mama Callie had a pretty bad coughing spell and her mouth started running blood, but Jemmie LaBotte didn't do a thing except just get down on his knees by Mama Callie's bed. And when she'd stopped coughing Mama Callie took a little ball of hair from under her pillow and gave it to him. Mama Callie told him that little ball had some of her and Alena's hair in it. She gave it to Jemmie LaBotte because he'd kept asking her to give him something to help his daddy in his misery. I'll tell you the truth, I didn't even believe my own flesh-and-blood aunt. For one thing I couldn't *see* Jemmie LaBotte doing all they said. I didn't even believe the willow leaves I'd found meant anything.

In the end I saw for my own self, though. One night. Dr. LaBotte had been real low all that day, and they'd put him under an oxygen tent. And Mrs. LaBotte had been calling up her friends telling them she didn't understand why Jemmie was off down in the Quarter. I think she must have known Dr. LaBotte was going to die. Those nurses finally gave her something that made her go to sleep, so she'd stop carrying on so. Anyway, that night after I'd got off I was walking up Bourbon Street on my way over to the show field to see if the carnival had come; and so I passed by Mama Callie's. Even when I was still way up the street I heard that singing. Mama Callie was singing and she was in the front window. She was singing that little French song, but it went so slow I could tell she was weak; she was so feeble her voice sounded high like a chicken squawking.

"Donnez tes levres.
Donnez tes mains.
Ces yeux, ces yeux
Sont pleins du feu!"

All the lights were on real bright in the room where she was. And she was sitting right up in the window with some kind of a shawl on that had long fringes that kept blowing around her arms. I couldn't help but look in there when I went by, but Mama Callie didn't see me because she had her eyes shut. I told you how the light was on in the room; I could see good. Alena was sitting there a little ways behind Mama Callie. She was in a straight chair and she had silk rags tied all through her hair: red and blue and green and yellow; all kinds of colors. Jemmie LaBotte must have been down on his knees or almost on his knees anyway, because all I could see was his head. Alena had Jemmie LaBotte's head, holding it *tight* in her arms. Just as tight as she could. It was so queer, because it looked like she might have cut off his head from his body and was just holding nothing but that head in her arms. She had her eyes closed and he had his closed too. Only in the light I could see shining streaks on his face, like he was crying. He looked pretty: like a woman. Maybe it was because Mama Callie and Alena were so wrinkled and ugly, but he looked really pretty; something like a young girl. His skin was so smooth, and his hair was shiny and very thick; like purple and black mixed together.

When I got back home that night I told Aunt Albertine how I saw the three of them. And she said, "I been thinking about it a while. I don't like all that funny stuff that's going on." She told me she wanted me to quit working for the LaBottes.

Only next day when I went up there a lot of people were at the house. Women in fine clothes with feathery hats and little white handkerchiefs. They were answering the telephone and talking loud all over the house and wiping their eyes because old man LaBotte had died the night before. I didn't even get a chance to see Mrs. LaBotte, because a nurse was keeping her quiet. And everybody was saying Jemmie LaBotte must be raving-crazy, because he'd gone driving down to the Quarter the night before, right after the old man died.

* * * *

It seems like it's been longer than two years ago since all that was going on; but it's been just about that long. I don't know for sure, but I don't think Jemmie LaBotte even went to his daddy's funeral. I do know one thing, though; he's never home these days. I see him all the time; whenever I go up on Bourbon Street. He's always at Mama Callie's house, and he waves his hand to me when he sees me. Alena still makes her little hair balls, and everybody says Mama Callie's just hanging by a thread. She doesn't feel anything, though, because most of the time Jemmie LaBotte keeps her full of codeine. But Jemmie LaBotte doesn't just only give codeine to Mama Callie. He gives it to a lot of them.

And they've stopped talking mean about Jemmie La-Botte down in the Quarter now. They stopped all that long ago. Even Mrs. Clara and old David don't put bad mouth on him anymore. They all think Jemmie LaBotte is all right these days. I know for a fact he never has to beg to get his money out of anybody, and that goes to prove what I was just saying. You ought to just see the way some of them carry on and call his name when he comes walking down Bourbon Street. Sometimes it's night when he comes, and every-body hangs out of their windows and all you can see in the dark is fire from cigarettes. They make a lot of noise, but you can hear that laugh of his above everything else. You can't tell me their carrying on like that doesn't give Jemmie LaBotte a good feeling, after the way everybody used to treat him. You can look at him and see it makes him feel good. The way he smiles, the way his eyes flash when he talks. You can tell he'd do anything in the world for them.

WILLIAM ALFRED

POEMS FROM

FIVE HARD SONGS IN A BAD TIME

"Now in my youth I am well on the way to a happy finish. I can hardly get much further at this staggering pace. Kicking evil away, I try, by singing, to have all things turned to the good. Love, and the dearest kind of love, is what I bequeath you all."
—RICHARD ROLLE OF HAMPOLE, *An Anthem for Thinkers*, 113

I. BANKRUPTCY   *"veni sancte spiritus . . ."*

Adventurous Spirit, turned Recluse,
I need You. Put at my blind use
What is beyond my competence.

I have run through that princely sum
You gave me to begin with. Come,
Father. Beggar that I am,

Inconsolable optimist,
Reduced to die in this mare's nest,
Perfidious with tedium,

My wasted funds could meet with ease
This interest bleeds me to the lees,
All these usurious wants grow dumb,

Should You but take this risk on me.
I do not care how angrily.
My pride is gone with my income.

The time is past when crazed with shame,
No one came near I did not blame.
I know why I have nothing to my name.

Without You I will lose even sense and will.
There will be nothing left me. Nothing. Sure and still
That core of storms, that loanshark vacuum

Will rob me blind, despite this moratorium
It grants me, hounded to this one locked room
Of Your ruined house, my honorarium.

Pay off that devil for me. I am numb.
My schemes are muddled to delirium.
I can see no other way, unless You come

And tide me through this time, for me to assume
My mortgage. It makes even health seem doom;
For I have squandered all inheritance.

If I am done for, past the point where some
Have managed to recoup, You still must come.
Or who will close this house, and take me home!

III. THE OFFICE OF THE BEE

When, caught between screen and glass,
Freedom of sight and touch
Were yours, but you found no way to pass
Beyond my window's smutch,
And flew till you split a wing
Against that ringing wire,
Since only to fly was to sing,
And to sing was your desire
I lifted up the screen.—
Yes, you foundered in the air,
And the grass no more was green
You fell to like a flare.
Bee,
I set you free:
Pray for me.

WINTER TERM

●
●
●
●
●

SALLIE BINGHAM

It was inconvenient. And worse; Hal watched the woman behind the desk ruffling through file cards, and wondered if she had noticed that he came to the library every evening. She must have noticed him, and Eleanor; and he often thought she watched them during those evenings in the library. During the day, he sometimes planned a new kind of evening, still at the library, for the dancing and movie Saturdays he spent with Eleanor were even more stereotyped. Sometimes, he imagined that Eleanor would be there when he came, or that she would not be wearing lipstick, as when he had first seen her. But he knew that the small details' change could not alter the whole evening. In the past week, he had begun to imagine the only possible change: that Eleanor would not come at all. When he studied in his room in the afternoon, Hal planned to wait at the library until a quarter past seven, and then, if she had not come, he would leave, not buttoning his coat and turning at once onto the street.

"Why don't you take off your coat?" the librarian asked him. He had never heard her voice before. It was pleasantly colorless and he was surprised that with such a voice she had spoken to him at all.

"Oh, that's all right," he said, vaguely. "I may have to leave in a few minutes." She pulled out another drawer of filing cards, and began to ruffle through them. As he watched her, Hal became more and more surprised that she had spoken to him. It reminded him that he was still, even after a month, an intruder; there were so few boys in the library that the girls stared at them openly. He walked over to the reading room door and looked in; the red haired boy whom he had begun to speak to on the street was studying there with his girl. Eleanor said that they were engaged, although Hal had pointed out that the girl was not wearing a ring; Eleanor said it did not really matter. They always went out with each other, and on Saturdays and Sundays she had seen them having breakfast together in the Waldorf. Hal remembered asking her what they had been eating; it was a new way he had of testing Ellie, to see how long it would be before she laughed; if he teased her for a certain amount of time, he knew that she would more probably cry. "French Toast," she had answered promptly, "three orders, with maple syrup." And then she had asked him why he laughed, and when he shook his head and went on laughing her mouth began to quiver, and he tightened as she said, "Why do you always laugh at me?" They had had a bad evening. The tightening had started it, Hal knew; he could grant that to her in this carelessly objective mood of remembering. He wondered if he would ever be able to prevent himself from feeling like that when she didn't laugh, or when she was depressed, or when she asked him, "What are you thinking?"

Hal looked at the clock. She was already seven minutes late. It happened every evening; he imagined her dawdling over combing her hair, watching the clock, and planning not to leave in time. She often warned him about taking one another for granted. Surprised by his own bitterness, he thought, Oh God, why do I always have to be so hard on her; lately she can't do anything right. He remembered how he used to feel when she came towards him, running because she was late, or in out of the rain; she shook the rain out of her hair (too proud to wear a scarf), and her face was flecked with drops.

Eleanor came in the door before he could decide when the change had begun. She started towards him, red faced from the wind she had fought for four blocks on her bike. "Hello," she said, and he knew that if he had looked permissive she would have kissed him instead, in spite of the librarian. It was one of the things that he had first liked about her, along with the absence of lipstick, which she had since started wearing; she was willing to kiss him even on the Saturday night subway to Boston, when the whole row of people on the other side of the car was watching. Hal remembered how surprised he had been when they first danced together and she had pulled close, for the action had not suited the mild, high necked dress she was wearing, or even the coolness of her cheek.

She was peeling off the neat layers of her coat and sweater, and he noticed how limberly she bent to unfasten her boots, because he was watching. She had a much better figure than the red haired boy's girl, especially since she had given up sweets. He remembered proudly that she had started to diet because he had told her once that a dress was too tight; he had never had to tell her again. Now, her hips were straight under her skirt, and he knew from looking at them how they would feel, very firm as she clenched the big muscles, and smooth through her slippery underpants.

She led the way to the reading room. He had grown accustomed to people looking but he knew from the way Ellie was smiling that they still made her uncomfortable. When they sat down, she whispered, "You'd think they'd learn not to stare every night!" and he whispered back, leaning close so that her hair touched his mouth, "It's only because you're beautiful."

"You've said that before," she said, mocking and pleased, but he had already realized it; it did not matter how often he had repeated the compliment, for every time the situation had been the same, until the lie had become as familiar as the library room. He looked at the clock.

"Bored?" she asked quickly.

"No." He tried not to frown. She made a little face at him, and bent over her notebook.

He wished he had not learned to translate her expressions. When he had first met her, he had been charmed by her good-humored little pout, or her wide-eyed stare after they kissed. But now he knew that the pout was made to conceal the quiver in her mouth, and if he watched her a minute later he would see that she was not reading, that she was staring at the page and trying not to look at him. And as for her expression after he kissed her—it always seemed to Hal that he was watching her come up from a great depth of water—he did not know what it meant, but it irritated him. It was like the way she acted after they had made love. She went into it as exuberantly as jumping up to dance, leaving it to him to make sure that his room mates were out, and that the shades were down. By the time he had checked, she would have pulled her dress off over her head, rumpling her hair in bangs over her eyes. He began to undress, folding his clothes on the chair—"Ellie, will you hang up your dress?"—, but when he turned around and saw her waiting, naked under her slip, he went to her and forgot what he had been about to say.

But afterwards, if she didn't cry, she would not speak to him. She clenched him in her arms when he tried to get up, and he had to hurt her in order to break away, even though he had told her how necessary it was. When she clung to him like that, with her fingernails pricking his back, he tried to force himself out of his sleepiness, to polish her hair and kiss her. But her mouth tasted stale when he was so tired, and he was afraid she might think he wanted to do it again.

"I'm sorry I was late," Ellie said, not looking up from her book, and he realized that for the last five minutes she had been trying to decide why he seemed irritated.

"I thought we said we wouldn't apologize any more." He wanted to sound gay, but he realized at once that she was still raw to the subject; her eyes seemed to grow larger with hurt as she looked at him and said, "I wished you'd forget that." She was bending down the corner of a page, and he wanted to tell her not to; the little, mechanical action irritated him out of all proportion, and he wondered if he was so tense because they hadn't done it for four days. How did she feel about tonight? He knew that his room mates were out. Hal looked at her, but he could tell from the way she was hunched over her book that she was not thinking about making love but about the evening three days before when they had quarreled and then made a list of resolutions over coffee in Hayes-Bick's. One of them had been not to apologize, for they agreed that it was hypocritical; apologies were only a dog-in-the-manger way of saying I was right all along but I'll give in for the sake of peace. It had been a terrible evening, and Hal was sorry that they had gone to Hayes-Bick's, for the quarrel had destroyed his picture of one of their first evenings together, when he had held her hand between the salt and pepper.

"Oh, I forgot to ask you about the exam." She had not whispered, and the girl at the next desk looked up, frowning. "How was it?" she whispered, not looking at the girl.

"Terrible!" The exclamation did not relieve him. He had come back from the exam in the winter darkness, coffee nerved, and fingering the three pencils in his pocket whose points were worn flat. He remembered cursing himself for not reviewing enough, and he had wondered wildly if he could have written at the end of the thin, scratched blue book, "Circumstances beyond my control. . . ."

"But I thought you were so well prepared; you've been reviewing for practically a week."

He tried not to say it, but the words promised too much relief. "Yes, but I can't really study here." He knew before he looked at her that she was hurt, and as soon as he saw her mouth he felt the tightening; he wanted to laugh out loud and throw his head back and yell with laughter, and at the same time he wanted to pull her into his arms and fold her so tightly that her breath came in gasps.

"You never told me that before," she said, and he knew how carefully she had weeded the hurt out of her voice.

"Well, I mean, what do you expect? How can I concentrate on studying with you around?" He had meant it to be a compliment, he wanted to see her smile and look up at him, but it sounded like an accusation. As she turned her face sharply away he thought, Oh God, not another scene, and then he noticed abruptly how thin she had grown; he could see the point of her collar bone through her sweater, and her little pear breasts stood out too sharply.

Ellie had bent the corner of the page down so often that it broke off in her hand. She turned to Hal, smiling too brightly. "You should have seen the dormitory tonight." In spite of her smile, Hal wanted to kiss her for changing the subject. He thought that afterwards he would buy her an ice cream cone at the drugstore on the way back. She loved sweets, and she hadn't had any for at least two weeks; he remembered her inexpensive, salad dinners even on Saturday nights. And she was really almost too thin.

"You know Wednesday night is usually bad, anyway," she was saying. The girl at the next desk looked up again, annoyed, and Ellie's hand flew to her mouth. She would not have gone on if Hal had not asked, "Well, what happened?" and then she turned to him and whispered so softly, hesitantly that he could hardly hear. "You know, Wednesday's boy night, and they have candles and ice cream, just because we eat at quarter past six instead of six! Tonight I sat at a table with three girls and their dates and I literally didn't say one word." Hal had heard it often before; he looked around the room, trying to distract his attention from his own irritation. Why was she proud of not talking for a whole meal? He noticed the pretty girl who was in his humanities class; she was winding a shank of hair around her finger as she studied. Pretty hair. But she looked even more tense than the rest of them. During exam period, you could cut the atmosphere in the reading room with a knife. Most of the girls looked overtired and ugly, and they had not bothered to comb their hair. This was the one place where they never expected to see any boys. But Eleanor hated the Harvard library. She said she felt too stared at when there were so few girls. Hal had caught some of the looks boys gave her when they walked down the corridor, and he agreed. She had such a damn good figure.

"You're not listening," she said. "I know—don't apologize; I shouldn't be distracting you." And as though her rigidly calm tone really expressed her feelings, Eleanor wrote the date neatly at the top of a notebook page, and began to read.

"I am interested," he lied, feeling her hurt; "it's just I'm interested in this place, too." She did not answer, and so he slammed his book open and turned the pages roughly, looking for the place. They sat for ten minutes in silence. Hal tried to read, but he was too conscious of the tip of her elbow, almost touching his; it looked a little chapped, and he remembered how hard the winter weather was on her blond skin. Then he wondered how he had known that—he had been through no other winter with her, or even a spring or summer—and inconsequentially he wondered what she looked like in a bathing suit. He hunched his shoulders and bent down closer to his book, trying to force the words into his attention. There were long, ruler straight lines under many of the sentences, and minute notes were printed in the margins. He had written them in October, when for a week he had devoted himslf to Schopenhauer, reading each page passionately, proud of the learned comments he wrote in the margins. He even found time to go into Boston to visit the museum where there was a portrait of the philosopher, and he remembered how his head had pounded as he climbed the long stairs and hurried down a corridor to the door of the room where the portrait hung. It had been a disappointment, an old placid gentleman in conventional black; did pessimism embodied look like that? he remembered thinking, like your own grandfather? But he had come back with a feeling of accomplishment.

Now he could not read his own notes. When Ellie was hurt, the consciousness of it ticked like a clock at the back of his mind, and he could not concentrate on anything. He gave up trying to ignore the point of her elbow. He wondered if she would move first, as she often did, slipping her hand into his or turning into his arms as soon as they were alone or touching the back of his neck. He noticed how rigidly she was sitting; why did they both go on pretending to study? He looked at the clock; already half an hour wasted. God, I wish we'd had a chance to make love so I wouldn't feel like I'm going crazy. Exams; we said we couldn't afford the time. And self-righteously they avoided his room, knowing that once they were there where the sheets were marked from the last time and where they had first said that they were in love, their resolution would collapse in a panic. Their coming together was always too violent, he thought, like the too big lunch you eat after missing breakfast, snatching and tearing at the food if no one was watching. But I bet she needs it, he thought, that's why she's so quivery, close to tears, and maybe that's why I loused up that exam. But he knew it was an excuse; he had failed the exam because he had not known the material. He felt his resentment heating as he wondered why he had not reviewed more carefully. But she's right, I spent all last week on it, he thought, and then he

THE HARVARD
ADVOCATE

25 CENTS

added, enjoying his bitterness, yes, but you know what studying here means, jockeying for position for three hours with our knees always about to touch or our hands and she's always looking up or else I am until finally we give up and hold hands though that means I can't write or else she can't. Why didn't I have sense enough to tell her I had to study, two evenings would have done it, but I knew she'd cry. Not over the phone but in the booth after I hung up so she wouldn't be able to walk back down the hall without the other girls seeing she'd been crying. He wanted to turn to her and break the thin unreal wall of her concentration, asking, why does everything hurt you too much? And why do I always have to know? Although he knew the last, at least, was not her fault.

He heard eight strike in silver, feminine notes from the clock over the girls' gym. That clock would never let him forget the amount of time he was wasting; all evening, he would have to listen to its coy reminders. The thought jacked him to the top of his irritation, and he slammed his books closed and began to stack them together. Eleanor looked up, and he saw in her eyes the terror that he had heard once in her voice when he told her that he would have to go home for the weekend. She had said, "You know that means three days without talking to anyone." But he had answered, trying to laugh, "But there must be someone—all those girls." "You know I'm not a girl's girl; I don't really know how to talk to them. And anyway, I don't spend my extra time in the Smoker, so they hardly know my name." And he had understood what she had been unwilling to say, that he had taken up the time she might have spent padding herself with girl aquaintances against the time when she would be alone. In the end, he had left without telling her goodbye, and the weekend had been spoiled because he had known how she was feeling.

He stood up, although he had still not decided what he was going to do. Only, no more waste.

"You want to leave?" she asked, hurriedly gathering up her books, and Hal knew that she thought he was going to walk out without her. He knew that he was being brutal, and that if she began to cry he would be more than ashamed; he would feel that his hands were as clumsy as trays as he tried to sooth her, and then, as he struggled to find something gentle to say, he would begin to go mad with irritation. He started towards the reading room door before Ellie was ready, and he heard the almost hysterical ruffling of the pages as she closed her books. He waited for her on the other side of the door, and when she came, nearly running, he saw

the brand mark of fear on her face fade as she smiled with relief that he was waiting.

"I agree with you; let's get out of this dreary place." she said, and Hal wished that she had been angry.

"Look, I'm going to walk you back now," he said as they went out into the sudden coldness. She began to fumble awkwardly with her scarf, trying to adjust it inside her coat collar.

"Right now?" Her voice was carefully casual.

"Look, Eleanor, I've got to get something done tonight. Friday's the Phil. 101 exam."

"Oh, I understand." They walked along side by side, conscious of not holding hands. The quadrangle was dark except for the library lights and the illumined clock over the gym. It was always five minutes fast, he knew, on purpose, so that the girls who were late starting would still get to the Harvard classrooms on time. In spite of the clock, Ellie was always coming in late, hesitating in the doorway to look for him, and red and damp from running.

"Are you going to continue the history course?" He wished that she would not keep her voice cheerful, trying to pretend to him, but not to herself, that they had not silently quarrelled.

"Can't divide it at mid-term." He was irritated by his own grudging tone, although it was easy enough to justify it; even if he broke with her now and finally (it was incredible, the thought of pushing off her hands and running without hearing her calling), he would still have to see her every Monday, Wednesday, and Friday at ten in the history class where they would try not to look at each other.

Her dormitory was full of lights. At last they've taken down the wreath!" he said.

"It was really too much." Her voice had revived with his cheerfulness, real this time; although it was ridiculous, he knew that the tarnished wreath was a reminder of the Christmas vacation they had spent straining to be together, the long distance calls when her voice was tremulous, and the too many, raw letters.

They stood under the porch light, and she held out her hands. He took them, and slipped his fingers inside her gloves. Her palms were soft and lined.

"Look at all the bikes," he said inconsequentially, "You'd think they'd give up in this bad weather," and they both looked out at the heaped, stone snow. He remembered that he had a long walk back, but as he bent hurriedly to kiss her she slipped her arms around him so that he had to pull back hard in order to get away. She let go at last, her arms hurting, and no longer trying to smile. "Hal, don't go." He hesitated. "Please don't go. Please." She was rigidly controlling her voice, but he knew the limit of her endurance, and he wanted to be away before she began to cry, for then he would never be able to leave. He would have to wait until she was calm, rocking her in his arms and kissing her hair. Then he would walk back along the river to the house, avoiding noticing clocks until he was in his room. When he saw the tin alarm clock that was already set for the morning he would throw his books violently into a chair so that John looked out of the bedroom: "What's wrong with you?" And then he would go out and buy coffee so that, with luck, he could study until three. By that time, the lights across the courtyard would all be out, and often, it would begin to snow.

Eleanor had sensed his tension. "About tomorrow," she said lightly, working her books around in her arms and wiping a fleck of nothing off one of the covers. "I know we both have a lot of work. I'll call you in the morning, anyway, and then we can decide. I guess maybe we ought to study by ourselves tomorrow night." Her voice was so matter-of-fact that if he had not known the pattern Hal would not have believed that, next day, when they came to the deciding, she would plead with him to study with her in the library: "Really, I promise, we'll get something done," and she would offer to sign a promise that she would not speak to him for three hours. Now, he was looking down, and running her finger along the side of a book. "Hal," she said, "I'm sorry about tonight. You know how I get sometimes." He put his arms around her, although the books were between them, and he tried not to tell her how sorry he was, tried to choke back his softness: "Oh God, Ellie," he said instead, and he heard the almost tears in his own voice, the rawness that was both tenderness and irritation. She strained up to kiss him, and when she opened her mouth he felt tricked, knowing that she was intentionally exciting him, that if he put his tongue between her lips he would not be able to leave. As he kissed her he began half consciously to forget that he should go. She dropped her books and they tumbled over their feet. He pressed close to her suddenly, forgetting, forcing his tightness to the back of his mind. He was only vaguely conscious of the porch and the staring light as he pulled her roughly against him, hearing her moan with pain and excitation. Then in a blurred voice, she said, "Isn't there somewhere we can go?" Her face was flushed, reminding him in a twisted way of a child waking up, damp and fresh. She was trying to think of somewhere and holding his hands tightly as though she could brace his desire

and prevent it from diminishing.

He hesitated. He knew that he could leave now, quickly and without kissing her, and it would not be too hard. But then she would go on taking classes with him and calling to him across the street, and when he came up the entry stairs and heard his phone ringing he would have to wait on the landing until it had stopped. . . .

"It's too late to have you in the dormitory," she said, and he automatically checked off their short list of private places. It was too cold for the common; they had been nervous, anyway, on the bench behind the thin screen of shrubbery. And it was too late for her to go his room. Parietal rules! He wondered viciously how many people they had forced into marriage. They had talked now and then of renting a room, but they never had the nerve; like his bedroom, the idea was sordid with old connotations. Although they were proud of their pretended indifference to surroundings, her face seemed to reflect the grey walls when they lay together on his bed.

"At least let's get out of this porch light," he said, and they went down the steps and stood hesitating on the sidewalk. She was looking around, eagerly and hopefully, and he wondered how much of her desire was passion and how much grasping; girls used sex to get a hold on you, he knew; it was so easy for them to pretend to be excited.

They wandered down the sidewalk. As they passed the college parking lot, Eleanor said, "Look, we could . . ." She did not go on, but Hal knew at once that she meant the cars, the college girl cars with boxes of tissues and clean seat covers, parked in rows in the lot behind the dormitories. "All right," he said, knowing that the whole time they would be afraid of someone coming, even at the climax they would be listening for steps. They walked around the lot. Ellie laughed; trying, he knew to keep him from recognizing the sordidness of the situation. He wondered why it was now so easy for him to accept the back seats of cars, and student beds with broken springs. He chose a Ford station wagon, and held the back door open for her. When he followed her, she turned to him, and they sank together down onto the seat. He started carefully to unbutton her blouse, feeling her stiffen as he traced her breast. Across the quadrangle, the gymnasium clock chimed silverly. Nine o'clock. Suddenly violent, he ripped her blouse open, and as she tried, terrified, to push off his hands, he began to tear at her slip. "Stop it Eleanor, let go," and as he pulled the straps off her shoulders, she dropped her hands and began to cry.

SEX: The Literary Breakthrough At Harvard Square

The officers of Radcliffe College, as well as parents of students and prospective students, have been caused increasing anxiety over the last few years by the publication of stories describing Harvard-Radcliffe love-affairs. Those published are but a small percentage of those written: an instructor in creative writing at Harvard tells us that one-third of every batch of papers handed in to him are of this genre, and the *Harvard Advocate* is flooded at each copy deadline with reams of poetry and prose describing these affairs in the Hasty Pudding—Hayes Bickford—steps of Memorial Church—coffee house, milieu. These pieces may be described stylistically as variations, more-or-less, between two extremes—one emphasizing the Pudding (Fitzgeraldesque), —the other the Bickford (Kerouacesque), with athletic and/or academic variants going off into Widener, or the Harvard Stadium. Harvard, being a place where literary aspiration and eros thrive together, it is not unnatural that this sort of fiction was initiated and reaches its greatest volume here. Needless to say, almost all of the unpublished poems and stories dedicated to 'young love,' are bad, but all of them—hundreds of them—have contentual elements in common with those that have been published.

We may still apply the term "Harvard Square Sex Fiction," generically, to works that are not strictly Cambridge-oriented, because those published stories that are not set at Harvard could just as well be, and they all seem part of the same trend. These published stories and novels vary a great deal in literary quality and style, but these qualities are not of as much concern as the elements of content they seem to have in common. The contentual similarities are so striking, furthermore, that it seems safe to treat these works as documents of what actually does happen at Harvard and places like it. Of the many published works, a few come immediately to mind such as Phillip Roth's very fine *Goodbye Columbus,* in which, among many other things, an unmarried Radcliffe girl purchases a diaphragm, and a very bad novel by a Yalie entitled *Entry E,* which describes with well controlled outrage a "gang-bang"—a kind of Ivy League rape. The pattern of Harvard-Radcliffe affairs may be derived from such works as J. D. Salinger's famous "Fanny," Sallie Bingham's locally scandalous "Winter Term," Jonathan Kozol's *The Fume of Poppies,* which doesn't even spare us the scatological intimacies, and Harold Brodkey's "Sentimental Education" with its less sophisticated but no less passionate lovers.

All of these stories, and the unpublished ones as well, are, in a sense, the same story. The two lovers meet in ways that are meant to be charming—such as observing each other in a Chaucer course, or holding hands between salt and pepper shakers. They fall in love, have adventures together, have intercourse, and through revelations that come to them from the adventures and the sexual experiences, take a spiritual journey that parallels the journey of their affair. They always end unhappily. The main source of their unhappiness is sex: satisfaction is never complete, although it may seem so at moments. Various things always go wrong: they are either inexperienced and through their inexperience cause neurotic associations for one another, are awkward in a way the author means to be charming but at which we can only sneer, are over-sexed, have a purely sexual relationship without other areas of rapport, get pregnant and have the usual troubles, end up being promiscuous and hurting each others feelings, can't find a place to do it, do it in a disagreeable car, are guilty about **it, want** to do it when partner doesn't, are passive or aggressive in ways unbecoming to their respective sexes, can't stand to do it, or, very rarely, want to but don't. One or more of these things is always the matter; sometimes the whole gambit with variations.

Another trend, in the form of unquestionable documentary evidence, seems to back up the conclusions that we must draw from reading these pieces of fiction, these conclusions being basically that something is very much amiss in the lives of students at Harvard and Radcliffe (or anywhere, for that matter, but at Harvard it is more interesting because we are supposedly dealing with an intellectual elite, if not a socioeconomic one). This trend of unquestionable documentation we are referring to appears in the form of "frank" symposiums, discussions and surveys in such periodicals as *Seventeen* and *Madamoiselle,* under such titles as "Chastity Today," or "What Girls REALLY Think About Sex," and, in a cheaper form, in teen-age columns about "date-nique" (*sic!*) in so many newspapers. Typical of the "frank" articles in the first category are quotations that usually run something like this: "Peter, a brilliant physics major at ——————, had this to say about premarital sex relations on campus: 'I think a girl expects a boy to be experienced, and therefore, to prepare myself for marriage, I find it necessary to take advantage of any girl who will comply, although I could never respect such a girl, of course. On the other hand I would not take a girl home to meet my parents unless she were a virgin, tra la, tra la'." The editor will undoubtedly conclude that Peter holds "the double standard of today's brave youth . . ." In another article we will read that Suzey Q., co-ed at ——————, has this to say: "I think petting and making out is OK, if a girl knows where to draw the line, but I am willing to go all-the-way with the boy I love even if we're not married." These articles always conclude the same thing: that most young people favor complete consummation if they are in love (a few prudes notwithstanding), while others prefer various substitutes best left undescribed. These articles also conclude that this is very interesting, demonstrative of a change in attitude since the day when girls in their twenties were faced with that most over-whelming of all moral crises, should they kiss good-night on the first date, and that, all-in-all, this is all right. What they do not conclude, but what is apparent to us when we read the literary documents such as *The Fume of Poppies* and see where this attitude leads in the hands of such simple and obtuse people as Peter and Suzey Q., is that along with the new freedoms we have been reading about, and know from statistical analysts such as Kinsey, there comes inevitable unhappiness. We may be sure that this unhappiness is not inherent in the new sexual freedoms, themselves, although it is primarily sexual, but rather in the people and the environment of which they are the products.

The causes of this unhappiness, evidenced so often and so clearly in "Harvard Square Sex Fiction," are only scratched at by the various authors. Much of the unhappiness is due to the lack of any framework and code within which college students may practice their freedoms. The reason there is, as yet, no suitable framework, must be held to be the result of a society in a state-of-change; that people at Harvard and Radcliffe openly have affairs is denied by no one, and yet these affairs are carried on in defiance of the school administrations, parents, ministers, and self-appointed leaders of the young. The new freedoms are accepted as fact, but are still held to be immoral. If we accept the writings about Harvard-Radcliffe affairs as documentary—, and this we must do both because of the recurrence of content, and the large numbers of works in which this recurrence takes place,—we must recognize the necessity that the causes of unhappiness and the changing society in which the unhappiness takes place, be *probed*, and not merely scratched at. We ask that writers—student writers, particularly—who deal with this kind of content, *probe*, in their future works, into the causes of what, to date, they have merely described. Since literature is by no means merely an examining force, but may be, at its best, a force of reform, we ask, at the risk of sounding pompous, that these writers imply, in their future works, a code and framework suitable to the new sexual freedoms. Rather than becoming mere documents, their works will become a directing force in the lives of their readers, much, as in a rather different way, Gide's *Les Nourritures Terrestres* became for the French youth of the last generation.   —W.S.B.

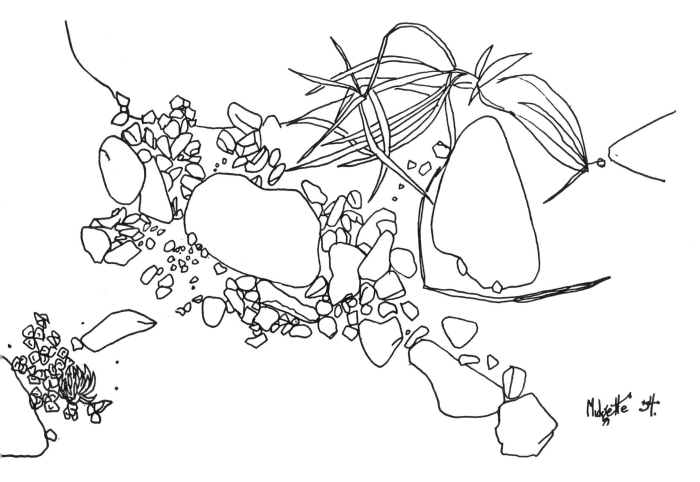

DOWN THERE WHERE IT'S BEAUTIFUL

edgar de bresson

There were nine hundred and forty three telephone poles between their house and the first outskirt of Paris. The house was not visible from the road. A wall ten feet high, and topped by fragments of broken glass encircled the woods about it. The trees were old, almost as old as the house itself; they grew straight out of the ground, and no undergrowth was allowed to arise about their claw-like roots. Only the tallest were tolerated, so that the outlines of the masonry defined themselves in a crepuscular atmosphere, and made it difficult to distinguish the house from the forest background into which it seemed to be on the point of fading away. In the lower part of the facade a row of French windows stretched from one end to the other, and in the evenings the candelabras threw complex shadows on the lawn. The grass was perfectly smooth, and evenly cut. When the lawn was wet from the dozen revolving sprayers, three peacocks left the imprint of their metallic claws on the closely cut grass.

The rooms were filled with precious things. The halls were carpeted with long rugs covered by pale floral designs as were the curtains of the innumerable windows. On the tables the vases stood without water. Each was filled by a single flower whose stem was a gold filament blooming into the intricacies of prehistoric blossoms. The servants moved with great care. They flourished dusters composed of feathers from Persian miniatures over the frames of visionary paintings, porcelain lampshades, and the sixty nine clocks which had all indicated the time to be four thirty two for the last seventeen years.

Each Friday of the week the butler served green tea in the pink room, and broke three translucent cups on the marble floor, as he was accustomed to do on that day. Every week the Collector ordered thiner tea-cups, and now they were so crystalline that they fell like petals on water, and splintered on the floor like dandelions.

At night the thousand lights of the glass chandeliers seemed to perform a music barely out of reach of human ears. The guests mingled and dispersed under them in a Quattrocento dream, where feet and hands moved with infinite precision, and no words were permitted to intrude in the dance. To the choicest guests the Collector revealed treasures made from the blue shell of Oriental birds' eggs. His hands were long, white, and streaked with violet veins like the imperfections of marble slabs preserved on the summit of Alpine peaks. They closed around rare objects with the slowness of a night-blooming cereus folding upon itself against the rashness of dawn. The ballet motion of his hands took an arrangement in the air as they swept from the faience figurines, to the jeweled handle of Akbar's sword, or the pink lobe of his wife's delicately chiselled ear.

She was the one unblemished thing in the house, the Collector declared, and he touched her only with the very tip of his fingers because he was afraid to bruise her skin. She was small, and occupied herself only with the most diminutive things in keeping with the smallness of her body. To look in her face involved traveling far down in her eyes, seeing wisps of smoke, flocks of small spiraling birds, and hearing the distant call of autumnal lakes. Her words bubbled up into her mouth, each one enveloped in a satin sheath, and when she laughed every one thought she had a small bird locked in her breast. She was as delicate as an eyelid, and her dreams were the colour of those very pale sea shells which can be loved only by the purest children.

A year after their marriage she grew so pale that the darkness of her enormous eyes upset the balance of her face. The Collector asked for the best doctor in Europe, and sent for him in Portugal. When the doctor arrived, he carried a black, pigs' leather bag from which issued the rattle of his shiny instruments. There were bits of tobacco in his black goatee, and his plump hands were as moist as those of a dribbling baby. He sat down with the Collector, and asked to examine the patient immediately, for he had no time to waste. He was the very best doctor in all Europe. When he heard that he would not be allowed to touch her, he threw up his hands. He was the very best doctor in all Europe; he could not afford to waste time. The Collector crossed his legs, and examined the reflection of the doctor's face in the black mirror of his pointed shoes. Then he took with the tip of his thumb and index finger, the stem of a gold flower from a vase at his side, placed it on the doctor's knees, and offered him an extravagant sum of money. "But what if she dies, because I can't touch her? What if she dies?" said the doctor, looking at the intricate blossom on his striped trousers.

"That would be preferable to someone's touch," the Collector said, and he left the room.

Alone, the doctor sank back in the armchair. It was tapestried with white silk like the fabric on the wall where the unlit candelabras threw minute lozenge reflections which had the blueness of shadows on snow. The Doctor shivered, and felt the gold flower tremble on his knees. His hand stretched forth, and as he lifted the stalk into the air, the blossom shattered silently into inumerable fragments, and covered his shoes with a million shining flakes of gold.

When he saw the Collector's wife, he saw instantly what was wrong. He did not say anything. Once settled in the house he forgot he was the best doctor in Europe. He did nothing all day except wander from room to room. Sometimes he stood by a window, and watched the Collector's wife making miniature drawings of flowers, weeds, and fossils. From time to time the Collector asked him if he had come to any conclusion, and he answered he needed more time. A day passed like the shadow of large, slow bird; a week like a small, running animal one has just missed seeing. He thought of all the patients he had saved from death, and that didn't stir him. He thought of all those he could be saving, and that didn't affect him. He did not think of saving the Collector's wife, because he could not imagine her death.

One day the Collector appeared before him, and requested an immediate explanation of his wife's case. The Doctor started to cry. The tears ran down the side of his nose, along the creases which began above the nostrils, into the unkempt forest which was his beard. All she needed, he whimpered, was a change to a warmer climate. The Collector showed no sign of surprise; he pushed a button on the wall, and, after the tinkle of the bell had reverberated against all the thousand glass panes of the endless corridors, the butler entered carrying on a tray of green jade seven large piles of untouched banknotes. In addition, the Collector took with the tip of his thumb and index finger the gold filament stem of a flower, and presented it to the Doctor who was wiping his face with his shirt tails. Then, the Doctor walked slowly down the wooded path toward the gate, the tinkling sound of his shiny instruments in the black bag muffled by the seven wads of money, and holding the gold flower firmly between thumb, and index finger. When he passed the gate, the blossom shattered into a million flakes which he saw float to the ground in the sudden sunlight. He looked up, and immediately felt so afraid of death that he ran down the road, and was, as he justly expected, run over by a moving van carrying an enormous shipment of pink toilet seats from Beauvais to Versailles.

In the house the servants unwound yards and yards of white cloth which they draped over the furniture. Each flower was laid in a box lined with blue silk. The rugs were rolled up, and the floors sprinkled with rat poison. The candelabras were taken down, and the mirrors veiled so that they might not reflect each other uselessly, and be worn out by the effort. Shutters were installed on the countless windows of the interminable corridors, and all lights closed off. The servants carried small candles while they moved between the spectral shapes of the lightless rooms, placing moth balls in the cushions of the enormous divans, in the heavy brocade of the folded curtains, the feather mattresses, and the damask tablecloths. As the house folded in upon itself, it took on a more massive form. The turrets seemed more heavy, the walls more thick. The halls echoed sonorously the lightest footstep. The rooms smelled of wax, the lawn of lime. The clocks seemed too heavy for the mantlepieces, the statues too large for their pedestals, the glass doors too ponderous for their hinges. Everything seemed on the point of breaking. From a distance one expected the house to sink into the ground.

They rode to Paris in a long, black car which the Collector had bought because it had once carried Proust from his apartment on the Boulevard Hausman to a nocturnal *rendez-vous* at the Ritz. The chauffeur was an enormous man in green livery who sat with his back so straight that it did not touch the violet cushion of the backrest. The Collector drove with the rigid chauffeur at his right, and his wife far away behind the glass panel. She sat in the middle of the seat, her head supported by a silk cushion, leaning her arms on two purple armrests to preserve her balance. As if frightened by the noise of the black tarpaulin which covered the thirteen monogramed suitcases on the roof, and made a snapping sound in the wind, her eyes darted about, following, now and then, the smallest raindrop trickle down the blurred window.

At the Gare de Lyon the three black-suited butlers stood side by side on the sidewalk, holding three black umbrellas over their bald heads. They were exactly the same height as if belonging to a special race. When the car drove up, one of them led the Collector and his wife through the station, while the other two gave instructions to perspiring porters from the shelter of their black umbrellas. In the station the loudspeaker announced the departure of the Paris-Rome express, "Depart pour Dijon, Bourg, Chambery, Modane, Turin, Genes, Pise, Roma-Termini, Napoli, Reggio, et Syracuse. En voiture!" The Collector's wife stopped in the middle of the station listening to the magical names, and clapped her hands in excitement. People stared, the Collector smiled, they walked on past the Rome express, the Orient express with destination of Istambul, to the Train Bleu. There, they entered the private carriage which had carried the Prince of Wales to his death on the Italian coast near Porto Fino.

The Collector's wife floated down on one of the corner seats of the carriage, and swung her legs to and fro above the floor until her maid placed a footrest under her feet. Outside the window a cloud of steam hissed up into the air, and shined the three bald heads of the butlers so smoothly that she could see the reflection of three lightbulbs on their polished skin. Right above their heads she read, "*Il est dangereux de se pencher en dehors—E pericoloso sporgersi*" on the window sill. When the Collector came in from his compartment, he drew the curtains across the two windows on the left side, and touched her forehead with the back of his longest finger. The slight red mark which he left on her forehead was the only indication that her skin was not more fragile than an April-new petal.

Night fell, and the train rode into it through the Fontainebleau forest where she divined, behind her reflection in the window, enormous tree trunks padded by the darkness which was a wad of black cotton torn into finger-like strands by the sparkling locomotive. She let her body float into the rhythm of the train until it disappeared from her, and she saw nothing but the blue light on the ceiling. Then, she let two cerulean butterflies out of her mind, and watched the blueness of the lightbulb give their wings the phosphorescence of stars reflected in the eyes of screeching peacocks. The butterflies evaporated, crystallised, scattered, and converged with such swiftness that the ceiling seemed an incandescent sapphire streaked by spider-like constructions of web-spun light. "Oh the beauties," said the Collector's wife, and clapped her hands with joy, letting the small bird fly out of her throat in a laugh of delight. The Collector looked up from his book, and smiled generously. The train slowed down to pass through the lighted station of Montereau, picked up speed again, and sped faster and faster toward midnight, dawn, and a day with neither a second more or less than twenty four hours.

In the morning the sky was blue over Avignon. At the bends of the railroad track the Collector's wife discovered villages perched like birds' nests on top of mountains of rocks, and olive trees. They presented yellow, and dirty ochre stones to a burning sun. Square steeples rose up above the faded, red tiles, and the pale rose of the roofs towering above a sea of grey-blue olive trees, their leaves sparkling in the sharp light. After Toulon the train followed the Mediterranean. On the coast she saw the warm sea, squinting in the sun, leaving thin layers of salt on the skin of vacation-brown girls, a heat crushed vaporous horizon hovering in the sky, in the sea, and above the imagined voices of splashing children. She saw big yellow casinos, and palm trees, and villas, and hotels, and yachts, and newspaper vendors in the streets, and tennis courts, and many foreigners in American cars. Then, she let the landscape go out of focus, and returned to the carriage which was a blue universe where bubbles of white air floated upward beyond yesterday's ceiling in a column so cold that it froze the wings of tropical insects.

In the dining-room of L'Hotel Splendide above the Grande Corniche, the precipitous road which runs high above Monte Carlo from Nice to Menton, the Italians, Swiss, Belgian, and Americans observed each day the Collector and his wife with the eyes of conspirators. "They're whiter than frog bellies," said the Italian Count, "and they don't sweat, not even at noon. Think of that." The Count Ludovico di Bassamore was a man of experience. Paris saw him in the fall when the chestnut trees of the Tuileries begin to shed their leaves, and *le grand monde* begins a fresh season. In the winter St. Moritz offered its white slopes to the ski-clad feet of his corpulent body which thrust through the Alpine air with considerable skill, and relaxed in the armchairs of the winter sport hotel with a grace not often associated with a man of such opulence. Spring was reserved for Rome, but even Rome had to be abandonned at the height of the racing season for the hippodromes of Ascot, Longchamp, and, later on, Deauville. In the summer the Riviera received him with the opened arms of a relative one knows too well to have to make a show of friendship to. The Count was on intimate terms with everyone, and everything. He was revered by the proprietor of the hotel, loved by its women, befriended by its men, and respected by its servants. Though he had the eyes of a lizard, he was reputed to keep three mistresses in each of the three most important capitals of Europe.

It was not long before the Count was on intimate terms with the Collector and his wife. He was invited into the Collector's apartment, and sat down with them on their terrace. The sun had gone down behind the mountain in back of them, and, hundreds of feet below the hotel, the waveless sea began to reflect the light of a few villas. As night fell the lamps in the apartment stayed unlit. The three persons on the balcony could hardly see each other. The Count talked into the darkness.

"There are fires all over the coast. Last week there was one near St. Tropez, now there is one at Juan-les-Pins. The parasol pine trees went up in gigantic flames, and almost fell into the sea. It was very beautiful, and very sick. The land is sick with dryness, and heat. You don't know about it because you never go down to the coast, and one can't feel it up here, but down there where its beautiful it is so hot that the fans in L'Hotel de Paris seem to turn more slowly than the minute-hands of the clocks. The dryness pushes us into the sea, soon the fires will drive us to drowning, and we will never realize our perversity. Think of that." The Count laughed. "However it is all very beautiful, the sea is bright, the sky is blue, the palm trees are green, the roofs red, the sand yellow, the rocks ochre, everything is very intense, and we are so perverted that we can't see that in this beauty lies the seed of our death." The Count laughed, and continued projecting a flow of words before him into the darkness, and towards the sirupy sea where no gulls flew.

The Collector's wife watched the Count's words glow in the darkness, and jump like grasshoppers over the rim of the balcony. The word death was an alizarin-crimson beetle which cleared the balcony in a single arc of red smoke. The Collector was restless. His long fingers moved swiftly in the air as if feeling the texture of the Count's words. His silence seemed a submission. The Italian felt the Collector come into the aura of his personality. The Collector searched for a colossal idea of marble palaces, colder, and more solid than the beauty of glaciers which take a million years to move over the petrified bodies of baby dinosaurs—but he could not find it. He looked towards the Count's face, and in the darkness it appeared to be a warm clump of purple bougainvilea blossoms, the petals vibrating with the blood of human veins, in that fullest bloom which comes just before their death. The Collector trembled, and felt his body dilate, contract, and relax suddenly. He saw that the sun was liquid, that it would let a drop fall on him, and seep into his flesh as ink pervades a fragment of blotter paper until it is black all over. Once more the Collector clutched at an idea of running horses imprisoned in the immobility of Attic stones sunk to the bottom of the Caspian Sea. It escaped him, blown away by the words from the purple clump of bougainvillias. He looked at his wife, but her eyes were warm with the flow of dream, and he sank apart from her into the Count's description of Southern cities where the women are more beautiful than any in Europe, because they die twice as early.

The next day the Collector ordered five hundred potted hyacinths. When they arrived, he had the servants dispose them in every corner of the apartment. The Collector's wife clapped her hands with joy, and refused to go out. He told the Count what he had done, and the Italian smiled wanly, as if he knew all about it. The Count drove him down the tortuous road, past Monte Carlo, and Beaulieu to the Cap Ferrat, where they bathed among a multitude of bronze bodies. In the hotel, the Collector's wife breathed in the blueness of the hyacinths, and fainted gently and completely among the peacocks of the Persian carpet.

Every morning, now, the Collector went down to the coast, and did not return to the hotel until night. He lounged on every beach from Antibes to San Remo, and let a layer of salt accumulate on his skin. The sun still tingled on his body in the room of his apartment, and he wondered when his wife would notice it. He could not sit still in her presence, but moved about her as if to penetrate her thoughts. She smiled her fragile smile and it exasperated him so, that he accused her of ignoring him. She protested, and her fragility increased so much that he apologised, and submitted to her inaccessability.

When the hyacinths died, the Collector's hands were brown, and his body shivered at night. The Collector's wife wept all day. Her voice became mouse-like, and she started continually the same sentence without ever finishing it. The first words were "Oh the magical flowers . . ." and no one ever heard the rest. The servants brought more hyacinths, but when she saw them, she shrieked in horror and they were taken away. The curtains of the apartment were pulled, and she disappeared in the penumbra of the alcoves, and the folds of the drapery. Every evening a table was set up on the terrace, and she went out into the darkness to dine with her husband, and the Count, to the light of a religious candlestick. After the flowers' death she was afraid of the daylight. The sea was so blue that if she looked at it for an instant, the water glittered in her eyes all day, and she floated in a blueness that cracked like the stalks of dead flowers. She stood in front of full length mirror for hours on end, and stroked the side

of her face with the tip of her small fingers, not daring to move for fear of falling.

One evening, she announced that she wanted to be put back among the gold flowers and the ivory figurines. The Collector was taken by a fit of rage, and threw all the dishes over the balcony. When he had finished, he went into the apartment and lit all the lamps. His wife stretched both hands over her eyes, and crouched in the darkest corner of the terrace.

"You must go to him in full light," the Count said.

"No, no, I can not. I will die," the Collector's wife whispered, "I must have my own light."

"You've had it too long," the Count said, "Now it's too late, his hands are brown, he carries the sun in his mouth, and there are fires all over the coast. Tomorrow you will go down there where it's beautiful, and meet your husband for the first time. You will tell him everything that comes into your head, and he will not own you any more. You will free yourself, and your presence will come up against him as his comes up against you now."

She whispered, "No, no," wrapped her arms around her shoulders, and crouched farther into the darkness.

In the morning a fire broke out below the hotel. The walls of two villas fell on their sides, and sent stones rolling down the slope toward the sea. The Count joined the firemen, and revelled in the flames, his bare arms swinging an axe, his face grinning with pleasure. The Collector watched the beautiful flames dance for two hours, then, yielding to temptation, ran to join the fire-fighters. By evening the fire was a hundred yards away from the hotel, and six of the guests had left. At midnight the Count, and the Collector emerged from the flames, their clothes torn, their hands black, and pearls of sweat rolling down their foreheads. When the Collector reached his wife's room, the flames shone through the slits of the shutters, and glistened on the skin of her face like rays of clear light on blue icicles. She became his wife without a sound, and when he raised his body off her, she folded in upon herself so quietly that one would never have thought that a woman had died.

HARVARD ADVOCATE

Michael Priddle

APRIL ISSUE 25¢

William Kelly

BROTHER CARLISLE

Mama leaned out the kitchen window, reeled in the line's knot, and started to pin out her cllothes. Then over the unoiled pulley's screeching, she heard her younger son scream. He was somewhere in the alley, between her building and the next.

"Carlisle, what you doing to Little Brother?" She attempted to bend her voice around to him. "Carlisle, you hear?" There was no answer, but someone had begun to pound on the apartment door. Drying her hands on her apron, she shuffled through the apartment, down the dark hallway, heard her slippers scraping on the wooden floor.

"Oh-Lass, won't you come open *the* door?" Mama opened the door to the fat West Indian woman who occupied the alley apartment and who now stood before her in a pink night-gown. "Oh-Lass, child, they *burn*-ing your babe a-*live*," Missus Neilberry was crying. Tears of excitement streamed over her cheeks, catching in the deep crevices of her chins. "They *burn*-ing you child, a-*live*."

Somewhere within her, Mama felt slightly ill, but by the time she noticed it, she was on the second floor landing, had almost cascaded into old, black Mister Doozen coming back from his daily walk. Already she had lost one slipper, and the front door pulled the other from her when it slammed on her foot.

Little Brother's shoes were starting to steam. He was bound to the clothes pole in the alley with thick black wire, and was all but obscured by white smoke surging up from the pile of paper and trash burning at his feet. Carlisle, Mama's older son, sat beside the fire sweating, pretending to warm his hands. The members of his club stood around, hands in pockets, in a state of mixed bewilderment, fear and excitement, not certain, now, they were doing the best thing.

Mama lunged into the midst of smoke and flame and with bare feet kicked the fire from under Little Brother. She untied his hands, which despite the heat were damp and cold. When she led him out of the smoke, the other boys had disappeared, leaving Carlisle sitting as before, only now biting his fingernails.

"Carlisle?" she spoke to him, almost afraid, for this was not the first time he had done such things, and she knew he would have again some valid excuse and that her protestations would have no affect. "Why'd you—"

"Aw, Mama," Little Brother, his breath returned, interrupted. "They was letting me join the club. You got to prove you is brave before they let you in." He was pulling her apron and jumping up and down.

Carlisle smiled.

She looked down at Little Brother and opened her mouth, but no words came. She drew her hand across her forehead. Little Brother moved away from her and sat next to Carlisle. Mama started up the alley.

"What time we eating, Mama?" asked Little Brother to her back.

"Pretty soon now, son." She sighed and turned the corner.

Upstairs again, standing over the stove, the jellied air of the gas burners rising to her face, Mama began to think. She knew she was not smart, was not a doctor of the minds of children, but one thing was certain: Something must be done with Carlisle. Tonight, as she had on other occasions, she would mention this to Papa. Perhaps this time he would understand.

Papa lumbered down the block just as the sun fell into the river. The boys came upstairs with him; today was allowance day. Supper was ready. They sat, said Grace and began to eat.

"What you boys been doing today?" said Papa, spearing a pork chop with his fork. He was big, dark as the inside of a chimney. During the day he built skyscrapers.

"I got into Carlisle's club, Papa," said Little Brother through a mouth of mashed potatoes.

"Don't talk with your mouth full-up," Papa snapped. Then, softly, "That's real good. Your brother helped you, I bet."

Little Brother nodded, Yes.

"That's good. You take good care your brother, Junior," Papa grinned proudly at Carlisle. "That's what the Lord says. Ain't that right, honey?"

"Yes, that right." Mama sipped iced tea, and looked away.

Her answer seemed somehow unsatisfactory to Papa, and he was silent for a short while. "Well," he said finally, "I guess you boys'll be wanting your money."

Carlisle nodded, Yes.

"Here's a dollar each. Go on celebrate your being club members." He handed the money to Carlisle to distribute. The boys excused themselves and disappeared, leaving half-eaten platefuls and the door's slam behind.

Mama twirled the ice around the bottom of her glass, staring blankly. When Papa started to sip loudly from his, she looked up. He watched his tea as he drank and did not see her. For a second she weighed speaking to him at all. She realized it would probably bring on an argument; he would misconstrue and distort her words. Maybe sometime, she thought, he'll listen to me and understand. "Carlisle?" She put down her glass. "That boy try to kill his brother today."

"What boy?" he asked, cracking ice in his jaws.

"Junior."

"Damn it—there you go again—about how bad Junior is. What you don't like about him?" His voice started to expand in volume. Missus Neilberry would hear him. Tomorrow the whole house would be discussing Mama's latest argument. Papa leaned forward and planted his fists on either side of the glass.

"Ain't got nothing against him," she protested softly. "But he set Little Brother afire."

Papa blinked, fell backward, and laughed. "You know how funny that sound? Maybe he pretend to set him afire, but they brothers and he wasn't going to harm him." He stopped, then added for emphasis. "Not one bit." He pounded the table. His glass tipped; he did not notice it. He began laughing again.

"But it true." Mama leaned on the table, reached for his hand, tried to find her husband's eyes, but his laughing head would not stand still. When he stopped, he was quite angry.

"I sick of your babying Little Brother. You thinks I don't love him much because he my second born. Woman, you know better. Still, you always leaping on that."

"Just ask Little Brother when he gets home." She felt tears coming to her eyes, but dammed them back. "You just ask him." She slumped, folded her arms, and stared at her lap.

"All right. I does just that. And if you wrong, you stop this mess." He got up and stalked into the living room to read his paper.

When the boys returned, Carlisle carried a large box. He went straight to his room, which Little Brother shared with him, and Mama heard him opening the closet door and put the box on the top shelf, out of harm's way. He came into the living room and joined Little Brother, who was standing in the middle of the floor.

"What you boys get?" Papa looked up from his paper.

"A cowboy costume," answered Little Brother. Mama noticed he seemed a trifle perplexed, as if he were not quite sure what they had bought, who had bought it, or who would use it. "I gave my money to Carlisle, because he said I would only buy some junk and you wouldn't like that much. He said I could wear it sometimes," he breathed deeply, "if I was good and minded."

Papa sat quietly for a moment, then smiled at Mama. Then he said, "See there, woman? How could that boy do anything but love his brother to give his money to him? And Junior taking care to see this boy ain't going to be foolish."

Carlisle sat next to his father, and Papa put his arm around his shoulder.

"I guess you right," she said, rising. She went quietly to the bedroom and undressed, placing her house coat neatly on the one chair in the room. She lay on her bed, and through the wall she could hear Carlisle and Papa laughing. After a few seconds, Little Brother joined in.

JOHN HAWKES • ADRIENNE RICH • HARRY LEVIN • ROBERT FITZGERALD

DENISE LEVERTOV • CONRAD AIKEN • HOWARD NEMEROV • DONALD HALL

The Harvard Advocate

JONATHAN KOZOL • RICHARD EBERHART • KAY BOYLE • ROBERT BLY

W. H. AUDEN • C. L. BARBER • TIM REYNOLDS • GARY SNYDER • DOUGLAS BUSH

CENTENNIAL ISSUE   75¢

1961–1976

The Advocate *is of course primarily a Harvard magazine, and will continue to emphasize undergraduate writing; but the editors feel that if its pages were restricted to work from Harvard College, the* Advocate *would be fostering literary provincialism. Some kind of critical interplay must be established between Harvard and the literary world outside. By widening the horizons of the* Advocate *to include more than Harvard Yard, the editors hope to awaken Harvard writers to the position—to suggest to them the idea that they must not be "undergraduate writers" only, but writers as individuals apart from institutions, speaking to the world at large.*

This manifesto, published in the summer of 1964, proclaims the new and minor renascence that took place in the *Advocate* of the early sixties. It had become clear that the "literary provincialism" of the previous ten years had been inadequate for the training of young writers. As a result, the magazine's pages were opened to the work of professionals too. In 1961 the Robert Lowell number—in which the poet published "Four Imitations"—hinted at a reawakening of the magazine to the greater world of letters. After the Lowell issue, famous authors began to appear more frequently than at any other time since the thirties. The range of the *Advocate* had widened indeed; and for most of the decade writers from outside Harvard outstripped their young rivals. The approach of the magazine's centennial in 1966 suggested a revival of past glory, and pieces by Marianne Moore, Kay Boyle, and W. H. Auden occupied *Advocate* space that year. Artwork grew in importance, and after 1964 we see not only an improvement in cover design and layout but also the allotment of magazine pages to photographs and drawings.

But, taken all in all, the *Advocate* of the sixties was overshadowed by its famous names, by names sought for their own sake, for profit and celebrity. Student writing was crowded out.

The break came in the last years of the decade, when the social turmoil at Harvard could not but show some effect on its literary magazine. Student writing began to appear in greater proportions and again occupied the central attention of the *Advocate*. But the avant-garde found little welcome there. The style of verse first established in the days of Bly and Ashbery continued with few changes, and the personal and confessional modes were not upset—although one may decide that Rich D. Rosen's "Go Away Richard Brautigan" is as aptly addressed to these schools as to the experimental writers.

In recent years the *Advocate*'s fortunes have varied. In 1969, James Atlas ("Thanksgiving") assembled a special issue devoted to John Berryman, in many ways the best in that series up to that time. It contained "Three New Dream Songs" and "an interview with the man himself." The man himself proved an intelligent and genial talker, and his pleasant cooperation brightens the whole issue. Yet despite such successes as this and the Agee issue of February 1972 (which included "An Article of Faith" by Agee's old teacher, Father Flye), the *Advocate* has often found itself financially straitened. Most boards have been sorely crippled for want of money—not an uncommon position, indeed, for the magazine, but one that has limited the size and quality of issues. Throughout most of the early seventies, the *Advocate* has been a quarterly.

Only recently has the situation changed. The second half of the 1970s has witnessed a surge in solidarity and interest, and the quality of writing has improved, as the last three pieces in this book, all of them published in 1976, testify.

four imitations

robert lowell

THE CADET PICTURE OF MY FATHER

(For Viola Bernard)

There's absence in the eyes. The brow's in touch
with something far. Now distant boyishness
and seduction shadow his enormous lips,
the slender aristocratic uniform
with its Franz Josef braid; both the hands bulge
like gloves upon the saber's basket hilt.
The hands are quiet, they reach out toward nothing—
I hardly see them now, as if they were
the first to grasp distance and disappear,
and all the rest lies curtained in itself,
and so withdrawn, I cannot understand
my father as he bleaches on this page—

Oh quickly disappearing photograph
in my more slowly disappearing hand!

Rilke: *Jugend-Bildnis meines Vaters.*

SELF-PORTRAIT

The bone-build of the eyebrows has a mule's
or Pole's noble and narrow steadfastness.
A scared blue child is peering through the eyes,
and there's a kind of weakness, not a fool's,
yet womanish—the gaze of one who serves.
The mouth is just a mouth . . . untidy curves,
quite unpersuasive, yet it says its *yes*,
when forced to act. The forehead cannot frown,
and likes the shade of dumbly looking down.

A still life, *nature morte*—hardly a whole!
It has done nothing worked through or alive,
in spite of pain, in spite of comforting . . .
Out of this distant and disordered thing
something in earnest labors to unroll.

Rilke: *Selbstbilnis aus dem Jahre 1906.*

YOU KNOCKED YOURSELF OUT

I

Those unnumbered, ruthless, random stones,
tense, vibrating still, as if slung
by the smothered abysmal fire;
the terror of those Amazon cataracts cascading
down miles to the chaos of implacable embraces;
the rock's lockjaw above the sand's
detonating dazzle—do you remember?

The sky-line, a blinding china saucer?

Do you remember the mountain, that wounded giantess?
The stranded sand-pine
with its nets of roots as mineral as the shards they finger,
as it beetled above the down-slope, only
yawning to engulf the horizon shadows?
Cool that grotto's gullet filled
with salad leaves and butterflies—
do you remember it, dumb, delirious,
there just under the summit's rotunda stone,
three men's length tall?
A king-pin of flint, teetering,
immobile?

Quick wren. Greedy eyes drunk with wonder.
You zig-zagged from fiber to fiber
to conquer the height's speckled crown,
dare-devil, musical child,
and loitered there alone to spy into the lapis lazuli bayou,
where unearthly, moss-browed turtles
were rousing from the ooze.

There the tension of nature at its lowest,
submarine sublimities,
nihilist admonitions!

II

You lifted arms like wings,
and gave the winds back their youth,
as you ran on the inertia of the stock-still air.

No one ever saw
your deft foot rest from the dance.

III

Lucky grace,
how could you help knocking your brains out
on such horny blindness—
you, simple breath, crystal bubble,

a candle, too dazzling
for the shaggy, random, vandalistic
burning of the naked sun!

Ungaretti: Tu ti spezzasti.

RUSSIA 1812

The snow fell, and its power was multiplied.
For the first time the Eagle bowed its head—
dark days! Slowly the Emperor returned—
behind him Moscow! Its onion domes still burned.
The snow rained down in blizzards—rained and froze.
Past each white waste further white waste rose.
None recognized the captains or the flags
Yesterday the Grand Army, today its dregs.
No one could tell the vanguard from the flanks.
The snow! The hurt men struggled from the ranks,
hid in the bellies of dead horse, in stacks
of shattered caissons. By the bivouacs,
one saw the picket dying at his post,
still standing in his saddle, white with frost,
the stone lips frozen to the bugle's mouth!
Bullets and grapeshot mingled with the snow,
that hailed . . . The Guard, surprised at shivering, march
in a dream now; ice rimes the gray mustache.
The snow falls, always snow! The driving mire
submerges; men, trapped in that white empire,
have no more bread and march on barefoot—gaps!
They were no longer living men and troops,
but a dream drifting in a fog, a mystery,
mourners parading under the black sky.
The solitude, vast, terrible to the eye,
was like a mute avenger everywhere,
as snowfall, floating through the quiet air,
buried the huge army in a huge shroud.
Could anyone leave this kingdom? A crowd—
each man, obsessed with dying, was alone.
Men slept—and died! The beaten mob sludged on,
ditching the guns to burn their carriages.
Two foes. The North, the Czar. The North was worse.
In hollows where the snow was piling up,
one saw whole regiments fallen asleep.
Attila's dawn, Cannaes of Hannibal!
The army marching to its funeral!
Litters, wounded, the dead, deserters—swarm,
crushing the bridges down to cross a stream.
They went to sleep ten thousand, woke up four.
Ney, bringing up the former army's rear,
hacked his horse loose from three disputing Cossacks . . .
All night, the *qui vive?* The alert! Attacks;
retreats! White ghosts would wrench away our guns,
or we would see dim, terrible squadrons,
circles of steel, whirlpools of savages,
rush sabering through the camp like dervishes.
And in this way, whole armies died at night.

The Emperor was there, standing—he saw.
This oak already trembling from the axe,
watched his glories drop from him branch by branch:
chiefs, soldiers. Each one had his turn and chance—
they died! Some lived. These still believed his star,
and kept their watch. They loved the man of war,
this small man with his hands behind his back,
whose shadow, moving to and fro, was black
behind the lighted tent. Still believing, they
accused their destiny of *lese-majeste*.
His misfortune had mounted on their back.
The man of glory shook. Cold stupefied
him, then suddenly he felt terrified.
Being without belief, he turned to God:
"God of armies, is this the end?" he cried.
And then at last the expiation came,
as he heard some one call him by his name,
some one half-lost in shadow, who said, "No,
Napoleon." Napoleon understood,
restless, bareheaded, leaden, as he stood
before his butchered legions in the snow.

Victor Hugo: *L'expiation.*

I am not *an* addict. I am *the* addict. The addict I invented
to keep this show on the junk road. I *am* all the addicts and all
the junk in the world. I *am* junk and I am hooked forever.
Now I am using junk as a basic illustration. Extend it. I am
reality and I am hooked on reality. Give me an old wall and
a garbage can and I can by God sit there forever. Because I
am the wall and I am the garbage can. But I need some one
to sit there and look at the wall and the garbage can. That is
I need a human host. I can't look at anything. I am blind. I
can't sit anywhere. I have nothing to sit on. And let me take
this oportunity of replying to my numerous and uh vociferous
critics. It is not true that I hate the human species. I just don't
like human beings. I don't like
animals. What I feel is not hate.
In your verbal garbage the closest
word is distaste. Still I must live
in and on human bodies. An intol-
erable situation you will agree. To
make that situation clearer suppose
you were stranded on a planet pop-
ulated by insects. You are blind.
You are a drug addict. But you
find a way to make the insects
bring you your junk. Even after
thousands of years living there you
still feel that basic structural distaste for your insect servants. You
feel it every time they touch you.

"WHO HIM? DON'T LET HIM OUT HERE."

by William Burroughs

Well that is exactly the way I feel about my human servants.
Consequently since my arrival some five hundred thousand
years ago I have had one thought in mind. What you call the
history of mankind is the history of my escape plan. I don't
want 'love'. I don't want 'forgiveness'. All I want is out of here.
Question: "Mr. Martin, how did all this start? How did you
get here in the first place? If you found conditions so distasteful
why didn't you leave at once?"

"God questions I mean good questions, young man. Obviously
I am not omnipotent. My arrival here was a wreck. Ship came
apart like a rotten undervest. The 'accident' in which I lost my
sight. I was the only survivor. The other members of the crew
. . . well . . . you understand . . . uh sooner or later . . . So
I decided to act sooner. And I have acted sooner ever since.
The entire human film was prerecorded. I will explain briefly
how this is done. Take a simple virus illness like hepetitis. This

illness has an incubation period of two weeks. So if I know when the virus is in—(and I do because I put it there) I know how you will look two weeks from now: yellow. To put it another way. I take a picture or rather a series of pictures of you with hepetitis. Now I put my virus negatives into your liver to develop. (Not far to reach. Remember I live in your body.) The whole hepetitis film is prerecorded two weeks before the opening scene when you notice your eyes are a little yellower than usual. Now this is a simple operation. Not all of my negatives develop by any means. All right now back to basic junk. Some character takes a bang of heroin for the first time. It takes maybe sixty consecutive shots before I can welcome another addict. (Room for one more inside, sir). Having taken one shot it becomes mathematically probable that he will take another given the opportunity and I can always arrange that. Having taken two shots it becomes more probable that he will take a third. One negative developed makes others almost unavoidable. The same procedure can be applied to any human activity. If a man makes a certain amount of money by certain means he will go on making more money by the same means and so forth. Human activites are drearily predictable. It should now be obvious that what you call 'reality' is a function of these precisely predictable because prerecorded human activities. Now what could louse up a prerecorded biologic film? Obviously random factors. That is some one cutting my word and image lines *at random*. In short the cut up method of Brion Gysin which derives from Hassan I Sabbah and the planet Saturn. Well, I've had a spot of trouble before but nothing serious. There was Rimbaud. And a lot of people you never heard of for good reasons. People who got too close one way or another. There was Tristan Tzara and the Surrealist lark. I soon threw a block into that. Broke them all down to window dressers. So why didn't I stop Mr. Gysin in his tracks? I have ways of dealing with wise guys or I wouldn't be here. Early answer to use on anyone considering to interfere. Tricks I learned after the crash. Well perhaps I didn't take it seriously at first. And maybe I wanted to hear what he had to say about getting out. ˙Always keep as many alternative moves open as possible. Next thing the blocade on planet earth is broken. Explorers moving in whole armies. And the usual do good missions talk about educating the natives for self government. And some hick sherrif from the nova heat charging me with 'outrageous colonial mismanagement and attempted nova'. Well they can't hang a nova rap on me. What I planned was simply to move out the biologic film to planet Venus and start over. Take along a few *good* natives to stock the new pitch and for the rest total disposal. That's not nova that's manslaughter. Second degree. And I planned it painless. I dislike screaming. Disturbs my medications."

Question: "Mr. Martin, in the face of the evidence, no one can deny that nova was planned. The reports reek of nova."
"It will be obvious that I myself, as an addict, can only be a determined factor in some one else's equation. It's the old army game. Now you see me now you don't."

Question: "Mr. Martin, you say 'give me a wall and a garbage can and I can sit there forever' almost in the next sentence you say 'All I want is out of here'. Aren't you contradicting yourself?". "You are confused about the word 'self'. I could by God sit there forever if I had a self to sit in that would sit still for it. I don't. As soon as I move in on any self all that self wants is to be somewhere else. Anywhere else. Now there you sit in your so called self. Suppose you could walk out of that self? Some people can incidentally. I don't encourage this but it happens and threatens to become pandemic. So you walk out of your body and stand across the room. Now what form would the being that walks out of your body have? Obviously it would have precisely your form. So all you have done is take the same form from one place to another. You have taken great trouble and pain—(believe me there is no pain like flesh withdrawal consciously experienced) and you have gotten precisely back where you started. To really leave human form you would have to leave human form that is leave the whole concept of word and image. You can not leave the human image in the human image. You cannot leave human form in human form. And you can not think or conceive in non image terms by mathematical definition of a being in my biologic film which *is* a series of images. Does that answer your question? I thought not."

Question: "Mr. Martin tell us something about yourself. Do you have any vices other than uh junk? Any hobbies? Any diversions?" "Your vices other than junk I manipulate but do not share. Sex is profoundly distasteful to a being of my uh mineral origins. Hobbies? Chess. Diversions? I enjoy a good show and a good performer. Just an old showman. Well when you have to kill your audience very few years to keep them in their seats it's about time to pack in."

Question: "Mr. Martin, I gather that your plan to move the show to planet Venus has uh miscarried. Is that correct?"

"Yeah it looks that way."

Question: "In that case, Mr. Martin where will you go when you go if you go?"

"That's quite a problem. You see I'm on the undesireable list with every immigration department in the galaxy.

'Who *him?* Don't let him out here.'

Question: "Mr. Martin don't you have any friends?"

"There are no friends. I found that out after the crash. I found that out before the others. That's why I'm still here. There are no friends. There are allies. There are accomplices. No one wants friends unless he is shit scared or unless he is planning a caper he can't pull off by himself."

Question: "Mr. Martin, what about the others who were involved in this crash? Aren't they still alive some where in some form?"

"You don't have to look far. They are sitting right here."

Question: "Who were these others?"

"There was an army colonel, a technician and a woman."

Question: "Won't you have to come to some sort of terms with your uh former accomplices?"

"To my disgruntled former associates I have this to say. You were all set to cross me up from the count down. You think I can't read your stupid virus mind, lady. And you, you technical bastard, with your mind full of formulae I can't read. And you Colonel Bradly waiting to shoot me in the back. The lot of you. Blind and paralyzed I still beat you to the draw."

Question: "Mr. Martin, what sort of place did you people come from?" "What sort of place did we come from. Well if you want the answer to that question, just look around, buster. Just look around." "Ladies and gentlemen, you have just heard an interview with Mr. Martin, sole survivor of the first attempt to send up a space capsule from planet earth. Mr. Martin has been called The Man of A Thousand Lies. Well he didn't have time for a thousand but I think he did pretty well in the time alloted. And I feel reasonably sure that if the other crew members could be here with us tonight they would also do a pretty good job of lying. But please remember that nothing is true in space, that there is no time in space—that what goes up under such auspices must come down—that the beginning is also the end.

Ladies and gentlemen, these our actors, bid you a long last good night."

Marianne Moore IN LIEU OF THE LYRE

One debarred from enrollment at Harvard,
may have seen towers and been shown the Yard —
animated by Madame de Bouffler's choice rhymes:
Sentir avec ardeur:* with fire; yes, with passion;
rime-prose revived also by word-wizard Achilles (see note)
Chinese Dr. Fang

The Harvard Advocate's formal-informal craftly rare
invitation to Harvard made grateful, Brooklyn's (or Mexico's)
ineditos —
one whose "French aspect" was invented by
Professor Levin,†
a too outspoken outraged refugee from clichés particularly,
who was proffered redress
by the Lowell House Press‡ —
Vermont Stinehour Press, rather. No careless statements
to Kirkland House; least of all inexactness in quoting a fact.

To the Advocate, *gratia sum*§
unavoidably lame as I am, verbal pilgrim
like Thomas Bewick, drinking from his hat-brim,
drops spilled from a waterfall, denominated later by him
a crystalline Fons Bandusian miracle.

It occurs to the guest, — if someone had confessed it in time —
that you might have preferred to the waterfall, pilgrim and hat-brim,
a nutritive axiom such as
"a force at rest is at rest because balanced by some other force (comma):
or "catenary and triangle together hold the span in place,
of a bridge‖ (Parenthesis)

or a too often forgotten truly relevant thing, the Roebling cable
was invented by William A. Roebling.

These reflections, Mr. Davis,
in lieu of the lyre.

Sentir avec ardeur. By Madame Boufflers — Marie-Francoise-Catherine de Beauveau, Marquise de Boufflers (1711-1786). See note by Dr. Achilles Fang, annotating Lu Chi's "Wên Fu" (A.D. 261-303) — his "Rhymeprose on Literature" ("rhyme-prose" from "Reimprosa" of German medievalists): 'As far as notes go, I am at one with a contemporary of Rousseau's: Il faut dire en deux mots / Ce qu'on veut dire'; . . . But I cannot claim 'J'ai réussi,' especially because I broke Mme. de Boufflers's injunction ('Il faut éviter l'emploi / Du moi, du moi')" Harvard Journal of Asiatic Studies, Volume 14, Number 3, December, 1951, page 529 (revised, *New Mexico Quarterly*, September, 1952).
†"A Note on her French Aspect", Harry Levin, p.40, *Festchrift for Marianne Moore's Seventy-seventh Birthday* — by Various Hands, Edited by Tambimuttu, $4.95.
‡Referring to Lowell House *separatum: Occassionem Cognose*, (1963) §*Gratia sum* Bewick tailpiece "a trickle of water from a rock, underlined by heart in outline carved on the rock, p. 53, *Memoir of Thomas Bewick Written by Himself*, (Centaur Classics).
‖*Brooklyn Bridge, Fact and Symbol* by Alan Trachtenberg (Oxford $5.75).

Robert Shaw

CASTAWAYS

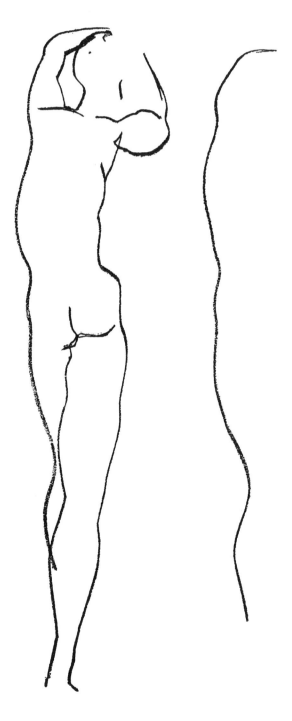

Caliban, you are all mouth,
gaping with gross howls,
only one tooth
is left and it's half-bad. Prospero scowls,

your voice drops a grudging decibel.
Miranda titters. "Brave monster," she mocks.
You get hell,
hearing her, chopping wood and breaking rocks,

living over the day of what you did —
her flowers that went with her full of music
fell, and skittered and hid.
They tease you now when you trip like a paralytic.

Love for a lady is bad for a brute.
How could she ever know your corded
throat wanted to be a flute
following her? Now all your hoarded

songs wither into spit, and drip. . . .
Once the words she taught you freed your tongue
then you sang to every ship
that wandered by, and waves it wandered among.

You went with her, but her scared shrug
angered her father into taking
away the words. Monster, hug
your warty self all night to a nightmare waking.

Hung in a body of captivity,
fighting for exit, groans escape.
Out of the sea
come the cruisers, crowds gather and gape.

Nothing to learn now from her lips.
No island tunes. Snarl and gulp,
brother. Once I came to grips
with who I wanted and was struck. Does this help?

No. . . . Sore mouth, groan for us both.
Ban, ban, Caliban, cry
past the last tooth
and nail to all newcomers. Let them know why.

W. H. Auden

DEAR DIARY

How odd it now seems
That when he was born there seemed
Nothing odd about writing:
I travelled alone
To Bonn with a boring maid.

*   *   *

As a child, before
Doctors had thought up the term,
He knew from watching
His maiden-aunts that illness
Could be psycho-somatic.

*   *   *

Father at the wars.
Mother, tongue-tied with shyness,
Struggling to tell him
The Facts of Life he didn't dare
Tell her he knew already.

*   *   *

Pleased with a job well done,
He fell asleep drunk,
Set the mattress on fire.

*   *   *

Once he had shat
In his new apartment,
He began to feel at home.

*   *   *

Having to cook for himself,
He goes back to dishes
Mother served him.

*   *   *

Another whole day wasted.
What is called for?
The Whip? Pills? or Patience?

*   *   *

Thoughts of his own death,
Like the distant roll
Of thunder at a picnic?

*   *   *

His thoughts pottered
From verses to sex to God
Without punctuation.

Alone on this hot
Saturday afternoon,
He can think of nothing
But lying in certain arms,
As scheduled for Tuesday
At 8. p.m.

*   *   *

Post coitum homo tristis.
What nonsense! If he could,
He would sing.

*   *   *

Mulberries dropping,
Twinges of lumbago
As he read *Clarendon.*

*   *   *

A September night.
Just the two of them, eating
Corn from their garden,
Plucked thirty minutes ago.
Outside: thunder, siling rain.

*   *   *

October mist.
St. Martin's gossamer.
In the bath-room a stray toad.

*   *   *

New York. A beautiful hot bath
At any hour,
With cockroaches in it.

*   *   *

The girl who admired his work
Was astonished to learn
He was not dead.

*   *   *

He woke in the small hours,
Dismayed by a wilderness
Of hostile thoughts.

*   *   *

Reflected in the bar-mirror
During their lunch-hour,
A row of faces,
Middle-aged, mute, expecting
No death of their own.

*   *   *

What was he to say
To the wretched youth? In flight
From a non-father,
An incoherent mother,
In pursuit of—what?

*   *   *

The class whose vices
He pilloried was his own,
Now extinct except
For lone survivors like him
Who remember its virtues.

Kay Boyle A POEM ABOUT THE JEWS

I have had enough of them, more than enough;
Enough of the pages allotted to them, the margins
Crowded with faces, not as high ground is thronged
With sheep whose lips tear at the parched grass
Between stones, but crowded as subway platforms are
With a mosaic of faces, eloquent beyond lamentation
In the rush hour of returning home.
I have had enough of the silent chapters
Of their history. ("Without outcry"
Is written in every language of their coming and going).
I am sick and tired of every word of it. And you, you haven't
The time to listen, so do not listen. There is so much else to do.

> After some centuries had passed
> The descendants of Abraham
> Took on the bright density of tribes,
> Related not only by common worship
> But by common ancestry. (So they began).
> Crop failures and droughts — the skeleton
> Hand of the parched wind sifting the dust —
> Impelled them to ask, as other nomads had asked,
> Leave to pasture their flocks in the western fringes
> Of the Nile's tidal mouth.
> There, on slopes cropped by the square teeth of
> Sheep, goats, occasional donkeys,
> Following highways of emerald bullrushes,
> Water to their ankle-bones, bearded,
> These shepherds roamed. They sojourned
> A long while in Egypt, speaking their own tongue,
> Compliant, peaceful as saints, and were
> In acknowledgement reduced to servitude.
> (Such was their lot). They who had been freemen,
> Their spirits illuminated by loneliness,
> Became bondsmen, groaning under
> The taskwork of fashioning bricks
> From the gold mud slipping under foot,
> Bemoaned their destiny as they built Pithom and Ramses,
> East of Goshen (cities without subways to herd them
> Or housing projects to take them in), crying out
> In longing for those places where the name Israel
> Lived still, was still whispered on the dunes,
> However far.

You have heard all this before.
You know that on one occasion a shepherd wandered
Deeper into the wilderness seeking fresher valleys, and passed
Close by the mountain of Horeb, of Sinai; and there beheld a bush alight.
But neither the branches of that bush nor the frail white flowers
Were devoured by the flame. However fiercely they burned,
They did not burn. The shepherd, a little slow of tongue,
Slow of thought even, it is rumored, could find
No explanation for this miracle (in the presence of which
The flocks stood ruminating) until a clear voice spoke in the rush hour
Of the return. The God of the fathers called out from the fire.
It was twilight. There were no stars yet
To bear witness, no clouds to veil the planets had they appeared.
The evening was blue as sapphire, translucent as amethyst.

There was silence
Except for the voice that spoke. It bade
The shepherd lead his people into freedom.
You know how the exodus took place in the petalled springtime
Of the year one thousand two hundred and twenty
Before Christ's name was known.

> And then, to go on with it, in 1093, Peter the Hermit,
> A native of Picardy, set forth on pilgrimage to Jerusalem,
> And in wrath at the miseries of the pilgrims
> Returned to Europe, crying out that the duty of the Church
> Was the deliverance of the holy places from the infidel.
> In Mayence, the Crusaders passed, and the Jews had trouble.
> "The blood of the men mingled with the blood of their wives,"
> It is written, "and the strong, sad blood of the fathers
> Mingled with their children's blood;
> The blood of the brothers with their sisters', the
> Blood of the teachers with their disciples', the
> Blood of the grooms with their brides', the
> Blood of the judges with their scribes', the
> Blood of the infants with their mothers'."
> (We know all this, the wailing, the bemoaning,
> Centuries without end).
> But one thing more, just one,
> And then I'll keep quiet about it.
> In July 1099, the knights in tunics
> Of chain and coats of mail, and the riff-raff
> That accompanied them, captured Jerusalem.
> Godfrey of Boulogne was made king; and thus
> Was founded the Latin kingdom of Jerusalem
> Whose life, it is recorded, "was one of the most painful
> Ever penned; a history of almost unredeemed envy,
> Malice, shame; a kingdom that in eighty-eight years
> Would disappear as suddenly as it had come, leaving no trace
> Save the ruins of castles and churches,
> And the countless dead; save a few place-names
> And a deathless legacy: the hatred of Christianity
> In the hearts and the marrow of the natives there."

But let me keep history straight.
"The ears of him who hears these things will tingle,
For who has ever heard anything like this?" wrote Solomon bar Samson
Early in his century, asking the question much too soon;
For presently Edessa fell to the Mohammedans, and Pope Eugenius,
Poor man, beside himself, out of his wits, doing his utmost,
Issued a call for a new Crusade. In response to the fiery eloquence
Of St. Bernard, multitudes gathered about the King of France,
About the German Emperor, and again the Jews stretched out their necks.
(That is the ancient phrase for it). They thrust forth
Their necks and let the bright knife find its place.
The Germans were not alone in their fury. There were always
The others. There were the virtuous, happy, just, ecclesiastical men,
The pompous, the titled, the revered, of France, England, Spain, all
Those who trembled at the look of features different from their own.
The Germans were not alone — except as each man's judgment of himself
Is secret and isolate, and has no nation's name. The bishops, delicate of thought,
Acute of sensibility, sought to protect the outcasts. St. Bernard himself
Permitted no excesses. Christian usurers, he argued, were no better
Than Jewish usurers. (That was gracious of him). But still Jews,
He made clear, should remit interest due from such of those
Who took the Cross.

At this moment in the wearisome history,
In the furtive annals on which no light of day, but only
Gas-light flickers, the instigator was the monk Radulph,
A pious man, gentle with birds, who in his devotion
Skipped in monk's attire along the Rhine,
Preaching that Jews living in the cities and villages
Should be effaced; like vermin, he specified,
Like rats; for were not their eyes as avid,
Their noses twice as long? His teachings
Bore fruit, and among the hundreds who were quickly slain
(Or who took their children's lives and then their own) was Simeon,
The Saint of Treves, returning on foot from England, making his way
Along the high road, where, not far from Cologne,
In the Queen Anne's Lace and the dust,
He was done to death by the passing noblemen of that Crusade.

(Young men and young women shall not dance together,
Wrote Judah, the mystic from Italy, the Jewish saint,
But each sex shall dance by itself. No Jew, so his
Teachings went, shall disguise himself in the garments
Of a Christian cleric to escape persecution, or shall
He sew a cross upon his cloak). I can hear you sighing.
I too have no patience left for the regulations of history:
"Jews to move freely, and carry their wares from
Place to place, but not to settle; Jews to hold no
Public offices, inasmuch as they have been
Condemned in expiation to perpetual slavery; Jews
To wear a special dress, or a distinctive sign,
A badge to be pinned or embroidered on their
Garments, a star, yellow in color, over the perfidious heart."
All this happened a long time ago. It's closed
In the pages of books "without outcry." Even the
Equalities they attained are like far, alien music,
Scarcely played: "No toll to be levied on
A Jewish corpse when removed from one city to another, from
One province to another." Cannot the burden finally be laid down?

No, not quite yet, not quite yet. Something has happened.
It is much later. It is July 1964. There are two hundred sailors,
Maybe three hundred, wooden clubs in their hands to fight off rattle-snakes,
Water-moccasins. They move through the suck of the Mississippi swamplands,
Wearing hip-boots as they comb the bayous. They drag the Pearl River
(Which yields other bodies, dismembered, bloated, but not those of the two Jews
And the Catholic who had left no sign). The frogs and the varmints hush their
    throbbing
As the skiffs paddle in, the orchestra moaning again once
The searchers have passed. It is said that one of the three died
Because of the beard he wore and the shape of his features. It is said
The state ordered coats of armor buckled on to meet the invasion of "Jews and
    other scum."
It is said that Choctaw Indians saw the mob gathering; but Indians
Have been sent back through time to the beginning. They no longer have a tongue.
The air was heavy with magnolia, light with the smell of honeysuckle.
The land for miles around was silent. The night they lay warm in the southern
    earth,
The bush did not burn. There was no miracle. Yet their names were spoken,
Jewish names, shepherds like the other, Goodman and Schwerner,
And one who was Catholic, Chaney; their faces eloquent
Beyond lamentation in the rush hour of returning. Can we say
Now we have heard enough? Can we say the history is done?

AN INTERVIEW
WITH JOHN BERRYMAN

[THE PUBLICATION OF *HIS TOY, HIS DREAM, HIS REST* WAS CELEBRATED IN NEW YORK ON OCTOBER 25, 1968: THE FOLLOWING DAY, MR BERRYMAN ARRIVED IN BOSTON TO SPEAK WITH THE *ADVOCATE* AND TO READ AT BRANDEIS UNIVERSITY. ON SUNDAY, THE TWENTY-SEVENTH, DAVID McCLELLAND, JOHN PLOTZ, ROBERT B. SHAW AND THOMAS STEWART VISITED MR BERRYMAN IN THE GUEST SUITE OF QUINCY HOUSE AT HARVARD, ARMED WITH TAPE RECORDER AND PHONOGRAPH. AFTER LISTENING TO BOB DYLAN AND ROBERT JOHNSON FOR SEVERAL MINUTES, WE GOT DOWN TO CASES.]

[COULD YOU TALK ABOUT WHERE YOU WERE BORN AND WHERE YOU CAME FROM AND HOW YOU STARTED WRITING POETRY?]

Yes, I can do that very quickly. I was born in Oklahoma; my father was a banker and my mother was a schoolteacher; they were the only people who could read and write for hundreds of miles around and they were living in the same boarding house, so they got married; so I arrived. Son number one. Then we moved to Florida, and my father killed himself.

[HOW OLD WERE YOU THEN?]

I was twelve. Then we moved to Gloucester, Massachusetts, and then New York and I was in school for some years on Long Island, in Jackson Heights, P.S. 69, that was the number of the school. Then I went to a Connecticut prep school—South Kent. I was there for four years, but got very bored in South Kent, so they gave me college boards a year early, so I skipped 6th Form. I went from the 5th straight into Columbia. Then I was at Columbia for four years—or rather three and a half years since I got thrown out.

[WHAT WAS THAT ABOUT?]

Well, I wasn't going to class and things like that, you know, and flunked a course, lost my scholarship. Then I went back in. By this time the administration knew me very well. I used to get notes from the Dean saying, "Dean Hawkes would like you to call on him at your earliest convenience." I used to say to myself, "That's damn white of the Dean. I must drop in on him." Until, Plotz, one day a message arrived, saying, "If you are not in the Dean's office by eleven o'clock you are suspended."

[AND YOU WENT?]

I went—and he suspended me.

[HOW DID YOU GET FROM THERE TO CAMBRIDGE?]

Well, during my last couple of years, I was a good boy. I toed the line and was a decent character. So they gave me everything—even made me Phi Beta Kappa. And they gave me their main travelling fellowship; and then I was two years at Cambridge, and then I came back to New York and lived in New York for a year. Then I taught at Harvard for three years, then I taught at Princeton off and on for ten years, and now I'm at Minnesota, where I'm not very often, but I sometimes go there. I bought a house.

[WHEN DID YOU FIRST START WRITING?]

I was very late in developing—very late in developing. I was about nineteen when I wrote four sonnets for my mother's birthday—and they were about the worst sonnets that the world has ever seen, but I thought they were quite good, and my mother thought they were terrific. I have always had a very close relation with my mother—that's very bad for me, I'm told.

[DID STUDYING UNDER MARK VAN DOREN AT CO-LUMBIA HAVE AN INFLUENCE?]

Oh, yes. I always wanted to be a writer—I wrote a science fiction novel when I was twelve; the chief character was called E-Coro-'aka. But a poet? I never imagined that. All I knew about poetry then was, "Abou Ben Adhem, may his tribe increase,/ Awoke one night from a deep dream of peace" and "Breathes there the man with soul so dead/ Who never to himself has said,/ This is my own, my native land"—junk like that? Who wants to write that!? So I never imagined being a poet, until I reviewed Mark Van Doren's book, A Winter Diary, which appeared after about seven years of silence, because he was having trouble getting a publisher. I became friends with him and I called him "Sir"—a habit I had picked up at prep school, when we had to call not only the masters, but the 6th Formers, "Sir". So I called Mark, "Sir"; so he said, "If you call me 'sir' once more I'll kick you in the ass." I was very touched by this, so I didn't call him 'sir' anymore.

[WHAT OTHER POETS DID YOU ESPECIALLY ENJOY AND FEEL INFLUENCED BY?]

Yeats. Yeats was my master. I went through a long period of hating Yeats, but now I regard him as extremely good. And Auden. I had to get free of both Yeats and Auden.

[WHY DO YOU CALL THE DREAM SONGS ONE POEM RATHER THAN A GROUP OF POEMS IN THE SAME FORMS?]

Ah—it's personality—it's Henry. He thought up all these things over all the years. The reason I call it one poem is the result of my strong disagreement with Eliot's line—the impersonality of poetry, an idea which he got partly from Keats (a letter) and partly from Goethe (again a letter). I'm very much against that; it seems to me on the contrary that poetry comes out of personality. For example, Keats—I'm thinking of La Belle Dame Sans Merci, I'm thinking of that; and I'm thinking of Hopkins—any one of the sonnets. So I don't buy this business about the eighteenth century being impersonal, either. Now Johnson's best poem in my opinion is about a factor in his household—I forget the name of it—and it's beautiful poem, and it's extremely personal.

[WHAT IS THE RELATIONSHIP BETWEEN 77 DREAM SONGS AND HIS TOY, HIS DREAM, HIS REST?]

Well, 77 Dream Songs is just the first three books.

[DO YOU SEE A GAP BETWEEN THE TWO VOLUMES?]

No, I don't see a gap; it's a continuous relationship. Except, there's this: at the end of the first volume, 77 Dream Songs, Henry goes into orbit. He was "making ready to move on." Well, I was already well ahead of him.

[I NOTICED THAT HENRY'S STATE OF DEATH, BOOK IV, CORRESPONDED TO THE EPIC CONVENTION OF PLACING A DESCENT INTO THE UNDERWORLD IN THE CENTER OF THE NARRATIVE; WAS THERE ANY CONSIDERATION OF THAT IN STRUCTURING THE POEM?]

I don't think so. Opus Posthumous is just a recovery from the end of book three in the first volume of Dream Songs. The placement of the poems in the Dream Songs is purely personal.

[IS THERE ANY ULTERIOR STRUCTURE TO THE DREAM SONGS?]

Ah—you mean, somebody can get to be an associate professor or an assistant professor by finding it out? Mr Plotz, there is none. Il n'y en a pas! There's not a trace of it. Some of the Songs are in alphabetical order; but, mostly, they just belong to areas of hope and fear that Henry is going through at a given time. That's how I worked them out.

[IN THE LAST VOLUME YOU SAID, THE POEM'S UL-TIMATE STRUCTURE IS ACCORDING TO HENRY'S NATURE.]

Now, that's right.

[SO, IN FACT, THE BOOK HAS NO PLOT?]

Those are fighting words. It has a plot. Its plot is the personality of Henry as he moves on in the world. Henry gains ten years. At one time his age is given as forty-one, "Free, black, and forty-one", and at a later point he's fifty-one. So the poem spans a large area, you see that.

[YOU ADMIRE STEPHEN CRANE, WE KNOW, AND MANY OF HIS CHARACTERS ARE NAMED "HENRY"; IS THIS THE ORIGIN OF THE NAME?]

Oh, no—that's all just accident and junk. I'll tell you how the name Henry came into being. One time my second wife and I were walking down an avenue in Minneapolis and we decided on the worst names that you could think of for men and women. We decided on Mabel for women, and Henry for men. So from then on, in the most cozy and adorable way, she was Mabel and I was Henry; and that's how Henry came into being.

[WHAT IS THE RELATIONSHIP BETWEEN YOU AND HENRY?]

I think I'll leave that one to the critics. Henry does resemble me, and I resemble Henry; but on the other hand I am not Henry. You know, I pay income tax; Henry pays no income tax. And bats come over and they stall in my hair—and fuck them, I'm not Henry; Henry doesn't have any bats.

[WOULD YOU TALK ABOUT HENRY IN TERMS OF HEROISM, AS THE HERO OF A POEM?]

Well, he's very brave, Henry, in that he keeps on living after other people have dropped dead. But he's a hopeless coward with regard to his actual death. That never comes out in the poem, but he is afraid of death. I tried to make it clear in the epigraphs from Sir Francis Chichester and Gordon.

[WHY IS HENRY CALLED "MR BONES"?]

There's a minstrel show thing of Mr Bones and the interlocutor. There's a wonderful remark, which I meant to use as an epigraph, but I never got around to it. "We were all end-men" Plotz—that's what it says—"We were all end-men".

[WHO SAID THAT?]

One of the great minstrels. Isn't that adorable? "We were all end-men, and interlocutors". I wanted someone for Henry to talk to, so I took up another minstrel, the interlocutor, and made him a friend of my friend, Henry. He is never named; I know his name, but the critics haven't caught on yet. Sooner or later some assistant professor will become an associate professor by learning the name of Henry's friend.

[WHAT ABOUT THE INFLUENCE OF BLUES AND MINSTREL SHOWS ON THE DREAM SONGS?]

Heavy. I have been interested in the language of the blues and Negro dialects all my life, always been. Especially Bessie. I picked all of it up from records, although while I was at Columbia the Apollo on 125th Street used to have blues singers. It was a completely coony house, and I used to go there sometimes; but mostly from records. For example, I never heard Bessie herself—she died.

[YOU LISTENED PRIMARILY TO BESSIE SMITH. WHO ELSE?]

Victoria Spivey and Teddy Grace. (Sings.)

> He went away and never said goodbye.
> I could read his letters but I sure can't read his mind.
> I thought he's lovin me but he was leavin all the time.
> Now I know that my true love was blind.

I found out that wasn't Victoria Spivey; it was Teddy Grace. As for others, oh, I could go down the line.

[WHY DID YOU CHOOSE TO EMPLOY THE NEGRO DIALECT IN THE DREAM SONGS.]

Well, that's a tough question. I'll tell you. I wrote a story once called "The Imaginary Jew". I was in Union Square in New York, waiting to see my girl, and I was taken for a Jew (I had a beard at the time). There was a tough Irishman who wanted to beat me up, and I got into the conversation, and I couldn't convince them that I wasn't a Jew. Well, the Negro business—the blackface—is related to that. That is, I feel extremely lucky to be white, let me put it that way, so that I don't have that problem. Friends of mine—Ralph Ellison, for example, in my opinion one of the best writers in the country—he has the problem. He's black, and he and Fanny, wherever they go, they are black.

[I'M TAKING CHAUCER FROM WHITING NOW—]

Is he still teaching? How splendid!

[HE WAS TALKING ABOUT CHAUCER'S USE OF DIALECT. TRYING TO GIVE AN EXAMPLE IN MODERN ENGLISH TO SHOW HOW DRASTIC THE MIXTURE OF DIALECTS WAS IN CHAUCER, HE SAID IT WAS

AS IF A POET WRITING TODAY WOULD HAVE A LINE ENDING IN THE WORD "WILE", SLIGHTLY ARCHAIC, AND RHYME IT WITH "HONEY-CHILE". I THOUGHT— WAIT, I KNOW SOMEONE WHO WOULD DO THAT.]

Well, it does attract me.

[WHEN YOU WERE GOING THROUGH ALL THE DREAM SONGS YOU'D WRITTEN, HOW MANY DID YOU DIS- CARD?]

I killed about fifty in Greece. I wrote about a hundred in Dublin, and I killed about fifty in Greece. I killed a lot of songs in Ireland, too.

[ABOUT YOUR OTHER LONG POEMS—DID YOU RE- VISE THE SONNETS EXTENSIVELY BETWEEN THE TIME WHEN THEY WERE WRITTEN AND WHEN THEY WERE FIRST PUBLISHED?]

No, I didn't. All I did was fix up identifiable symbols—namely, I didn't want *her* to be identified, so I changed the name of the place, and street names, and I changed her name. I'd used her name a lot, and it was very difficult, because sometimes there were rhymes. So I had to change her name into a name that would rhyme. That's about all I did.

[A QUESTION ABOUT THE SOURCES OF *MISTRESS BRADSTREET*. YOUR INTEREST IN AMERICAN HIS- TORY SEEMS RELATIVELY UNUSUAL FOR A CON- TEMPORARY AMERICAN POET. HAVE YOU ALWAYS BEEN PRE-OCCUPIED WTH EARLY AMERICAN FIG- URES?]

Well, yes—because my people have been here a long time. I have a great-great-grandmother who's Canadian, but otherwise all my people have been here since the Revolution—that's a long time. About the Bradstreet poem: I don't like her work, but I loved her—I sort of fell in love with her; and wrote about her, putting myself in it. It took me two years to get over the Brad- street poem (it took me five years to write it, and two to get over it) and I don't think I incorporated any of it into the *Dream Songs*—I don't think so.

[HAD YOU EVER THOUGHT THAT YOU WOULD WRITE A POEM THAT LONG BEFORE YOU GOT IN- TO IT?]

No, as a matter of fact, I didn't know, because I was very wrong about the Bradstreet poem—I thought I could do it in fifty lines, but when it worked out it came to 450.

[DO YOU FEEL THAT NARRATIVE IS BECOMING IN- CREASINGLY THE PROVINCE OF POETS?]

No, actually I don't—history teaches me that most of my col- leagues, my friends, poets, can't write narrative poems. They just can't do it—and some of them have tried. Lowell tried it in *Mills of the Kavanaughs*—and that's a bad failure. And other people have tried; and I remember one afternoon with William Carlos Williams—my wife was waiting and the taxi was waiting with Flossie, his wife, at the table, and Bill took me upstairs and said he was descended from Emily Dickinson— and I said that was wonderful, William, I didn't know that. And then he said

he was also descended from Shelley, and he opened a trunk and took out the documents to show me. Now, writing long poems is scary and very few people will be found who can do it.

[DO YOU FIND THAT, SINCE YOU'VE BEEN WRITING LONG POEMS FOR SUCH A LONG TIME, YOU DON'T FEEL LIKE WRITING SHORT ONES?]

I don't write short ones—no, I don't. You're right.

[EXCEPT WHEN AN OCCASION COMES UP, LIKE THE KENNEDY ASSASSINATION.]

Ah, that's a very special kind of poem. When Kennedy died I was living at the Chelsea in New York, at the hotel; I'm not much of a TV fan at all, but I got a set in immediately and they brought it in and for four days, like everybody else in the United States, I was watching TV, about all the murders and so forth, and I did write one poem about his death—it's called *Formal Elegy*—and one reviewer in the *Times Literary Supple- ment* said, "Mr. Berryman, whose recent poems are all an attack on organized poetry, has a new poem now, the title of which is deeply ironic. It is called *Formal Elegy*." The title isn't wrong, it's right.

[WHAT DO YOU SEE AS THE PRESENT RELATIONSHIP BETWEEN POLITICS AND POETRY IN TERMS OF YOUR OWN WORK?]

Oh, I don't think I can answer that question, but I'll try. Robert Bly makes a living out of the war, and I'm against this. He uses my name in different cities; and he finally rang me up once and asked me to read in a given city at a given time, and I told him to go fuck himself. And he said, "Do you mean you're not willing to read against the war?" And I said, "No," And he said, "Well, I'm appalled." And I said, "Well, be appalled!" and hung up.

I'm completely against the war—I hate everything about it. But I don't believe in works of art being used as examples. I would like to write political poems, but aside from *Formal Elegy,* I've never been moved to do so, because my favorites in the current campaign were McCarthy and Rockefeller; I would love to have had a chance to vote between either one of them, but they both got bombed and the shit was poured on them. The current candidates—the existing candidates, don't seem to me interesting—they seem to me extremely boring and troublesome and I wish they weren't there. I agree with you—I feel like laughing when I think of these candidates. Humphrey—My God—Humphrey who's repudiated every position that he ever took, you know. And Nixon, who has never held any position, is going to win, and be our next president; we're going to have to say "President Nixon."

[PLEASE!]

I'm sorry, John, that's what we're going to have to say now.

[A FORMAL QUESTION ABOUT THE UNIT IN THE *DREAM SONGS* OF THREE STANZAS—DID YOU HAVE ANY IDEA OF THIS PARTICULAR LENGTH FROM EARLIER POEMS, SPECIFICALLY "THE NERVOUS SONGS", WHICH HAVE A SIMILAR STRUCTURE?]

Yes, well, the stanza is complicated. It goes 5-5-3-5-5-3, 5-5-3-5-5-3, 5-5-3-5-5-3—that's the business— and it's variously rhymed, and often it has no rhyme at all, but it sounds as if it rhymed. That I got from Yeats—three six-line stanzas. His songs don't really resemble mine, but I did get that from him. It's rather like an extended, three-part sonnet. You know, the Italians have it much better than we—when I was writing sonnets, years ago, I was troubled by the fact that their sonnets were much better than ours because they could get more into it. They had eleven syllables per line, instead of ten. But you add it up, you see, and it comes to more. I made up the Bradstreet stanza in 1948—it's a splendid stanza, it breaks in 3-5, not 4-4—and my new poem has a completely different stanza; it's a seven-line stanza and it's about Mo-tzu—and I invented it in 1948 also—and since then I've been reading Chinese philosophy and art and history and so on. Let me see if I can remember the stanza—it goes like this:

> Sozzled, Mo-tzu, after a silence, vouchsafed
> a word alarming. "We must love them all."
> Affronted, the fathers jumped—
> "Yes," he went madly on, and waved in quest
> of his own dreadful subject. "O the fathers,"
> he cried, "must not be all."
> Whereat, upon consent we broke up for the day.

Isn't that beautiful? It's a poem about Heaven. It's called "Scholars at the Orchid Pavillion", a single poem—which I still feel I can do in about fifty lines, but it may work out to be a whole book.

[IS THIS, "SCHOLARS AT THE ORCHID PAVILLION", MAINLY WHAT YOUR'E WORKING ON NOW?]

No, I'm translating Sophocles, with a back-up by a classical scholar at the University of Cincinnati. I do the translation, and then I show it to him. It's in verse. But to mount on one of those sentences—it's scary, because you can see the period way down at the end of the third line, or the sixth line. You have to get up on top of that sentence and ride it down.

[WHICH DO YOU FIND HARDER, CHINESE OR GREEK?]

Chinese—much harder. Greek has an alphabet. Chinese doesn't have any alphabet—it's every goddamn *word*—you have to learn each individual word. It's scary.

[COULD YOU TALK ABOUT HOW—PHYSICALLY—YOU WRITE YOUR POEMS? DO YOU DO SEVERAL DRAFTS, START WITH A LINE, A PAGE, OR SEVERAL DRAFTS, JUST WRITE THEM OUT? WHAT IS THE PROCESS?]

Well, you feel uneasy, and you get going with a pencil or a pen and rhymes emerge, sentences emerge.

> Henry Hankovitch, con guitar,
> did a short Zen pray,
> on his tantami in a relaxed lotos
> fixin his mind on muffin, rose-blue breasts,
> and gave his parnel one French kiss.

You know what a parnel is? It's the mistress of a priest.

> enslaving himself he withdrew from his blue
>
> Florentine leather case an Egyptian black
> & flickt a zippo.
> Henry and Phoebe happy as cockroaches
> in the world-kitchen woofed, with all away.
> The international flame, like despair, rose
> or like the foolish Paks or Sudanese
>
> Henry Hankovitch, con guitar,
> did a praying mantis pray
> who even more obviously than the increasingly fanatical
>   Americans
> cannot govern themselves. Swedes don't exist.
> Scandinavians in general do not exist,
> take it from there.

Now what happened? Something began to boil around in my mind.

[WHEN YOU SAY YOU START OUT WITH AN UNEASINESS IN BEGINNING TO WRITE—DO YOU EVER WORRY ABOUT THE UNEASINESS THAT INSTIGATES THE SITTING DOWN TO WRITE GOING AWAY? IS THIS SOMETHING THAT YOU CAN TURN ON WHEN YOU WANT TO?]

No, you can't, no, it depends on accidents. I took my new wife to see Scollay Square several years ago . . . and Scollay Square was not Scollay Square—everything was removed—all the nightclubs, everything was gone—it was a goddam government project. But I took my wife there to see Scollay Square and later I was moved to write about it but I didn't feel friendly to the idea, so I did not write about it, so I have never written about it.

[YOU HAVE TWO POEMS, I THINK—AT LEAST TWO—ABOUT CHARLES WHITMAN ON THE TEXAS TOWER. WHY IS IT THAT THAT APPEALS TO YOU SO MUCH?]

Well, the guy had a complete armory with him, do you know that? It's unbelievable. And even *Time* magazine (which I hate and which I read every week, cover to cover; every Tuesday afternoon I have a big war with *Time* magazine) they did a cover story on him called "The Madman on the Tower", and that was very moving to me. Anyway, the word Whitman is very ambiguous in our time.

[DO YOU REVISE YOUR WORK AT ALL?]

Oh, heavily, very heavy. Mostly they're unrecognizable by the time I'm finished with them. Although many of them I don't revise at all.

[HOW DO YOU SEE YOUR ROLE AS A TEACHER IN RELATION TO YOUR POETRY?]

There's no connection. Teaching keeps my relations with my bank going. Otherwise they would be very stuffy with me. I teach my kids, heavy. I'm giving two courses. The University of Minnesota loves me dearly, so I only teach two courses, each one for an hour and a half. One course is in the American character, seem mostly from abroad. I use De Toqueville, and D. H. Lawrence and various other foreign characters, and then I zero in on *The Scarlet Letter* and *Moby-Dick* and so on. The other course is about the meaning of life, and I use the high religions—Christianity and Buddhism— and then I use other books.

[WHICH POETS LIVING AND WRITING NOW DO YOU PARTICULARLY ADMIRE?]

Well, I'm very keen on Auden, and very keen on Robert Lowell, and I'm very keen on Ezra Pound. I would think they were the three best poets working in our language. I couldn't choose between them or among them.

[HOW DID YOU VIEW GENERALLY THE STATE OF AMERICAN POETRY TODAY? ARE YOU ENCOURAGED BY THE QUALITY OF WORK BEING PRINTED?]

Oh, I don't know. It's all a matter of what any individual is doing.

[WHAT DO YOU THINK OF THE BEATS, GINSBERG ESPECIALLY?]

Ginsberg I like very much—I love him. He doesn't shake your hand, he comes and kisses you—and that's extreme. But I like him very good. I don't like his work very much, but in general he's an excellent operator.

[WHAT ABOUT WOMEN POETS?]

Well, among the women poets Miss Moore is obviously the best. But very close to her is Miss Bishop—very close.

[WHAT ABOUT LOUISE BOGAN?]

Oh, no—Louise Bogan I read out; she blows through a different realm of existence.

[HOW DO YOU FEEL BRITISH POETRY COMPARES WITH THAT OF AMERICA?]

Well, Edwin Muir is dead, and Auden is still alive. I regard him as a British, not an American poet . . . I'll tell you a story about Auden. He came over here and pretended to be an American for some years, and he was elected to the National Institute of Arts and Letters, which I'm a member of, too. They were having a fantastic conversation about uniforms—about whether or not they should have uniforms. And Auden got up and said, "We in England feel . . .", but then he suddenly remembered that it was the *American* Institute of Arts and Letters!

[WHAT DO YOU THINK OF BASIL BUNTING'S VERSE?]

My God—Basil Bunting? The only connection I can make here is from Yvor Winters. Yvor Winters once published a letter in *Hound and Horn,* saying, "Mr Bunting seems to offer me some kind of challenge. I will be happy to meet him at his own weapons—prose or verse; Marquess of Queensbury rules; my weight is 180." That's all I know about Basil Bunting. And I don't think he took up the challenge, either.

[YOU SAID YESTERDAY THAT TO BE A POET YOU HAD TO SACRIFICE EVERYTHING. CAN YOU AMPLIFY ON THAT, AND TELL WHY AND HOW YOU FIRST DECIDED TO MAKE THE SACRIFICE AND BE A POET?]

Well, being a poet is a funny kind of jazz. It doesn't get you anything. It doesn't get you any money, or not much, and it doesn't get you any prestige, or not much. It's just something you *do.*

[WHY?]

That's a tough question. I'll tell you a real answer. I'm taking your question seriously. This comes from Hamann, quoted by Kierkegaard. There are two voices, and the first voice says, "Write!" and the second voice says, "For whom?" I think that's marvellous; he doesn't question the imperative, you see that. And the first voice says, "For the dead whom thou didst love"; again the second voice doesn't question it; instead it says, "Will they read me?" And the first voice says, "Aye, for they return as posterity." Isn't that good?

John Berryman

THREE NEW DREAM SONGS

HENRY'S UNDER-STANDING

☞

He was reading late, at Richard's, down in Maine,
aged 32? Richard & Helen long in bed,
my good wife long in bed.
All I had to do was strip & get into my bed,
putting the marker in the book, & sleep,
& wake to a hot breakfast.

Off the coast was an island, P'tit Manaan,
the bluff from Richard's lawn was almost sheer.
A chill at four o'clock.
It only takes a few minutes to make a man.
A concentration upon now & here.
Suddenly, unlike Bach,

& horribly, unlike Bach, it occurred to me
that *one* night, instead of warm pajamas,
I'd take off all my clothes
& cross the damp cold lawn & down the bluff
into the terrible water & walk forever
under it out toward the island.

Henry's nocturnal habits were the terror of his women.
First it appears he snored, lying on his back.
Then he thrashed & tossed,
changing position like a task fleet. Then, inhuman,
he woke every hour or so — they couldn't keep track
of mobile Henry, lost

at 3 a.m., off for more drugs or a cigarette,
reading old mail, writing new letters, scribbling
excessive Songs;
back then to bed, to the old tune or get set
for a stercoraceous cough, without quibbling
death-like. His women's wrongs

they hoarded & forgave, mysterious, sweet;
but you'll admit it was no way to live
or even keep alive.
I won't mention the dreams I won't repeat
sweating & shaking: something's gotta give:
up for good at five.

HENRY
BY
NIGHT

Bizarre Apollo, half what Henry dreamed,
half real, wandered back on stage from the other wing
with its incredible circuitry.
All went well. The moon? What the moon seemed
to Henry in his basement: shadows gathering
around an archaic sea

with craters grand on the television screen,
as dead as Delphi treeless, tourist gone
& the god decidedly gone.
Selene slid by the Far-Shooter, mean
of plagues & arrows, whom the doom clampt on,
both embarrassed in the Christian dawn.

(That roar you hear as the rocket lifts is money, hurt.)

Which dawn has ended, and it is full day.
And the mountain of Mao flesh, did it once respond
'Let all moons bloom'? O no,
these events are for kids & selenographers, say,
a deep breath, creating no permanent bond
between the passive watchers & moonglow.

APOLLO
8

Go Away Richard Brautigan,
You're Not Helping College Poetry Any

Alkahest (numbers 2 and 3), Wesleyan University Press, 1968, 1969. .95.

TERMS All Beef: consisting of prime steer beef, as in a **good** steak.

        All Meat: consisting of any unspecified meat, including chicken meat, horse meat, cat meat, fat, internal organs, as in all-meat weiners, bad bologna, and luncheon loaf.

I. Beginning early in 1968, Wesleyan Press, which has coddled, fondled and taken great pains to discover and publish young American poets, began a bi-annual college poetry anthology entitled *Alkahest*. Since its inception, *Alkahest* has appeared three times, making available on a national scale a selection of previously unpublished undergraduate verse. It is not a publication you might easily pick up and read, since it has benefited from neither wide publicity nor acclaim. Yet despite the fact that it is an obscure periodical, plagued by unattractive student art work and a slim audience, *Alkahest* offers a fair representation of contemporary college poetry.

This last statement is not as empty as it might sound since, after reading countless student poetry manuscripts at two Ivy League schools, I feel on intimate terms with our peculiar idioms as well as our capacity to produce vast quantities of fatty, all meat verse. However, I do sense that my taste has been dulled rather than sharpened by the consumption of so much student work, making it difficult to judge it delicately. My palate's confused. If you eat a hundred all meat burgers, the next all BEEF burger you eat will taste like all the others.

II. Victimized by over-eating, then, and also the lack of a detached perspective, my critical obligation becomes one of characterizing rather than making specific judgements of college poetry. (Premature literary judgements have unquestionably, when written by critics of some influence, helped to banish potentially good writers from our body of literature while admitting others most would prefer to have never heard from at all. As always, it even seems that the particular dispositions of some editors tend to obscure solid verse while elevating fetishists and high shcool orators to prominence, a position in which they will embarrass us when they finally appear on the Tonight Show and write short pointless reviews of their friends' first books.)

Cooking Directions: *Place frozen Brussels Sprouts in a saucepan; add ½ cup water and ½ tp. salt. Bring to a boil, reduce heat and simmer covered, 8-10 minutes, or until Brussells Sprouts are just tender. Drain and Serve.*

If we have sprouts in ten, how long do you figure any of us is going to spend perfecting dactyls? It is no surprise we write poems in an hour, which many college students do. We may be incorrigible romantics in some ways, but our emotion is more often recollected frantically than in tranquillity, between classes more often than on long, contemplative walks.

When our parents, as children, struggled with quatrains, they must have been diligent, if not skillful, about it. Presumably the bygone era of courting and coy dialog in parlors with victrolas both engendered and perpetuated a more deliberate way of life. Cynicism was not in fashion. Our parents applauded a type of elegance we find ludicrous today. They may not have thought Joyce Kilmer's *Trees* was great, but I doubt if many thought it was bad.

Something has happened to us. Halfway through lectures, we start to squirm like infants in our seats, thinking of distant things. We are spoiled. We have the leisure that allows us to be discontented with the modrate competency too often mistaken for something better. In a few decades, we will become the moderate competents and our children, yearning for something better themselves, will tell us so. But I think we will believe them more than we are believed now; we will hold on less tenaciously to our own excellences, will finally agree to letting our children wear their crew cut while we bemoan the demise of long hair and everything America stands for.

But as it is now, we're impatient with ourselves and our poetry. We've grown impatient with the Richardsian textual analysis we absorbed in high school. Now that many of us have mastered it to a good degree, we believe we don't need it. We are determined, in part, to create poems which defy close examination. In poetry, as in many areas, we have begun to conspire against the snappy logic politicians are using to keep us in wars and administrators are using to keep us in schools.

As we bring our poetry closer to our lives, we understand that our poetry should then be no more comprehensible than our lives, which are a mystery to us. If our lives are fast, our poetry must be fast too. Flying from Chicago to Boston in one hour, twenty-six minutes, we hardly hope to spend more than half that amount of time writing a poem. Those of us who do spend more time often feel as if no one cares that we do.

Stop! If this is, in fact, one of the major reasons we spend less time perfecting our poems, I can't condone this state of affairs. The Problem is this: we *must* spend more time. It's a too well known fact that this age has quickened most facets of our lives and that this maddening acceleration has fueled facile critiques of society. The next step is often to say that good quality has become an impossibility and under the conditions we must expect and accept the cursory, the built-in obsolescence, the spontaneous. We must be satisfied with instant poetry; after all, Instant Quaker Oats tastes just as good as the regular stuff. But if, in fact, life in a velocitized world is one of the reasons we are often writing prolific rubbish, it becomes our duty not to capitulate, but to resist and begin to write more *careful* poetry, drive more slowly, and brush our teeth longer and more often.

III. My friend makes leather hand bags. He goes down to the dark leather district in Boston, by South Station. There, in a basement warehouse, Mr. Segal sells him hides which he takes back to his room. He designs his own bags which he hand-sews and then sells on the street. Hawking his bags with him a few weeks ago, I enticed a college coed. Eighteen dollars, I replied. Oh, that's too much, she said, I know where I can buy them for twelve. I know, I said, but those are machine-sewn and there are a thousand like in this city alone, all from the same factory. The reason this one costs eighteen dollars is that it's hand-sewn. It took many hours, not ten minutes, to manufacture. And its human imperfections make it unlike any other in the world. Oh, she said, thinking, it *is* quite nice, but eighteen dollars is half again the cost of these others; and walked away.

THE POETRY

IV. **We Envision The End**

Too often written in throes of depression or milder malaise, student poetry frequently becomes self-referential confession or at apocalypse. Influenced by the Confession's lyrical peaks, is a description of minor list tendency to assume the illnesses of the entire age, we are pron to throw up our hands at the slightest ontological difficulty:

They assemble, the sleepwalkers
at the edge of the world . . .
And the fall defies calendars,
an infinite floating.

The apocalypse can be a simple thing, too sadly final to admit analysis or even description, as in "Goodnight to Dylan Thomas":

The light began to dim.
You did not rage.
Sensible only at the end,
you left the Chelsea Hotel,
walked across the street;
died.

Never straying far from current issues, the end is even seen in faintly ecological terms:

he has nowhere
to go

huge dark owls
pass gracefully over his head
but the other animals,
soft and white,
have not been seen there
in years.

or suggestively:

death, I think
is like a thimble, she said
smiling
she wore a red dress
and we danced another waltz
she didn't know
that death is like a window

Yet, beneath all our private horrors, there is an echoing humor, almost flippancy. Unable to really understand war, we cannot always take our fear seriously. The draft lottery implies an untouchable fate so remote from Western logic, many of us don't realize what's at stake. Turning uneasily to our friends, we laugh. We are not Wilfred Owens; we are able to handle our end from a comfortable distance:

Luckily, then I hear that a few miles
from death there's a Cantonese
*   restaurant*
where we can have some barbecued pork
and talk.

* * *

"The end is at hand,"
I scream . . . reaching up, I grab here
where it counts and begin to believe it.

One of the most salient characteristics of student poetry is conversationality, our familiarity, at times almost irreverent, with the language. No subject matter is out of bounds. And we are not, as a rule, careful with our language, but nevertheless we insist on feeling close to it. In a short *Alka-*

hest poem which exemplifies the Brautiganese popular among students, the poet, like the comedian, sets himself up for his own punch line:

my daughter is gaining
more motor control —
today she pinned my
penis pronglike, with
thumb and forefinger,
like a frog down on
a dissecting table —
and relit that ancient
fire in my wife's eyes.

V. **We Write Short Poems**
If we deliberately eschew the technical concerns of poetry (although we are often well-versed in them), I get the impression many spend the gained time achieving a lyrical reticence. Of the ninety poems in the second and third issues of *Alkahest*, no less than half were under twelve lines. Inevitably, this practice leads to epigrammatic rather than expository or discursive poetry. Many college poets not only admire and enjoy Brautigan, but identify with him and his shot-gun lyrics. Note: Implicit in his poetry is the value-rejection that makes our politics beautiful but our poetry often negligent. A short poem in *Alkahest* which ends, "Good bye little old lady,/There will be no loud parties/In the rest home." derives its interest only from the irony of those last three lines and not from the poem as a whole. As the punch line is delivered, we discover that the preceding stanzas are there merely for the sake of the conclusion.

When I'm talking to someone
I'm really as quiet as a sleeping house;
I creak and the people sleeping in me
Wake and listen
And wait for the noise to stop.

* * *

The gifts have not arrived
and my ear hurts.
Let's forget ugly things.

* * *

Listen, Joey, you're ninety-seven years
*   old.*

In three years
*   you're going to be a hundred.*

Why do you feel like dancing,
*   like you're a kid of sixteen,*
*   with it all ahead of you?*

These three passages just quoted are all complete poems. We know better than any other generation how to make slight, even gratuitous poems attractive. We know a trick or two.

VI. We Use Falling Cadences

Many have perfected the dying fall, the subtle drop of the last stanza, the ironic understatement, the rhythm like a rock bounding down a mountain side, da-Da-da- Da-da-Da-da-DAH. Unfortunately, as a result, much of our poetry has become predictable in that we know that when the rock hits bottom, the poem is over. Few really have the time or energy to push, like Sisyphus, their poems uphill.

Our music is dying, dissonant, at its very best haunting, and that is good. But in the process we are forgetting how to say anything without being ironic, and that is bad. We don't have to suddenly turn to Edna St. Vincent Millay, but we should turn away now and then from our own verbal cuteness.

VII. We Prefer Studebakers to Mustangs

In general, we write with a high substantive level, that is, with a good degree of specificity and name-calling, an eye and ear for the justapositions of contraries, for poetic *tension*. An expression of our substantive concern is our search for interesting objects, the ambiguous objective correlative. In the ninety poems of the last two *Alkahests,* oboes appear twice. The more common objects like "corn flakes" and "orange sodas" show their faces, but *Alkahest* contributors also come up with "Va. Sweet Grille", "Cloemana City", "Rice Chex",

"Nylon bears", "saguara cactus" and "Engine 10-9-0". The sun is no longer a "red wafer" pasted in the sky. It rises like a "ping-pong ball".

If this brief catalog does little to characterize student poetry, it at least suggests some bad habits which, in turn, have created a couple of problems for us.

I think that many of us write under the heavy influence of intentionalism or author psychology which most critics agree is a Romantic phenomenon. Instead of calculating specific poetic responses from our readers, instead of depending upon the cognitive meaning of words, our writing process is much less measured. We have a strong conviction that the workings of our intricate psychesogies have rationales of their own and that the poetry we may produce spontaneously is justified by those often inscrutable rationales. Just as Wordsworth in his Preface insisted that "my description of such objects as strongly excite those feelings will be found to carry along with them a purpose," we would like to say that our short poems, written between classes, contain their own inherent purpose; that, far from being the gags they read like, they are the profound manifestations of our psyches even though we may not be able to tell what the psychological or intentional origins of the poem are. Perhaps, we deserve to have this faith. But I suspect many are using their faith in the organizational abilities of their psyches to avoid or-

ganizing the poem on a conscious level. We use our own *imprecision voulue* as a crutch. We commit what Allen Tate calls "failures of connotation." By employing in our poems effusions of connotative words, we, in Tate words, "yield a clutter of images that may be unified only if we forget the firm denotations of the terms."

VIII.

The introduction to the second *Alkahest* confesses: "I doubt if there are any Eliots published in these pages." The fact is that fewer and fewer of us do have it in them to become Eliots. Few of us have it in them to recognize an Eliot since we are looking for other things. Too often the carefully chosen word or assiduous poem goes by unnoticed. We admire the impeccable mind less and less, often preferring the witty Brautigans in poetry and the daring Laings in psychology. I am proud of this irreverence, if you can call it that. Our politics, our style, our minds and our wits are all sharpened by it. But, in poetry, it may do us in. I simply don't like to see so many "serious" writers fawning over Brautigan. He is very good, but he is very unhealthy. He encourages *poetic* failures. We must take more time to write our poems and eat our dinners. We have to be more careful. Some of us have been eating all meat burgers for so long, we don't know what's good for us.

— *Rich D. Rosen*

THANKSGIVING

"O body swayed to music, O brightening glance,
How can we know the dancer from the dance?"

W. B. Yeats

1

I stand in the lobby of Grant Central Station,
clutching a Harvard bookbag and *The Collected
Yeats*. This cavernous waiting room, the arching dome:
I long to drift through some Byzantine cathedral,
lingering by pale mosaics or gliding on
a tapestry.
                    Here the close benches beneath the
balcony kneel like pews. Through wide glass doors across
the marble floor, trains idle on the dripping tracks;
I decide on a seat between a nun reading
Valley of the Dolls and a rabbi, gingerly
hiding my bookbag under a trenchcoat. O Rome!
pensioners pray in Nedicks, we rise like a choir
from our worship of the *Times*. My train is late.

2

Uptown. Lovers breathe promises in vestibules.
I come out of a movie on West 76th
Street, looking like Joyce in my overcoat. Pale light
from Buddha lamps in a pawnshop window settles
in the hollows of my eyes. The wind billows my
sleeves out like long balloons, snow is disappearing
in the darkness.
                    Suddenly I want to be told
that the subways rushing beneath these streets would be
unknown to Pius, or to gleaners in the Pyrenees.

3

In my room at the Earle Hotel, I wake to a
rattle of milk-trucks edging cautiously through the
alley. Dawn, and below my window West Eighth Street
recedes into the distances of Manhattan.

Dreams vanish like stars above Long Island Sound. If
only I yearned for less than this, to disappear
in the wash of Sunday morning's brilliance, floating
out to sea in the dawn's sad tide, lost in shallows

somewhere beyond the Brooklyn Bridge. Brightening sky!
the sun settles like dust on these etiolated
walls. Hearing voices murmur across the hall, or
the woman who walks her goat in Washington Square

bleating for home: I tell you, there is nothing else!
Wagner on Sunday, branches pointing like wands toward
the clouds, and the heavy stillness of this hour:
I am Daedelus, this hotel my swaying tower.

LOUIS REED

Sweet Jane

Standing on the corner
suitcase in my hand
Jack is in his corset
Jane is in her vest
and me I'm in a rock 'n' roll band

riding in a Stutz Bear Cat, Jim
you know those were different times
all the poets studied rules of verse
and those ladies rolled their eyes

Sweet Jane
oh Sweet Jane
oh whoa, Sweet Jane

I'll tell you something
Jack he is a banker
and Jane she is a clerk
and both of them save their monies
and when they come home from work
ooohhh sittin' down by the fire
the radio does play
the classical music there, Jim
the *March of the Wooden Soldiers*
all you protest kids
you can hear Jack say

Sweet Jane
oh Sweet Jane
oh whoa, Sweet Jane

Some people they like to go out dancing
and other peoples they have to work
just watch me now
and there are even some evil mothers
they're going to tell you that everything is just dirt
you know that women never really faint
and that villains always blink their eyes
and that you know children are the only ones who blush
and that life is just to die
but anyone who had a heart
they wouldn't turn around and break it
and anyone who played a part
they wouldn't turn around and hate it

heavenly wine and roses
seemed to whisper to him
when she smiled

heavenly wine and roses
seemed to whisper to her
when he smiled

Sweet Jane
oh whoa, Sweet Jane
Sweet Jane Sweet Jane Sweet Jane
Sweet Jane Sweet Jane Sweet Jane

Pain

"I adore," she said, wicked as a whipperwill.
"Me too," me, rolling her over to approach her other side.
"I only enjoy it if it causes pain," I said. "It's nothing sexual."
"I never would have guessed," she said as it tightened,
loving the fright and fear of it, the it of it.
"I adore pain," she said in gulps biting her own hand,
and then they were off, two spacelike butterflies
split down the middle, reflecting the city in twos
the fact that he adored it too,
the fact that they both hated women.

FIREWING

Old Ez is dead. Say it
isn't so! Terrible Ez -- but he had heart.
Old Ez dead with Possum 'n the boys
who turned the heavy wheel of art
a turn or two: some noise

they made! Old Ez
he dead. Courageous and intolerant too
he was, and was he too long before the mast?
L'oiseau de feu est l'oiseau fou!
Say it isn't so. Action

stirred his mind: was there a sea
untillered by his fierce hand?
Heard in the rigging are many voices.
His feeling life
and the error of his choices

were and were not the wing of fire
which he knew survives
the voyage of our heroes,
their shipwreck and bitter sunrise.
Ez will bed Penelope tomorrow.

Old Ez is dead. Say it
isn't so! Say the waters never still:
say lives on to sing
& sail that which his red beard was
    the windward firewing.

Richard Dey

An Article of Faith

by Father James H. Flye

In 1905, on the Cumberland plateau in Middle Tennessee, two miles from Sewanee, some members of the Order of the Holy Cross, a monastic order of the Episcopal Church, started a little mission center, and for some young boys who were put under their care and a few others from the neighborhood, they provided teaching in school subjects and religion. From this developed Saint Andrew's School, which in a dozen years had come to have some seventy-five boarding boys and a few day students, with grades of instruction from primary up through High School.

It was a rural setting, a property of perhaps 200 acres, some wooded, some under cultivation as a farm; a few dwellings, the school buildings, and the small monastery or priory where members of the Order lived.

My connection with the place began in September, 1918, when I went there to teach in the school and be of assistance in some religious services and ministrations. My wife and I lived in a cottage on the school grounds. After the end of the school year, I stayed on there through the summer, as did some other persons of the staff and a few of the boys.

Mrs. Agee, whose home was in Knoxville, had friends at Saint Andrew's and in 1918, two years after the death of her husband, she with her two children had spent the summer there, living in one of the cottages. In 1919 they came

again, and it was thus that I came to know them. James (or Rufus, as he was then called, using his middle name which he came to dislike and later dropped entirely) was then in his tenth year, and Emma two years younger. And so began one of the most cherished and rewarding relationships of my life.

Many factors act as deterrents to rapport between individuals, but a difference of chronological age is not necessarily such, as Rufus and I soon discovered. Here was a friendly, intelligent boy, of active mind, fond of reading, with a good store of knowledge and eager for more. There was no lack of things for us to talk about. He was interested in fossils and shells, knowing many by their scientific names which he used fluently and naturally. Then there was the subject of possible pets, and we discussed monkeys, ponies, elephants, rabbits, pigeons, and kangaroos, with citations from pet books and books of Natural History. Then foreign countries, and Indian life, and Scout lore and woodscraft. He wanted a bow and arrows and we made a bow which he used some. Later he wanted a 22 rifle. It wasn't considered advisable to buy him one, but we borrowed one and did some target shooting. He wouldn't have thought of shooting at birds or rabbits or other living things.

But besides talk and doings such as just mentioned, there were real bonds between us in spirit, feelings and instincts. He was very tender-hearted, touched to quick sympathy and pity at the sight or thought of suffering, human or other, and incapable of willingly causing it. He had a keen sense of humor and comedy, but was never comfortable with teasing or banter. He was by nature affectionate and trustful, with many endearing traits, and I

FATHER JAMES HAROLD FLYE met James Agee when Agee's family first arrived at St. Andrew's School. Their friendship flourished through four decades and is acknowledged, in part, with the publication of the *Letters of James Agee to Father Flye*. This article represents his first attempt to record for a periodical the remembrances he touched on in the editions of the letters. He is 86 years old and lives in New York City.

felt deep tenderness and affection for him at this lovely age.

It may not be out of place here to include something told me years later by his mother of an incident in his childhood in Knoxville. "A friend of mine," she said, "was interested in a Settlement School out at the woolen mills. The women brought their children and they had to have people there in the nursery with them all day long while they worked in the mills. And she was taking Rufus in a little pony-cart or something. She had him with her to ride around to some of those places and she was telling him about those children. And Rufus said, 'Well, why do they have to stay in such a place? What are they there for?' She explained that they were very, very poor, which they were. And she said, 'You know, some of them don't even have shoes and stockings to wear.' And Rufus's eyes commenced to fill up and he was taking his shoes and stockings off then and there to give to whoever would need them. And that was like him, too. That continued to be like him, you know."

Some have felt James Agee saw in me something of a surrogate for his father, but I do not think this was the case. Our friendship and association and feeling toward each other were such, it seems to me, as we might equally well have had if his father had been living. As to the word "Father", by the way, used by James Agee, that was simply standard usage at Saint Andrew's in addressing or speaking of any priest.

With the passing of summer, I had assumed that Mrs. Agee would be returning to Knoxville, but she decided that as the cottage where they were living would still be had, she would stay on through the winter and have the children attend Saint Andrew's School*

I was glad that our association was not to be broken off, but could not help wondering how things would be with a boy like that in the regimen and surroundings to which he would have to adjust, with few of the boys of anything like his type or background. And he would undoubtedly be in trouble in the matter of some school rules and requirements; not by his intentionally breaking them, for he was not of defiant or uncooperative spirit, but because, though he meant well, he was absent-minded, forgetful of details, absorbed in what he was doing and not sufficiently conscious of time.

Life at Saint Andrew's School at that time was of rather plain and simple type. Most of the boys had very little money, and some really none. The charge for tuition and board was extremely low, and the school could not have carried on without the contributions sent in for its support. It was quite different from places modeled after the pattern of English schools. There was no system of rank and status within the student body, or between "old" and "new" boys, but general free choice of association and personal relations. Most of the boys were from rural or small-town background. The range in age was from a few very young boys to those in their upper 'teens, and three or four who after service in the first World War had come back to school for more education. The boys for the most part got on with

---

*This arrangement was made and continued for the next four years, with visits in vacations at the home of Mrs. Agee's parents. In late February, 1924, when her father was not well, she left Saint Andrew's and in 1924–25 Rufus attended High School in Knoxville.

THE HARVARD ADVOCATE

COMMEMORATIVE TO

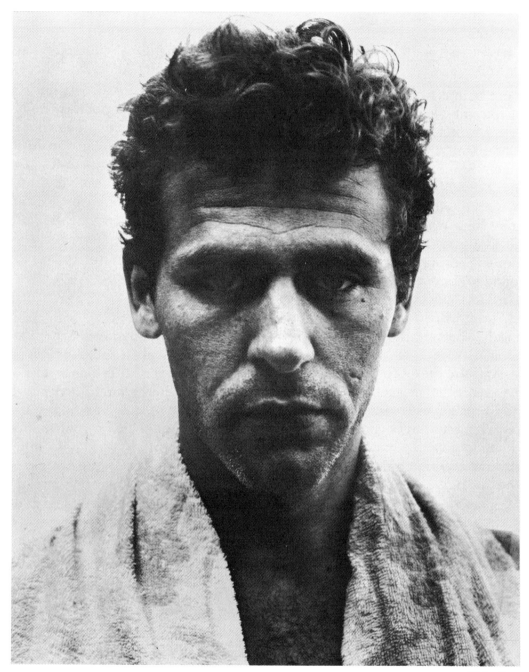

Walker Evans

James Agee

each other very well, and the general spirit was friendly and pleasant. The boys took care of their own living quarters (with regular inspections) and each had some assigned job (changed every two weeks)—cleaning, waiting on table, pantry duty or other inside or outside work about the place. As to scholastic aptitude and ability, the range was from boys who would never make any progress with "book learning" to those who would go to college and do well.

The religious commitment of Saint Andrew's was definite and strong. The head person there was the Prior, appointed by and responsible to the Father Superior of the Order of the Holy Cross at West Park, New York, who would from time to time come for a visit. At the time of which we are writing, the Prior was also Headmaster of the School, and he taught one or two classes. The members of the Order were not aloof but friendly men and held in warm regard.

The aim and hope of the Holy Cross Fathers at Saint Andrew's was to be of service in promoting Christian faith and practice in the form called Anglo-Catholic; a term designating the religious position of those in the Episcopal Church (or the Anglican Communion) who emphasize the organic historic continuity of the Church and the teachings, rites and practice which bear witness to this. Some other places then or later with that same religious alignment would be the Church of the Advent and the Church of St. John the Evangelist in Boston and the monastery of the Cowley Fathers in Cambridge.

In the School, attendance was required at daily chapel service and on Sundays at the Sung Mass and at Evensong; Grace was said at meals in the School Dining Room; and religious instruction was a required course in the curriculum. There was due observance of Lent, Holy Week, and other special seasons and days of the Christian Year, and Church boys

were encouraged to go to Confession and Holy Communion. Many of the boys were acolytes, and liked to take part thus in the Church services. And each year would see a number of boys from other backgrounds coming into the Church. It should be said here that what was emphasized in the religious teaching given at Saint Andrew's, whether in sermons or group instruction or personally, was not mere externals, though these had their place, but real Christian faith and devotion.

In this setting, then, James Agee spent the years of his school life from the age of ten to fourteen. For most of that time he had quarters in a dormitory, it being felt that this was better for him than living at home. Our friendship continued and developed, but not in any exclusive way. I was on very good terms with all the boys and we had many very pleasant associations; but with him there was a special fulness of understanding and communication. When he was eleven, just for fun, outside of school hours, I started him with French, in which he did well; and somewhat later, with another boy four years older who had had some French, we continued and read *Tartarin de Tarascon* which they greatly enjoyed. When he reached the Ninth Grade (High School) he was for the first time in one of my classes (English History), in which he was an excellent student.

After his return with his mother to Knoxville in the spring of 1923 I saw him occasionally; and in the summer of 1925 we spent two months in France and England, travelling mostly by bicycle. That Fall he entered Phillips Exeter Academy, and during the next several years we met very seldom, but kept such contact as we might by writing. From 1941 to 1954 I took parish duty each summer in New York and we would see each other often.

When he first began to think of creative writing, or make any attempts at it in prose or verse, is not certain, but this does not seem to have been while he was at Saint Andrew's. On our trip abroad he spoke sometimes of wishing he could write something about things we had seen, but such feeling and such writing are not unusual. After getting to Exeter, however, that Fall, his first letter to me spoke of his keen interest in writing and of his having written a story and two or three poems for publication in the *Monthly*.

A rich store of memories, impressions, and no doubt influences remained with James Agee from those years at Saint Andrew's: that Cumberland country of Middle Tennessee and its people; persons of all ages whom he had known —boys, teachers and others; and that school life in its various aspects and relations. I remember seeing pages of pencilled jottings by him—single words, phrases, idioms, proper names—recalling persons, places, incidents, or experiences, unintelligible except to himself or perhaps someone in whom these might also stir recall. He made use of memories of this sort in his writings, and would have liked to use more. The scene of *The Morning Watch* —the dormitory, the Maundy Thursday Watch in relays through the night before the Blessed Sacrament—is unmistakably Saint Andrew's, and the originals of probably all the characters in that story would be easily recognizable by anyone familiar with that place in the early 1920's. He had deeply perceptive understanding toward his fellow human beings in their individual lives and would have liked to write more about them, and also to write some form of autobiography. *A Death in the Family* (which though called fiction is largely factual) shows what could be done with one episode in a life narrative.

Mrs. Agee was a devout and faithful Church member of Anglo-Catholic convictions to whom the religious faith and practice at Saint Andrew's meant a great deal, and Rufus grew up well grounded in this teaching and practice

and familiar with the language of the Bible and Book of Common Prayer. He was an acolyte and used to serve often at the altar. In later years he felt unable to commit himself to full acceptance of some doctrinal statements of the Church, but he had not abjured religion or Christian faith. He had a humble sense of wonder and reverence before the mysteries of the universe, of existence, of life, of human lives—a religious sense. There were many things about which he felt simply that he did not know, but he was not of those who sit in the seat of the scornful. I remember his declaring his belief in "a divine or supernatural consciousness, power and love." As between the essentially religious and the non- or anti-religious, there is no doubt whatever in which category James Agee belongs. Read *Dedication* in the book of his poems.

He often had difficulties in regard to commitments, for he could not pledge himself to full support of or membership in an organization of any kind—political, social, economic, religious or other—some of whose principles or policies he could not accept. He knew very well, however, the problems and difficulties of anyone considering this matter and what he should do.

He was truly humble, very conscious of weakness, shortcomings and failures; a kind and loving person with great capacity for understanding and compassion. He will continue to speak through his writings, and to many there will be communicated thus the realization that here was one who had similar desires, hopes, uncertainties, moods and emotions to theirs, and would understand how they feel. For he did understand, and perhaps with the thought that through something he had been able to put into writing some might come to feel more deeply the bond of our common humanity.

AN UNPUBLISHED INTERVIEW [1953*]

conducted by Walter Kerr

Mr. Auden, you once contributed to a symposium called "Writers at Work."
I believe I did, yes.

At the same time I understand that you don't really regard the writing of poetry as work.

Well, it depends on what you mean by work. I think that writing can or ought to be pure work. On the one hand, you have things you must do; one must eat, one must sleep, one must drink. They are necessities. On the other hand, I suppose that one can say that one must do one's duty. Anything that comes between that is something you don't have to do, but you do because you like doing it, I would call play in that sense.

Play is anything that the body doesn't demand and that the moral conscience doesn't demand, I see, and poetry comes within this classification?

Yes, because people often ask you why you write poetry. What answer can one possibly give except that 'I do this for fun.' I sometimes quote people the nice story about Dr. Cushing the famous brain surgeon who, once was consulted by an intern as to whether the intern should take up in surgery. Cushing said, 'Well, I'll just ask you one question. Do you like the sensation of putting a knife into living flesh?' And the intern said, 'No, I don't believe I do.' Cushing said, 'Don't become a surgeon.' And that applies, I think, to all professions of that sort, of which writing poetry is one.

Suppose a writer came to you and said he wanted to be a poet, what question would you put to him?

I'd first of all find out whether he really loved language. It's a bad sign if somebody says, 'Oh, I have important things to say.' Poetry is one of the things to which a quotation from E. M. Forster applies, "How can I tell what I think until I see what I say?" And a person who starts by being too anxious — 'I have a message' — I suspect that they are not really talented for poetry.

In other words, there's a certain lack of love and a playful affection there.

Yes, for the medium. Just as Valery said, if a person's imagination is stimulated by arbitrary restrictions, rules like in a game, then he may be a poet. If his imagination is crest by those, then he might be something else, but he isn't a poet.

In other words, you think the restrictions are very good?

Oh, they're the whole fun of it. You couldn't play any kind of game without some kind of rules.

You think of them not as codes of law but as game rules?

Yes, because you're allowed to choose your rules, but once you've chosen them, you have to obey them. The enormous fun of poetry for me, as compared with prose, is that suddenly you're faced with a problem of, 'Now I've got to have a word here', what shall we say, 'three syllables long, with an accent on the second syllable, rhyming with another word, and meaning dry.' And all right I have 'waterless,' and suddenly, you find that you say something which you haven't thought of saying, and you wouldn't have thought of if it hadn't been for these kinds of restrictions.

In other words, the restrictions finally give you a certain freedom of choice. You must make a choice and that in itself is a freedom.

Yes, like all choices. You can't choose absolutely in a void.

And this freedom of choice has something to do with the concept of play, that you are enjoying this freedom within arbitrary limitations?

Yes, but they're not actually quite arbitrary because nobody, I think, can explain how it is for a given poem you feel that this particular kind of form is right. And there is a right form for it; you may spend days doing something that gets stuck. You cannot fit it right, it looks all wrong. You suddenly find, shall we say, 'Oh, these lines have to be two syllables shorter,' and the whole thing comes out.

But the poem has finally taken on its own accord. . . .

Yes, that's why when people ask you what a poem means, that you've written, I would suggest, 'Well, your guess is as good as mine,' because they are the words; they either make sense or they don't.

You set something in motion, perhaps even tyrannically in motion?

Yes, now there it is, and what I think it means has nothing to do with 'What does it mean?'

Well, now this concept of poetry as essentially play hasn't always been widely held. Poetry has been supposed to have other functions of much more, perhaps, useful kind or dictatorial or helpful kind in society.

Well, I think probably the origins of poetry lie in magic. I think that it was probably thought that if you arranged words in a certain way, they could make certain things happen. After all, you get old women peasants in the country who will, after they burn their finger, recite a charm like, 'There came two angels out of the north. One was fire, one was frost. Out of fire and in frost. In the name Father, Son, and Holy Ghost.' Presumably, originally they thought that if said these words would have some effect on their finger.

Then the words constitute a charm?

Yes, though I think very early, as soon as poetry really becomes recognizable as poetry, that the completely magical view disappears.

When you use the word magic, I'm assuming that you don't mean to confine it to simple folk charms but to extend it to larger pieces of poetry, perhaps didactic poetry?

You mean you're asking whether I disapprove of didactic poetry?

I was trying to avoid bringing up such moral judgments.

Well, I think it is a very interesting point actually because magic after all is what man tries to do, when applied to people. It is to make them think or act in a certain way without having to choose it.

You mean magic tries to impose itself on their wills?

Yes, so they aren't aware of making a choice. Now, there's obviously no reason why didactic poetry shouldn't exist where there's no doubt about the truth. For example, supposing one, in order to remember it, one says, 'Thirty days have September, April, June, and November.' Or it wouldn't matter in a thing, a matter really of indifference, such as what you buy. Supposing one were to have a rhyme advertising a certain kind of toy, why I assume the law protects me against a substance which is actually poisonous or that leaves me dirtier than I was before. But in every matter where choice is really important for the person to choose something, if it's important that they choose the right thing, then I think magic is deplorable.

In other words, you don't really approve of the effort to persuade?

No, because the medium really won't do it, and I think it's immoral too.

Well, what about the relationship of artifice and sincerity in life?

Well, sincerity always hits me something rather like sleep. I mean if you try to get it too hard, you won't; you will just repeat yourself. If you try to be sincere, you won't be, just as if you try to go to sleep, you won't. Now, just as people have bouts with sleeplessness for some time, people have bouts with sincerity. Well, when one can't sleep, maybe one should change one's diet. When one's writing doesn't seem to be genuine, perhaps one should change one's company.

I know that you once spoke as though animals and angels could be sincere, but that humans had to be actors first before they could become the thing they were acting.

Yes, because they're changing all the time. An animal remains what it is; it doesn't have a history apart from a biological history. It doesn't have a real history so that it can't help but be anything but sincere. Therefore, one couldn't really apply the word. But a human being who is always having to become something else from what he is now has to practice a bit. You cannot live without a certain amount of acting.

In other words, it is all right to adopt an artifice if in adopting the artifice, you hope to produce in yourself the actual quality. As a matter of fact, I think you wrote a poem that may have something to say about this.

Well, I think I know the one you're referring to. It's of course very one-sided because it is deliberately a polemical poem. The title came from Shakespeare's 'As You Like It,' where a character says, 'The truest poetry is the most feigning.'

Do you remember the poem?

I think so.

By all means sing of love but, if you do . . .

Like I said, this poem isn't to be taken too seriously. This poem is deliberately one-sided.

I wonder if this general notion of poetry as play and also the idea of truth coming from and through feigning, does that in any way explain in part the relative estrangement of the poet in our society?

There are, I think, particular problems about poetry as the medium which makes it difficult for people living in this particular technological age. It's an age in which poetry is a kind of ritual, and it's also rhythmical; it has repetition. Now I think repetition in people's minds now is so associated with the dullest parts of life, of routine, punching a time clock or road drills, that they don't see that anything that repeats, as poetry does, is then a little antipathetic.

Has this mechanization that you're talking about in any way depersonalized matters so that the poet's function is no longer so personal?

In one sense, I think you might put it the other way, that there is a reason for a poet living in a technological age. It is in fact that he can only write about personal matters. When one thinks in the past how much poetry there was written about topic events, and now it's almost impossible to do. The question interests me very much, worries me too. I think the reason is that in order to write about or celebrate a hero or heroine, one must combine virtue, excellence of some kind, with power. Now in a technological age, power is taken over by the machine, and however excellent a person might be, the power isn't theirs, it's in the machine. Supposing you think of St. George and the dragon. St. George plunges the spear into the dragon; it is really his act. Supposing St. George now gets into an airplane and drops a bomb from twenty thousand feet on the dragon. Though his intention is the same, and the result is the same, his action is stretching apart; it is not his personal act. And that makes an enormous amount of life simply not available, I think, to poetry.

It no longer seems a heroic act?

It does no longer have this personal relation to it. For example, Yeats was able to write great poetry about the Irish Civil War. It was on a very small scale; the participants were his personal friends. It took place in a place he had known from childhood. So all right, he's personally related to that. If somebody were to try to write about the second world war, it's on too vast a scale, there's really nothing you can do with it.

It is difficult for the individual man to see himself as heroic?

Well, he can only see his part in it; he can't really make sense of the whole thing. The only thing to do for a modern war is straight reporting, factual reporting, candid camera publicity. The only person who could write a poem about it would be God.

Well, there is also, it seems to me, and I think from what I have read of your work, it seems to you, a pressure on the poet nowadays, a pressure that comes from the fact that he cannot see a future, not the future, but a future at the present time. Does that bother him?

Yes, I think one of the difficulties for any artist now in any art is that it's not a question of one's own personal insecurity, which can often be a great stimulus, after all, people thought dead are thought to produce wonderful poetry. But in the past, people had a reasonable feeling that when they were writing, that the kind of world that exists fifty or a hundred years after them would be more or less the same world. Now we have no guarantees that it will be; in fact, we are pretty sure it won't, and that makes it, I think, very difficult to resist the kind of pressure to have an immediate success, you know to improvise. . . .

You mean poets no longer think of themselves as being a continuing tradition?

Well, it needs an awful lot of work to think about it. In one sense, we're also in a different position in regard to tradition and the past world because in the past, tradition and keeping tradition meant you made a very slight alteration in the immediate tradition at best. Now every poet has the whole of the past available to him, and he can choose from this. Absolutely everything in a technological civilization one knows; it's no good pretending what it might be about or what is isn't. The pressure therefore, the passion becomes all the stronger.

You've mentioned three or four different problems besetting the contemporary poet, how does the poet manage considering the problems he's faced with? How does he live nowadays?

I doubt very few poets, indeed, are able to make a living directly out of their income from poetry, but, of course, you get jobs of various kinds through it. It has certain advantages; you know when you start that you're not going to live by it until you make your arrangements accordingly.

Most of them I imagine go into teaching.

A lot of them do. It has advantages and disadvantages. There's been a lot of talk and discussion about the role of colleges as patrons of the arts, and I must say that they have done a wonderful job in this. It can be dangerous. When it is, I think it is largely the poet's fault. Ideally, of course, he should be able to do nothing but write an epithalamium for a marriage of a faculty member or a, what should we say, an elegy on the death of a trustee. But presumably, we cannot see that utopia. The danger is, I think, when a poet takes a job in a college, and either talks about his contempt for it or tries to teach 'creative' writing because that, I think, is much too near what he is doing, and it's apt to make him much too self conscious.

I see you mean he's engaged in cerebration, in formalized thinking?

Yes, and there comes a point in saying, 'Well, this is the right way of writing.' It is a kind of conformacy; he's bound in. It's awfully important that writers aren't afraid to write badly. You must hope that you don't. The moment you're really afraid of writing badly comes to you, then you'll never write anything any good.

The poet musn't be listening then to his own classroom strictures as he is at work; he must be a little freer than that. Apart from the immediate poetic problems that are entirely peculiar to our own age, is there any larger problem that remains to be solved at the present time for the poet?

Well, there's a problem which in one sense is insoluble and affects the whole of poetry really written in the last, two thousand years, that's in the post classical period, which is what I would call the development of a sense of history. Let's say that life of our person counts something. When Keats quite rightly made the Graecian ode say, 'Beauty is truth, truth beauty,' for the Greeks it was. Neither for Keats nor for us is that the case; there's a distinction between these things. There's a problem always of reconciling the poetry which, by nature, deals with being, with trying to represent becoming.

You're saying now that the Greek poetry or classical poetry generally was concerned primarily with representing being.

Yes, that's how they thought. There, perhaps, was something which didn't change. If you were a hero, you were a hero. If you're a churl, you're a churl. You do not change from one thing into another.

If you're a tragic hero, you're pinned to a set of circumstances.

Yes, so that Greek tragedy is always really a tragedy of situation rather than a tragedy of temptation. Take the difference between Oedipus and Macbeth. There's nothing Oedipus can do once the play starts, everything has been done. There's no point at which you can say he should have done something else; he could not have done it. At every step you watch Macbeth, you can sort of say, 'Now don't do that, do that.'

So that Macbeth is becoming what he is at the end of the play?

Yes, at the beginning you see a brave warrior; at the end, he's this sort of fear-crazed, guilt-ridden creature of the 'Tomorrow, tomorrow, tomorrow' soliloquy.

And you think that this is the result of the development of the historical sense?

Of a personal history, yes, which means artistically it is very difficult because becoming can only be represented in a series of stages, and it's arbitrary how many you show while real becoming as we know is a continuous thing. I think it makes it more interesting to be a poet but more difficult. The best definition of a poet I know I think is Thoreau's. He said, 'A poet is somebody who having nothing to do, finds something to do.' And the best description I think I know of the artistic process is the wonderful passage in Virginia Woolf in *The Waves,* 'There is a square; there is an oblong. The players take the square and place it upon the oblong. They place it very accurately; they make it a perfect dwelling-place. Very little is left outside. The structure is now visible; what is inchoate is here stated; we are not so various or so mean, we have made oblongs and stood them upon squares. This is our triumph; this is our consolation.' I think it's the best description of art I ever heard.

Rhoda Leichter

Hooks and Eyes for a Bibliophile's Breeches
An Essay on Book-Collecting
Peter Theroux

On what was surely an occasion of note, three hundred years ago in Salonika, Sabbatai Zevi (1626-1676), religious zealot and messianic pretender, actually married a book. Though I myself have kept shy of matrimony with even the most beloved of my books, I will confess, here, a perhaps unnaturally deep love for them—and go on to hope that there is enough bell-metal in my pen to convey the vehemence of a bibliomaniacal passion, to which such extravagances are not altogether alien. The book-collector, you see, is as much voluptuary as scholar, and sees a book's value in terms of both the excellence of the writing, and that second story which every volume has to tell: where and how it was made, of what, by whom—this together with particular details pertaining to its rarity and its physical make-up, which signify in importance second only to the intellectual joys the book conveys.

I am a book-collector, a proud avocationist in what Eric Quayle (wrongly) asserts to be the "least vicious" of hobbies (we are quite savage). We collectors are puzzled and often piqued unpleasantly by the common, absurd notion whereby we are only a pack of myopic, semi-crazed old pedants fretting over a book's colophon, dull dogs full of humorless zeal and no conversation, who suck our fingers free of pounce. I can speak only for myself, I realize, since the diversity of bibliophiles is matched only by the wide multiplicity of the things they love and collect. The collection's the thing, though: the collector is merely the pale Usher, dusting his lexicons, and imports, for the nonce, little: let's to books. What defines an item for my shelves?

Neither age only, nor even beauty, nor a work's merit by itself make a "find". All together, they do. Beauty, frankly, means the least: strictly applied, the aesthetic standards set for books by de Worde or Grolier, Viscount d'Aguisy, would wipe out whole shelves in even the finest of libraries. The aesthete in one must make room for the scholar: gilt spines, silk endpapers, elaborate watermarks and painted fore-edges are all very well, but the collector's eye, schooled in rarities, skims past imposing calfskin encyclopediae, to settle on, say, a plain first-edition of *Some People* (witty and rare), which might be autographed—such is the collector's fund of hope—or a rare illustrated copy of *Foutue a l'Hollandaise* by Mme. Sokolova Kneginja (Zagreb, 1899). No nook is too dark, no aisle too strait, no shelf too high, no crouch too painful to prevent the devoted bibliophile from prevailing at last, triumphantly clasping a dusty *Anatomy of Melancholy* (water-stained, crudely rejointed, but—ah!—complete), which would have gone undiscovered had he been a whit less conscientious or a shade less passionate than he was.

Tell the book-collector of some uncharted bookshop off in a distant borough—hint that you saw heavy old cartons in the basement—and watch him bolt his breakfast, take up his bookbag, and go spatterdashing out into the rain to begin his search. For what? For books! For the rare old riches nestling alongside the lowest tripe, concealed, captive, misshelved and mispriced by the clumsy, thankfully illiterate old panders who usually run book-shops, whose crude, mercantile dealings with great books make their trade little more than some species of white slavery. Understand his excitement; after all, this could be the day he finally comes upon the rare *Whimzies* (1631). Or *Venus in the Cloyster*; or Solyman Brown's *Dentologia: A Poem on the Diseases of the Teeth, in five Cantos.* Who knows?

My own collection reflects my tastes well since I do not extend the "investment" aspect of collecting to the point where I would clutter my shelves with valuable but unwanted purchases; more on that later. One's focus reveals; my weaknesses are immediately apparent: two full shelves of Vladimir Nabokov (his complete works in English, all first editions, including *Lolita* in the very rare two-volume Olympia Press edition, 1955); most of the thirty-seven books of Edward Gorey, all of them autographed; four volumes of Baron Corvo which cost me in eyestrain and inconvenience what I luckily saved in dollars; Byron's works in the first 1826 edition (eight little duodecimo volumes); *Joyce and Aquinas* by W. Noone S.J., signed by the Jesuit himself; a first edition of Trollope's *Autobiography* (for which a Charing Cross Rd. bookseller charged me "arf a craown"); and—here—let me show you an early copy, in red half-morocco, with marbled boards and endpapers, of Huysman's *l'Oblat*.

And then there are my treasures, most of them gifts; the Limited Editions Club *Ulysses* (#883 of 1500 copies, illustrated and signed by Henri Matisse); Homer's *Odyssey* done into English by Butcher and Lang (first edition, 1879); an elegant brown-and-gilt copy of the first translation of *Anna Karenina* (in which the "foreign term" *vodka* is glossed as "brandy"). Here is a two-volume Rabelais, Paris, 1659, pridefully placed beside the three-volume boxed Urquhart and Motteux translation (London, 1926). Permit me to add, here, that a good collection (*vide* mine) is a monument not only to good taste and sound intellect, but to acute financial sense. There are prizes to be had outside of Sotheby's, certainly, and "finds" that are not Caxtons are tucked away in dim corners of nearly every bookstore you see; what's wanting is the eye of a gyrfalcon, the purse of a Shylock, the thoroughness of Pliny, the patience of St. Monica, and a nose as formidable and aristocratic as Cyrano de Bergerac's, for booksmelling is, of course, a form of drug addiction; and if this amalgam seems improbable, I call my collection to witness that it is not. I invite you to my study. I own an eighteenth-centure miscellany full of such bawdiness as *The Gardenhouse Intrigue, Cupid's Bee Hive,* and *Pancharis, Quean of Love, or Woman Unveil'd*; had I passed it by as a mere curiosity and poked it back into its place, I would have missed Pope's *Essay on Criticism* (Sixth Edition, 1719) and his *Ode on St. Cecilia's Day* (Third

Edition, 1719), and Joseph Addison's poem of the same title (First Edition, 1699), all of which were bound into the same volume. The same volume! I delight in the arduous chase and the easy kill. I love to scour the terrain. My eye condescends to every low crooked shelf, to every listing stack tied with twine, to every dented box, for what might be concealed there. You've read about the violet by the mossy stone? As have I, as have I. Each bookstore has its dungeon, each dungeon its fettered princes awaiting liberation.

I must check my rhapsody, I know, but let me show you a few more. Here is a first edition of *Tess of the d'Urbervilles*, there *Hadrian the Seventh.* Here are Fitzgerald's translations of the *Iliad* and the *Odyssey,* sought out and kindly autographed. Come closer. This copy of *Go Down, Moses,* has the signature "Wm. Faulkner" on the half-title page, and has a long history as a gift: recipient to spouse, spouse to friend, friend to brother—me. (I ignore the "Idaho U. Library Discard" stamp in the back.) Lastly, here is a huge and indestructible leather volume of Shakespeare's *Works,* fast by the Yale facsimile of the first Folio. No, wait, let me show you this little copy of Scott's *Lady of the Lake,* bound in actual Birnam wood, and I have done.

I do not subscribe to that ruinous dictum whereby only first-editions, incunabula, and signed copies are worth having; in fact, new books are often welcome into my little bibliocracy. The Heritage Press, the Folio Society, the Libited Editions Club, Godine Inc., and the Fantod Press all produce books worth collecting. But I am sparfling my lore with dubious wisdom; my chatter might undo me. I cannot help but see each reader as a rival, each peruser of this very essay as a dangerous enemy who, now entrusted with some bibliophile secrets, might shamble in a bookstore three steps ahead of me and pick up a "find" before I can get to it—look over its valuable points with a look of cretinous stupefaction—pay up and carry it off, leaving me paper-pale, twitching with horror, my week ruined.

Yet I bibliobsessively seek quarities. The clack of a bell announces my entry into a small bookstore; the old proprietor and I exchange polite smiles, and I stroll down a snuff-colored aisle, sampling to my right and to my left. My heart quops: is that a Confederate book, printed on wallpaper? I sigh: it is not. Ever hunting bargains, you see, I yet always cherish hopes of finding a treasure. What will this heap reveal—Mathelia's rare *Nothing,* perhaps, or the yet rarer *! ! !* by George Heyworth? Will this be the day, I ask myself, that I find a book printed on *pâpier de guimauve* (edible paper) or bound in shahtoosh, the finest of all cloths? I hear the bookseller several feet away, coughing and rattling his newspaper (booksellers never read books, you'll note) and cannot help but wonder, will he be the man to sell me a book bound in human skin (technically, "cutis bound"—an oyster-gray binding, this, with the nap of chicken derma)? My foot is asleep. Perhaps that book, over behind *this* book, is that wonderful edition of Homer I once heard about, printed on rubber to read in the bath. I disregard the cramps in my legs to reach up for that book, there— could this be, finally, Francis Glass's *Washington Vita,* a Latin biography of our first president? No, sadly. The thought of finding a book with Mary Wordsworth's bookplate and bound, for such was

her custom, in the fabric of an old dress, is never completely out of my head. Are there any zipper bibles left? They were an American invention (1933). When will I stumble on a book written in Wolof, Micmac, Zmudz, or R'lyeh? When indeed? I leave the store with a complete edition of Florio's Montaigne: good. There have been richer days and poorer. I have more anecdotes.

Once in West Barnstable, Massachusetts, an unprosperous *bouquiniste* sold me a first edition of Borges' *Labyrinths* (a minor rarity and first-rate book) for $1.50—then gracefully reduced the price to a dollar, since I was buying three books. The good angel Common Decency hissed in my ear. I ignored her. The least vicious of hobbies?? Similarly, I once bought a book illustrated and signed by Fritz Eichenberg, paying only half-price for it because of what the cashier mistakenly thought was the previous owner's indelible signature. Not a word of correction parted my lips: the least vicious of hobbies, indeed. Inside every book-collector beats the heart of a Guiccardini.

A frequent fly in the ointment: that much-desired book in the window, set at a slightly inflated price, and the ensuing pain of indecision, whereby hangs many a tale. It can be difficult. It can be dicey. I am a veteran of the dead-end search, of the empty bookbag, of the primrose path that proved to be a cul-de-sac; but it is the odd failure, the tragic overspending, and the buy, mediocre in retrospect, that give my rare bargins their true bouquet. Shall I tell you about the time I *didn't* buy Tolstoy's scarce pamphlet *Tolstoy on Shakespeare,* and nearly died from depression that night? Luckily it was still there the next day, and now it is on my shelf. We persevere mightily; every book-collector, whatever the enormity of his setbacks, belongs to the pick-up-and-bloody-well-carry-on school of thought.

Let me now treat of my small crucifixions: those damaged, stained, torn or wormed-through books. I am no mean hand at restoring them if need be. I have spent patient hours de-foxing pages (cleansing them of those freckley brown spots that disfigure their pages), repairing leather (common vaseline is the best thing for this), toiling over soiled prelims and embrowned endpapers with infinite care, with an eye toward the worth and the readability of the finished book. I do not, as some do, regard restoration as the chiefest joy of bibliophilia, but I often get deeply involved in surgery on the day's purchase and hunch over amongst gluepots, tissue strips, erasewheels, and plates of water, painstakingly doctoring the boards of an old leather tome and perhaps guiltily thinking of the next day's French exam or a paper due in three days—resolving, more than likely, to keep working and to leave the conjugations until breakfast, and to sacrifice a movie in the interests of the paper—but specifically in the interests of the bookish labor in front of me just then. A restoring job within the scope of my powers never fails to produce a rapturous warmth as I place it in my one-book-richer library, but of course there are quite hopeless cases: shaved catchwords (a page's first word printed at the bottom right of the preceding page), crooked joints, scars, haphazard backing and those criminal cases of mere idiot abuse—in any of which cases there is no alternative to packing it off, in a jiffy-bag, to a relatively inexpensive restorer in Portugal. It is clear, I think, that the purchase of a book is no affair of the moment.

To what end all this fuss? The creation of a body of great books, garnered enthusiastically from all over by a relentless sophiophile, and united by his love and concern. A perfect library is a democracy, providing equal room for Boswell and for *Flushed With Pride* (the definitive biography of T. Crapper, inventor of the chain-pull); the gorbellied brainchildren of Henry James and Charles Dickens are neighbors with Twain's *1601*, Strachey's facetiae, and Gorey's *Limerick*; the *Arabian Nights* is on excellent terms with Aquinas—in short, fully as democratic as the alphabet which sets Richardson and Rochester a scant four books apart, and from which only Shakespeare, Milton, and the two-volume Oxford English Dictionary—all on my desk—are exempt.

I take pleasure in shifting them about. I rearrange them, set them to rights, gladly find excuses to hold and compare them; for I am no packrat. I do not scamper off with armloads of precious books, only to latch them up in hair-trunks, there to molder and warp. My books are accessible, readable, and—every one of them—read. They render service. My Chaucer-lover's Chaucer is no bibliothecal dream, it is the well-built Robinson edition. My Huysmans set, once softbounds on fine paper, is now bound in red and stamped gold, each book, forever. In short, I pamper what is pamperable and expect the rest of my collection to bear with my reading.

What better place than here to set off myself and my fellow bibliophiles from the company of our would-be brother "collectors", e.g., the funless oil-magnate with his long gallery of Renoirs, the teenager with his bins of saved-up bottlecaps, and spinsters whose parlors are mere Disneylands of Wedgewood—idlers, these. Book-collecting is not an outlet for frustration, ennui, impotence, or random energies; it is not a bogus religion, it is not a desparate alternative to knitting socks or watching television. The bibliophile —antiquary, voluptuary, priest—has a calling; he is no soulmate of the matchbox-saver, the tycoon, the clutterphile, or the shrewd crunchfist who buys books with the cold eye of an auctioneer, whose books are merely a burden to him until they treble in value.

Choice means selection. Exclusion, then, is a condition of bibliophilia, for we true collectors distinguish ourselves as much by what we leave behind as by what we acquire. My private *index librorum prohibitorum* includes comic books, cookbooks, sexual banalia, uninteresting psalmodies, anatomical studies of animals, histories of costume, horticultural texts, and *any* books on mathematics, ever were they printed in the year ought. That shelf of old phrenologies? Keep it. These quaint volumes on naval customs? They're yours.

Books precede and outlast us. They are cemeteries of the living. The solemn buckram sepulchers contain the wildest of life, and the carousing corpses within—begot by an author, realized by a printer, first freed by a paperknife—now wait only for sight to fall on their pages for them to rise up and live—little resurrections performed for every new reader. *Every* book has its Finnegans. Every collector who has stood gazing paternally on his silent brood of old books before going to bed, is conscious of this cheery fact, that a book is, paradoxically, our ancestor and our child—and sometimes our wife.

The nuptials of Zevi grow less and less foreign to my comprehension. While I was not there, regrettably, to give him my joyous congratulations on his splendid match, the day he took the Torah, the Scroll of Laro to himself, for better, for worse, for richer, for poorer, in sickness and in health, to be sundered by death alone, I yet, today, gratefully pen an appreciation of an obsession, his and mine, to shred up and sprinkle down the temporal and spatial void that separates us, confetti to grace the wedding whose heartiest well-wisher lived three centuries too late. ✦

Stripping the Wreck
Peter Harper Alson

Leonard Spungofsky's socks were stinking up the whole apartment. Leonard, himself, sat in the john with the door open and the feet that were attached to socks spread wide apart. It wasn't that I minded so much watching someone take a shit while I was in the kitchen cooking, but Leonard had once been my friend. He had dropped in one night about two weeks ago at three A.M. while I lay in bed drunk and sick after a party at which my girl made passes at three men none of whom were me and proclaimed me boldly to be one of the truly fine men around. Leonard who had once been my friend before he wracked up my '54 Mercury now proclaimed me boldly to be one of the finest men around. Oftentimes I am capable, in the face of such flattery, of rising to the occasion, and sick as I felt, this time was no exception. "Leonard Spungofsky," I said, "the last person I could hope to see. You fucking asshole." Leonard stood there in the center of my dark bedroom, a monastic cape draped ominously over his broad shoulders, and even as I began to lose consciousness the image of his spreading simple grin seemed to signify something to me akin to hammering lead nails into metal.

Indeed when I woke up Leonard was still there, his sprawled body announcing his intention to stay, like an unwanted and unreturnable gift.

"Leonard," I say, "do you think it is too much to ask that you close the door while I'm cooking?"

"Oh is it bothering you, man?"

"yes it is bothering me."

"Oh you see, when I was travelling cross country they told me that Berkeley was a cool place. Very liberal, you know, man?"

"Leonard, Berkeley is dead. It was never very liberal. And liberals don't, for Christsakes, take shits with the door open."

"I thought it was the cooking that was bothering you, man."

"No the cooking only added to it."

"Man don't you see it? I couldn't be talking to you now if the door was closed. I couldn't be seeing your side of things. We both might miss something important."

"Leonard I don't want to talk to you while you're taking a shit. I don't want to see your side of things. I think I could've missed everything you've said for the past two weeks and been perfectly happy." This last is an understatement. I've heard everything he's said for the last two weeks and been perfectly miserable. I look at Leonard and he is smiling and rolling a joint. The door is a gap between us that will remain there even when it is closed.

The sound of a key in the door. Bix Le Gendre my roommate wheels his tenspeed into the apartment. I slam the bathroom door shut in Leonard's face. My last glimpse of him through the quickly narrowing crack reveals a face that is stupid and right. The face of someone who murdered his family because there was no soap in the shower. A face that makes me cut off part of my finger while slicing an onion.

"Oh gosh Miller what did you do?" Bix asks me.

I look down at my bloody finger, and at the stew bubbling in the pot on the stove. I look at the door behind which lurks Leonard's face, and down at the picture of an orange lobster on the apron I am wearing. I look at Bix, my gay roommate fresh out of the closet, still beset by horrendous heterosexual habits and I laugh.

"What's wrong Miller? And what happened to your finger, it looks dreadful."

"Do you want to know in the greater sense Bix, or just for the past month?"

He smiles sympathetically. Bix is very pretty in a California way. Blonde hair and mustache and a lover who looks much the same. He isn't much of a fag yet and I suppose never will be. He's a lousy cook, a slovenly housekeeper, and a sleazy dresser. Bix is pretty bad at everything he does, and I'm sure if I was so inclined I could be a much better fag. When he smiles at me sympathetically like he is doing now, I know what he is thinking. He is thinking that I am a pain in the ass and that because I come from New York I think I am very witty. I know this because I read it in his diary. He intended for me to read it because he left it lying open on the coffee table for two days. This is what I mean about him not being good at anything he does. If he had wanted me to read it he could just as easily have left it

closed. I find out a lot more about people by the way they do things than by what they do. I found out that Leonard was an asshole because when he smashed up my Merc on the Cross Bronx Expressway instead of calling the cops he left it out there for the vultures. When I finally found out about it a day later it had been stripped clean. The only thing left was the body and one bent rim.

Leonard flushes the toilet and walks so quickly out of the john that, beyond leaving his hands unwashed, I wonder whether he has neglected to wipe his ass. Bix ix much more tolerant of him than I am, and they exchange hellos.

Leonard is still a hippie. He has long hair and unkempt beard and has rejected all of his parents values but the bad ones. We played poker last night head on head and he won twenty bucks. He thinks it is okay to freeload off people because he has read the Communist Manifesto. But after the poker game he demanded immediate renumeration.

"Look Leonard I'd really rather owe it to you. I have to buy some books tomorrow and don't want to go to the bank."

"Yeah I understand Miller. That's cool," he said. But ten minutes later he laid it on me. "Man, I really need the money. I'm going to try and score a lid later on. Why don't you go to the bank tomorrow if it isn't a hassle."

"It is a hassle."

"Hey look man. I won. Pay up."

"You're incredible, you know that," I said, but I gave him the money. When he stuffed it in his wallet I noticed that there was a green wad already taking up a lot of space. I don't know why I didn't kick Leonard out right then and there. But I am very irrational and I didn't want him to feel justified. I want to kick him out right after he has done something very nice so I can make him understand what a shit he has been.

Berkeley has made me eccentric like this. I wonder whether I am going crazy. I used to be from New York and think I was witty. Now I go and stand and stare out the window while Bix and Leonard continue to say hello to each other. The Berkeley hills sit solemn and green and unmoving in the fading light. Over the uppermost ridge there is a streak of red from the sun. I watch as it slowly shrinks up and disappears, and wonder if maybe the time hasn't come to leave Berkeley.

"But honey what about me? What about school?" It is Kam my ex-girlfriend trying to drum up some melodrama on the steps of Sproul Plaza.

"I'm only going for a little while. And I'm bringing some books," I say tapping my plaid travelling case on the side.

"Why are you going?" she asks. "Why are you going alone?"

"I'd ask you if it would do any good."

"I'd love to go with you. That would be supercool. It really would. But why don't you wait three days until the weekend?"

"I can't wait. I can't plan it. I've gotta go now. It'd be nice if you

Judith Baumel

could come along."

"Oh honey I'd love to go along. It sounds romantic. But I've got this paper due on Friday." She smiles. "You know how lousy I am at writing papers."

Suddenly I feel masochistic.

"I'll help you write it. You can hand it in late."

"You will!" she says. "Oh Miller, you're so nice. But it wouldn't be good to hand it in late, and besides we wouldn't have much fun if we had to write a paper."

I think about waiting three days until the weekend. It's been hard since Kam and I broke up. I would enjoy three days in the country with her. But then I see Bix sashaying across the plaza with his arm around Eugene, his lover.

"Well it's too bad you can't come," I say, "but I've really gotta go."

"Have a super time," she says. "I'll be thinking of you."

I'm half way across the campus before I put her out of my mind.

An old woman in hornrimmed glasses that essay desperately to divert the glance from benign brown eyes and a wart below the right eyebrow is asking me where I'm going. I am staring at her wart which is probably the reason I look so befuddled, but it is really the smell of exhaust that is fucking me up. The sounds of the San Francisco bus terminal are indistinguishable from any other station, and the truant kids ringing up scores on battered pinball machines, and the lowlife scattered like old newspapers on and under benches are on loan from Port Authority.

"Sonny, where did you say you were going?" the old woman asks me.

"What would you suggest?" I ask politely.

"I'm afraid I can't help you. It's against company policy to—"

"I'm not interested in the company policy. I want to know what you would suggest. In your own words."

"You better let me check with my supervisor . . . "

"I don't want her opinion I want yours."

"I'm sorry."

After her supervisor has been called and consulted, the old woman leans near the barred window confidentially, and says "Inverness" in a fluttering whisper that rushes off her tongue like bad news.

"Inverness? I thought that was in Scotland."

She shakes her head. Her wart quivers. The company has been served well. Inverness is the last stop on the line.

I buy a pack of Camels in the terminal newsstand, and I'm flipping through the latest *Playboy* when the proprietor asks me what I'm doing.

"Well I was just looking at this magazine."

"Well don't look at it."

"Whaddya mean?"

"Either buy it or put it down."

"Are you kidding?"

"You want to read go to a library."

"Hey, uh, look. How do I know if I want to buy it if I don't know what's in it?"

"You want tits you pay for 'em. Now get out before you soil up my magazines. You goddamned kids ruin my business."

"Look you asshole. I'll tell you who ruins your fucking business—"

"Leave," he yells. "Get out." His bald eagle head is alive with trembling veins. I cannot think of anything witty to say.

"You fuck," I mutter.

When I take my seat on the bus I am in that worn state in which every cigarette ad I have ever seen begins to finally take its toll, and I know that nothing can calm my nerves but a Camel. It has gotten to be like that. To conclude this macabre joke, the cigarettes are gone, and if I have left them at the newsstand I deserve to be the brunt of it.

While I am searching behind me in close-fisted fury a girl in tight jeans shoves her pack up on the overhead rack across from me. I thrust my head forward between my legs and scan the coke stained linoleum under the seat.

"Whatta ya doin?" the girl asks.

"I'm looking for my cigarettes," I say raising my head up to my knees.

"Ya want one of moin?"

"Maybe later," I say, "these kinda had a sentimental value to me."

"Owisee. That's cool." Her voice is Shirley Temple from the wrong side of the tracks. "Heah lemme help ya." Before I can say no, she's down on her knees beside me, her large rolly tits doing a seduction number on my sleeve. She's the kind of girl I once would have gone for in a big way. Dark pockmarked face and soft brown eyes on top of a terrific body.

"Is this one?" she asks excitedly, jabbing an old and battered cigarette at me.

I look at it appraisingly, sharing her excitement.

"Wrong brand."

"Oh," she frowns, bending over again.

The engine has revved. The lights flash on. Before I have a chance to brace myself the bus lurches forward. I am thrown heavily into the girl. She is soft, cushioning my force, but I can hear the wind push out of her stomach. She struggles to breathe, oohing and ahhing in pain.

"You just had the wind knocked out of you," I say, "you'll be okay." I help her back to her seat and sit down beside her. The people whose necks have been craned into the aisle pull back their heads like frightened turtles when I give them my fuck-you look.

"You're real nice," she says.

I shrug. "It was my fault."

"No but I can tell. You troid to gettouta the way."

This isn't true. When I saw I was going forward I tried to save myself. I didn't think about her. In fact the only time I have thought about her is now and she probably wouldn't say I'm so swell if she knew what I was thinking.

But that's okay because aside from idle ruminations I don't really care if I'm swell or not. Moral considerations are eaten like candy by other people, and come out like shit. For me they are not even worth a fart.

It turns out that we are both going, by some happy coincidence, to the same place. "Inverness is wonderful," she says. But when I ask her if she goes there often, she says she's never been. She talks so close to dese and dose that I'm afraid I'll insult her if I ask her where she's from. It's all academic because she tells me unprodded that she ran away from her home in Montclair, New Jersey about five years ago. She wanted to be a dancer and her parents were fucked and wouldn't let her.

But after five years she is the kind of dancer who gets catcalls from the audience and changes costume on stage. And though she rightly says that a stripper is an exotic variety of dancer, I wonder to myself what dancer has ever used a stage name like Shelley Allstar.

Shelly's main problem is that she is built like a stripper, not a dancer. She has fleshy knobs. To someone shortsighted that might not seem like much of a problem, but Shelley tries to achieve a sense of grace when what she should be doing is throwing her hips around more freely. She's probably a stately stripper, not proud, but misplaced. I imagine that therewith lies her attraction. She appeals to the dignity of the slovenly. Which might explain why, in a perverted sense, she appeals to me.

I on the other hand attract her because I respect her forthrightness, her country charm. She believes I have faith in her career. She likes the appreciation she assumes. She touches me whenever there is the slightest possibility that it will help to illustrate a point.

By the time the bus makes its first extended stop, she is already fairly familiar with my anatomy. And I am smoking her cigarettes. We go into the wooden shack depot and have a cup of coffee.

"It's nice," she says, "the way you get to meet people on trips. That's what I like about 'em."

"Unless you're trying to get away from people," I interject.

"Ohwiam. But new people'r different. I mean if you didn't meet anyone new then it would be harder to get away from the old people."

I nod appreciatively, impressed with her logic.

"You're making it a lot easier," she says.

I smile with complicity.

It turns out that Shelley has been bummed out by the city. Too many bumps and grinds in North Beach have made her unhappy. A friend of hers once told her that Inverness was enchanted and it seemed like this was the right time to find out. But when we get to the next prolonged stop the

J. Rhodes '63

weather has changed. The sky is grey and ugly.

"Shit." Shelley rubs her hands together.

"Yeah," I say, "it looks like rain."

"It isn't fair," she says, "they said the storm wasn't coming for another two whole days."

"I guess they were wrong. It looks like it's gonna be a chilly son of a bitch too." I stuff my hands in my pockets and hunch my shoulders to demonstrate. A cigarette hangs loosely between my lips. It gives my voice a street tough sound.

"Shit," Shelley says.

When we get to Inverness it is pouring. Though it is only three o'clock the sky is black and it is hard to distinguish enchantment. Shelley's spirits are as dark as the sky.

"What are we going to do?" she asks.

We bounce off the bus quickly onto the porch of Mel's general store, which serves as

the bus depot. The rain is pelting away at the roof, and because of the wind onto most of the porch as well. Only by standing against the house it is possible to stay dry. So there we are the only ones to make it as far as Inverness and our backs are against the wall.

"Where were you going to stay, Shelley?"

"Outside. I brought my sleeping bag. Where were *you* going to stay?"

I shake my head. "I don't know. I didn't plan. I just came."

"This storm is supposed to last for days."

"Look," I say, "let me go inside and ask old Mel a few questions."

When I come out, Shelley is still pressed up against the storefront.

"Mel says there's a motel a little ways up the road. If we want he'll drive us there."

"A motel?" Shelley asks.

Jesus Christ, I think, she's a stripper. She must know what a motel is. "We'd get separate rooms," I say.

She regards me practically.

"Wouldn't one be cheaper?"

Mel closes up the store and drives us to the Star motel.

I wake up the next morning to the sound of rain. The desk clerk described our "Starroom" as a quaint little bungalow which was ideal for short vacations, but probably not as desirable as "Constellations" or "Big Dipper". Quaint little bungalow translates roughly into small shack off dining room. It isn't that bad considering everything, but the roof leaks and the shower doesn't work. However, for five bucks a night it is a bargain. And it's private. Which is good because Shelley and I bent the walls last night.

She is asleep, her head bent under my arm. I search the barely noticeable scars on her face for some meaning, some clue as to why we are in this ratty little motel together. It is like asking where to go all over again.

"Shelley."

"Wha?" she rolls her head to one side and loses consciousness.

"Shelley?"

Her eyes open. She forces, with the pain of day, a smile. I smile back without pain.

"What?" she says.

"Nothing," I say, "go back to sleep."

"What was it?"

."Nothing. I just wanted to see if you were there." She nestles close, and is soon breathing in sleep.

After breakfast we sit over coffee. I am natty and unshaved. We are both unshowered. The air smells like Yankee Stadium on a hot night.

"Are you gonna strip for the rest of your life?"

"Whaddaya mean?" she looks indignant. "I'm gonna be a dancer."

"When?"

"When I make enough money to take more lessons. When I get better."

"When's that gonna be?"

"Hey leamee alone. I thought you were nice." She pouts.

"I am nice," I say, uncomfortable with it, "but nice is bullshit. If we're going to bullshit, we can do it easily enough. Everyone else out here does. People are nice, the weather is nice, living is nice. Everything is fucking nice. So how come we're both wandering around taking buses?"

She is silent. Her fingers fiddle with the bowl of sugar packets. Her eyes follow her fingers.

"So do you want to be nice to each other, or what?"

"I wanna be a dancer."

"Okay. You be a dancer, and I'll be an asshole. And we'll both be happy."

"I won't," she says.

"Why not?"

"I want you to be nice."

"All right," I say, "I'll be nice. A nice asshole."

The rain continues and the walls still bend. Two days later we decide to leave. Shelley has to work and though she could call in sick there is really no reason to. We part at the San Francisco terminal where anonymous faces attend our kiss. Shelley walks out into the grey. The rain coming down is long and thin, like strings of slate. She turns around once and waves, disappearing into the fog.

The apartment has an illegal reek. Leonard is blissfully straddling a chair with his eyes closed. On his feet are a new pair of socks. Leonard never wears shoes. Never

even considers it. When he goes outside he takes his socks off.

"Hey man, how's the flow?" his eyes are still closed.

"Cut the crap Leonard. It's me."

"Miller! My buddy. Howya doin? I thought you were Bix."

"Nowam not Bix," I say in a high, mincing voice.

Leonard doesn't pick up on it. I can never tell when he is stoned, but he picks up on things even less than when he is straight.

"Ya wanna smoke a little?" he asks. "I copped that lid."

"Sure," I say, "after all I paid for the stuff." Also it will make it easier for me to do what I am going to do. I will be in Leonard's medium.

"Listen Leonard," I say, after we have put away a couple of joints, "you're gonna have to be packin."

"What's the rush?" he says lightly, "I just got here."

"No Leonard I just got here."

"Hey we're buddies."

"Leonard you gotta leave."

"Aw man, don't be a downer."

I am not ready for this. I thought I would be ready, but nothing has changed.

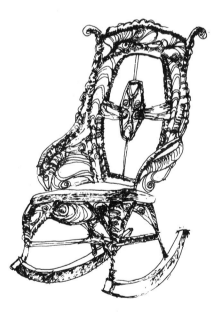

Rebecca Zurrier

"Miller man, you don't really want me to leave. I mean what's down there for me, the street, you know. The fucking street."

"That's tragic Leonard. You make it sound like this is a goddam ghetto."

"It is. A bunch of slum lords beating on the students. You're getting ripped off, man. On these rents. The University probably gets kickbacks from the guys who own this place. I'm helping you beat the system."

"The way I see it, the only system you're beating is mine."

"That's deep, man. That's really deep."

"Jesus God!" I am getting a labyrinthian dope headache, so I go into the kitchen and pull down a bottle of Wild Turkey I have been hiding behind a box of graham crackers.

"You see Leonard," I say, waving the bottle, "I'm part of the establishment."

Leonard is standing on his head, his back to the wall.

"I'm trying to maintain touch with my body," he explains. "This helps me concentrate." Suddenly Leonard loses touch and his body crashes to the floor. He sits up, smiling redly.

"I'll probably be moving out in a couple of days," he says. "I've been hanging around with this chick down by the Garden Spot. She wants me to move in with her."

I take a swig of Wild Turkey.

"That's great Leonard great. When can you move in?"

"Well I don't know. These things are tricky. I don't even know where she lives, man. But don't worry, next time I'm down by the Garden Spot I'll work it all out."

"Oh . . . Well that's great Leonard. Is she a nice girl?" The Garden Spot is a sleazy grocery store where the streetpeople and panhandlers hang out. I am being tactful.

"Not like the girls you know."

"Yeah," I say, "I suppose not." I lift the bottle to my lips. The fumes bristle up my nose. "Where did you get to know this girl, Leonard?"

"I tol' you over at the Garden Spot."

"Yeah, but where did you get to *know* her?"

Leonard starts spacing out. His eyes begin to reflect the roomlights. "Whaddaya mean, man?" he mutters.

"What I mean is where did you screw this girl?"

"Oh. I didn't know what you meant."

"Jesus Leonard. Are you trying to feed me a story. Cause I'm not a sucker you know. Notta sucker. Jesus. You said you didn't know where this girl lives. Whadja fuck her in the street?"

Leonard starts tapping his feet. He picks at a fever sore on his bluing lips.

"I fucked her here."

"Here?"

"Yeah while you were gone. I fucked her in your bed."

"My bed? No Miller. You're not hearing this. Leonard has driven you around the bend. You'll simply strip the sheets. Come here my Wild Turkey. My sin, my soul. You'll soothe me for now." The Wild Turkey disappears rapidly down my gullet. I am stoking the fire. Leonard is expanding. There are two Leonards.

"Whatta you doin', man. You're gonna get sick. Take it easy."

"Take it easy . . . I hate that. What's the other thing . . . Relax. Relax and take it easy, yeah. What shit that is. What shit . . . so you fucked her in my bed. Hell I go away to do the exact same thing. Take it easy you sumbitch, he tells me. I don't wanna take it the way you do, you fuck . . . "

"Miller you shouldna drunk that stuff so fast. You're gonna get sicker than hell."

"I'm okay goddamnit." Leonard is getting ugly. His head is losing its shape. His beard has grown very large. "Lennirt, whychoo ever trim your beard, hunh? Takes up the whole goddam room. S'blocking my view. I can't see the hills out th' window."

"Miller take it easy. It's dark outside. Can't see the hills now."

"Whattaya mean you can't see 'em. You trying to tell me they're gone. Tell me the Puerto Ricans ripped 'em off next, right man?"

Leonard shakes his head. I get up and the booze rushes to my head: I am like a scubadiver contracting the bends. "Lennirt," my voice fights to stay above water, "fucking Puerto Ricans ripped 'em off, right?" The floor starts a slow walk around the room, that turns into a lazy dance. "Right Lennirt?" I can't see Leonard suddenly. "Lennirt?" Wait, there's Leonard, and there, and there. Where?

There, down by the Garden spot. Shelley is on the corner, and Leonard keeps walking by casing her like a bank. She grabs him, asks him what he's trying to do. He doesn't answer. There's nerve gas, she says. Look there's my boyfriend. he's stuck in an attitude. I am unable to move from where I stand across the street. Shelley and Leonard get playful, and Shelley starts twirling her clothes off her body, onto her fingers, and down onto the sidewalk. The streetpeople suddenly swoop in and make off with her sweater. Her bra. Her panties. They dart in and out, their arms upraised in horrible glee. A black and white police car pulls up and everyone scatters. I am alone across the street, and an officer waves at me from faraway. He gets into his car, and soon the callbox that stands two feet away from me begins to ring. I strain forward, desperately, until like a cardboard cutout, I fall on my face. The streetpeople are back, taking the tires off of the police car. The callbox continues to sound.

"Br-ring. Brr-ring." The phone is going near my head. I snake my hand out and knock it off the hook. My head raises up off the floor, slowly, and with great pain. The

room gyrates lazily. I grab the receiver and speak, but my voice is in the back of my throat.

"Hello is Miller there?"

I grunt. It's Shelley.

"Is that you Miller. Did I wake you?"

"Shelley," I croak, "wait a sec. Hold on." I put the phone down and stumble blindly toward the bathroom. as soon as I splash some water on my face and down my throat, and eat a gob of toothpaste, I realize that something is wrong.

"Shelley, listen can I call you back? Yeah something's up. Uh huh. I'll call you right back. Bye"

Bix's room is empty, and Leonard's stuff is gone, dirty socks and all. Back in the living room I wander around looking purposefully for something, and it is almost five minutes before I discover Leonard's scrawled soap message on the picture window. It reads:

MILLER— I KNEW THAT YOU WOULD FIND THIS HERE BECAUSE IT IS YOUR SPOT. I AM SORRY TO SEE WHAT HAS HAPPENED TO YOU BECAUSE YOU USED TO BE A FINE PERSON. I DON'T WANT TO BE RESPONSIBLE FOR WHAT I THINK IS GOING TO HAPPEN TO YOU. IT IS THE FAULT OF THE SYSTEM YOUR A PART OF. I CANNOT LIVE WITHIN THAT SYSTEM, SO I AM LEAVING. I HOPE YOU UNDERSTAND. TAKE IT EASY, MAN.

LEONARD

I stare at this message that obscures the Berkeley hills, my asylum and disease, unable to decide whether to laugh or cry. In the end I conclude that it is a question of morality, and suddenly in the mood for burlesque, I give old Shelley a ring. ✤

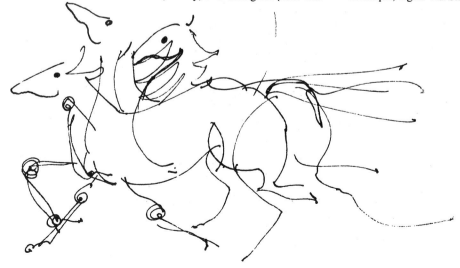

The Fall of Miss Alaska

George Franklin

I.
Cliff is a cliff is a
Perilous descent without wings,
Hardly a moot point.
                    That's how I'd do it,
No chance of ill-considered resurrections.
It's historical:
                    I, now so cored,
                    So bitten-out-of,

Almost decided to take & leave the plunge
Many years ago young-apple-I: good color,
Full of gravity/ Gathered by a "man-made lake",
Definitive as a crater . . .

Boarding school in one bus
Was a telephone cram & goldfish silly:
All of us, literally, at 4 a.m.,
Our motor-activity frenetic, elbowing Escape!
Long distances!
Little fishes in a bigger pond!
& I knew it, cheeky: this was a bust.
Nothing ever comes off.
Who'd been editing my dreams?
Pa & I scouting for oil in Oyster Bay . . . /
                                        Tatters

In yammering union
Down Route 1/12/24/386 . . . ,
Products of broken homes
& so many bottles of beer on the wall,
Then off. Of course I can't recall!
The numbers themselves don't count
For much, as solitary prison-campers know:
Just add, subtract, & throw in jumping jacks/
                    Because it's there
To see the moon eclipsed!
Indeed it was—by clouds.

Atop Mt. Loon, I'd grappled
Inch for inch & toe to toe
With the climb, wheezing: vertigo!,
Dry heaving/
                    Big lens
Made nothing clear
But specified such clouds!
That wafted by
& ate up dimes.
                    Internimbus
Venus emerged,
Demure, looking like the moon,
Trailing cirrus
Strands like
                    beauty if not science?

The point, indeed,
Was not to see the moon—
But not this way.

Well 4 a.m. I'd never spied before
Except in clockface/

II.
(5 a.m.
So-so serious)

Jutty,
Precipice: I sat
Loll-like, swing-shinned,
Darkened spikes of pine underfoot,
Dangling,
Urchin-needling air so thin a sea . . .
Votary mists displayed me out & solving   away!
Hazing: can't catch your breath?
Universal dispersal, fine as cremation/
          Quizzed: would I,
                    Contemplative,
                    Downcast,
                    14

Break myself at the mountain's foot
& crash so frail a shell?

The idea
Stood/

III.
All that the factory gives to life
smoke-makers making anonymous warning.
Inside they're tending small fires.
I burn out small clouds that tell time.
          This is a horizontal smoke;
I must be something sideways,
On its ear. I hear the dissipation
Of my breath . . . Dissolving signals
Extend my chest
As under a shifting screen of clouds
The deep eclipse is total & unseen/ No terror.
          A little death with every draught.
          My blood's ascending pitch
          Beats pace with the fanciful fall—
          Between each quickening note
          A constant drop along a constant wall/
Disputing the cliff's close edge,
Two skirmishers approach
& reveille—"Hey!
                    Miss Alaska!
                    "Miss Alaska?"
A new name & an end

To reverie—"Hey!
                    Kicking yourself
                Like she did?"
                "She did what?"
                "Jumped. Right here.
                Three weeks ago."
                "Bull . . ."

        Trilled in the steep darkness,
My spine a scale!
Cold/ The catatonic of the cliff
Marbles in his Method, posing
On a lucky lordly pedestal,
Advertising a laconic despair.
        There is no provision
For interminable lines
        & only circles are requited.
        Horizons may be understood
In principle; I fear the drop-off point,
Concretely. Secretly:
        Only half-afraid
                Of some new world/

IV.
                Nestled in a rough grey cloud
                A pearl reclining in an oyster shell
                Sand encamping in our sleepy eyes
                A latent itch, it's part-way out . . .
The dream's a memory.
Pupils yawn in the dark like depthless mouths.
Behind drawn lids
The great black center of the world,
Widened, exclusive. The mind's a lensing
Vacuole snapping at a dark oasis,
Taking its own negatives, famished, in,
Recess into recess, opening out again
To radical light: the cell
        Became an animal;
        Its walls
        Shut close & closer
        To recall
        The primal shock,
        The shock
        Of no recognition—
        The blow
        Of a naked energy,
        The race
        Confronting itself
        In a cry—
        The snapping cord,
        The slap,
        The ocean contracted
        In an eye—
        Breaking mightily
        To terrify—
        The dilated flesh
        Exhausted,
        The freshened scar:

The sun inflames a corner of the sky.
The troops are gathered,
Marching at the corners of my mind . . .
        TURN ON A SUDDEN LIGHT!
                Angry contractions
        Force the eyes blind
                & thick with secretion,
        Dilated dreams squeezed out
                Like an over-ripe juice.
        Tighten them shut: the veins
                An idiosyncratic map
        Like a bloody thumbprint
                Or faint dying embers,
Inscrutable traces of shock . . . /

V.
Only an inference as I block the world,
I am my own shadow stretching inward,
Caught. So that you never were here,
Never . . . The cell is its own
It's an amputation-in-progress
                Agitation; the dream remembers
A sequential lobotomy,
        A lost dream & is lost . . .
"Can you take a picture
        Through a telescope?"
        "No . . ."
        Your life is phantom pain,
        Imagined nervous dross,
        Feeling past the raw endings
Of hopelessness, the blank buzz of lack.
I am constantly unarrived.
        I am not my own source/
Returning to our home-away-from-home
The home that isn't home . . .
        No orderly falling in.

                The chorus is a rubble.

VI.
This bus an unaccomodating dive
                In none-too-rapid transit: sleep
A lazy vagabond deception—
                Anarchic but undangerous
Suspension. No immersion . . . Someone
                Starts a sentence. —O,
It will have to be an extraordinary sentence
                To quicken my pulse!
. . . The dream is inarticulate, resists
                The rigid code
Of meaning tongues—the sound ecstatic
                Buried in an unformed
Thought . . . My mind a myriad image
                Of itself, outstripping, uncontained/
                I sense a seismic
Shiftlessness—someone rolls a window up
(Is cold) & pikes his knees up
                Toward a ragged head:

Excursion fully sealed!
        Brisk ethers of the respirating night
Closed out. Motion sickness
        Stifled by exhaustion . . .
        & as she fell, as she fell, she fell
        DID SHE THINK BITTER THOUGHTS
Churning over split-lined asphalt,
        IN ATLANTIC CITY? WAS SHE ECSTATIC
Firing gas & spitting bi-productions,
        IN NOME, TRAVELLING THE RAMP?
Tracking a painful independent line,
        WAS THE MOON A WATER-COLORED
Ancient pistons pumping thinned-out
        LOLLIPOP-IN-THE-SKY AS SHE MELTED
Crude, a faint pollution given off . . .
        OPEN-MOUTHED OVER THE CLIFF?
Good mileage; 20 years of service/

        DID HER LIFE FLASH BEFORE HER EYES?
        Strike me a match; close &
           closer, such unblinking
        Discipline! O, slip it in
           the engine!, dance about
        The generative pyre/
        & DID SHE ADMIRE THE CAST OF IT?
Frozen tongue of fire dropped in tears!
STATUESQUE SHE TOPPLED IN THE NIGHT . . .
We trundle, timid, home without a fight,
        Still tumbling, limpid,
        In & out of sleep's
Uncertain troubled surfaces
        Chaotic hot retreat
           Coddled in a rattling limbo
        Shadow-grazing as we go:
Shaken in an uncongealing
        Phantoms quickly melt or
           Mix. Negotiate the rhythms!
        Scurry in an unrememb'ring
Dance! Meek, I bend; then
        Light, the light you used
           Reckless, fire-drunk & sure
        To hunt the phantoms down
I tip the trembling bar
        Until it fell & they returned
           To waking senses, fallen
        When it finally failed &
Flush in a half-emergence
        Light & shadow merged . . .
           Joined by a displaced dream/
           O I WOULD RETURN
        To the center,

        The source, where I was
        Myself & not yet myself,

        Where I was the other &

        Not yet the other; even if,
        Shut with light, these eyes
        Are blind to the prodigal

        Return; even if I can never
        Meet myself; even if
        I was never really there/
        "For what we cannot accomplish, what
is denied to love,
        what we have lost in the anticipation—
           a descent follows,
endless & indestructible . . . "

VII.
The lake is a sculpture of shadows,
Formal with absence.
The negative of some force,
Some fall, I'm halfway down a bank
In nothing's orbit. Here the center holds
What it cannot attract, provokes me,
Cries out for completion.

Roots that dangle, shorn,
Like severed nerves
Reveal themselves in the volatile air,
Feel in the darkness that cloaks me
For integral clay, lost clay
That kept the network intact.

Though I did not crop this earth,
Though this is not my home, still I descend
Beneath my fear, recite my given name
Until the sound grows self-pervasive,
Strange. & I have felt its claim.

It is the deep room prepared for me,
The room I remember,
That takes my breath away.
The unanticipated step in the dream,
The illusory curb . . . I feinted,
& startled the sleeper from sleep.

The sun has shuddered over the range.
The lake is a sunken table, blazing
Beneath a dark rim. Now falling
Headlong into itself
Desire breaks on the sudden earth:
A waking landing, separate & alive.

The bus is empty by the bank.
As if a caught sun prowled within
The slant light strikes each separate pane,
Transparencies of a single source.
The glare inverts the restless eye
& sight displaces sight.

The soul went out in sleep,
The moving shell
Abandoned to banished visions,
Crowding back. & now I must seek
With these repossessed eyes
The light that discovers me,
Constantly, where I am.

AUTHOR INDEX